Contents

This book is dedicated to the memory of
Brian Stone
(1919–1995)
Reader in Literature at The Open University

Approaching Literature

Shakespeare, Aphra Behn and the Canon

edited by W.R. Owens & Lizbeth Goodman

in association with The Open University

Preface

Shakespeare, Aphra Behn and the Canon is one of four books in a series entitled *Approaching Literature*, which is designed to offer students an introduction to various aspects of literary study. The aspect on which this book focuses is the concept of the literary canon – the body of texts and writers traditionally regarded as 'great' and thus possessing special authority. As you work through this book, you will investigate the complex process by which certain authors and texts are canonized; you will also explore how and why the traditional canon is being challenged by critics who want to open it up to a much wider range of authors and texts.

In examining these large issues, we have decided to concentrate on drama, and on four plays in particular. William Shakespeare is of course the most celebrated example of a 'canonical' author: his plays are published in innumerable editions, taught in almost every school, college and university, and performed all over the world. We have chosen to look in detail at three of his works – a history (*Henry V*), a tragedy (*Othello*) and a comedy (*As You Like It*). But alongside these we include a lesser-known play – Aphra Behn's comedy *The Rover*. This was first performed in 1677, and its history since then illuminates many of the issues around the canon: although Behn was one of the leading playwrights of her time, and *The Rover* was a great success, she virtually disappeared from view for over two hundred years. It is only in the last few years that her plays have been revived on the stage. As more and more of her works are published, it is clear that she is now in the process of entering the canon – or perhaps already has. A new edition of *The Rover* is provided here, including full explanatory notes.

The book opens with a chapter analysing the concept of the canon and offering definitions of key terms such as 'drama', 'theatre' and 'performance'. After a short chapter on the kind of theatre Shakespeare was writing for, and the language of his plays, the book proceeds to deal with each of the four plays in separate chapters. A key concern of each chapter is to examine the connections between live performance and recorded performance on audio cassette, video, television and film. The chapters on *The Rover* and *As You Like It* include extended discussions of specially produced video performances of these plays. Other issues addressed include the representation of race and gender in the theatre, Englishness and cultural identity, and the relevance of historical context to an understanding of the plays. A brief concluding chapter picks up once again the debates surrounding the canon. Each chapter gives suggestions for further reading.

The production of this book has been very much a collaborative effort. The academic editors and authors would therefore like to thank their Open University colleagues – Julie Bennett, Kate Clements and John Pettit (for their work as Arts editors in shaping and clarifying the text), and Marilyn Brooks, Tony Coe, Anthony Coulson, Jonathan Davies, Julie Dickens, Robert Doubleday, Janet Fennell, Nick Furbank, Cicely Palser Havely, Eddie Head, Nick Levinson, Graham Martin, Lesley Passey, Stephen Regan, Jill Tibble, Nora Tomlinson, Trevor White and Amanda Willett. Thanks are also due to the external assessor, Professor Judie Newman, for her valuable comments.

W.R. Owens and Lizbeth Goodman

W.R. Owens is Staff Tutor and Senior Lecturer in Literature
at The Open University
Lizbeth Goodman is Lecturer in Literature at The Open University
Kate Clarke is Lecturer in the School of Humanities and Education, and
Assistant Registrar (Academic Quality) at The University of Hertfordshire;
she is also a tutor with The Open University
Roger Day is Lecturer in Literature at The Open University
Simon Eliot is Staff Tutor and Senior Lecturer in Literature at
The Open University

Part One

Chapter One

The idea of the canon

by Lizbeth Goodman

'The canon' defined

If you have already come across a definition of 'the canon', it may have been something like 'those works of literature that are considered especially worth studying'. But this seemingly straightforward definition immediately raises further questions. *Which* works? *Who* considers them worth studying? And so on. Such questions can only be answered if we move towards a more considered definition of 'the canon', and that is what we are aiming at in this book. We will use a variety of approaches: for example, we will look at a number of *definitions and critical accounts* – ranging from scriptural and historical ideas, to more contemporary approaches. But we will also examine the term by looking at *examples*, by studying plays, literary scholarship and performance history in some detail. As you explore these definitions and examples, you will need to work in an active and questioning way so that you can put together your own definition of the canon.

In 1986 Graham Martin – then Head of the Literature Department at The Open University – outlined some thoughts on 'the canon' for debate among his colleagues as they were beginning to plan a new course, *Literature in the Modern World*. I'd like you to read his notes now, identifying the questions that he raises:

> Dictionary definitions of 'canon' specify 'a body of sacred writings, accepted as inspired, which the Christian Church authorizes as the principal guide to faith and morals'. There is also the narrower sense of 'the Shakespearean canon', or 'the Defoe canon', composed of those works held to be by the author, as distinct from those spuriously or merely conjecturally attributed to him. It is the first sense that is in question in talk about 'the canon of English literature'.
>
> Yet there is clearly a huge difference between a collection of sacred writings held to be of divine origin, and the long historical sequence of humanly produced writing that we now call 'literature'. There is, for example, the question of authority. Who decides that certain sacred writings are 'canonical' and that others are not? The leaders of the relevant religious institution. But in the case of literature? We may, perhaps, think of educational institutions (universities, schools, exam boards) as exercising a similar authority, but no more than a loose analogy can be claimed. For one thing, the distinction between canonized and uncanonized literary works has never been binding; and for another, it is always imprecise. Then further, as time passes, opinions change. Since new novels/poems/plays continue to be published, there are always new candidates for whom 'canonicity' is claimed, and yet others whose past achievement of 'canonicity' begins to be questioned – perhaps denied altogether. The very criteria by which 'the canon' is assembled can be seen to undergo a process of

continual, sometimes striking, change, and those today who feel the need to 'challenge the canon' are taking part in a well-established cultural process. So, while institutional authority is crucial in setting up 'a canon of English literature', and in authorizing accredited members of the institution to make the canon an effective public presence, there is no question of its content being – however fiercely defended – 'fixed' or 'sacred', i.e. uniformly characterized by a common element.

This quotation defines the canon in an introductory way, but that's not the only reason why I chose it. Notice that it

(a) refers to the scriptural background to the idea of the canon

(b) refers to 'the canon of *English* literature' – an important term when we are studying William Shakespeare and Aphra Behn

(c) addresses other key issues around the canon: for example, who decides what is to be included and excluded, and on what grounds?

In fact, these are the main issues in this chapter, and we will begin with the first point – about the scriptural background. How does the sacred status of scripture relate to the status of the literary canon?

Scripture and literature: defining canonicity

In Graham Martin's reference to sacred writings, he explained that certain books of the Bible are generally regarded as divinely inspired and are thus judged to be canonical.

I would like you now to think about the following question and to note down your answer: in what senses do you think scripture and literature are similar, and in what senses different? Consider, for example, who writes them.

D i s c u s s i o n

Both tend to take the form of written records of stories, myths and ideas (they are *texts*). But whereas authors of scripture are in many cases anonymous (and 'divinely inspired'), authors of literature are almost always identifiable people – even if we see them as inspired by 'genius'. There is a further difference between scripture and literature: the classification of certain works (and not others) as 'divine' is authorized by the Church, whereas with literature it is less easy to identify who decides which authors and texts are worthy of inclusion in the literary canon. ■

That brief discussion emphasized the differences rather than the similarities. But at this point it is interesting to note that, recently, more and more literature courses have included the Talmud, the Koran, the Bhagavadgita and the Bible as texts that benefit from two kinds of literary analysis.

First, all of these texts can be studied as stories, as sets of narratives including mythic characters and events. The gospels in the Bible, for instance, can be studied as competing versions of the same story, told by different authors (or at least different narrative voices, for the 'authorship' of the Bible is an uncertain entity indeed). Secondly, all of these texts have been tremendously influential in the development of literature itself: all were used as models for the styles, characters and values of 'literary' texts that followed. For example, the medieval mystery plays are based on gospel accounts of Christ's birth, death and resurrection; John Milton's epic poem *Paradise Lost* (1667) deals with the events recounted in Genesis, and most of Shakespeare's plays are infused with Christian morality.

The interpretation of religious texts, from whatever culture, may seem to have little relevance to our discussion of the canon. But as many recent critics have argued, the very development of literature may be related to the decline of religion in the modern world. As secular life and ways of thinking have replaced the structures of morality and values previously enshrined in organized religions, a gap has opened; people have often filled this gap with literature, arguing that literature can convey some higher truth, some artistic and aesthetic ideal, some 'values'.

You may or may not agree about the role of religious writings in relation to the idea of 'the canon', but it is important that we consider a range of views if we are to undertake a serious investigation.

Loading the canon

When I was researching the background for this chapter, I found many and varied sources from which to choose: I found practical criticism of literature, and elegant arguments about the integrity of 'literary texts' (though that term is rarely defined). I also found all manner of reactions and challenges to that position, especially from cultural and feminist critics. But what I want to offer here is not theory, but rather a more introductory, even common-sense, position. I have already found it useful to quote Graham Martin, and I also looked at the work of his predecessor as Head of Literature at The Open University – the late Arnold Kettle. In a book first published in 1951, Kettle attempted to explain the relevance of literature to life and I think that, in so doing, he got to the root of the 'canon question'. Referring to the English novel, he wrote:

> It is impossible to evaluate literature in the abstract; a book is neither produced nor read in a vacuum and the very word 'value' involves right away criteria which are not just 'literary'. Literature is a part of life and can be judged only in its relevance to life. Life is not static but moving and changing.

> (Kettle, *An Introduction to the English Novel*, 1983 edn, p.12)

Here Arnold Kettle gets to the heart of what makes literature interesting: it is not just its artistic merit, or the status of its author, but the joy of reading and of engaging with ideas, characters and situations that conjure new ideas, suggest unexpected connections and open up fresh perceptions about life. And, as Kettle reminds us, life keeps changing. So too does literature, and so too, it follows, should our ideas about what makes and keeps literature valuable, relevant, 'canonical'. In his reference to life as 'moving and changing', Kettle also introduces a crucial element for this book: drama involves performance – movement, speech, changing scenes and sets and time-frames, all made literal in three dimensions when a play is staged or recorded in visual media. And with new technologies, the

5

forms of presentation of 'drama' keep changing and developing as well. So the idea that literature is alive and changing is one with particular relevance to our study of plays.

In setting out the views of Martin and of Kettle, I have entered into a dialogue with them. I have selected them for reproduction and comment, and rejected others as less helpful. This is not to say that the definitions above are any less subjective or biased than any others, but rather to point out that to define terms is a tricky business, and one of the pitfalls of any field of study is an account that seems too 'objective'. While I don't want to suggest that there are no terms, or that defining terms is too awkward or difficult, I do want to stress that defining terms always involves value-judgements and choices. I have so far offered only two views, both quite complementary. Of course there are many others, and of course you will question the ideas offered here and compare them with your own.

So, the defining of the term 'canon' is, to give in to the obvious pun, 'loaded'. **What if we set aside the two views offered above and try to construct our own definition of 'the canon'? Could you write a sentence or two to define the term, and suggest a few of the authors who are usually included in the canon?**

Discussion

Here's my best shot at it:

The term 'the canon', at a very basic level, refers to the set of authors and literary texts that has been passed down from age to age, generation to generation, with a stamp of approval – with a reputation for being 'great'. So the canon, until recently, might well have included only Homer, Dante, Chaucer, Milton, Shakespeare, and also perhaps Wordsworth, Dickens … ∎

But as soon as I provide this list of 'canonical' authors, you can see quite plainly that it is partial, and that it depends on value-judgements. In fact, there are two major kinds of value-judgement implicit in it – the 'official' and the 'personal'. My list is 'official' in that it is composed of the authors whom I would most expect to find listed as 'canonical'. Yet it is also personal: it includes only authors whose work I find inspiring and relevant.

We are all inevitably influenced by general cultural ideas of value when we set out to define terms on our own. This is not limiting, but rather potentially exciting as it also means that we engage in a debate with our cultures when we offer our own definitions. Each time we discuss the canon, we all enter into the process of evaluating literature and its authors – and we do so with the backing of a certain tradition or accepted set of ideas behind us (the 'official version'), but also with our own personal preferences and objectives somewhere in the frame as well. Thus, as Martin pointed out above, we won't be engaging in some completely new and unheard of attack on the canon, but will rather join a distinguished list of thinkers who have long questioned the canon in its various forms. As we explore the terrain, then, we can keep in mind the range of questions posed by contemporary critics. For instance: why are most of the canonical authors white men? Why is English the language in which we study most of this work, and why do students in many countries study a canon of mostly

English authors? These questions are crudely formulated, but no less interesting for all that: each will be explored in the pages of this book.

They are also a crucial part of the question that was raised a little earlier: how is it decided which works of literature – drama, novels or poems – will be accepted into the canon? Here we need to consider the concept of 'good writing' (and who determines what is 'good'?). We also need to look at the issue of 'textual integrity', or the idea that a work of literature should be judged for its artistic merit on aesthetic criteria, and deemed acceptably canonical if it meets those (subjective) criteria. The process seems to involve evaluating works of literature – but perhaps we need to explore this a little further, asking ourselves whether there might not be many kinds of value or merit that any text and author might possess.

The canon 'fired'

On several occasions so far, I've used the term 'literature' as though it is a straightforward term. But is it? We can, perhaps, all accept that 'literature' in the broadest sense is applied to three main 'literary' genres (prose fiction, poetry and drama), but the two extreme views outlined below demonstrate that the jury is still out on the question of what precisely makes literature 'literary', let alone 'canonical'.

The first, long-held view (so common that attribution to any particular critic would be misleading) is that literature is a particular kind of writing which is concerned with its own style, and which aims to inspire imagination and creative thought rather than merely to convey information or express political or personal views. Of course it is easy to criticize this definition: you might well argue that most 'literature' expresses the political and personal beliefs of its author, whether implicitly or explicitly. And indeed, what is valued as 'literature' by some will seem to be 'philosophy' or 'politics' or 'history' to others, depending on who reads it, when, and why/how it is read. Still, this first definition of 'literature' is as good a starting-point as any; we have no more precise term available to us and, besides, this view of 'literature' is the building block for the commonest idea of 'the literary canon'.

A very different view is offered by Terry Eagleton, the Thomas Warton Professor of English Literature at Oxford University, who has famously questioned the very nature of 'the literary canon'. He argues that the term 'literature' is problematic. Even a train timetable, Eagleton argues, may be read as literature if the person reading it does so in order to think about philosophical ideas of time and travel, or as a structure for considering the aesthetic placement of words and figures on the page as 'poetry'. For this reason Eagleton defines literature as 'highly valued writing', and goes on to argue that the definition of 'literary value' is unstable, shifting, subjective.

The following excerpt from Eagleton's work gives you a flavour of his approach. As you read it, make notes on what you think may be of value in his approach to thinking about the canon:

The reason why it follows from the definition of literature as highly valued writing that it is not a stable entity is that value-judgements are notoriously variable ... the so-called 'literary canon', the unquestioned 'great tradition' of the 'national literature', has to be recognized as a *construct*, fashioned by particular people for particular reasons at a certain time. There is no such thing as a literary work or tradition which is valuable *in itself*, regardless of what anyone might have said or come to say about it. 'Value' is a transitive term: it means whatever is valued by certain people in specific situations, according to particular criteria and in the light of given purposes.

(Eagleton, *Literary Theory*, 1983, p.11)

Discussion

One thing you may have noted is the radical edge to Eagleton's writing. Indeed, he is well known as a Marxist literary and cultural critic whose ideas inspire both respect and consternation, depending on who reads his work, when, for what reason and in what context. At one level Eagleton's literary criticism may itself be regarded as 'literary' in that it is eloquently written and soundly argued; if polemic and politics necessarily detracted from 'literariness', then Shakespeare himself would be discounted as an author of 'literature'. In fact, Eagleton is also an accomplished playwright, and his sense of style informs the treatment of his subject-matter, as in much 'literature' and 'literary criticism'. Still, there is the question of 'literary value' to be considered. Criticism such as Eagleton's may not be valuable in itself, but it does serve a definite purpose: it adds significantly to our understanding of the complexity (and excitement) of thinking about the canon. If we are inspired to think and re-think issues such as the idea of the canon, surely this is more interesting and more educational than simply accepting the views and value-judgements of previous generations? ■

I interrupted Eagleton in mid-flow. Let's see what else he has to say on the subject. **As you read the rest of the extract, try to identify the intended readers. Is he writing for a world audience, or is he addressing (and referring to) a specific culture? For instance, whose history is 'our history'?**

It is thus quite possible that, given a deep enough transformation of our history, we may in the future produce a society which is unable to get anything at all out of Shakespeare. His works might simply seem desperately alien, full of styles of thought and feeling which such a society found limited or irrelevant. In such a situation, Shakespeare would be no more valuable than much present-day graffiti. And though many people would consider such a social condition tragically impoverished, it seems to me dogmatic not to entertain the possibility that it might arise ...

(Ibid., pp.11–12)

Discussion

It's not absolutely clear what Eagleton means by 'our history', and you were hampered by seeing only an extract, taken out of context. But he seems to be referring to *English* history or society. Most readers of Eagleton's book would, in the first instance, have been students and fellow academics in the UK, though the book later reached a much larger international audience.

But with this book, as with all writing ('literary' or not), the language in which it is written determines to a very large extent the people who will read it: Eagleton's book is in English. ■

That said, what do you make of the idea that, given a transformation of (our) history, 'Shakespeare would be no more valuable than much present-day graffiti'?

D i s c u s s i o n

One could resent such a suggestion. If you are reading this textbook as a student, you might well think it insulting to suggest that the author who is to be your major focus may not be so highly respected in future. Eagleton's comments are intended to be provocative, and I include them here to initiate debate. This is *not* to say that you, the reader of this book, should take Eagleton's views as a definitive statement, but rather to say that the kinds of question he raises are extremely useful. Eagleton hasn't said that Shakespeare is unimportant, or that graffiti are unimportant. You may value graffiti quite highly, particularly if you are a visual artist or political activist, or if you're interested in the everyday language of expression. What Eagleton has said is that the value of graffiti, like the value of all writings (including those by Shakespeare), is determined by the people who read them. So your estimation of the importance or 'literary value' of Shakespeare may be different from mine. Eagleton himself has written at length about Shakespeare and his work; far from negating the importance of 'the Bard', Eagleton is interested in the continuous process of revaluing literature in changing cultural circumstances. ■

Englishness and Bardolatry

Both Martin and Eagleton raise, in different ways, the issue of 'Englishness', or the distinct cultural identity of England and its associated concerns, patterns of speech and writing, and sets of values or standards for social conduct and literary achievement. The concept of an *English* literary canon assumes the use of the English language, and it assumes a focus on English writers and/or texts dealing with English themes, history or attitudes.

Where does Shakespeare fit into this? One of the most basic reasons why he is so widely considered a canonical writer is to do with his Englishness – not only the fact that he was born in England, but also his long-standing status as 'the Bard of Avon'. Shakespeare, the Bard, enshrines the ultimate figure of the great writer; his image and symbolic identities are associated with the English countryside, theatre, social customs and entertainments, as well as with more literary ideas about his contributions to the development of poetic and dramatic form. The Shakespeare phenomenon is often referred to as 'Bardolatry' – cultural worship of a writer who is said to embody the genius and values of a nation. But as we shall see in Chapter Two, the facts of Shakespeare's life are not clear: what we 'worship' is a later idealized version of the great writer, not an actuality – not even a memory.

There is a further complication in relation to Shakespeare and other playwrights: we need to take account of the distinct aspects of 'dramatic literature' and theatre, because the possibilities of performance introduce a new set of questions and issues in relation to the idea of the canon. I will have more to say about this later, but first I want to go deeper into the issue of which authors are selected for canonization – from which groups, and from which countries.

'Entry requirements' for authors

Following on from our consideration of Englishness as the framework for much debate about the literary canon, let's stop to consider the international, or cross-cultural, implications of the canon. As usually studied in England, the literary canon might include a wide range of work, some taken from international cultures but all translated into English. It might include classical Greek texts such as Homer's *Iliad* and *Odyssey*, and plays by Euripides, Aristophanes and others; it might also include Italian Renaissance works such as Giovanni Boccaccio's *Decameron* and Francesco Petrarch's sonnets. But overwhelmingly it would include works written in some form of English – from *Beowulf*, the medieval mystery plays, William Langland's *Piers Plowman* and Geoffrey Chaucer's *Canterbury Tales*, on through Edmund Spenser's *Faerie Queene*, Shakespeare's sonnets and plays, the poetry of John Donne, Milton's *Paradise Lost*, famous novels such as Daniel Defoe's *Robinson Crusoe*, Henry Fielding's *Tom Jones*, the works of Charles Dickens, poetry by the Romantics such as William Blake, William Wordsworth, Samuel Taylor Coleridge, John Keats, Lord Byron and Percy Bysshe Shelley, right up to and including a wide range of more recent poetry, drama and prose fiction.

Most of the work in this version of the canon is written by men. If we make an effort to take account of writing by women, we might include lyric poetry and dramatic fragments by the Ancient Greek poet Sappho, plays by Aphra Behn, novels by Jane Austen, the Brontë sisters and George Eliot, poetry by Elizabeth Barrett Browning, Christina Rossetti and Emily Dickinson. But these are exceptions: until the late nineteenth century, very little writing by women was attributed explicitly to them as women (rather than written anonymously or under male pseudonyms), and very little was published or printed in some form that would allow it to last. Furthermore, it has only been in the past few decades that feminist scholars have influenced the reviewing of the canon, partly through searching for writing by women of previous eras – and partly through re-evaluating writing by modern women. Similarly, writing by people of colour was not – until very recently – acknowledged as important enough to publish, let alone canonize.

At this point in the chapter, let's summarize the key issues that we have just been looking at. **What concerns have emerged in this subsection and the preceding one?**

10

I found:

(a) Englishness
(b) the English language
(c) Bardolatry
(d) performance
(e) gender
(f) race. ■

I'd like to discuss some of these issues a little further. Of the male canonical authors already mentioned, you will note that many are *English*: Langland, Chaucer, Spenser, Shakespeare, Milton, Defoe, Fielding, Dickens, Blake, Wordsworth, Coleridge, Keats, Shelley – even Byron, though his parents were Scottish – were born in England, and many of them write about England. Thus we return, yet again, to the related concepts of language, cultural identity and Englishness. Of course there are many exceptions, but they are, well, exceptions: for every Homer or Boccaccio, there are dozens of English authors whose work is regularly included in courses on 'Literature' and 'Great Writers'.

This is so even in colleges outside England, and I think there are several reasons for the 'Englishness' of the traditional literary canon. For example, English authors were writing 'literature' long before the white settlers who took over the lands of North America and Australia, for example, had (or made) 'national identities' of their own. So, to begin with, the literature of colonial North America and Australia was largely composed of English 'classics'. Later, of course, distinctive forms of North American and Australian literature began to develop. In the USA, the field of American Literature has grown quickly and steadily, but it is interesting to note two trends with regard to the US literary canon.

First, it still tends to include a good deal of English writing (by Chaucer, Shakespeare, Milton, Donne, Keats and Dickens, for example), in addition to what are usually considered the 'American classics' – *Moby Dick* by Herman Melville, *The Scarlet Letter* by Nathaniel Hawthorne, *The Old Man and The Sea* and *The Sun also Rises* by Ernest Hemingway, *Light in August* and *The Sound and the Fury* by William Faulkner, and *The Great Gatsby* by F. Scott Fitzgerald.

Second, courses on 'The Great Writers' or on 'Classical and Scriptural Backgrounds to Literature' are not at all uncommon, even in the 1990s and in the more 'radical' universities and departments – perhaps because many students need (and want) to read the 'classics' before moving on to consider 'alternatives' to them. At entry level, US universities frequently offer courses with such titles as 'From Beowulf to Virginia Woolf'. This indicates that Virginia Woolf (again, an English and middle-class author, writing primarily in the 1920s and 1930s) is the most recent and 'radical' author yet to be firmly canonized.

We have seen, then, that the traditional literary canon – even when studied outside the UK – has a high degree of Englishness. It is also (and this is a rather different point) dominated by works written in English. For an author, whether he or she writes in English can be a crucial 'entry requirement', because the dominance of English as a 'world language' (a dominance achieved partly through colonial rule) has tended to exclude many authors who didn't write in English. Further, the process of deciding what gets translated into English, and when, is a crucial part of the process of canonization – and involves not only judgements about the 'literary' or 'aesthetic' value of a work, but also issues of political power and social control.

To return to our list of canonical authors: you may have noticed that it does not include any playwrights, except for Shakespeare, and indeed few playwrights have yet been accorded official canonical status. Behn's canonical status is less well established than Woolf's, partly because her work was neglected for so much of the period of modern literary scholarship, but partly because of her chosen genre: she was primarily a playwright. If we were to name the best-known twentieth-century playwrights writing in English, we would probably include W.B. Yeats, Oscar Wilde, Arnold Wesker, John Osborne, Joe Orton and Harold Pinter (all of them British or Irish authors), perhaps adding North Americans such as Tennessee Williams, Eugene O'Neill, Arthur Miller and David Mamet.

Challenging the canon

To summarize the situation so far: you have looked at the similarities, and differences, between scripture and the literary canon. You have also seen that the question of how the canon is constructed raises a raft of issues – about Englishness, the English language, race, gender relations, and so on. The question of which works should enter the canon is clearly problematical. But we have not challenged the basic assumption that there is a choice to be made. We have not challenged the idea that there is, or should be, a canon – a way of valuing literature, of separating the good from the bad, the literary from the journalistic, the 'classic' from the merely 'popular'.

The position we are coming to, it seems, is that value-judgements are attached to any body of work; these judgements will alter from age to age, and indeed what is 'classic' may become classic in part because it appeals to the popular imagination. The idea of the canon is just that – an idea – and cultural change will affect it. So, rather than accepting that the rules of canonicity are 'handed down from the mount', we might decide to challenge those rules. How would we go about it? Well, one way would be to argue with definitions and terminology, as we've begun to do in this chapter. But it's far more interesting to read texts and enter the process of evaluation in a more active, personal way. If we do so, we can challenge the existing canon by composing our own lists of what is valuable, for each of us, today.

What if you wanted to include, in a revised canon, a range of plays by women and black authors? Whom would you include? How would you even begin to compose such a list, given that the traditional canon (of plays in English, primarily by white British men) governs both what is available in print and what is taught on the courses you're likely to be offered?

If you wanted to challenge the existing drama canon, you would have to look around and assess the 'value' of the work of playwrights from many countries. Even if you confined yourself to British and American writers, you might want to include dramatists such as Caryl Churchill, Sarah Daniels, Susan Glaspell, Lorraine Hansberry, Jackie Kay, Megan Terry and Timberlake Wertenbaker. There are some recent textbooks that help to put the work of such authors into perspective, mainly written by feminist academics and critics. But as you searched for new authors and texts for possible canonization, you would probably find that the textbook and resource material you discovered tended to refer to women's work, and work by black authors or working-class authors, as 'marginalized voices'. This suggests that, in the complex process of canonization, the issue is not solely the quality or value of individual authors or texts. ■

Now of course I am not arguing that Shakespeare should be replaced by Behn or Churchill, but rather that we will get the most out of Shakespeare if we read his work with an awareness of the cultural legacy or reputation which goes before it, and with the idea that the canon could be, if not dispensed with, then at least enlarged. Here we return to the idea of Bardolatry, and the wider, non-literary cultural status of the name 'Shakespeare'. Firm historical evidence tells us relatively little about him (as the next chapter reveals), yet what critics such as Gary Taylor (*Reinventing Shakespeare*, 1990 edn) have labelled 'the Shakespeare Industry' draws in tourists to Stratford and London, keeps theatre companies afloat, and stimulates the production of numerous well-edited and inexpensive texts for performance. Bardolatry reinforces the idea of the canon even as it tends to overshadow the possible value of other works, by other authors.

So, while I hope that you will enjoy reading and learning about Shakespeare, I hope that you will also keep an open mind about the canon as you read this book, thinking through for yourself the very strong reasons why other authors might also be given space in a newly expanded canon.

Canonizing and analysing dramatic literature

When we study plays, we engage with the idea of the canon in a very particular way: it is different from what happens when we study other types of literature. To understand this, we must first agree on a rough set of definitions of 'drama'.

Let's begin by looking at the relationship between 'drama' and 'literature'/'literary criticism'. Literary criticism has developed as a form of analysis of literature, mainly in the twentieth century (though it could be argued that it has its origins in the writings of Plato, Aristotle and other classical authors). Before the twentieth century there was a wide body of writing about literature, but the role of the 'critic' or 'academic' was not so clearly separated from the role of the 'creative writer'. In previous eras, many authors of literature – for instance, the poets Wordsworth and Coleridge – wrote 'literary criticism' of their own and other authors' work. But it is mainly since the 1960s that literary criticism has been recognized as a distinct theoretical field, peopled mainly by academics, though of course some creative writers are also academics and/or literary critics. The range of perspectives within literary criticism is very wide – from the view that the text should be read with no regard to the author or social context, to the view that the text should be read in relation to the views of its author and with regard for the positions of its readers in different ages and cultural contexts.

One of the most influential English literary critics in the twentieth century has been F.R. Leavis. His views on literary criticism are best known from his books *The Great Tradition* (1948) and *The Common Pursuit* (1952), where the focus is mainly on prose fiction and poetry rather than on drama (and there is no mention of performance). Another prominent twentieth-century critic, the American Harold Bloom, has specialized in writing about the nature of literary influence, and how canons of literature are formed by the impact of one strong 'influence' on another. In *The Anxiety of Influence* (1973) he conceives of poetic influence in terms of generational tensions and conflicts between fathers and children. As well as giving priority to male influence (hardly mentioning women authors or readers), Bloom's theory develops entirely in relation to poetry. Such a theory gives us little help in determining the literary or cultural 'value' of the work of a female dramatist such as Behn, even though – as we shall argue in the pages of this book – her work was very clearly influenced by Shakespeare's, and has since been a major influence on other writers and on the re-evaluation of the very concept of a literary canon. Bloom's more recent work, for example *The Western Canon* (1994), argues for inclusion of Shakespeare next to Dante at the very centre of the Western canon; not only is Shakespeare supremely important, argues Bloom, but his work is a kind of yardstick by which the work of other authors can be measured. Even here, Bloom does not discuss 'drama' as such, though his high valuation of Shakespeare lends the Bard a distinct position in the field of 'dramatic criticism' as well.

The field of literary criticism has an uneasy relationship with the field of dramatic criticism, even for more radical scholars. For instance, Raymond Williams – the late Professor of Drama at Cambridge University, who was well known as a leading cultural critic of his day – pointed to some of the difficulties with the term 'drama':

> The word *drama* is used in two main ways: first, to describe a literary
> work, the text of a play; and second, to describe the performance of
> this work, its production. Thus, the text of *King Lear* is drama, and
> Shakespeare, as a writer, a dramatist; while a performance of *King Lear*
> is also drama, its players engaged in a dramatic activity.
>
> (Williams, *Drama in Performance*, 1991 edn, p.159)

Williams wrote this in the early 1950s (the book was first published in 1954). His words marked one of the first major modern evaluations of a difference between plays and performances, though he argued that the one term was perfectly adequate to refer to both. Later – in his 1976 book of definitions of cultural terms, *Keywords* – Williams referred to a developing 'problem' of defining drama as opposed to literature:

14

Steadily, with the predominance of print, *writing* and *books* became virtually synonymous; hence the subsequent confusion about *drama*, which was writing for speech.

(Williams, *Keywords*, 1976, p.153)

As early as 1954 Williams had explored the relationship between 'drama' and film (in *Drama in Performance*), and in later books – *Television* (1976), and *Culture* (1981), for instance – he considered the impact of television and other technological developments in relation to the written word. In many ways he was ahead of his time and pointed the way towards the more complex treatment of literary terms that we must apply in the modern world.

Why might it now be confusing to use the single term ('drama') for both literary texts (plays) and performances? What has changed or developed since the 1950s to further complicate the matter?

D i s c u s s i o n

The rapid development of technology in the 1980s and 1990s has meant that it is now possible to have access to performances on audio cassette, record and CD, on video, television and film, and in multi-media forms such as CD-ROM. The single term 'drama' would have to refer to far too many kinds of performance, some of which bear little resemblance to any play text. ∎

Let's begin with some definitions, which are based on the ones I offered in another book in this series (*Literature and Gender*, 1996). The three key terms for discussion are 'drama', 'theatre' and 'performance', with a fourth term, 'production', defined within these.

(a) **Drama** is the form of literature written for performance and – along with poetry and prose fiction – is one of the three major literary genres. The standard drama text is the play, and the standard form of literary critical analysis of play texts is 'dramatic criticism', which will tend to focus on the language of the play text, its literary qualities, the history of the text and its publication.

(b) **Theatre** is the forum where plays are performed; it is a broad term, and includes the physical space for performance (the stage), the area reserved for the audience, and the backstage area. It can also refer imprecisely to 'drama' and to the study of drama. 'Theatre studies' is the term for study of the theatre, including plays in performance (in theatre settings) but also theatre history, the history of individual plays in production and of playwrights in their historical and cultural contexts. Theatre studies – as opposed to 'dramatic criticism' – tends to pay particular attention to the space in which a drama text is performed, the cultural context and economics of production, the role of the audience in interpreting that text, and the effects of lights, costumes, sets and props on the reception and interpretation of any play or performance.

(c) **Performance** is an even broader term. A 'performance' differs from a 'play': the play is the text, which may be performed; the 'performance' is the new entity that is created when the words of the play text are directed, acted, interpreted in three dimensions on stage, or for audio productions. Each time a play is performed, the resulting 'performance' is unique: it is influenced by the size and constituency of the audience, the actors' success or failure in delivering their lines and realizing their parts on any given night, and many other factors.

But the term 'performance' is also applicable to theatrical events that are not based on the text of a play. Much contemporary theatre work is 'devised' – inspired and collaboratively created in a group process, with no single identifiable author and no single set script. In addition, some plays are written and performed in non-theatre spaces. For such performances, the terms 'theatre' and certainly 'drama' do not quite fit.

The fourth term that needs defining, because it is related to all three points above, is 'production'. A production of a play is the set of performances comprising one 'run' of a play – one director's choice of casting and interpretation, enhanced by the chosen designer's setting and the input that the selected group of actors (the cast) make to the interpretative process of performing. So a given production of a play begins with the play text (if there is one) and is made up of all the performances of the play in that run.

Performing the canon

Many aspects of both plays and performances can help us explore the idea of the canon: audience interaction is part of the total performance of any play, and the spoken language sounds different depending on the nationality and vocal range of actors (assuming for the moment that we are dealing only with English-language performances). Accents matter, costumes matter, the choice of location for each performance matters.

Also, of course, the medium matters. As we saw when discussing Williams's definitions, it is only quite recently that we have had to consider the differences between, on the one hand, 'performing Shakespeare' live and, on the other, recording plays on audio cassette or radio, video or television or film or CD-ROM, or using forms of 'new technology' that are continually arising. In this book we consider the texts of Shakespeare's plays, but we also refer to a range of media and performances to illustrate the interpretative process involved in translating a play text into per-formance.

The medium in which any performance is realized has an important impact on the canonical status of the text itself. For instance, it is usually true that more people see film productions than see any given live stage production. When we refer to the adaptation of any play to the medium of film, we usually refer to a visual interpretation with a monolithic quality of its own. For instance, Laurence Olivier's 1944 film version of *Henry V* becomes **the** *Henry V* (the canonical film version) until it is challenged by a new production of equal 'weight', such as (many argue) Kenneth Branagh's film version of 1993. Similarly, Orson Welles's 1951 *Othello* becomes **the** *Othello* on film. Film is often more accessible than live theatre, especially now that video cassettes can be rented. In addition, the canonical film performances by Olivier, Welles and others are often (illegally) taped from television broadcasts. In this way the canon on film reproduces itself, and the very wide range of lower-budget, less 'mainstream' film productions hardly gets noticed. This is even more the case with stage productions, which are by their very nature more selective in terms of audiences (people must be able to travel to see them) and in terms of longevity (theatre is ephemeral).

How do we discuss an ephemeral entity such as 'theatre' alongside the long-standing range of definitions and cultural constructs attached to the idea of 'the canon'? Answer: carefully, step by step.

The structure of the rest of the book

This first chapter has laid out the contours of the debate: the ideas developed here will be returned to, again and again, as you read this book and consider its application to play texts and performances.

In Chapter Two, 'Shakespeare: theatre poet', we consider the complex question of how ideas about an author have been constructed, drawn together from patchy historical evidence. We examine the kind of theatre Shakespeare worked in; how his play scripts were published; and, finally, some of the unique uses of language and verse in his drama.

In Chapter Three we offer a close reading of the famous history play *Henry V*, giving detailed guidance on reading the play and understanding Shakespeare's language and frames of reference. The play can be studied as a literary text and historical document that reframes real events from English (and French) social history and warfare. This chapter deals with the play as particularly concerned with masculine values, attached to the public sphere of political authority, government, war and also religion. In fact, the 'Englishness' of the play is tied up with the treatment of religion as an important frame for the action and character development, especially for the main character, King Henry V – a Christian monarch, by whose values the other characters and the events are measured. The chapter also highlights the depiction of class issues in the play, in the contrast between the 'low-life' characters and the courtiers. It argues that relations with women are seen largely in economic terms: women are presented as bearers of male children, the 'vessels' that carry on royal lineage and ownership of land and, therefore, power. Because the focus is principally on the play text, this chapter comes closest to what we have labelled 'dramatic criticism'.

In Chapter Four we study the tragedy *Othello*, considering the text in its social context and with regard to the changing perception of race issues and gender relations from Shakespeare's day to our own. We read the play and analyse specific scenes, but then go on to offer cultural and social interpretations of the events and dramatic techniques, in order to show that the play was both 'of its time' and relevant today. In considering the performance history of the play, we engage with controversial subjects such as the representation of race in the character of Othello, and the representation of gender and sexuality in the character of Desdemona – showing how these can be 'read' in performance through basic consideration of the visual and symbolic sign systems of the theatre. This chapter takes what we have loosely termed a 'theatre studies' approach.

In Chapter Five we introduce Behn's comedy *The Rover*, partly as a point of comparison with Shakespeare's work. Behn was a 'Restoration' playwright, working in the later seventeenth century – a very different social, political and theatrical context from Shakespeare's. Yet by looking at a play by a woman from roughly Shakespeare's period, we can compare the representations of gender issues and power issues in society and in the area of performance. Behn is also useful if one wants to assess the fluctuations in the English literary canon: we look at how popular her work was in its own day, consider why her work fell into relative neglect for so long, and then ask why scholars and theatre-makers have recently re-discovered her as part of a re-focused canon. This chapter begins with a study of Behn's play text in relation to its cultural context and production history ('theatre studies'), and then moves on to its potential for modern adaptation through live performance and recording for video ('performance studies').

Then in Chapter Six we look at a further play by Shakespeare, the comedy *As You Like It*. Here, as in Chapter Three, we consider the common Shakespearean themes of the 'real versus the ideal', and the individual within – and in exile from – society, and we ask whether these themes in performance add to our understanding of how and why Shakespeare came to be canonized. This chapter moves furthest towards a 'performance studies' approach, as it discusses the play text mainly in connection with its potential for performance; it gives examples from recent productions, and the inside-story of the play's development – from reading and auditions to workshops, rehearsals, and performance for video.

In each of these chapters we pick up and develop ideas about the canon set out in this first chapter. Then in Chapter Seven we review these ideas with reference to the four plays studied, in order to develop a new perspective on the canon as well as on each of the plays. We are aiming for a larger understanding of the nature of drama and theatre, which will contribute to our understanding of play texts and performances.

Some themes are common to all the chapters. For instance, the theme of gender relations is important in the study of all four plays, both in terms of characters and situations within the plays, and in terms of the reading, viewing and interpretation of the plays today. Gender issues are discussed at many levels throughout the book – with reference to the use of language, the representation of male access to the realm of war versus female access to the domestic realm, the treatment of Englishness as definitively masculine, and also in the construction of female identity within plays by a man (Shakespeare) and by a woman (Behn). Gender issues and the representation of power in performance are discussed in relation to the treatment of women by men, and in the significance of cross-dressing, which is a major theme in two of the plays (*The Rover* and *As You Like It*).

Another theme that is explored in all four plays is the relationship between the play text and its 'playing out' in terms of our developing understanding of drama, theatre and performance. Each chapter engages in a different way with the interpretative power of performance, the ability of the director or actor or designer or student/reader to engage with a text and imagine it in three dimensions. In Chapters Five and Six we have offered the inside-story of the live performances and Open University/BBC video productions of *The Rover* and *As You Like It*; and elsewhere we consider other film and video performances – all as part of the study of texts and performances in relation to the overall idea of the canon.

Summary

Our strategy in this book is to help you to understand the way in which the interpretation of texts and performances varies according to context. So we'll take different approaches to each of the plays discussed. With Shakespeare's *Henry V* we focus tightly on the *text* of the play. Next, with *Othello,* we look at the author's intention and the social context of the work. Then we offer a contrast: in Behn's *The Rover* we have a different author, writing in roughly the same period but with a very different view of gender and power. Finally, with *As You Like It*, we consider the role of the reader and audience today as interpreters, as part of the active process of canonizing and reviewing literature.

I hope the broad range of ideas covered in this chapter helps you to think about three related issues:

(a) what the term 'canon' means, or might mean

(b) how many variations and perspectives there can be on the idea of the canon

(c) how different frameworks for analysis lead to different definitions, ideas and approaches to the study of literature.

Further reading

Baldick, C. (1983) *The Social Mission of English Criticism*, Oxford University Press.

Bloom, H. (1994) *The Western Canon*, Harcourt Brace.

Davies, A. and Wells, S. (eds) (1994) *Shakespeare and the Moving Image*, Cambridge University Press.

Eagleton, T. (1983) *Literary Theory: An Introduction*, Basil Blackwell.

Eagleton, T. (1986) *William Shakespeare*, Basil Blackwell.

Gorak, J. (1991) *The Making of the Modern Canon: Genesis and Crisis of a Literary Idea*, Athlone Press.

Kamps, I. (ed.) (1995) *Materialist Shakespeare: A History*, Verso.

Novy, M. (ed.) (1993) *Cross-cultural Performances*, University of Illinois Press.

Ryan, K. (1989) *Shakespeare*, Harvester (2nd edn 1995).

Taylor, G. (1989) *Reinventing Shakespeare*, Oxford University Press.

Wayne, V. (ed.) (1991) *The Matter of Difference: Materialist Feminist Criticism of Shakespeare*, Harvester Wheatsheaf.

Wells, S. (ed.) (1990 edn) *Shakespeare: A Bibliographical Guide*, Oxford University Press.

Shakespeare: theatre poet

by W.R. Owens

The purpose of this chapter is to give you some basic information about William Shakespeare and the theatre he wrote for, and to say a word or two about the language of his plays. A great deal has been published on all these subjects, and if you want to explore them in depth you should consult the books listed at the end of the chapter. However, this chapter – though short – will give you the preparation you need before you launch into detailed study of *Henry V.* We begin by asking what is known about the playwright himself.

Who was William Shakespeare?

As we have seen from the previous chapter, the name 'Shakespeare' has acquired a unique cultural status. Within the space of a hundred years, between the 1660s and the 1760s, 'Bardolatry' elevated him to his present, unrivalled position of supremacy within English literary culture, and his plays to the status of canonical texts. Yet, extraordinary as it may seem, we know relatively little about the life of this most famous of writers. Unlike many of his opinionated, flamboyant contemporaries in the Elizabethan theatre, Shakespeare seems to have had little desire for self-promotion. Nor, although respected as a highly successful dramatist, was there any cult of him as 'the great canonical author' in his lifetime. Much of what we know about him is derived from public documents – legal records and the like – which give us hardly any insight into his personality. As a result, much of what has passed for Shakespeare biography is sheer speculation.

We do not even know for certain the exact date of his birth. The baptismal records of Stratford parish church show that he was baptized on 26 April 1564. Tradition has it that he was born three days earlier, on 23 April (St George's day), but this may simply reflect a patriotic wish to have the 'national poet' born on the day of the national patron saint. His father was a prosperous glove-maker who, though probably illiterate, proceeded through a series of minor public offices in Stratford to become an alderman and, in 1568, high bailiff (or what we would now call mayor). Later, though, he fell into debt and was taken off the town council.

William Shakespeare was probably educated at the local grammar school, where the masters would have taught him some Latin, history and biblical studies; they may have taught him a little Greek, but most of the teaching would have been done in Latin. The standard of teaching would have been high but, unlike many grammar school boys, Shakespeare did not go on to university.

Chapter Two

Instead, at the age of eighteen he married Anne Hathaway. Their first child, Susanna, was born after only six months, to be followed by twins, Hamnet and Judith, two years later in 1585. We have little certain knowledge of what Shakespeare did for the next seven years, but it has been suggested that he joined a touring group of players, before establishing a career in the London theatre as an actor and playwright. We can infer from an attack on him by the dramatist Robert Greene in 1592, who called him an 'upstart crow', that by the age of 28 he had achieved sufficient success in his chosen profession to arouse jealousy. By 1595 he had written several history plays, four comedies and two tragedies, and had collaborated on several other plays. He also kept up his career as an actor: it is reported that he took 'kingly parts', as well as playing the role of Adam in *As You Like It*, and later made a notable appearance as the Ghost in *Hamlet*. He went on to write plays at the rate of about two a year, and the three we will be studying in this book all come from the middle part of his writing career. *Henry V* and *As You Like It* were, it is thought, first performed in 1599, and *Othello* in 1604.

Between 1592 and 1594 the theatres were closed because of an outbreak of bubonic plague. When they re-opened, the London stage was dominated by a company called the Lord Chamberlain's Men. Shakespeare bought a share in the company, and went on to become its resident playwright. The company was based at a playhouse in Shoreditch known as the Theatre, and many of Shakespeare's early comedies and history plays were produced there. When, in 1597, the landlord threatened to evict them, Shakespeare and the other shareholders responded by dismantling the theatre and using the timbers to build the Globe on the south bank of the Thames. It was for this new theatre that Shakespeare wrote his greatest and most famous plays – comedies such as *Twelfth Night* and *As You Like It*, and tragedies such as *Hamlet, Othello, King Lear* and *Macbeth*.

Opened in 1599, the first Globe Theatre had a short life. In 1613 it was burned down when a cannon set fire to the thatched roof during a performance of Shakespeare's *Henry VIII*. It was rebuilt with a tiled roof but later demolished in 1644. Now, in the late twentieth century, a replica has been built on the same site, with a thatched roof as in the original – but made fire-resistant by modern chemicals. This project is the result of a long-cherished dream of the US actor and director, the late Sam Wanamaker.

Shakespeare was to work in London for many years, though he accumulated substantial property and land investments in Stratford and retired there towards the end of his life. He died in 1616 at the age of 52, and this time there is no doubt that it was St George's day: 23 April. He is buried in Holy Trinity Church, Stratford. Although we know little about him as a man, several accounts suggest that he was much loved by his contemporaries in the theatre. Fellow playwright Ben Jonson – though not an uncritical admirer – described him in his *Discoveries* as being 'honest, and of an open and free nature; had an excellent fancy, brave notions, and gentle expressions'. It seems, though, that Shakespeare was not a great 'company keeper', which is hardly to be wondered at – given the amount of work he had accomplished by the time of his death.

What was it like to see a play at the Globe?

Going to the public theatre in Shakespeare's time was a much riskier experience than we are used to today – and may have seemed more exciting. At the most trivial level there was the risk of getting soaked if you were a 'groundling', as standing spectators were called: the Globe was open to the sky. More seriously, in a society which had little or no control over public health, any congregation of people represented a serious threat of transmitting disease. The Globe was reputed to be able to hold up to 3,000 people and, since it was a smallish building, this meant that many people were packed together. In such circumstances infectious and contagious diseases are easily passed on, as are fleas and lice. It is hardly surprising that, when plague threatened, theatres were almost the first places to be closed. Public disorder was another risk: the Globe was cheek by jowl with bear-baiting pits and brothels and the unruly elements associated with them. Tudor England had little in the way of an organized police force: if things got out of hand, it was difficult to keep the peace. Finally, fire was a constant hazard; as we have seen, the Globe was in fact burnt down accidentally.

The most important pictorial information we have about Elizabethan public playhouses is a copy of Johannes de Witt's sketch, made in c.1596, of the interior of the Swan (overleaf). There has been enormous debate among scholars about the physical structure of such theatres, but I think we can assume that Shakespeare's Globe would have been very similar to the Swan, round or polygonal in shape, with a thatched roof for the galleries. As can be seen, there were three tiers of galleries (with the higher ones costing more to enter). Admission to the 'pit' or 'yard' where the groundlings stood cost a penny, the lower galleries twopence, and so on. The stage was a raised platform that projected out into the middle of the pit, so that the audience surrounded it on three sides, standing or sitting close to the action. At the back was a 'tiring-house' where the players changed (or 'attired') and from which they entered the stage through doors. Above the tiring-house was a balcony or gallery which could be used as a playing area, or for musicians. Half the stage was covered by a roof, which was supported by two wooden pillars and was known as the 'heavens'. On top of it was a 'hut' which contained the machinery for lowering objects and people, and from which stage-hands could produce thunder and lightning effects, trumpeters could sound fanfares announcing performances, and so forth. For further special effects there was at least one large trap-door in the stage.

Although props and stage effects were used at times (and we can see a simple bench in the de Witt sketch), the Elizabethan stage was bare of scenery. This does not mean that performances were drab: a good deal of time and money was spent on elaborate and colourful costumes (clothing being an important indicator of social status and occupation in the period). We also know something about the acting-styles of the time: Shakespeare's characters sometimes talk about the way in which particular gestures should accompany particular emotions, so we can infer that the acting was more conventional, more stylized, than we expect today. We also know that there would have been a lot of acrobatic 'tumbling', clowning, fencing, dancing and music. Some of the leading actors became very famous, with

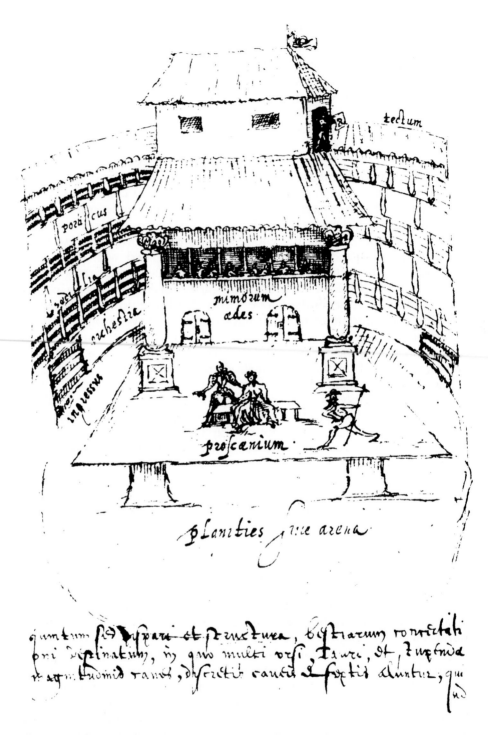

Figure 2.1   The Swan theatre, *c.*1596. The original drawing, by Johannes de Witt, survives only in this copy by Aernout van Buchel. We cannot be sure how accurately de Witt drew the original, or how faithfully van Buchel made his copy: *ingressus*, for example, may not mark the actual entrance, though *mimorum ædes* ('actors' house') is the 'tiring-house'. Note the trumpeter at the top of the hut. Photograph: Mansell Collection.

parts being written very much to display their talents. For example, Will Kempe, the resident comedian in Shakespeare's company, was probably the first Falstaff, while Richard Burbage, perhaps the most celebrated of the Elizabethan actors, won a huge reputation for his performances in the lead roles in *Othello, Hamlet* and *King Lear.*

Because of the lack of visual illusion, spectators would have had to use their imaginations actively, and a good deal of their attention would have been focused on the language of the play. Elizabethan culture was still very much an oral one, in which people would have been more accustomed than we are to following and responding to complex poetical speech. Action would be rapid, with one scene flowing into another with nothing more than a rhymed couplet to indicate the end of one and the beginning of the next. Finally, of course, there were no actresses: the parts of women were usually played by highly trained boys whose voices had not broken.

The audience at a playhouse such as the Globe would have represented a cross-section of Elizabethan society, with up to one in five Londoners being a regular playgoer. It should be stressed that plays such as those by Shakespeare were *popular* entertainments, by no means restricted to – or only addressing – the well-educated or socially superior. One observer reported that they were attended by 'water-men, shoemakers, butchers and apprentices … mechanics of all professions', while another drew attention to the numbers of 'nobility' and 'very honourable and handsome ladies' in the audiences. In the early part of the seventeenth century, however, there was a gradual shift away from the popular, outdoor playhouses towards new indoor theatres that catered for a more socially restricted audience of wealthy patrons who could pay higher admission charges. As we shall see in Chapter Five, by the second half of the seventeenth century outdoor theatres had disappeared completely in London and had been replaced by two indoor theatres.

The publication of Shakespeare's plays

It may come as a surprise to learn that fewer than half of Shakespeare's plays were published in his lifetime. *Othello*, for example, did not appear in print until 1622. Nor is there much evidence that Shakespeare was responsible for these published texts. Rather than thinking of himself as writing for publication, it's more likely that he thought of himself as writing for the stage, producing a dramatic script that would then be adapted and revised as part of the collaborative process of theatrical production. The plays he wrote would not have been regarded as his personal property, but were owned by the company who commissioned or bought them from him. As far as we know, he would have begun by writing out a draft in longhand. This would then have been rewritten, copied out neatly by a scribe, submitted to the Master of the Revels to be checked as suitable for performance, and censored if necessary. This version would have been turned into a 'prompt book' which, with stage directions, would form the basis of the production. Actors would not have been supplied with full copies of the

THE
CRONICLE
History of Henry the fift,

With his battell fought at *Agin Court* in
France. Togither with *Auntient
Pistoll.*

*As it hath bene sundry times playd by the Right honorable
the Lord Chamberlaine his seruants.*

LONDON

Printed by *Thomas Creede*, for Tho. Milling-
ton, and Iohn Busby. And are to be
sold at his house in Carter Lane, next
the Powle head. 1600.

Figure 2.2 The titlepage of the first quarto edition of *Henry V,* which was published in 1600. Quarto editions have a smaller format than folio editions. British
Library c12g22, reproduced by permission of the British Library Board.

text: they would have been given only their own parts and cues in hand-written copies in the form of scrolls.

This meant that the concept of a complete play only came together in performance, and the text would have been subject to alteration during rehearsals. It is worth considering the implications of this. We are so accustomed to thinking of Shakespeare's plays as *books* – fixed, unalterable, even revered entities – that it requires an effort of imagination to think of them instead as the raw material of live theatre which would change and develop through experimentation, improvisation, rehearsal and performance.

Playscripts were valuable assets to acting companies, who went to considerable lengths to prevent them from being published. Nevertheless, in the absence of copyright laws, there was little protection against piracy and some plays were published in quarto form. ('Quarto' comes from the printing process in which sheets of paper are first printed with *four* pages on each side and then folded twice and bound together in 'gatherings' to make a small-format book.) Nearly half of Shakespeare's thirty-eight plays were published as quartos between 1594 and his death in 1616, and quarto versions of individual plays continued to be published throughout the seventeenth century. The texts were of varying accuracy: the more corrupt ones, where the sense is sometimes difficult to make out, are often referred to by modern scholars as 'bad' quartos, and there is much controversy as to their origin. Were they illicit transcripts, taken down in shorthand by some member of the audience, or do they represent the text as memorized by an actor?

In 1623, seven years after Shakespeare's death, two of his actor colleagues collected his plays together and published them in a more formal edition known as the 'First Folio'. (Again, 'folio' is from printing: in this case *two* pages are printed on each side of sheets of paper which are then each folded once. The more pages printed on sheets and the more times they are folded, the smaller the format of the book. Hence a folio is the largest size of book.)

There are very significant differences between the texts of quartos and the First Folio, and Shakespeare scholars have debated these energetically. Whereas in the past the folio text has been regarded as more authoritative, many now consider that the quartos, even the 'bad quartos', may represent crucial evidence of how the plays were actually performed on the stage. Some have even argued that, in cases such as *King Lear*, the quarto and the folio differ so radically that they represent what are virtually two distinct plays, and that they should be published as independent texts.

The important point to remember when you turn to study a Shakespeare play is that your modern edition has been constructed by scholars who have had to make many decisions about which words to print as Shakespeare's. There is not a single play where we can be certain that all the words we are reading are exactly the ones Shakespeare wrote. Most editors include an account of the textual problems they have had to consider, and list variant readings from quarto and folio texts.

Figure 2.3   The titlepage of the First Folio edition, published in 1623. The engraving of Shakespeare is by Martin Droeshout. British Library G11631, reproduced by permission of the British Library Board; photograph: Mansell Collection.

Language and poetry in Shakespeare's plays

Although they are primarily concerned to establish an authoritative text, editors try to make Shakespeare's language as accessible as possible to modern readers by modernizing the spelling, punctuation and other typographical features of the original such as use of capital letters and italics. (You might like to compare your modern edition of *Henry V* with the extracts in Figures 2.4 and 2.5.) Despite these efforts, some aspects of the language used by Shakespeare remain strikingly different from the English language we write and speak today.

One obvious difference is that some of the words used by Shakespeare have fallen out of use completely. When Pistol in *Henry V* (II.1.106–7) says that he will 'sutler be/Unto the camp', most readers now need to be told that a 'sutler' is someone who makes a living selling provisions to soldiers. Other words have altered in their intensity: a famous example is in Othello's final speech, where he refers to the murder of Desdemona as an 'unlucky deed' (V.2.337). This is not to be read as understatement: 'unlucky' had a much stronger meaning then, carrying overtones of grave misfortune. Hardest of all to spot are cases where a word has changed its meaning over the years, but where the modern meaning – misleadingly – makes a kind of sense in the context. An example of this is where Othello is described (IV.2.138) as having been 'abused by some most villainous knave', where 'abused' does not mean insulted, as we might think nowadays, but 'deceived'. Because of these shifts in meaning and use, modern editors provide notes to help explain such words. It would be wrong to exaggerate the difficulty posed by this, or by unfamiliar grammatical constructions. It is often possible to get the drift of what a character is saying from the context, but when you pause to look more closely at particular passages, you will need to use the notes to your text to make sure you fully understand the words.

The authors of the following chapters will have much to say about particular linguistic and stylistic features of the texts as they work through them with you. Before you turn to these, I want to say a brief word about perhaps the most important feature of Shakespeare's plays – the fact that they are largely composed of poetry, not prose.

What distinguishes poetry most obviously from prose is that it is arranged in lines of a particular length, and these lines are given a rhythmic, or metrical, pattern. This pattern is achieved by arranging stressed and unstressed syllables within the line, and it is possible to analyse, or 'scan', a line of poetry to work out its metrical pattern. In scansion, the mark '/' is used to indicate a stressed syllable, while 'x' indicates an unstressed syllable. Each unit made up of stressed and unstressed syllables is called a 'foot'. In English, the most common foot is the *iamb*, which is an unstressed syllable followed by a stressed one (x /), as in the word 'tŏdáy'. The next most common foot is the *trochee*, a stressed syllable followed by an unstressed one (/ x), as in the word 'ríddlĕ'. Others include the *anapest* (x x /) and the *dactyl* (/ x x), which are triple rhythms, rising or falling respectively as in 'ŏvĕrcóme' and 'cértăinlў'.

Lines of verse are described according to the number of feet they contain, as follows: monometer (one foot), dimeter (two feet), trimeter (three

Enter Thambassadors from France.

Now are we well prepared to know the Dolphins pleasure,
For we heare your comming is from him.

Ambassa. Pleaseth your Maiestie to giue vs leaue
Freely to render what we haue in charge :
Or shall I sparingly shew a farre off,
The Dolphins pleasure and our Embassage ?

King. We are no tyrant, but a Christian King,
To whom our spirit is as subiect,
As are our wretches fettered in our prisons.

Therefore freely and with vncurbed boldnesse
Tell vs the Dolphins minde.

Ambas. Then this in fine the Dolphin saith,
Whereas you clayme certaine Townes in *France*,
From your predecessor king *Edward* the third,
This he returnes.
He saith, theres nought in *France* that can be with a nimble
Galliard wonne : you cannot reuel into Dukedomes there:
Therefore he sendeth meeter for your study,
This tunne of treasure : and in lieu of this,
Desires to let the Dukedomes that you craue
Heare no more from you : This the Dolphin saith.

King. What treasure Vncle?

Exe. Tennis-balles my Liege.

King. We are glad the Dolphin is so pleasant with vs,
Your message and his present we accept :
When we haue matched our rackets to these balles,
We will by Gods grace play such a set,
Shall strike his fathers crowne into the hazard.

Figure 2.4 The French ambassadors' visit, as given in this first quarto edition of *Henry V.* Compare the text with Figure 2.5, an extract from the First Folio edition. British Library c12g22, reproduced by permission of the British Library Board.

feet), tetrameter (four feet), pentameter (five feet), hexameter (six feet), heptameter (seven feet), and octameter (eight feet). By far the most widely used of these are the tetrameter and the pentameter.

The particular form of poetry that Shakespeare used is known as *blank verse* and, if you have not studied it before, it is important that you understand its basic structure. Blank verse is arranged in unrhymed iambic pentameters. This means that a perfectly regular iambic pentameter line will have five stressed syllables, or beats, with five unstressed syllables, making ten in all. Here is a short speech from *Henry V* (I.2. 122–4) to illustrate this. Say the lines aloud, tapping your fingers to count out the five stresses:

Your brother kings and monarchs of the earth
Do all expect that you should rouse yourself,
As did the former lions of your blood.

Figure 2.5 The French ambassadors' visit, as given in this First Folio edition. British Library G11631, reproduced by permission of the British Library Board.

I have marked it as if it were in absolutely regular iambic form, but of course no one would actually *speak* the lines like this. Here is how the main stresses might fall when the lines are spoken:

> Your brother kings and monarchs of the earth
> Do all expect that you should rouse yourself,
> As did the former lions of your blood.

You will see that, in my version, only four syllables in the first and third lines are given a full stress, and only three in the second. But you might want to scan the lines slightly differently: for example, you may feel that 'As' should not be stressed.

Because iambic pentameter – especially in its unrhymed, 'blank verse' form – often resembles ordinary speech patterns very closely, it is possible

31

to read it for the sense alone, not attending to the metre. In my view, however, the underlying iambic beat or pulse is extremely important in giving the lines their sense of movement and flow, and it is worth spending a little time making sure that you can identify it. Indeed I would go even further and argue that actors should not ignore the form of the verse in performance, but should indicate, if only by the slightest of pauses, where each line ends. It seems to me, though many actors and directors would not agree, that we should always be aware that we are listening to poetry as distinct from prose.

Those three lines from *Henry V* are a relatively simple example of Shakespearean blank verse. What you will discover as you proceed in your study is that Shakespeare can achieve the most amazingly complex effects within this strict metrical form. To end this discussion of language and poetry in his plays, let us look very briefly at a famous speech from the second play you will study, *Othello*. The hero, Othello, has been persuaded by Iago that his wife has been unfaithful, and he determines to kill her for this. Iago pretends to advise Othello to have patience, pointing out that perhaps his mind will change.

> OTHELLO Never, Iago. Like to the Pontic sea,
> Whose icy current and compulsive course
> Ne'er feels retiring ebb, but keeps due on
> To the Propontic and the Hellespont,
> Even so my bloody thoughts with violent pace
> Shall ne'er look back, ne'er ebb to humble love,
> Till that a capable and wide revenge
> Swallow them up. Now, by yond marble heaven,
> In the due reverence of a sacred vow
> I here engage my words.
>
> (III.3.450–59)

It is, I think, easy enough to work out the meaning of the words here. Notes to the text tell us that the 'Pontic sea' is the Black Sea, the 'Propontic' is the Sea of Marmora, and the 'Hellespont' is the Dardanelles. Othello is comparing the motion of his own 'bloody thoughts' to the irresistible onward motion of the Pontic as it surges through the Propontic towards the Dardanelles and into the Mediterranean. The lines could be scanned in different ways, depending on what effect the actor wanted to achieve. But responding to, and giving expression to, the stress patterns in a speech like this involves much more than a mechanical counting of syllables. What we sense – particularly when reading the passage aloud – is that the rhythm of the lines, the forward rush of the clauses, enacts in the movement of the speech the rush of the mighty stream as Othello is swept along on the purposeful current of his passion. In such a passage, we see why Shakespeare is described as a 'poetic dramatist': the poetic language and expression here are a crucial part of the dramatic means by which we come to understand and respond to the character of Othello.

Further reading

Berry, C. (1993 edn) *The Actor and the Text*, Virgin Books.

Dobson, M. (1992) *The Making of the National Poet: Shakespeare, Adaptation and Authorship, 1660–1769*, Oxford University Press.

Gurr, A. (1980 edn) *The Shakespearean Stage, 1574–1642*, Cambridge University Press.

Gurr, A. (1987) *Playgoing in Shakespeare's London*, Cambridge University Press.

Holderness, G. (ed.) (1987) *The Shakespeare Myth*, Manchester University Press.

Hussey, S.S. (1982) *The Literary Language of Shakespeare*, Longman.

Schoenbaum, S. (1977) *William Shakespeare: A Compact Documentary Life*, Clarendon Press.

Thomson, P. (1992) *Shakespeare's Professional Career*, Cambridge University Press.

Wells, S. (ed.) (1986) *The Cambridge Companion to Shakespeare Studies*, Cambridge University Press.

Wells, S. (ed.) (1990 edn) *Shakespeare: a Bibliographical Guide*, Clarendon Press.

An English history play: reading and studying Henry V

by Simon Eliot

Introduction

In case this is the first Shakespeare play you have studied, I shall try to give you as much practice as possible in close reading of the text. But because, like most plays, *Henry V* was originally written to be performed, I shall discuss some of the features of the Elizabethan theatre for which Shakespeare wrote. I shall also occasionally refer to two film performances of *Henry V* – Laurence Olivier's of 1944 and Kenneth Branagh's of 1989. It will be very helpful if you can watch at least one of them (they are widely available on VHS video cassette), and even better if you can see a live performance.

In considering the play in this way, it's important to remind ourselves that film, television and theatre productions make for very different sorts of performance, with different advantages and disadvantages. For instance, in the theatre a member of the audience can choose to look at any part of the stage and at any actor or group of actors in sight; the viewer of a film can only look at what the camera is prepared to show, and in the detail and at the angle and in the light the director chooses. (A modern theatre director can, of course, use sophisticated lighting, but this would not have been available to Shakespeare: performances in the Globe took place in the afternoon in broad daylight.)

To give another example: in representing Agincourt, limitations of space and cast mean that a theatrical performance must represent the battle, as Shakespeare puts it, 'With four or five most vile and ragged foils/Right ill-disposed in brawl ridiculous' (IV.Chorus.50–51). In a film (given enough money) the director might be tempted to recreate a 'realistic' battle with hundreds of extras (as Olivier does). Although at first glance this would suggest that film and TV, with larger budgets, would have an advantage over the theatre, this is not necessarily the case because it can lead to distortions of the text. For instance, *Henry V* contains only one scene that represents the battle of Agincourt, and that is a comic one featuring Pistol. Both the Olivier and Branagh productions, however, spend a lot of time on the battle, and one could argue that such a preoccupation unbalances their interpretations. These points should be borne in mine when we are discussing performances on film. But before we pursue these and other issues, I want to map out Chapter Three.

The chapter is divided into five unequal sections. Section 1, **Themes in the text**, is much the longest and explores a series of themes that run right through the play:

1 the king's search for justification
2 modesty and pride
3 money and the making of deals

4   the omnipresence of death
5   the rhetoric of politics
6   the king as an actor.

For each theme we will work our way through the play, looking for interesting examples so that, by the end of the final theme, you should know the text quite well. Although the themes are distinct, you will find that they overlap and relate to each other. For instance, Henry's avoidance of pride (theme 2) is part of his 'deal' with God (theme 3), which in turn relates to his attempts to justify himself to God and man (theme 1). Many of the themes will touch on the tension between what the characters say and what they do – between (and this is a very common Shakespearian idea) appearance and reality. This is strongest in themes 1, 5 and 6 but it crops up frequently elsewhere. Of course, appearance and reality are central to the play in another way: the Chorus is forever reminding us of the gap between the reality of Henry V's life and what we see portrayed on the stage. It is only appropriate that, in this play which refers explicitly to the limitations of the theatre, we find that one explanation for the gap between appearance and reality is that a successful political and military leader has to act many parts according to the demands of the time, just like an actor in a theatre. By the end of theme 6 we should be in a position to appreciate the irony that, although the audience knows that it is only an actor who is portraying Henry, the king portrayed in *Henry V* is himself a supreme political actor. In other words, the audience understands that the actor acting an 'unreal' part may be as close as we can ever get to what the 'real' Henry actually did and was. Later on you will be studying *As You Like It* where Jaques comments that 'All the world's a stage,/And all the men and women merely players' (II.7.140–41); in one sense *Henry V* is a serious exploration of that idea.

Section 2, *Henry V*: **history and the canon**, deals with the play as it relates to history and to the idea of the canon. Being a play, the text was subject to much alteration in performance, so we always have to ask ourselves what precisely is being canonized. But *Henry V* raises particular problems about the canon, because the very historical figure of Henry was 'canonical' long before Shakespeare wrote about him.

Section 3, *Henry V*: **politics and performance**, carries on the idea of performance by looking at the political significance of the play as it might have struck audiences contemporary with Shakespeare.

Section 4, **The contrary Chorus**, returns us to the text of the play to look at the way in which the 'appearance and reality' theme can be observed in the relationship between the Chorus and the rest of the play, and between the Chorus and the theatre to which he frequently refers.

Section 5, **Conclusion: 'In little room' and in 'Small time'**, brings together some of the themes of Section 1 and places them very briefly in the setting of the Elizabethan theatre.

If you have not already done so, you should now read *Henry V*. Getting hold of the Olivier and Branagh videos would also help, though don't worry if you can't.

(Note that all quotations in this chapter are taken from The New Penguin Shakespeare edition of *Henry V*, edited by A.R. Humphreys, 1968.)

1 Themes in the text

Theme: 'Upon the king' – the search for justification

Let's begin by looking at an early scene in the play. In Act I, Scene 2, Canterbury presents the justification for Henry's invasion of France. It takes the form of a long-winded argument about whether or not the Salic Law – which forbids descent of the crown through the female line – applies to France. The important matter, however, is whether it provides justification or not.

Why is Henry so keen to have his act justified? In one sense the answer is obvious: as he himself asserts, he's a lawful Christian king; his acts must therefore be lawful and, if possible, justified by the Church: 'My learnèd lord, we pray you to proceed,/And justly and religiously unfold' (I.2.9–10).

But the speech is more than an invitation to deliver judgement. It is a warning against the dangers of ingenious but false argument. It is also an explicit warning about the horrors of war:

> For God doth know how many now in health
> Shall drop their blood in approbation
> Of what your reverence shall incite us to
> …
> For never two such kingdoms did contend
> Without much fall of blood …
>
> (I.2.18–20, 24–5)

What would you say Henry was most worried about in this speech?

Discussion

It is that he might be drawn into a war in which all the suffering was unjustified because the cause was not true; he thinks of those

> whose guiltless drops
> Are every one a woe, a sore complaint
> 'Gainst him whose wrongs gives edge unto the swords
> That makes such waste in brief mortality.
>
> (25–8) ∎

'Mortal' was a common synonym for a human being in Shakespeare's plays (hardly surprising in a period when, with high infant mortality rates and low life-expectancy, death was frequently an early and sudden visitor). Even in Shakespeare's comedies we are reminded of our brief span ('Lord, what fools these mortals be!', says Puck of the human lovers in *A Midsummer Night's Dream*). Thus 'mortality' here stands for humanity, a humanity whose common characteristic was that it did not last long ('brief mortality').

Having set up this vision of vulnerable and temporary life, Shakespeare intensifies its poignancy with the image of the just (or unjust) sword making 'waste' even in the ranks of the briefly living. Henry's argument is reminiscent of another much later in the play. **Can you think of another occasion in the text when the link between the suffering of brief mortality and the justice of the King's cause is discussed?**

Discussion

The debate between Williams and the disguised Henry in IV.1. We shall look at this in greater detail later, but it is worth reminding yourself now that the context of the debate is set by Williams's moving vision of death in battle:

> some swearing, some crying for a surgeon,
> some upon their wives left poor behind them, some upon
> the debts they owe, some upon their children rawly left.
> (IV.1.134–6) ■

To return to I.2: have you noticed that, in the first scene in which he appears, it is Henry, and only Henry of all those on stage, who seems fully aware of the horrors of war? Canterbury describes war, but it is in terms of a jolly enthusiast wishing to recreate the glories of Henry's great uncle, the Black Prince (the 'lion's whelp'):

> Whiles his most mighty father on a hill
> Stood smiling to behold his lion's whelp
> Forage in blood of French nobility.
> ...
> And let another half stand laughing by,
> All out of work and cold for action!
> (I.2.108–10, 113–14)

'Stood smiling to behold', 'stand laughing by': it is as though the other characters were merely spectators in a sort of rhetorical game whose terrible outcome in the real world only Henry saw clearly.

Given that he does see vividly the inevitable pain and suffering of war, it is Henry who needs the clearest legal and moral justification for it. He looks, quite naturally, to the Church to provide it – and it does. (Why it does is explained in the very first scene of the play.) To present a justification, and even more to accept it, is to take intellectual and moral responsibility for the actions that flow from it. **How does Henry accept this responsibility? Please look at I.2.29–32.**

Discussion

He doesn't. He lays the responsibility squarely on the Archbishop:

> For we will hear, note, and believe in heart
> That what you speak is in your conscience washed
> As pure as sin with baptism.
> (I.2.30–32)

In other words, he will believe whatever he is told. Why Henry adopts this position is one of the questions explored in themes 5 and 6. ■

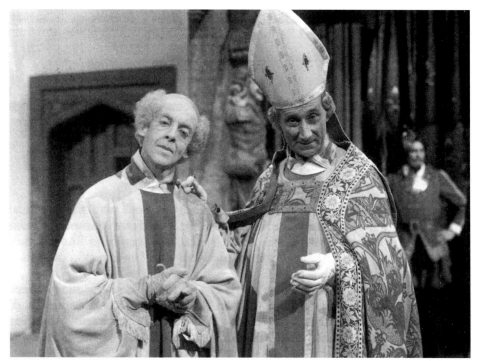

Figure 3.1 An up-beat *Henry V*: the Salic Law scene played for laughs, with Robert Helpmann as the Bishop of Ely and Felix Aylmer as the Archbishop of Canterbury in the film directed by Laurence Olivier, 1944. Two Cities, courtesy of The Kobal Collection.

Figure 3.2 A sombre *Henry V*: the Salic Law scene as power-politics, with Charles Kay as the Archbishop of Canterbury and Kenneth Branagh as Henry in the film directed by Branagh, 1989. Renaissance Films/BBC/Curzon Films, courtesy of the Kobal Collection.

Despite this invitation, the Salic Law speech clearly doesn't quite satisfy Henry's wants, for at its end, he repeats his question:

> May I with right and conscience make this claim?
> (I.2.96)

The Archbishop, being a perceptive and obliging politician, reads Henry's unspoken need and provides him with the ideal answer, one that both justifies his action and relieves the burden of personal responsibility:

> The sin upon my head, dread sovereign!
> (I.2.97)

Thus morally bolstered, the king is now ready to deal with the practical strategic problems posed by the Scots (a subject tactfully ignored by both Olivier and Branagh). Once that is done, he has the leisure to find another person who will take a share of the responsibility for his invasion of France – the Dauphin.

Please look at Henry's speech (I.2.260–98) and see how many times the king lays the blame on the Dauphin for the terrible consequences of war. **Then, thinking back to lines 222–34, ask yourself whether Henry was right to hold the Dauphin responsible.**

Discussion

I counted three occasions on which Henry points the finger at the Dauphin:

> and his soul
> Shall stand sore chargèd for the wasteful vengeance
> That shall fly with them:
> …
> And some are yet ungotten and unborn
> That shall have cause to curse the Dauphin's scorn.
> …
> and tell the Dauphin
> His jest will savour but of shallow wit
> When thousands weep more than did laugh at it.
> (I.2.283–5, 288–9, 295–7)

As Henry had already resolved to invade France (222–6) before receiving the tennis balls, the Dauphin's undiplomatic joke can hardly be said to be the cause of war. The 'jest' does however provide an additional justification, which helps Henry further divest himself publicly of moral responsibility for the invasion. ■

Dealing with the Southampton Conspiracy (Act II)

Let us look at another example where Henry uses others to underwrite his decisions morally. Please re-read II.2.

It is clear that Scroop, Cambridge and Grey are guilty of high treason in that their intention is to kill the king. The law is clear: death is the appropriate penalty. Even if this were not the case, policy would require their execution for Henry cannot afford to have potential traitors at his back while campaigning in France (he is already worried about the threat from the Scots: I.2). At the beginning of II.2 it is clear that both the king and his loyal courtiers know of the plot: 'The King hath note of all that they intend,/By interception which they dream not of' (II.2.6–7).

Why play this elaborate cat-and-mouse game with the conspirators?

D i s c u s s i o n

First, it fits in to a pattern of presenting Henry in some sort of disguise or playing some role other than his true one. (Later in *Henry V* the king will disguise himself and go among the common soldiers before Agincourt.) Second, it gives Shakespeare the chance to refer to an earlier part of the scene where Henry showed his common touch and his exercise of mercy. We have been told already that 'We are no tyrant, but a Christian king' (I.2.242) and one of the prerogatives of a Christian king is mercy. So, despite the urgings of Cambridge, Scroop and Grey, Henry releases the drunk who had 'railed against our person' (II.2.41). ∎

This incident, moreover, allows Henry to punish the conspirators without seeming vindictive for, in urging Henry to punish the drunk, they had sealed their own fate:

> The mercy that was quick in us but late
> By your own counsel is suppressed and killed.
> You must not dare, for shame, to talk of mercy,
> For your own reasons turn into your bosoms
> As dogs upon their masters, worrying you.
> (II.2.79–83)

Law and political necessity would have justified execution, but for Henry that doesn't appear to be enough: the conspirators must by their 'own counsel' be condemned.

The debate with Williams (Act IV)

Two of the themes we have been discussing – the king in disguise, and the re-direction of responsibility – come to a climax in the scenes before Agincourt and, in particular, Henry's conversation with Bates and Williams. Please turn to Act IV and read the Chorus and Scene 1 from the beginning to line 290.

The Act begins with the Chorus describing the night before Agincourt and contrasting the arrogant and confident French with the weary and apprehensive English. In order to raise its spirit, Henry tours his army – displaying yet again his sense of commonality ('And calls them brothers, friends, and countrymen') and conveying to the audience a sense of how dependent the English cause is on one man:

> That every wretch, pining and pale before,
> Beholding him, plucks comfort from his looks.

41

A largess universal, like the sun,
His liberal eye doth give to every one …

(IV.Chorus.41–4)

Henry then borrows a cloak from Sir Thomas Erpingham and declares:

I and my bosom must debate awhile,
And then I would no other company.

(IV.1.31–2)

It is significant that, in this highly political play about public figures, this is the first time the audience has seen Henry alone and thus in a position to deliver a soliloquy, the conventional way in which a playwright could convey the inner workings and thoughts of a character. In fact the soliloquy, and the prayer that follows it, are deferred by the entry of three sets of characters – Pistol; Fluellen and Gower; Bates, Court and Williams. This could have been used simply to confirm what the Chorus had already told us about Henry's beneficial influence on his troops, but Shakespeare does not do this. Henry, wearing Sir Thomas's cloak, is now in disguise and thus has dispensed with 'ceremony'; for better or worse Henry as a 'common man' (IV.8.51) will now be confronted with the truth unfiltered by reverence or fear. This change is marked by a change in the relationship between the actors on stage. In the 'little touch of Harry' episode, Henry had actively sought out the soldiers; now he remains passively in one spot while his soldiers inadvertently come to him.

It is a measure of the complexity and richness of this play that what we actually see is a muddle of reactions – from the comic (Pistol), through the practicalities of professional soldiers (Fluellen and Gower), to the rational anxieties of frightened men. The conversation with Pistol starts well with an unforced compliment to Henry, but it soon degenerates and ends with Pistol throwing an insult as he exits. Henry makes no direct contact with Fluellen and Gower. His third experience, with Bates, Court and Williams, quickly drifts into argument. Court has little to say, but Bates and Williams raise issues that require all Henry's much vaunted rhetorical talents to answer.

Henry begins by stressing the common humanity of the king (99–109); Bates takes this up and promptly identifies his wishes ('in Thames up to the neck') with those of the king; Henry responds by rehearsing what he will say on the day of the battle itself, namely that he would not want to be anywhere else but here. Bates responds in a way which makes clear that he doesn't fully accept the adequacy of Henry's 'common humanity' argument. Henry may share feelings with other men, but his position would mean that he was valuable to his enemy: Henry's life would be spared and a ransom paid; the common man could not hope for such salvation. In other words, what Henry describes as 'ceremonies' (102), Bates perceives as having substantial benefits in the real world.

Henry changes tack and lays stress on the moral justification of his invasion of France: 'his cause being just/and his quarrel honourable' (123–4). This again raises the issue of justification with which the play began and which we have been pursuing so far in this section, and it is at this point that Henry's most formidable opponent enters the argument. The exact meaning of Williams's snappish 'That's more than we know' (125) is uncertain: it could mean 'we are ignorant of that' or 'we haven't had that proved to us' or 'we are not yet convinced by that'. However, whatever the precise meaning, the moral circumstances of the common soldier are made clear: he is fighting, and might possibly die, for a cause of whose justice and honour he is uncertain. Bates's response in lines 127–9 is one particular defence: we should be unconcerned by the rights and wrongs of the issue, our obedience to our lawful monarch exonerates us. This sort of argument should be familiar to us in the twentieth century, for it is a version of the 'just obeying orders' defence which was not accepted by the Nuremberg War Crimes Tribunal after the Second World War.

Williams seems to accept Bates's argument, but he then develops it in an unexpected way for he turns it directly on to the king who must, he argues, take responsibility for the justice of the cause. **Please read Williams's speech (130–142). How would you summarize his case?**

D i s c u s s i o n

It looks like one single argument, but there is a case for regarding it as two related but distinct ones: the first is a general one about the anguish, pain and wild regret of those dying violently and before their time (this lies between lines 130 and 136); the second is a more theological argument about the moral state in which people die (137–42). Let's take them separately.

Williams doesn't pull any punches; he has already said that he is convinced that he will not survive another day ('but I think we shall never see the end of it': 89–90) so has no time for euphemism or courtesy. He begins with a vision of the Day of Judgement when the bodies dismembered in the battle are resurrected and reassembled. (In Shakespeare's day, and well into the twentieth century, one of the tenets of the Church was the belief in the resurrection of the physical body.) Very quickly, however, we move from a conventional image to something much more explicit and personal, Williams's own vivid and moving vision of death in battle:

> some swearing, some crying for a surgeon,
> some upon their wives left poor behind them, some upon
> the debts they owe, some upon their children rawly left.

Into these three crowded lines is packed the diversity of humanity and its response to suffering: from the brutish ('some swearing'), through the desperately practical ('crying for a surgeon') to the heart-rending ('upon their children rawly left'). The poignancy is made sharper by the very practicality of even the most moving of the responses, for what the dying men are most worried about is the economic consequences of their deaths on those they love – the 'wives left poor', 'the debts they owe', 'children rawly left'. In other words, the majority of Williams's examples illustrate not brutish or selfish dying thoughts, but loving and selfless ones.

This will be important when we look at Williams's second argument. 'I am afeard there are few die well that die in a battle' is the sentence that marks the transition from the first to the second argument. It looks back to the suffering Williams has just described and forward to what one might call the theological argument, for 'to die well' had a very specific meaning in early modern Europe: it suggested that you died with your property disposed of (through a legal will), at peace with family and friends and, most important of all, at peace with God with all your sins forgiven. If you could die with a piety on your lips surrounded by your family, and in your own bed, so much the better. Thus Williams's question, 'how can they charitably dispose of any thing when blood is their argument?', is apt. However, it is also a weaker argument, particularly for Henry who, as we have been told (see I.1.38–40), is skilled in theological argument. ■

Please read Henry's reply (IV.1.143–80). Try to summarize it in a few lines. Does it answer Williams's argument?

Discussion

Very roughly Henry's argument goes as follows. If a man, who has not sought forgiveness for his sins, dies accidentally while on a job, you do not blame the man who employed him: the employer did not intend his death and, anyway, cannot be responsible for the state of another man's soul. Every soldier should prepare for battle by having his sins forgiven him; if he dies, he will be in a good state; if he lives, God clearly intended that he should survive as an example to others.

As an answer to Williams's second argument, it is pretty good: 'Every subject's duty/is the king's; but every subject's soul is his own'. In other words, you cannot escape responsibility for your moral and spiritual state by just obeying orders. In the context of the play, however, there are certain disturbing features. It may well be that Henry didn't intend the soldiers' deaths when he launched the campaign, but death – and lots of it – is an inevitable result of war in a way that it is not in the cases of the son or the servant sent on ordinary commercial enterprises as described by Henry. In another context, Henry has already admitted this, as you may recall:

> For never two such kingdoms did contend
> Without much fall of blood, whose guiltless drops
> Are every one a woe, a sore complaint
> 'Gainst him whose wrongs gives edge unto the swords
> That makes such waste in brief mortality.
>
> (I.2.24–8)

This is surely very close to Williams's arguments. Even if we accept that Henry wins the theological argument on points, can we say that his response adequately justifies the 'waste in brief mortality' so vividly illustrated by the reference to the cries of the dying men? The point here is surely that, apart possibly from those who die swearing, there is no indication of wickedness in these cases. Indeed, it is quite the contrary: they are men dying with thoughts of the suffering of those they leave behind; and unless they are rich, a properly ordered death of the sort Henry recommends would have no effect on the fears they take into death with them. ■

It's an uncomfortable scene altogether: Henry can browbeat Williams but he cannot fully answer his questions. The argument changes direction (and becomes a matter of whether or not the king will be ransomed), but the issue is still unresolved at the end of the scene – with Williams threatening to fight it out if he survives the battle.

There isn't the space here (but see below, 'and profits will accrue') to consider how the conflict is resolved, but you might like to look at IV.7.122–78 and IV. 8.1–72 and consider the way in which Henry deals with the issue, first by proxy (Fluellen) and then by rewarding (or paying off?) Williams. It is by this time a comic scene, which emphasizes both Henry's common touch and his tolerance, but neither forgiveness nor reward is an adequate response to Williams's vision nor to his questions about kingly responsibility.

The debate within the King (Act IV)

Kingly responsibility is the theme of the sole soliloquy Shakespeare gives Henry, but if we expect it to take up the issues raised in the Williams scene, we shall be disappointed. In essence this is a variation on similar speeches (the most famous being 'Uneasy lies the head that wears the crown') in *Richard II* and in *Henry IV, Part 2*. However, the opening few lines do indicate that at least part of Williams's argument has struck home. **Look at IV.1.223–30 and see if you can find the evidence for this.**

D i s c u s s i o n
In listing the burdens the common man places on the king, Henry includes 'Our debts, our careful wives,/Our children' (IV.1.224–5), which exactly reproduces three of Williams's five examples. ∎

What is interesting about this speech is that Henry seems to accept the burden of responsibility as a natural and inevitable function of kingship: 'We must bear all. O hard condition,/Twin-born with greatness' (226–7). What he cannot acknowledge in public, in private he accepts as inevitable: the soliloquy is about the gap between the rewards of kingship ('ceremony') and its burdens, not about redistributing responsibility. This idea can be taken further. The soliloquy is interrupted by Erpingham, and when he exits Henry prays. Although not formally a soliloquy, a prayer in drama can function in a very similar way. The prayer begins as a conventional invocation to a God whom Henry, as we have seen, has always confidently claimed for his side. Having asked God to steel his soldiers' hearts, Henry suddenly slips sideways into something that has no logical link to what went before. It is some measure of the force of this subject that it breaks through for the first time at this critical point. Henry IV, Henry's father, had usurped the throne of Richard II and had later colluded with Richard's killer. Henry IV carried this stain of killing God's anointed king. Henry V fears that he has inherited that stain, and thus prays: 'O not today, think not upon the fault/My father made in compassing the crown!' (286–7).

Most extraordinary is the fact that the character who has devoted many of his public utterances to distributing responsibility elsewhere, is revealed – in the brief moments in which we hear him talking to himself and to God – as accepting in private more than his fair share of guilt and

45

responsibility. Indeed, by the end of the prayer the entire burden of responsibility is seen to be resting on Henry's shoulders. The private man from his prayers, and the public man from his deliberations, rises with the terrible recognition that everything is dependent on him alone: 'The day, my friends, and all things stay for me' (301).

Theme: 'O God, Thy arm was here' – modesty and pride

We have seen that Henry is eager to find justification for his actions – particularly the declaration and prosecution of war – by placing the responsibility for negative consequences on others' shoulders (the Archbishop, the Dauphin, the conspirators at Southampton, the French king). However, what is also striking is Henry's equal keenness not to claim responsibility for the positive consequences of his actions. Whenever glory, triumph or power are in the offing, Henry does his best to side-step them by offering them all to God.

Piety was an important component in the make-up of an ideal monarch, and the character of Henry has it in abundance. In the play it takes two forms. The first is the king's frequent acknowledgement that all his plans are dependent on the approval of God. This dependence, this need for God's co-operation, recurs frequently, particularly in the earlier part of the play. The second form of piety is the need to acknowledge God's participation in a successful outcome and to deny his own achievements in favour of attributing them all to God. Both these can be explained in terms of a Christian tradition which emphasizes the helplessness of mortal humanity and the need to avoid the cardinal sin of pride. Henry is always extremely careful to give the glory to God. The corollary of this, of course, is that characters marked down for doom are frequently characterized by displays of over-confidence, vanity and pride. **Can you think of an example of such hubris in *Henry V*?**

Discussion

You need look no further than the French nobles, and in particular the Dauphin. In II.4, for instance, the Dauphin inclines to underestimate the English (26–29), is warned by the Constable of the danger (29–40) and seems to accept the point: 'In cases of defence, 'tis best to weigh/The enemy more mighty than he seems' (II.4.43–4). ∎

In practice, however, all the French nobles are stained with pride and conceit and this blazes out in their conversations on the eve of Agincourt and in the morning before the battle. These are perfect examples of God-provoking arrogance and impatience and would have alerted a contemporary audience (should they have needed it) to the likelihood of a downfall:

> DAUPHIN Will it never be day? I will trot tomorrow a mile, and
> my way shall be paved with English faces.
>
> (III.7.77–8)

In the very next scene the Chorus makes this explicit:

> Proud of their numbers, and secure in soul,
> The confident and over-lusty French
> Do the low-rated English play at dice,
> And chide the cripple tardy-gaited night
> Who like a foul and ugly witch doth limp
> So tediously away.
> (IV.Chorus.17–22)

Quite apart from the dangers of pride, lurking in this image of night is the superstitious fear of what might befall those who 'chide' a witch.

Henry's defensive piety is present throughout the play, but is at its most active at the very moment when he might be most vulnerable to pride – after the triumph of Agincourt. Consider the following:

> Praisèd be God, and not our strength, for it!
> (IV.7.85)

>   O God, Thy arm was here!
> And not to us, but to Thy arm alone,
> Ascribe we all!
> …
>   Take it, God,
> For it is none but Thine!
> …
> And be it death proclaimèd through our host
> To boast of this, or take that praise from God
> Which is His only.
> (IV.8.105–7, 110–11, 113–15)

That this piety is an important feature of a great (and prudent) king is made clear by the fact that it is amplified by the Chorus at the beginning of Act V during the description of Henry's celebratory return to London via Blackheath:

> Being free from vainness and self-glorious pride,
> Giving full trophy, signal, and ostent
> Quite from himself to God.
> (V.Chorus.20–22)

As we saw earlier, Henry frequently attempts to find others to share in, if not to take over fully, the responsibility for the negative consequences of his acts (war, suffering, death). In this subsection we have seen that he is also inclined to shuffle off the positive consequences of his decisions (praise, glory, success). Thus at many crucial points in the play, Henry appears to be striving for a strange moral neutrality in which both the good and bad consequences of his acts are underwritten by others, human or divine.

Theme: 'and profits will accrue' – money and dealing in Henry V

At the beginning of Act II the Chorus presents us with a vision of 'all the youth of England', inspired by 'the mirror of all Christian kings', rejecting vanities in the pursuit of chivalric honour:

> Now all the youth of England are on fire,
> And silken dalliance in the wardrobe lies.
> Now thrive the armourers, and honour's thought
> Reigns solely in the breast of every man.
>
> (II.Chorus.1–4)

Yet what dramatic example of this heroic and noble preparation is offered in the scene that immediately follows? A collection of dubious hangers-on rowing about an unpaid debt in a low inn that has been (and, at the time of the play, possibly still is) a bawdy house. **Please read the last twenty lines of II.1. What motive does Pistol offer for going to the war?**

Discussion

> I'll live by Nym, and Nym shall live by me.
> Is not this just? For I shall sutler be
> Unto the camp, and profits will accrue.
>
> (II.1.105–7)

To 'nim' was to steal, and a 'sutler', as your notes tell you, was a seller of provisions to an army; thus Pistol and Nym were aiming to make somewhat dubious profits out of the war. ■

This is a far cry from the Chorus's noble vision, or is it? **Please re-read the Chorus and see if you can find another motive for the war.**

Discussion

> For now sits expectation in the air,
> And hides a sword from hilts unto the point
> With crowns imperial, crowns and coronets,
> Promised to Harry and his followers.
>
> (II.Chorus.8–11)

This is not a complete contradiction of what the Chorus had told us earlier about 'honour's thought/Reigns solely in the breast of every man'. A contemporary soldier would see no contradiction in fighting valiantly to capture a prisoner and then selling that prisoner back to his family for ransom. (Pistol parodies this idea in a scene with Monsieur Le Fer in IV.4.1–75.) However, it does qualify the rather over-simple version of motives that we had originally been offered. ■

This vision of England united in honour is further complicated by the Chorus's later description of Cambridge, Scroop and Grey, who have been bought by precisely the same currency – crowns – that had been promised to Harry and his followers: 'A nest of hollow bosoms, which he fills/With treacherous crowns' (21–2).

Henry V is full of deals, proposed deals and negotiations of deals, most of which are to do with money or power, or both. It is hardly surprising, therefore, that the low-life characters should, in their first scene, be wrangling about money and marriage ('and certainly she did you wrong, for you/were troth-plight to her': 17–18), and threatening violence ('I will cut thy throat, one time or another': 66), for they are merely paralleling the actions of their 'betters'.

To illustrate how widespread this 'doing of deals' is in *Henry V*, think back to Act I: you may recall deals being mentioned in this earliest part of the play. The play opens with the issue of Church wealth and how it is to be protected and, by I.2.133, the Archbishop is offering Henry 'a mighty sum' if he invades France. Later on we have the joke 'deal' from the Dauphin.

Throughout the play there runs a theme of offers, counter-offers, deals agreed or denied. This theme expresses itself most grandly in the international negotiations over Henry's claims to France, of which the Dauphin's 'mock' is only a part. Exeter continues negotiations in II.4.76–143, and a counter-offer is mentioned by the Chorus (III.Chorus.28–32). The final resolution is reached, with the help of an international negotiator (the Duke of Burgundy), right at the end of the play in V.2.

Within this structure of international deals is set the smaller-scale but still important late medieval chivalric idea of 'ransom'. Essentially this meant that if someone surrendered to you on the battlefield, you were able – once the battle was over and you had shepherded your prisoner safely away – to negotiate a ransom payment with his family for his release. Clearly this would only work if the prisoner came from a 'good sort' of family that had the wealth to offer in exchange. Obviously this form of dealing was at its most profitable with a member of the feudal aristocracy or a king, hence the appearance of Mountjoy bearing various offers for ransom in III.6.123–31 and IV.3.79–88, and hence the concern of Williams that, in the end, Henry would allow himself to be ransomed (IV.1.188–9).

This is no abstract literary convention. In the fifteenth century, prisoners from rich families were ransomed for huge sums and a lucky soldier could, with one affluent prisoner, make his fortune. On the other hand, for prisoners whose ransoms were set very high, it could mean a very long wait, albeit in comfortable conditions (ransomable prisoners were a valuable capital asset and thus tended to be cosseted). Charles Duke of Orleans, whom the real Henry V captured at Agincourt in 1415, was only released in 1440.

In other words, in *Henry V* prisoners became another form of commodity. The only developed example we have of this dealing in the play comes in the low-life parody of the chivalric process in IV.4 where Pistol makes a deal with Le Fer via the Boy as a negotiator: 'He is a gentleman of a good house, and for his ransom he will give you two hundred crowns' (IV.4.44–6).

Henry himself is very concerned with ransomable prisoners. Even *before* asking about the French or English dead at Agincourt, the king enquires of his uncle Exeter: 'What prisoners of good sort are taken, uncle?'

(IV.8.74). It is very noticeable that neither the Olivier nor the Branagh film versions include this question in their performance texts. Also excluded from both modern productions is Henry's order during the battle:

> Then every soldier kill his prisoners!
> (IV.6.37)

and Gower's subsequent, non-ironic comment:

> wherefore the King most
> worthily hath caused every soldier to cut his prisoner's
> throat. O, 'tis a gallant King!
> (IV.7.8–10)

The killing, or threatened killing, of the prisoners comes down through Shakespeare's historical sources and seems to have been a feature of the real battle of Agincourt in 1415. As valuable prisoners were captured, they would have been taken to the rear of the English army and held there. In a small medieval force there would be very few to act as warders so, if the French forces seemed to be rallying, the French prisoners might suddenly gain heart and attack the English from the rear. (Modern estimates suggest that Henry V's army was probably no larger than 6,000–7,000; the French army somewhere between 20,000 and 25,000.) To avoid this danger, and to protect his army, Henry is willing to see the prisoners lose all their value by being killed. Henry is 'gallant' in the eyes of Gower because he puts the safety of his army and of his cause above that of realizing a substantial profit. It is the killing of the prisoners that explains why Pistol, despite having captured Le Fer, is by the end of the play still poor.

If Henry is gallant, he is also politically pragmatic. Even the most serious and sacred moments in the play are tinged with his politically compelling need to achieve a compromise, to do a deal, to strike a bargain. Even when addressing his God, Henry can't resist negotiating:

> and I have built
> Two chantries where the sad and solemn priests
> Sing still for Richard's soul. More will I do ...
> (IV.1.293–5)

Less honest is Henry's response to Williams, to whose doubts he had no adequate answer in IV.1. When confronted by Williams again, and by his devastating straightforwardness ('Your majesty came not like yourself', IV.8.50), Henry's only answer is to pay him off ('fill this glove with crowns/And give it to this fellow': IV.8.57–8). Significantly Williams says nothing (his one response is to Fluellen). It would have been easy for Shakespeare to have written for Williams a couple of lines in praise of Henry of the sort that come frequently from Fluellen or Gower. He chose not to. Sometimes the silences of Shakespeare's characters are eloquent.

This theme of power, negotiation and money-dealing comes to a climax in V.2 which, in one sense, is nothing more than the international deal to which Henry's whole policy has been moving. Despite Burgundy's grandiloquence that does its best to hide the realities of power politics, Henry strips all away by saying simply: 'If, Duke of Burgundy, you would the peace ... you must buy that peace' (V.2.68, 70).

As the final scene is meant to provide an up-beat ending, things can't be allowed to grow too dark, so Henry's wooing of Katherine is presented in a mainly comic vein. However, even in the comic mode, the need to deal and bargain is not completely forgotten: 'and so clap hands, and a bargain. How say you, lady?' (V.2.129–30).

Ironically, the only Englishmen who don't seem to be able to get a good bargain are Nym and Bardolph; even their thieving is pathetically small-scale and unprofitable:

> Bardolph stole a lute-
> case, bore it twelve leagues, and sold it for three half-
> pence ...
> in Calais they stole a fire shovel ...
> (III.2.42–5)

Bardolph steals a 'pax of little price' (III.6.44) and is hanged, as is Nym (IV.4.71). Pistol, of course, lost his property (Le Fer) when the French prisoners were killed. It is at points like these that two of the important themes in the play, dealing and death, intersect.

Theme: 'for, lambkins, we will live' – death in Henry V

The subject-matter of *Henry* V concerns war and the build-up to war, so it is hardly surprising that death and the threat of death feature strongly in it. Two major conflicts are actually represented on stage (the siege of Harfleur: III.1–3; Agincourt: IV.1–8). In the latter, prodigious numbers of French are killed:

> This note doth tell me of ten thousand French
> That in the field lie slain
> ...
> Here was a royal fellowship of death!
> (IV.8.79–80, 100)

In contrast the English casualty figures are miraculously light, some twenty-nine being mentioned (IV.8.105–8); of those mentioned by name, only one – the Duke of York – features as a character in the play, and that in a minor way (he has just two lines). So it would seem that the English characters in an English play escape lightly. And yet this is not so, for the actuality or imminence of death permeates the whole play and affects many more than those who die at Agincourt. Paradoxically the English characters in the play die away from the major battles, their deaths being civil rather than military.

The death of Falstaff

The first actual death recorded in the play is a very significant one – that of Falstaff. Falstaff was the presiding comic figure in *Henry IV, Part 1* and *Part 2*. In those plays he had represented a sort of glorious lord of misrule, a huge figure of wit, coarse humour, bombast, large physical appetites (for food, drink and sex), cowardice and petty criminality. For Henry, or Prince Hal as he then was, Falstaff was both a rich source of warm and vivid humanity and a dangerous invitation to impiety, immorality and illegality. Falstaff's character was clearly a great hit with contemporary audiences (Olivier's production tries to illustrate this by having the groundlings react noisily to every mention of the character's name) and Shakespeare had, in an Epilogue to *Henry IV, Part 2,* all but promised his audience that Falstaff would reappear in a sequel: 'our humble author will continue the story, with Sir John in it, and make you merry with fair Katherine of France'.

Henry V is not quite the kind of play that is being promised there, is it? And, of course, it couldn't be. Again and again in the text we are reminded that Henry has now rejected the past represented by Falstaff (see, for instance, I.1.24–37, 54–69; I.2.251–4, 267–73; II.4.36–40, 134–7). He is now a just, responsible and sober king. The introduction of Falstaff as a character quite contrary to the new Henry would have seriously shifted the gravitational centre of the play. So, if Falstaff is to feature at all, it must be only by report, and that report must be of his extinction (as his influence has already been extinguished). As modern audiences are not assumed to know the plays that came before, both the Olivier and Branagh film productions find it necessary to include lines from *Henry IV* (both using the highly cinematographic device of the 'flashback') to explain what has happened to Falstaff.

Falstaff's death in *Henry V* is set firmly, as his life had been in the earlier plays, among the low-life characters Bardolph, Nym, Pistol and the Hostess Nell Quickly. For an Elizabethan or Jacobean audience this would have helped tie the new play into the two parts of *Henry IV,* because Bardolph and Nell Quickly feature in *Part 1* and *Part 2.*

The Boy's announcement of Falstaff's sickness breaks in upon the wrangling of Pistol and Nym (again, in the low-life characters, dealing and death seem closely connected). The impact, however, seems very temporary, and it is only with the Hostess's plea, 'As ever you came of women, come in quickly to Sir John … Sweet men, come to him' (II.1.112–13, 115), that the mood clearly changes.

The Hostess's emphasis is on their common humanity, all those born of a woman, which seems renewed in the face of death. How strange to call these three cantankerous and rather unappealing characters 'sweet'! **Why do you think that, at this suddenly serious moment, the Hostess uses this adjective?**

Discussion

You might argue that she wants them to do something, so she is flattering them as an inducement, and that may well be part of it. However, I think that there's more to it. She has emphasized their common humanity ('As ever you came of women'); in Falstaff she is witnessing the inevitable end of all who are mortal, and in the face of death those who survive become exquisitely precious. We have already been made aware of how acute a contemporary audience's sense of mortality might be, a sense akin to that which Shakespeare described in the last two lines of his Sonnet LXXIII:

> This thou perceiv'st, which makes thy love more strong,
> To love that well which thou must leave ere long. ■

As the Hostess expresses the desperate affection generated by imminent death, so her husband expresses the equally human, though less elevated, emotion of relief. At least it is not us: 'Let us condole the knight; for, lambkins, we will live' (II.1.122).

As the Hostess used the improbable adjective 'sweet', so Pistol bestows the equally unlikely noun 'lambkins' on his rough companions. There are two levels of irony here: one, the conscious joke of all these experienced cheats and rogues being described as something young and innocent; two, the unconscious dramatic irony of the implication 'like lambs to the slaughter'. Such an irony is not a vague, generalized, rhetorical point about 'brief mortality'. **Think about those whom Pistol addresses and those who surround him in the inn: how many survive to the end of the play?**

Discussion

Only one, Pistol himself. Bardolph and Nym are both hanged (IV.4.70–71), and Nell Quickly dies 'Of malady of France' (venereal disease) (V.1.77–78). The Boy, though not actually on stage at this time, also dies when the French attack the English camp (IV.7.1–2); we know from IV.4.72–5 that he is one of the boys mentioned. If we add Falstaff to their number, five out of the six low-life characters are dead by the end of the play. ■

Falstaff's death is anticipated in II.1 but is only finally reported in II.3. Between these two is another scene culminating in death – the execution of Cambridge, Scroop and Grey at Southampton. Scroop (although he does not feature at all in *Henry IV*) is identified by Henry as a close companion of his youth: 'Thou that didst bear the key of all my counsels,/That knew'st the very bottom of my soul' (II.2.96–7), and thus the betrayal is deeper and more wounding.

In *Henry V* this sense of betrayal works both ways. Henry, in the eyes of the low-life characters, has in a way betrayed Falstaff:

HOSTESS   the King has killed his heart.
…

NYM The King hath run bad humours on the knight, that's the even of it.

PISTOL Nym, thou hast spoke the right;

(II.1.84, 116–18)

Henry, as betrayed and betrayer, has had to distance himself from those who represented a past in which he was more credulous and more vulnerable. He goes to France disengaged from his past, more experienced – and less trusting.

The death of Falstaff as recounted by the hostess and commented on by her companions is a remarkable piece of writing for its restraint, its detail, its diversity and its humanity. It moves from the conventional signs of impending death ('fumble with the sheets, and play with flowers') and the cry of a repenting soul, through the Hostess's cheerful reassurances and jollyings along ('I hoped there was no need to trouble himself with any such thoughts yet') to her hand exploring his body for signs of life in a sad parody of her bawdy past:

> I put my hand into the
> bed, and felt them, and they were as cold as any stone;
> then I felt to his knees, and so up'ard and up'ard, and
> all was as cold as any stone.
> (II.3.22–25)

The creeping, dull relentlessness of Falstaff's dying is mirrored in the repeated phrase 'as cold as any stone', of course, but it is also psychologically apt: sometimes when people are trying to come to terms with a shocking experience (a road accident, say) they will often latch on to a phrase which describes that experience but which they have to repeat again and again in order to give shape to the event and to allow its reality to filter through, drop by drop.

It is worth noting that Falstaff, as Mistress Quickly points out, is making a 'good death':

> 'A made
> a finer end, and went away an it had been any christom
> child;
> (II.3.10–12)

something that those in battle – as Williams is to point out – can rarely do. Falstaff cries on God and then, in lines 26 and 28, denounces the indulgences of sack and women. As it was her profession, the Hostess is naturally reluctant to admit the latter. The Hostess frequently misunderstands or misuses words, and it is her confusing 'incarnation' with 'carnation', and her defence of his 'handling' of women, that allows the account of Falstaff's death to modulate from the grim 'cold as any stone' to the warmer recalling of his character:

HOSTESS 'A could never abide carnation, 'twas a colour
he never liked.

BOY 'A said once, the devil would have him about women.

...

BOY Do you not remember, 'a saw a flea stick upon Bardolph's nose, and 'a said it was a black soul burning in hell?

(II.3.31–3, 37–9)

A joke against the red nose of Bardolph the drinker still stings enough for him to reply bleakly and sharply:

> Well, the fuel is gone that maintained that
> fire – that's all the riches I got in his service.
>
> (II.3.40–41)

And with that dismissive epitaph (which returns us to the theme of money) the episode concludes. Nym's brutal 'Shall we shog?' brings the survivors back to the world of immediate necessity and to the parasitic, profitable life anticipated by Pistol: 'Let us to France, like horse-leeches, my boys,/To suck, to suck, the very blood to suck!' (52–3).

Henry and death

It is ironic that the longest description of death in the play is that of a character who does not appear in it. Though Falstaff is invisible from the beginning and dead by the end of II.3, the audience is not allowed completely to forget him. In IV.7 Fluellen is drawing an awkward parallel between Henry and Alexander the Great, during which he observes that, when drunk and in high anger, Alexander killed his friend Cleitus. Gower interrupts and defends Henry by saying: 'Our King is not like him in that: he never killed any of his friends' (IV.7.38–9).

Fluellen objects that he hadn't finished his argument, and that the last part was to be a contrast between Henry and Alexander:

> FLUELLEN   As
> Alexander killed his friend Cleitus, being in his ales
> and his cups; so also Harry Monmouth, being in his
> right wits and his good judgements, turned away the
> fat knight with the great-belly doublet – he was full of
> jests, and gipes, and knaveries, and mocks; I have forgot
> his name.
> GOWER Sir John Falstaff.
>
> (IV.7.42–9)

Fluellen must be the only person who has forgotten Falstaff's name, but what do you think of the contrast he is presenting, and of Gower's objection? Think back to what we have seen of Henry, and to what we have discussed in this section.

Discussion

As king, Henry is indeed quite unlike the Alexander who is presented by Fluellen: Henry is sober, moderate and rational. The first evidence that he could lose his temper comes a few lines after this debate: 'I was not angry since I came to France/Until this instant' (IV.7.53–4). But this only serves to reinforce the fact that he hadn't been angry until then. The contrast is between the drunken Alexander killing his friend, and the rational, sober Henry turning away his enemy. This is such an abstract argument that

Fluellen cannot even remember the man's name, but Gower can. It is Gower who unwittingly, in correcting and informing Fluellen's argument, creates doubts in the audience's mind. Falstaff's relationship to Henry, whatever it was, was not that of enemy. 'He never killed any of his friends', Gower says. But is that true? As we have seen, Nell Quickly, Nym and Pistol believe that Henry's actions did indirectly kill Falstaff. ∎

In Southampton Henry has Lord Scroop executed ('thou that didst bear the key of all my counsels'). Later, in III.6, Fluellen tells Henry of Bardolph's execution:

> FLUELLEN Bardolph, if your
> majesty know the man: his face is all bubukles, and
> whelks, and knobs, and flames o'fire; and his lips blows
> at his nose, and it is like a coal of fire, sometimes plue,
> and sometimes red; but his nose is executed and his
> fire's out.
> KING We would have all such offenders so cut
> off ...
> (III.6.98–105)

All these killings are, of course, in one way or another fully justified and rational. Falstaff has to be rejected because he represents a self-indulgent misrule which no just king could condone; necessity of state (and not the king's personal wrongs) justifies the execution of Scroop; and law and diplomacy ('for when lenity and cruelty play for a kingdom, the gentler gamester is the soonest winner') justify the execution of Bardolph (and, presumably, Nym). The paradox underlying the Fluellen/Gower debate is that a rational and sober king may find himself, out of moral and legal necessity, killing his erstwhile friends.

All the deaths in *Henry V* occur off-stage and are reported to the audience. The last death alluded to in the play, but occurring outside its time span, is Henry's own. In the Epilogue the Chorus observes: 'Small time, but in that small most greatly lived/This star of England'.

We shall be discussing later what a contemporary audience would have known of the story of Henry V (see pp. 77–9, 'Henry V as a figure in history and literature'), but there is little doubt that most would have known that his reign was brief and that his triumphs in France were short-lived. In a play that is frequently concerned with brief mortality, it is significant that an audience would go away having been reminded in the last few lines of the play that even its central figure did not last long.

Theme: 'There's nothing so becomes a man' – the rhetoric of war, the rhetoric of peace

There are at least two speeches in *Henry V* that seem to have an independent life – the one before Harfleur (III.1.1–34) and the one before Agincourt (IV.3.18–67). Lines such as 'Once more unto the breach, dear friends, once more', 'Cry, "God for Harry, England, and Saint George!"' and 'We few, we happy few, we band of brothers' resonate far beyond the confines of the play. The danger of this, of course, is that we are inclined to detach them from the context of the play and view them as set pieces to be performed independently of their textual surroundings. Let us resist this temptation and instead look at these speeches and others in the light of what we have already discovered about the play and its characters.

Before Harfleur: 1

Please turn to the beginning of III.1 and read the entire speech (1–34). **From what the Chorus has told us and from what we learn in the first couple of lines of Henry's speech, what is happening just before the speech?**

Discussion

Henry has rejected the French deal and Harfleur is being besieged. After all Henry's dire warnings about the horrors of war in I.2., the explosions and trumpet calls implied by the stage direction 'Alarum, and chambers go off' must have made the audience jump, particularly as the Chorus had asked it to *imagine* all these things rather than expect them in reality. 'And down goes all before them' (III.Chorus.34) suggests that a breach has been made in the defensive wall of Harfleur. However, despite this, the English have failed to take the town and are, indeed, retreating from the breach. Henry's speech is therefore designed to rally his dispirited forces. ■

There is a sort of heroic desperation in the first two lines, something that offers the stark alternatives of death or glory. Indeed, throughout the play Henry reminds the audience that he is not, in the French campaign at least, a man of moderation and compromise: he is determined to take all or break all. **Can you think of other occasions in the play where Shakespeare makes this clear?**

Discussion

In I.2:

> France being ours, we'll bend it to our awe,
> Or break it all to pieces. Or there we'll sit,
> Ruling in large and ample empery
> O'er France and all her almost kingly dukedoms,
> Or lay these bones in an unworthy urn,
> Tombless, with no remembrance over them.
> Either our history shall with full mouth
> Speak freely of our acts, or else our grave,
> Like Turkish mute, shall have a tongueless mouth,
> Not worshipped with a waxen epitaph.
>
> (I.2.225–34)

Again, in III.6, just after the dismissal of Bardolph to his fate, Montjoy enters to negotiate a possible ransom deal. Henry's reaction is intense and explicit: 'My ransom is this frail and worthless trunk' (III.6.152).

Figure 3.3 An up-beat *Henry V*: 'Once more unto the breach' set in a sunny landscape, with Laurence Olivier as Henry in the film that he directed, 1944. Two Cities, courtesy of The Kobal Collection.

Figure 3.4 A sombre *Henry V*: 'Once more unto the breach' set at night amid the glare of fires, with Kenneth Branagh as Henry in the film that he directed, 1989. Renaissance Films/BBC/Curzon Films, courtesy of the Kobal Collection.

Just before Agincourt Henry, stung by yet another attempt by the French herald to offer ransom terms, replies starkly:

> Bid them achieve me, and then sell my bones
> …
> They shall have none, I swear, but these my joints,
> Which if they have as I will leave 'em them
> Shall yield them little …
>
> (IV.3.91, 123–5)

Even in the light-hearted wooing scene, Henry makes clear to Katherine how absolute his views on France are:

> for I love France so well that
> I will not part with a village of it – I will have it all mine:
>
> (V.2.172–3) ■

Have you noticed how physical most of these images are? They concentrate on the body of the king, on its weakness, its vulnerability, its mortality: 'Lay these bones in an unworthy urn', 'frail and worthless trunk', 'sell my bones', 'these my joints'. There's not much here about 'the divinity that doth hedge a king' or the mystical idea of the king's body as an image of the state: it's all about the king as a vulnerable individual putting life and limb on the line. Given this pattern, we can begin to understand why Henry is so angry with Williams for suggesting that 'when our throats are cut he may be ransomed, and we ne'er the wiser' (IV.1.188–9).

In the French campaign Henry is assuming that his soldiers will commit their bodies in the same relentlessly absolute way. If they can't succeed in war, then they will befoul and besmirch the physical landscape of France with their bodies, killing those they didn't kill in battle, by creating disease through the decay of their corpses ('killing in relapse of mortality'):

> And those that leave their valiant bones in France,
> Dying like men, though buried in your dunghills,
> They shall be famed; for there the sun shall greet them,
> And draw their honours reeking up to heaven,
> Leaving their earthly parts to choke your clime,
> The smell whereof shall breed a plague in France.
> Mark then abounding valour in our English,
> That being dead, like to the bullet's crasing,
> Break out into a second course of mischief,
> Killing in relapse of mortality.
>
> (IV.3.98–107)

In these intense moments of war, this equality of desperate sacrifice allows Henry to think of the soldiers not as subservients but as equals, as 'friends'. **Can you remember another occasion on which Henry talks in such terms?**

Discussion

Significantly enough, it is in that other great set speech, the one before Agincourt: 'We few, we happy few, we band of brothers' (IV.3.60). ■

In some ways Henry is being presented as a 'modern' man in this play. The French are still old-fashioned enough to regard war as a sort of huge chivalrous game, the main purpose of which is to display the superiority of one's talents and possessions (think of the sniping conversation between the Constable, Orleans and the Dauphin about horses and armour at the beginning of III.7) and to gain additional wealth through ransoming prisoners and gambling for them. The French army was led by a group of roughly equal, competing lords who seem to have no concern for those they led. Henry's army has a single and responsible head and a clear chain of command (nobles–captains–soldiers). For Henry and his soldiers, war is a grim state:

> We are but warriors for the working-day;
> Our gayness and our gilt are all besmirched
> With rainy marching in the painful field.
>
> (IV.3.109–11)

The recognition of this grimness seems to bind then together ('*We* are but warriors'). It is therefore worth looking at the advice Henry gives to his soldiers as they battle for Harfleur, for it is advice he will apply as much to himself as to them:

> Then imitate the action of the tiger;
> Stiffen the sinews, summon up the blood,
> Disguise fair nature with hard-favoured rage;
> Then lend the eye a terrible aspect;
>
> …
>
> Now set the teeth, and stretch the nostril wide,
> Hold hard the breath, and bend up every spirit
> To his full height!
>
> (III.1.6–9, 15–17)

Look at the verbs in these two passages. **Does anything strike you about them?**

Discussion

They are all active verbs; it is not that war automatically changes men (as though they were passive victims). It is that men have to make a conscious, active effort to become war-like: they must 'stiffen the sinews', they must 'summon up the blood', they must 'lend the eye…'. All these events must be willed. But there's a further, more puzzling point. Consider the verbs 'imitate' and 'disguise'. These suggest that it is not simply a matter of calling up the war-like emotions: on occasions the soldiers must pretend to be what they are not. They must *act* the part. 'Now set the teeth, and stretch the nostril wide,' sounds almost like a director telling actors how to perform. We will consider in greater detail this business of assuming a role, when we go on to look at Henry's speech to the Governor of Harfleur. ■

As we have seen, there is much implied fellow-feeling in this speech; however, it is clear that Henry, although addressing his first remarks to all those besieging Harfleur, does go on to distinguish between parts of his army. In line 17, for instance, he turns to the nobility ('On, on you noblest English') and exhorts them to set a good example to those below: 'Be copy now to men of grosser blood,/And teach them how to war' (III.1.24–5), and then addresses their social inferiors: 'And you, good yeomen' (25). However, all are united again in the final simile: 'I see you stand like greyhounds in the slips,/Straining upon the start' (31–2).

This is a slightly curious image on which to end. The tone of the rest of the speech has been one of heroic endeavour, the similes (and they are mostly similes, not metaphors) comparing the men to siege weapons ('Like the brass cannon') and dramatic natural scenery ('As fearfully as doth a gallèd rock'), and their fathers to classical heroes ('like so many Alexanders'). Yet the exhortation ends on the image of a dog. Shakespeare's plays are full of images of dogs, but very few of them are favourable.

Think for a moment of the occasions in which 'dogs', 'hounds', 'mastiffs' or 'curs' are mentioned in the play: there are at least twelve instances of such imagery (if you have a computer and an electronic version of the play, you could do a search and find them all). To pick just a few: the Archbishop talks of the marauding Scots as dogs (I.2.219); both Fluellen and Pistol use 'dog' as an insult (for example, Fluellen, 'Up to the breach, you dogs!', III.2.20); the Dauphin refers to 'coward dogs' (II.4.69), Orleans to 'foolish curs' and Bourbon, in the anguish of humiliating defeat, has a vision of sexual violation:

> Whilst by a slave, no gentler than my dog,
> His fairest daughter is contaminated ...
> (IV.5.15–16)

But perhaps the most telling is the very first description the Chorus gives us of 'warlike Harry':

> and at his heels,
> Leashed in like hounds, should famine, sword, and fire
> Crouch for employment.
> (I.Chorus.6–8)

The dog image placed at the end of the heroic Harfleur speech thus gives it a strange twist, a sort of moral uncertainty. Are Henry's men to act like dogs in Harfleur? The next two scenes will answer this question and lead us to another of Henry's great set speeches, though one that in modern productions is often heavily edited or omitted altogether.

The thing to notice about the first part of III.2 is that, like II.1, it offers the low-life characters a chance to comment on the heroics that have just occurred. In the case of II.1, the Chorus's vision of 'all the youth of England are on fire' is immediately questioned by the sordid goings-on in Eastcheap. In III.2 it is made clear that Henry's rhetoric has not convinced everyone: of the low-life characters, only Bardolph seems inspired; Nym, Pistol and Boy all want to be somewhere else. It is only Fluellen's appearance that drives them forward.

Forward to what? If the low-life characters were unimpressed, how effective was Henry's rhetoric in achieving its goal? **What do we learn from the conversation of the captains in the second half of III.2?**

That, despite the heroic speech and the (presumably) heroic action that followed it, the town has not fallen. The Captains representing the four nations of the British Isles are wrangling: Fluellen doesn't believe that the undermining of the walls is being done properly, and Macmorris is frustrated that he has not been allowed to continue. Henry's army is divided and has not achieved even its first victory. ∎

Before Harfleur: 2

Please now read Henry's speech to the Governor of Harfleur (III.3.1–43). **How would you characterize it? What acts of violence does it concentrate on and whom does it single out as the major victims?**

D i s c u s s i o n

It is a speech full of threats that are illustrated by images of extreme violence. As you might expect in a ransacked city, its main victims are civilians. The examples Henry concentrates on are the weakest and most vulnerable – young women, infants, old men.

> Your fresh fair virgins, and your flowering infants.
> …
> If your pure maidens fall into the hand
> Of hot and forcing violation?
> …
> Defile the locks of your shrill-shrieking daughters;
> Your fathers taken by the silver beards,
> And their most reverend heads dashed to the walls;
> Your naked infants spitted upon pikes …
>
> (III.3.14, 20–21, 35–8) ∎

Did you notice the most common image? It is one of rape, of violation. In part this is nothing more than the literal truth: in a sacked town, rape and pillage will be commonplace. But it is more than this. Throughout the play there are contrasts drawn between the sexual forcefulness of the English and the effete qualities of the French, particularly the men. We have already seen Bourbon's vision of the dog-like English violating French daughters, but something similar has also occurred earlier in the play when the Dauphin observes that

> Our madams mock at us, and plainly say
> Our mettle is bred out, and they will give
> Their bodies to the lust of English youth,
> To new-store France with bastard warriors.
>
> (III.5.28–31)

In the final scene of the play (V.2) this theme returns, albeit modified. Henry comments that his love for Katherine stops him seeing further cities to conquer, and the French king observes:

> Yes, my lord, you see them perspectively,
> the cities turned into a maid; for they are all girdled
> with maiden walls, that war hath never entered.
> (V.2.315–17)

It is not just that rape happens in sacked cities, it is that the cities them-selves are female ('Till in *her* ashes *she* lie burièd'), and besieging and cap-turing them is a form of collective rape. (There is lurking in this whole business the pun of deflowering a city called Harfleur; such images as 'mowing like grass', 'flowering infants' are also part of this word-play.)

Violation, murder, conflagration: it's strong stuff and all of it is being threatened by this 'mirror of all Christian kings' (II.Chorus.6). **What is going on here? What is the king's argument in his speech at Harfleur?**

Discussion

Henry's argument is twofold. First, at the moment I can control my troops, but soon I won't be able to – and what happens then will be your own fault. Secondly, it will be your own fault because you are 'guilty in defence'; in other words, I claim Normandy as rightfully mine, and towns that resist me are resisting their rightful lord (an act that is, of course, treason – which, as we know from the Southampton scene, is punishable by death). ∎

If the Archbishop's Salic Law speech is right, then Henry's second argument is sound. But what about his first, that beyond a certain point he cannot control his troops? The text of the play would tend not to support this. On every occasion that we see Henry with his army, it is clear that the king is in control: he has that combination of natural authority and a close under-standing of his men's feelings which makes for a very successful and firm leader (remember how Henry is able to manipulate his soldiers' emotions whenever he addresses them). It is clear from his rigorous enforcement of the no-stealing rule (under which both Nym and Bardolph are hanged) that Henry is determined to get his army to conduct itself well (see III.6.104–10). During Agincourt he can order his men to kill their prisoners, which rep-resents a huge financial loss to them and him. After Agincourt Henry is ruthlessly in control of even the boasting of his troops, let alone their crimi-nal actions: 'And be it death proclaimèd through our host/To boast of this' (IV.8.113–14).

There is no doubt that Henry presents a terrifying vision of war in this speech, but about everything else concerning the speech there is much doubt. We have already seen that his claim about being unable to control his troops is dubious, but what about the assault itself? The speech assumes that another attack on 'half-achieved Harfleur' will be successful but, as we have seen, his various attacks on the breach so far have not been, despite his fine rhetoric. Furthermore, right at the end of the scene Henry admits that his troops are in a desperate condition: 'The winter coming on, and sickness growing/Upon our soldiers' (III.3.55–6). **Given all this, what is his underlying purpose in this speech?**

The extreme violence, the false claims and the actual physical weakness of his forces all lead to the conclusion that Henry here is being forced into psychological warfare. He is trying to terrify Harfleur into submission. And it works: coupled with the fact that the expected relief force from the Dauphin does not arrive, the speech opens Harfleur's gates and Henry's bluff is not called. He can enter the town as its rightful Christian lord showing 'mercy to them all'. ■

But what is the underlying reality of the situation? Henry's army, so heroically pictured by the Chorus at the beginning of Act III ('these culled and choice-drawn cavaliers'), has achieved but one victory (and that partly by deception), is weakened by disease and dissension (Nym, Pistol and the Boy versus Fluellen; Macmorris versus Fluellen), and is now going to retreat to Calais.

Throughout the play, gaps open up between what is said and what is done or what is proved to be the reality of the case; in other words, between appearance and reality. In Act I what starts as a cynical ploy by the Church – to distract the king – becomes an heroic crusade; in Act III what the Chorus and Henry present as an heroic crusade becomes, in the shadow of Harfleur's walls, a frightening *performance*, a piece of verbal terrorism that wins out when heroic deeds fail.

Henry's great speeches in the play are not, as they are often taken to be, simply the inspiring calls to action of a great soldier. They are also elaborate rhetorical devices, acting performances deliberately designed for particular effects. We should not forget the Archbishop's original description of Henry (so often omitted from modern productions on the grounds that it is just a piece of over-blown and sycophantic praise):

> List his discourse of war, and you shall hear
> A fearful battle rendered you in music.
> Turn him to any cause of policy,
> The Gordian knot of it he will unloose …
>
> (I.1.43–6)

Henry is a master of different sorts of language – of theology, of politics, of warfare – but they are all used as tools to achieve the practical aims of life: 'So that the art and practic part of life/Must be the mistress to this theoric' (I.1.51–2). In this play, language and acting are as much weapons of war as the siege engine or the sword.

Before Agincourt

With this in mind, let us look briefly at Henry's speech to his men before the battle of Agincourt. Henry's men, weary and disease-ridden, are retreating from the exhausting siege of Harfleur towards Calais. The French, in vastly superior numbers, block their way. Henry has, in his conversations with Williams and Bates, realized that despite Pistol's and Fluellen's admiration of him, some of his army are uncertain about his cause and doubtful of his commitment. He has to reassure them and give them something to fight for. How does he do this? Not, significantly, by raising the issues of moral justification that he had so many problems with in the Williams debate. I'm going to suggest that you divide the speech of IV.3 into three parts: lines 18–39, 40–59, 60–67. **What is Henry's main argument in each of the sections?**

D i s c u s s i o n

In 18–39 there is a series of negatives hovering around the word 'honour' (used three times in the first fourteen lines): more men would either increase the country's loss or dilute the honour by requiring it to be spread more thinly; those who fear to share this honour should be paid off. This is heroic but bleak, but the bleakness is ameliorated by the stress on the fellowship of death in the concluding two lines of this section. Here, unlike in the Harfleur speech, Henry makes no distinction between nobles and others: throughout the speech he seems to be addressing his whole army: 'We would not die in that man's company/That fears his fellowship to die with us'.

From this rather abstract idea Henry moves to the particular and becomes immediately more positive. During lines 40–59, by hanging his thoughts on the annual feast of St Crispian, he projects the coming experience of battle into the future, into a warm, familiar, domestic setting ('safe home', 'feast his neighbours', 'household words', 'flowing cups'). From that vantage point he looks back on the battle about to be fought. The wounds

Figure 3.5   An up-beat *Henry V*: the Battle of Agincourt as an epic clash of arms, in the film directed by Olivier, 1944. Two Cities, courtesy of The Kobal Collection.

Figure 3.6 A sombre *Henry V*: the Battle of Agincourt as mud, blood and desperate individual struggles; Kenneth Branagh as Henry and Brian Blessed as Exeter in the film directed by Branagh, 1989. Renaissance Films/BBC/Curzon Films, courtesy of the Ronald Grant Archive.

they are about to receive will then be merely scars, and the deeds they are about to do will become exaggerated by the re-telling ('remember, with advantages'). It is a brilliant rhetorical device that calms the anguish of anticipation by setting it in the mellow light of reminiscence. It is equally important to note that, although the mood has shifted, the theme of brotherhood, initiated in the first section, runs through this middle section of the speech as well. Harry the king and his nobles will be as familiar as 'household words'.

Having run as a subsidiary theme through the first two sections, brotherhood emerges predominant in the concluding section (IV.3.60–67). Underlining the difference between this and the Harfleur speech, Henry makes explicit what has been implicit throughout the rest of the speech: the trial of strength and courage that they are about to face together makes them all, the highest and the lowest, brothers. The speech ends neatly by returning to the place where it started, in England, with those 'now abed' (Westmorland's 'those men ... that do no work today!') and reversing the sentiment that has been heard from the Boy ('Would I were in an alehouse in London!', III.2.11) and from Bates ('he could wish himself in Thames up to the neck: and so I would he were, and I by him', IV.1.111–13) by suggesting that in the future it is those men now in England who will regret that they were not at Agincourt.

This speech is a remarkable performance which moves from an heroic contemplation of brotherhood in death to a vivid celebration of brotherhood in life. When Salisbury enters with news of the French preparing for battle, Henry can justly reply: 'All things are ready, if our minds be so' (IV.3.71).

For Henry the disposition of the mind is as important as the disposition of his troops on the ground. Certainly, as we have noticed before, the sense of brotherhood in arms distinguishes the English army from the French and seems to imply the superiority of the English. ■

We must, however, set this magnificent speech in context. Just before it, in his one soliloquy (IV.1.218–77), Henry speaks of those he has just called 'brothers' as 'fool' (228), 'the wretched slave' (261), 'such a wretch' (271) and 'gross brain' (275). What happens after Agincourt? Look at the scene when Henry once again confronts Williams (IV.8.57–61), the character who most profoundly questioned him and to whose anxieties the Agincourt speech was a partial answer. **What does Henry call him?**

Discussion

'This fellow'. 'Fellow' has a number of meanings in sixteenth-century English. In a term such as 'fellowship' ('Here was a royal fellowship of death!', IV.8.100) it could suggest the sort of heroic brotherhood referred to in the Agincourt speech. But when used on its own, it was more often dismissive and sometimes downright contemptuous; Orleans describes Henry as a 'wretched and peevish fellow' (III.7.129), and Fluellen describes Pistol as 'no petter than a fellow' (V.1.7). ■

We have already seen in another context that when Henry asks Exeter for details of the French prisoners, he makes a distinction between the 'good sort' and others. We might well defend this by saying that this is of monetary importance, and anyway refers to the French – who in the play have always been presented exclusively through their nobles. They were not told that this battle would make them all brothers. So how does Henry react to the list of English dead? By reading the names of those of noble or gentle birth, and then adding dismissively: 'None else of name' (IV.8.104).

The Agincourt speech is magnificent: it expresses what has often been observed of human beings brought together in a crisis, that common suffering breeds fellow feeling. It is, however, in all senses of the word an 'occasional' piece: it is delivered at a particular moment and is true for that moment and effective within it (it makes the soldiers fight better). But, like a lawyer's speech, it is a performance: it is appropriate, just and effective within its context but cannot necessarily be of use outside it. It is a skilled piece of rhetoric, a skilled piece of acting.

Think back for a moment to that description of Henry given by the Archbishop in the first scene of the play (I.1.38–59). Almost all the talents he describes there are related to argument and rhetoric. But, as we are reminded by almost every scene in the play, Henry is also a politician operating in the real world and carrying an immense responsibility. He is taking huge risks morally, politically and militarily. Shakespeare is not portraying a magisterially detached figure, but a talented leader on a knife-edge between triumph and disaster. He must use what talents he has in what circumstances he finds himself. Politics in the real world rarely allow even the most principled to act absolutely honestly or absolutely consistently. According to the Archbishop, Henry's rhetorical talents aren't exclusively technical: when he practises a particular rhetorical skill, the auditor wishes that the king were that sort of person:

> Hear him but reason in divinity,
> And all-admiring, with an inward wish,
> You would desire the King were made a prelate.
>
> (I.1.38–40)

The type of speech and the character who speaks it are here thought of as one. This is very close to the actor's craft, and in some sense one might think of Henry as using the rhetorical skills of an actor but within a political and military context.

Theme: 'A name that in my thoughts becomes me best' – the actor-king

Henry V is a very self-conscious play. It is full of references to the fact that it *is* a play (the Chorus will not let us forget the stage's limitations), and it contains allusions to other Shakespeare history plays – to the three parts of *Henry VI* and to *Richard III* in the Epilogue, and to *Henry IV* in the characters of Bardolph, Pistol, Quickly and, above all, Falstaff. At various points in both parts of *Henry IV*, Prince Hal makes it clear to the audience that he is aware of playing a part and, when the time comes, will play another. The Archbishop regards Henry's transformation as something close to a miracle (see I.1.24–37) but those play-goers who had seen the earlier plays would have had more warning and more understanding of the change. In *Henry IV, Part 1*, Prince Hal comments on his wild youth:

> Yet herein will I imitate the sun
> Who doth permit the base contagious clouds
> To smother up his beauty from the world,
> That, when he please again to be himself,
> Being wanted, he may be more wond'red at,
> By breaking through the foul and ugly mists
> Of vapours that did seem to strangle him.
> If all the year were playing holidays,
> To sport would be as tedious as to work;
> But when they seldom come, they wish'd-for come,
> And nothing pleaseth but rare accidents.
> So, when this loose behaviour I throw off
> And pay the debt I never promised,
> By how much better than my word I am,
> By so much shall I falsify men's hopes;
> And, like bright metal on a sullen ground,
> My reformation, glittering o'er my fault,
> Shall show more goodly and attract more eyes

68

Than that which hath no foil to set it off.
I'll so offend, to make offence a skill,
Redeeming time when men think least I will.

(*Henry IV, Part 1*, I.2.190–210)

This is worth quoting at length because it alerts us to a knowledge that many play-goers in 1599 would have had about Henry; namely, that he is a considerable actor who uses his talents to manipulate events and people's reactions to them.

The courtship scene

With this in mind, let us look at the courtship scene between Henry and Katherine (V.2.98–276). Please read Henry's account of himself in the two speeches which lie between lines 121 and 167. **How does he present himself, and do you think that the presentation is a fair one?**

D i s c u s s i o n

He presents himself as a rough soldier-king who appears to have 'sold my farm to buy my crown'; he then promptly acts out the part by trying to force a deal as though he were at an agricultural fair: 'and so clap hands, and a bargain' (129).

In the second speech he speaks to the Princess as a 'plain soldier' for he cannot act the lover: 'I cannot look greenly, nor gasp out my eloquence, nor I have no cunning in protestation' (142–3).

Most of the rhetorical performances we have so far seen from Henry have been in a military context, but they were different enough from each other, and complicated enough in themselves, to suggest that Henry at best is being disingenuous here. His arguments about constancy (151–65) display the eloquence that he denies. ■

Henry here is *acting* the part of a simple soldier-lover, he is adopting a role that suits the circumstances. It is a sort of constitutional fiction. After all, the constitutional reality is clear: to gain Katherine as his wife has been one of Henry's demands from the start (and one of the demands first granted: see III.Chorus.30), a demand reiterated at the beginning of the courtship scene (V.2.95–7). After Agincourt the French king is in no position to deny Henry anything (his complete weakness is demonstrated in lines 328–39). Nearer to the end of their scene, Katherine declares that she will leave the final de-cision to her father, and Henry responds: 'Nay, it will please him well, Kate – it shall please him, Kate' (245–6), where the auxiliary verb 'will' (usually implying no more than the future happening of something) changes to 'shall' (implying some degree of insistence). Henry is clearly in a position to insist.

The complete control exercised by Henry over the French court is fur-ther emphasized by his reaction to Katherine's conventional modesty: 'O Kate, nice customs curtsy to great kings ... and the liberty that follows our places stops the mouth of all find-faults' (V.2.265, 268–9).

'Nice' here means 'fine, delicately precise and subtle' and draws an implied contrast between the precise, over-refined rules of the French court and the bluff, honest, no-nonsense manners of the English. However, this point, as so many others in the scene, must have been lost on the Princess, whose English seems to be restricted to naming the parts of the body and trying a few other faltering phrases.

The rules of courtesy and conduct themselves, of course, encourage people to act a part rather than be themselves. We should not assume that it is only Henry who is acting a role here. Katherine in this scene presents the character of a well-bred, timid, easily shocked young woman, but if you think back to III.4, which shows the princess learning English from the 'old gentlewoman' Alice, we may see a somewhat different aspect of her character. She is rehearsing the names of parts of the body in English. (Have you noticed how insistent this text is in linking Katherine with the body?) Near the end of the scene she asks Alice the English for 'le pied et la robe' (III.4.46) and Alice replies 'Le foot, madame, et le count'. The joke is that Katherine slightly mishears, and detects no difference between the English 'foot' and the French *foutre* (fuck), or between the English 'count' (Alice's pronunciation of 'gown') and the French *con* (cunt). Her reaction is interesting: she is shocked and outraged, but that doesn't stop her from repeating the words twice (in 52 and 55). It is not surprising that most productions of the play point up the ambiguity by having Katherine appear simultaneously exited, amused and outraged at this point. However the director chooses to play this scene, it begins the close association of Katherine with images of the body and procreation which are to be developed in V.2.

One further point: the placing of III.4. **What does it immediately follow, and why do you think this juxtaposition might be important?**

Discussion

It comes immediately after the besieging and taking of Harfleur. Later (in V.2.312–22) it becomes clear that Katherine is associated by both Henry and her own father with those cities of France as yet unbesieged by English troops. This wooing scene might therefore be thought of as a form of siege warfare conducted by other means. ∎

We have seen that the ambivalent and amused Katherine of Act III does not quite match with the very proper princess outraged by the suggestion of a kiss in Act V. This is because both Henry and Katherine are acting out roles that help disguise the crude power politics underlying the scene. But it is not just politics: it is sex as well or, rather, fecundity and procreation. And fecundity and procreation have, in the context of the time, much to do with power politics. Let us untie this knot of images.

Burgundy's description of despoiled France between lines 23 and 67 in V.2 stresses the fertility of that country, even if that fertility has been temporarily thwarted or misdirected by war. **Can you pick out three examples of the imagery that helps convey this sense of fertility?**

Discussion

Here are a few I found:

> Dear nurse of arts, plenties, and joyful births,
>
> best garden of the world,
>
> Our fertile France
>
> Corrupting in its own fertility.
>
> wildly overgrown with hair,
>
> erst brought sweetly forth
>
> Conceives by idleness, and nothing teems
> (V.2.35, 36, 37, 40, 43, 48, 51)

But in fact you could have picked others, because the whole speech is bulging with images of natural growth (albeit of the wrong sort: weeds rather than cultivated plants). ■

Many times in his history plays Shakespeare uses images of nature run riot (particularly in a garden where nature should be ordered and regulated) to express and explore the problems of a country in turmoil. (If you would like to take this further, note that the most famous example occurs in *Richard II*: III.4.) This is by no means a fanciful parallel, for in pre-industrial society a nation's wealth and power were almost wholly dependent on its agriculture and thus on the fertility and cultivation of its land. In many such cultures the fertility of the land was closely associated with the fertility of women, so the close association in imagery we have seen between the princess and the land of France is no coincidence.

For monarchs, the fertility of their consorts had a more pressing and specific significance. In cultures which at least in theory were based on primogeniture (where the first, usually male, child inherits the title), it was very important that the line of succession from one king to the next be clear and legal, and the simplest way of ensuring that was for the eldest son to inherit the throne from his father. If it were less simple than that, then the throne (and therefore the country) might be threatened by instability as two or three equally legitimate successors disputed the crown and thus caused a civil war such as the Wars of the Roses. It is not by chance that *Henry V* opens with a debate about the Salic Law, which is concerned with the way in which power can or cannot be inherited through the female line. For Henry V, a son was vital to guarantee both the continuity of his family's control of the English throne and to validate his family's claim to the French throne. But, given the high infant mortality of pre-industrial societies, more than one son was necessary; thus not single but serial fertility was important.

These would not have been abstract matters to Shakespeare's contemporaries. The Wars of the Roses, which had been ended by Henry Tudor – later Henry VII, Queen Elizabeth I's grandfather – at the battle of Bosworth Field in 1485, may not have been within living memory, but on the collective memory they had left scar-tissue that was frequently picked by popular histories (such as the chronicles of Hall and Holinshed that Shakespeare used extensively as sources) and by plays (including most of Shakespeare's history plays). At the time of the first performance of *Henry V*, Elizabeth I (who had no children and was beyond child-bearing age) was facing the problem of succession. For an audience attending a performance of *Henry V* on a summer afternoon in 1599, the links between power, peace and fertility were not abstract matters: they were of immediate interest and concern.

Given this background, it's perhaps not surprising that images of political power, sex and procreation interweave throughout this scene to provide an undercutting commentary on the roles that Henry and Katherine appear to be performing: he is the ardent but bluff lover, she the modest and retreating maiden. Sometimes this undercutting imagery is stark and clear. To Burgundy's moving vision of a fertile France laid waste and to his plea for peace, Henry's retort is pure politics:

> you must buy that peace
> With full accord to all our just demands
>
> (V.2.70–71)

Of Katherine he says simply:

> She is our capital demand, comprised
> Within the fore-rank of our articles.
>
> (V.2.96–7)

Sometimes the threat slips out in the form of a simile, as when – attempting to speak French – Henry says:

> It is as easy for me, Kate, to conquer the kingdom as to
> speak so much more French.
>
> (V.2.183–4)

Some of the 'procreative' imagery is just as explicit:

> thou must therefore needs prove a good soldier-
> breeder. Shall not thou and I, between Saint Denis and
> Saint George, compound a boy,
>
> …
>
> He [Henry's father] was thinking of civil wars
> when he got me;
>
> (V.2.203–5, 223–4)

But more often it is contained within *double entendres* such as 'No, 'tis hereafter to know' (210), where 'know' is used in the Biblical sense. In Elizabethan English, to 'leap' also meant to mount sexually, so Henry's references to 'leapfrog' (136) and 'leap' (139) reinforce the sexual subtext of these exchanges, as does 'Lay on' (140–41) which at the time could be applied to both fighting and sex. This sort of linguistic ambiguity may have been particularly appropriate on the Elizabethan stage because, of course, the acting companies were exclusively male, the female characters being acted by boys whose voices had not yet broken. What effect this had on Shakespeare's audience is difficult to gauge: were the sexual references somehow downplayed by being part of this all-male exchange? Or were they given an extra, odd twist? Or was there such a willing (and perhaps automatic) suspension of disbelief that, within the performance, audiences actually saw the boys as women? In answer, one can only say that, whatever other theatrical limitations the Chorus apologizes for in *Henry V*, he never apologizes for the boys playing women.

Whatever the case, the sexuality bubbling beneath the enacted scene between Henry and Katherine is as nothing to the flood of often rather crass sexual jokes made by Burgundy on his return, between lines 277 and 310. The character whose first major speech explored – in lyrical, not to say grandiose, terms – the themes of fertility and abundance gone awry (for example, 'That should deracinate such savagery', 47), now returns for an almost music-hall exchange of sexual puns with Henry. In his edition Humphreys passes over most of these; it would be tedious to rehearse them all in detail, but here are some of the most obvious:

'apt' (281): sexually promising, as well as being an apt pupil

'circle' (289): magic circle was a sexual pun

'hard condition' (294)

'they will endure handling' (304–5)

and so on, and so on. (If you want the full details, refer to the notes in the New Cambridge Shakespeare edition of *King Henry V* edited by Andrew Gurr.) **Why do you think there is such a distinctive change in Burgundy's diction between his first and second entrance?**

D i s c u s s i o n

There are several reasons. Plays, even more than other forms of literature, have to satisfy many demands simultaneously. As you may recall from Chapter 2, Elizabethan and Jacobean plays seem to have attracted and held a very wide audience that was drawn from many social groups and educational levels. There would be those who came just for the spectacle, those who wanted lots of sex and violence, and those who expected magnificent speeches and much word-play. You could argue, therefore, that the *double entendres* provide the sex just as Harfleur and Agincourt had provided the violence.

You might also argue that the Duke of Burgundy, as an international mediator between France and England, was on his best behaviour in the early part of the scene; after all, the French king had not yet agreed terms and Henry had not yet formally proposed to Katherine. By Burgundy's return, virtually everything was in the bag and he could relax. (Notice that it is *only on his return* that Burgundy calls Henry, and Henry calls Burgundy, 'cousin' – a term implying near equality and closeness.) Finally, you might argue that although the scene starts formally with everyone playing their ascribed parts, the reality of the political and military situation keeps breaking through in the language and the imagery, so by Burgundy's second entrance he can afford to be honest about what is going on. As none of these three interpretations contradicts or mutually excludes the others, it is reasonable to suggest that all three go to explain this change in Burgundy's language. ∎

'Cheerful semblance': the necessity for disguise

We have seen how the rhetoric of love in V.2, or the rhetoric of war in the speech to the governor of Harfleur, or the rhetoric of fellowship in the Agincourt speech, are contradicted – or at least modified – by either the realities of the situation in which the speech is made, or by the events that follow it or, indeed, by both. The use of a particular sort of language or style implies that the character using it has adopted a particular role, is playing a particular part. Henry's language (and the attitudes and values implied by that language) change and change again as the play progresses. Henry's political aims are clear, but the means he uses to achieve them vary. His language and his character seem created for the occasion, for the achievement of a particular purpose. Once that is achieved, the language and the persona will change. Certain critics have observed an 'opacity' in Henry's character as portrayed by Shakespeare, which makes him difficult to understand, difficult to see into.

In practice, however, it might be better to describe the problem as one of 'mobility' or 'fluidity' of character rather than 'opacity'. Think back to the Archbishop's praise of Henry's character in I.1. Each time the king speaks a 'language', you expect him or want him to be that sort of person:

> Hear him but reason in divinity
> And all-admiring, with an inward wish,
> You would desire the King were made a prelate.
>
> (I.1.38–40)

This ability of the king to adopt or act a part recurs throughout the play. In II.2 he acts the innocent to entrap Cambridge, Scroop and Grey; later the Constable refers to Henry as 'Covering discretion with a coat of folly' (II.4.38); his threats to the Governor of Harfleur are a performance (he sounds angry but later admits that, until the boys were killed at Agincourt, 'I was not angry since I came to France': IV.7.53); before Agincourt, Henry is described by the Chorus: 'But freshly looks, and overbears attaint/With cheerful semblance and sweet majesty' (IV.Chorus.39–40).

After these public acts he adopts another disguise and confronts Bates and Williams. Williams, when accused by Henry, legitimately defends himself by saying 'Your majesty came not like yourself' (IV.8.50). Henry has no answer but to give Williams money. Perhaps Henry never can come like himself. Henry identifies 'ceremony' in IV.1 as the thing that separates a king from the common man. Ceremony in this context is, of course, the external trappings – the actions, clothes and symbols – that mark the monarch. Ceremony is the ritualistic theatre of power.

The Chorus's phrase 'cheerful semblance' is significant. There is no suggestion in the play that these various acts and roles and disguises Henry adopts are done for cynical or bad reasons. He dissembles before Agincourt, as any good leader must, to give his men heart. He terrifies the inhabitants of Harfleur in order to achieve a less bloody victory. He woos Katherine in order to disguise the crude fact that she has already been negotiated away by her father.

Figure 3.7 An up-beat *Henry V*: heroic Henry (played by Olivier), surrounded and enclosed by his well-equipped troops, receives the French envoys in the film directed by Olivier, 1944. Two Cities, courtesy of the Ronald Grant Archive.

Figure 3.8 A sombre *Henry V*: Henry (played by Branagh), standing on a cart full of corpses, is raised and separated from his troops after the Battle of Agincourt, in the film directed by Branagh, 1989. Renaissance Films/BBC/Curzon Films, courtesy of the Kobal Collection.

Henry V is a play about an heroic and successful king, but it is also about the sacrifices a king has to make in order to be successful. It is a play about the realities of leadership and the realities of power. A king hasn't the luxury of the private man: he cannot be one single personality, his state is multiple and episodic. As everything waits on him, he must do and be what the current circumstances require. It is not a coincidence that almost all Henry's great speeches are public occasions: he has only one soliloquy, and that is spent identifying the burden of his public role ('ceremony') and envying the privacy and continuity of the private man ('And follows so the ever-running year/With profitable labour to his grave': IV.1.269–70).

In being ever-changing to match the circumstances, in adopting the most effective language to achieve an immediate end, and then moving on, Henry resembles a type that would have been immediately recognized by an audience at the Globe: he resembles an actor.

2 Henry V: *history and the canon*

Shakespeare's play and history

We come now to the second of the five sections in this chapter, and it signals that we are shifting our focus to consider the relationship between Shakespeare's play and the historical record. It is important to remind ourselves that, although the play has contributed to the popular twentieth-century image of Henry V, it is in some ways only very loosely based on historical truth. After all, it was written nearly two hundred years after the events it portrays, and at a time when historically based narratives were expected to teach very particular values often firmly associated with the government of the day. Sometimes this results in no more than exaggerations of the scale of Henry's epic struggle (the size of both armies at Agincourt is exaggerated and the English losses in the battle are underplayed). Sometimes it is a matter of suppressing complications that might obscure the thrust of the story and its message. For instance, none of the following complications is acknowledged by the play: the fact that the French king, Charles VI, was subject to long bouts of madness; that the French Queen, Isabeau of Bavaria, was alienated from her husband and was frequently the focus for political discontent; that between 1415 and 1420 there were no fewer than three Dauphins (the first dying in 1415 before Agincourt, the second in 1417); and that by 1420 (the setting for Act V) the new Duke of Burgundy was firmly pro-English.

However, there are other suppressions that have a greater significance. Let us take just two examples. All the evidence suggests that the Southampton conspiracy (II.2) was not just a matter of weak men being corrupted by French gold. The real Cambridge-led plot was designed to replace Henry V with Edward Mortimer, fifth Earl of March, whose claim to the English throne was actually stronger than that of Henry's father. **Why do you think Shakespeare ignored this fact?**

Quite simply, to avoid any questioning of Henry's legitimate claim to the throne. In a play so preoccupied with justification of Henry's cause to God and Man (see I.1, I.2 and IV.1), you could not afford such an awkward detail. ■

Our second example comes from III.2, which shows the English, Welsh, Scottish and Irish captains during the siege of Harfleur. It's a curious scene, because it seems to set up a collection of characters and relationships that one might expect to be developed through the play as a comic sub-plot. In fact, only two of the characters appear again, and Jamy and Macmorris simply disappear from view. In representing all four kingdoms united in Henry's cause, Shakespeare seems to be making a powerful if unhistorical point. Although Henry is an English king leading an essentially English army ('On, on, you noble English', 'Whose limbs were made in England', '"God for Harry, England and Saint George!"'), the implication of this scene is that in practice the king was forging a *British* alliance. Of course, the political realities of Henry's time were quite different, as the references to the 'weasel Scot' in I.2.136–221 remind us. Scotland was an independent kingdom, Ireland's status was unclear and, although Wales was nominally subject to him, Henry had spent most of his youth fighting against those (such as Owen Glendower) who would have had an independent Welsh kingdom. Even Holinshed, one of Shakespeare's main historical sources, records both Welsh and Scottish mercenaries fighting at Agincourt – not for Henry but for the French. **Given all this, what job do you think III.3 is performing?**

Let us consider the realities of the period in which *Henry V* was written and first performed: the Earl of Essex was attempting unsuccessfully to bring Ireland under military control (see V.Chorus.29–34) and Elizabeth I's most likely successor, though nothing was made clear, was James VI of Scotland. In such circumstances, a suggestion of the four kingdoms bickering but nevertheless working together in some common (but English-set and English-led) purpose would be likely to go down well with both the audience and the authorities. Interestingly it is Jamy and Macmorris, the two characters who represent the most contentious countries, who do not reappear; indeed, many critics have argued that these two were later additions to the text and were therefore never properly incorporated into the play. Whatever the truth of this, it leaves one wondering about the significance – with James VI waiting in the wings – of having a Scottish captain, 'a marvellous falorous gentleman', called 'Jamy'. ■

Henry V as a figure in history and literature

In one sense the historical figure of Henry V (1387–1422) was 'canonical' long before Shakespeare wrote his play *Henry V.* There are incidents in English (and, later, British) military history that virtually everyone seems to know something about: the date of the Battle of Hastings, the Spanish Armada, the death of Nelson ('Kiss me, Hardy'), the Battle of the Somme, Dunkirk, the Battle of Britain. Among these we would have to list Henry V and Agincourt. This common knowledge that we possess is not simply the product of over one hundred years of compulsory state education. Its roots lie deeper. There is much evidence to suggest that Agincourt struck a chord in popular sentiment almost as soon as it had been fought. A number of ballads and lyrical poems were written within a few years of the battle, the most famous of which was the *Agincourt Carol*:

> Our king went forth to Normandy
> With grace and might of chivalry;
> Ther God for him wrought mervelusly;
> Wherfore England may call and cry
> *Deo gracias, Anglia,*
> *Redde pro victoria.*
> [Give thanks, England, to God for this victory]

The battle itself is one of the best documented of all medieval conflicts: there are at least seven contemporary chronicles that describe the conflict in some detail, and three of these were written by eyewitnesses. There were a number of accounts of Henry's acts, and at least one of them, *Gesta Henrici Quinti* (1417), was completed while he was alive. In the thirty years after his death a host of accounts of his life and deeds appeared from the pens of both English and French writers.

The interest in Henry and Agincourt did not wane with a new century for, sometime in 1513–14, during a brief campaign fought by Henry VIII in north-eastern France, a new English translation of a life of Henry V was produced (thus allowing this later Tudor Henry to see himself as carrying on the grand tradition of invading France). By the 1530s and the Reformation, writers were using Henry V's life, somewhat anachronistically, as an example of English resistance to the Papacy and European Catholicism. Hall's *Union of the Families of Lancaster and York* (first edition, 1542) and Holinshed's *Chronicles* (first edition, 1577), the Tudor histories from which Shakespeare derived most of his historical information, were in one sense just playing further variations on the theme of this heroic English king.

Indeed, Shakespeare was not even the first Elizabethan dramatist to tackle the subject. There seem to have been a number of plays presented during the 1580s concerned with the exploits of Henry, but the only one to have survived in even partial form – *The Famous Victories of Henry the fifth: Containing the Honourable Battell of Agincourt* – comes from a text printed in 1598, only a year before Shakespeare's play. Shakespeare's was not even the last word on the subject. A month or two after the first presentation of *Henry V,* a rival company of actors at the Rose Theatre on Bankside presented a new play, *Sir John Oldcastle,* which dealt with a Falstaff-like figure and placed him in the reign of Henry V.

The Agincourt theme proved a durable inspiration; it could be found cropping up again early in the next century in the form of a ballad written by Michael Drayton and published in 1605:

> Fair stood the wind for France
> When we our sails advance,

Nor now to prove our chance
Longer will tarry ...
Well it thine age became,
O noble Erpingham,
Which didst the signal aim
To our hid forces!
When from a meadow by,
Like a storm suddenly
The English archery
Struck the French horses.

Thus Shakespeare's *Henry V* does not exist in a historical vacuum: our attitude to it, and the attitude of earlier generations, is likely to have been influenced by the legendary status of the real Henry and by the multitude of other writings on the subject both before and after 1599. I will give but one example. Both the Olivier and the Branagh film productions make much of Agincourt: both introduce the images of the line of sharpened stakes to deflect the charge of mounted French knights, and both emphasize the impact of the flights of English arrows on the French army. (In Olivier's production, the sudden darkening of the sky above the French army reminds one irresistibly of Drayton's 'Like a storm suddenly'). But you will look in vain in Shakespeare's text for mention of sharpened stakes or flights of arrows. Indeed, *Henry V* does not include a single reference to that most important part of the English army at Agincourt, the bowmen. These images, and others that we commonly associate with Shakespeare's play, actually have their origin in this broader legendary context in which, though we hardly ever acknowledge it, *Henry V* is set.

To talk about *Henry V*'s being a canonical text therefore raises problems of context. Unlike most other Shakespearean plays, *Henry V* carries the cultural 'charge' that comes with tackling a subject of legendary status and that gives it a significance above and beyond the meaning of its text alone.

In what sense is Henry V *part of the canon?*

Canonization of literary texts is a tricky matter, doubly so where a performance text is involved. In one sense *Henry V* is obviously a canonical text by a supremely canonical writer. But Shakespeare was not always canonical and, even when he became so in the eighteenth century, his texts were frequently mauled almost beyond recognition by both editing and production. Given the legendary charge of its subject and the fact that the text of *Henry V* has been sliced in so many ways, we should be sceptical: does *Henry V*'s canonical status help us to understand the play or its historical context more fully?

The process of canonization has been regarded by some critics as a rather regrettable one: it seems to them to imply, on the one hand, uncritical and slavish acceptance of texts canonized and, on the other, a cruel exclusion and persecution of those texts not canonized. In practice it is not this simple. Canonization can often act rather like the Trojans accepting the Greek gift as 'just a horse': once it is within the walls, it can prove to be a very different beast.

For example, *Henry V* may well have been canonized partly because it seems to be patriotic. But in fact the play can be read as a much subtler, more complex text that, in some ways at least, subverts the original reasons for its canonization.

One of the ironies of the play's becoming a canonical work is that, from the early 1800s on, with the expansion of formal education and the cheapening of printing (thus creating the 'set book'), it is highly likely that more people *read* Shakespeare's text than *saw* it in performance. To put this another way: in becoming a supremely canonical work, the play for many became separated from the theatre, yet it was in the theatre that *Henry V* had originally achieved its canonical status.

3   Henry V: *politics and performance*

To understand *Henry V* more fully, we must also try to see it as contemporaries of Shakespeare saw it, not from a reverential distance as a great, canonized work but right up close as a current piece of entertainment. **What in the performance of the play do you think might have appealed particularly to an audience in 1599?**

D i s c u s s i o n

This is not an exhaustive list, but what about the following?

The action: the Harfleur and Agincourt scenes would have given plenty of scope, even if there were only a few 'ragged foils'.

The costumes: there were few props and less scenery on Shakespeare's stage, but a lot of time and money seems to have been spent on costumes. A history play with many court scenes (both English and French), and some battle-scenes, would have given the acting company many opportunities for visual display.

The comedy: the Eastcheap low-life scenes revive characters (Pistol, Bardolph, Quickly, etc.) already known from *Henry IV, Parts 1 and 2*, and would have been reassuringly familiar. (This is rather like the catch-phrases associated with radio comedy of the 1940s and 1950s; indeed, Nym has a catch phrase in this play: 'that is the humour of it'.) The bawdy comedy associated with Princess Katherine, and the Duke of Burgundy's *double entendres*, would have appealed in the way that bedroom farces and Donald McGill postcards might today.

The grand speeches: remember that many of Shakespeare's contemporaries would have come to 'hear' rather than 'see' a play (that's why we still call the spectators at an entertainment 'the audience'). Formal education in the sixteenth century put a very heavy emphasis on rhetoric, on the art of writing and speaking well and convincingly. Even those with little or no formal education, even those who were illiterate, would be used to hearing great prose in the form of the early English translations of the Bible, particularly the Geneva and Bishop's Bibles (not the Authorized, of course, because that was first published in 1611) and the Book of Common Prayer.

The patriotic pleasure of witnessing the English bashing the French. The French were, and continued to be right up until 1912–14, the traditional enemy. The re-creation of past military glories is a very common feature of popular culture (witness the large number of very successful movies about the Second World War, produced long after the event). There is some evidence that Shakespeare's version did not offer as much patriotic gratification as other plays on the subject. In the *Famous Victories,* for example, the Dauphin is present at the final scene and makes a personal and very humiliating submission to Henry. ■

Something that would have certainly appealed to contemporary audiences, but might escape our notice almost entirely, were the play's allusions to current political concerns. 'Almost' entirely because there is at least one occasion where a very topical allusion to the events of the summer of 1599 is made. **Can you remember where this occurs?**

D i s c u s s i o n

It occurs in the Chorus at the beginning of Act V when, in a description of Henry's triumphal return to London, we have the following lines:

> As, by a lower but loving likelihood,
> Were now the General of our gracious Empress –
> As in good time he may – from Ireland coming,
> Bringing rebellion broachèd on his sword,
> How many would the peaceful city quit
> To welcome him!
>
> (V.Chorus.29–34) ■

The empress was Elizabeth, the general was the Earl of Essex who had not yet returned from what was to prove a disastrous campaign in Ireland. Essex was to be executed two years later, in 1601. No doubt these lines were only spoken in the earliest performances, but it is some indication of how risky as well as how exciting working in the theatre might be.

This dangerous association between Shakespeare's company of actors (the Lord Chamberlain's Men) and the headstrong and foolish Essex did not end with this pointed and flattering reference in the Chorus of *Henry V.* On Thursday or Friday, the 5th or 6th of February 1601, a couple of days before the Essex Rebellion, Sir Gelly Meyrick and other supporters of the Essex cause crossed the Thames and met members of the Lord Chamberlain's Men at the Globe. At this meeting they requested that the company present Shakespeare's earlier history play *Richard II,* and promised them 40 shillings more than they would ordinarily get for such a performance. As *Richard II* was about the deposition of an anointed but ineffectual monarch by one of his nobles (Bolingbroke, later Henry IV, Henry V's father), the play was clearly dynamite in the current political situation. Nevertheless, it was duly performed at the Globe on Saturday 7 February. The following day the Earl of Essex rode into the City of London in an abortive attempt to raise an army.

The parallels between literature and life were not lost on even the most important figures in the realm. After the collapse of Essex's muddled rebellion, the Queen herself made the connection by observing to William Lambarde: 'I am Richard II, know ye not that?' The Lord Chamberlain's Men were very lucky to get away without being imprisoned.

Even more critical for an audience in 1599 would be the problem of succession. By this time Elizabeth was sixty-six and could not last much longer (she was, in fact, to die four years later). Upon the smooth and legitimate transition of power depended the stability of the whole state, and the fate of Protestantism in England (a Roman Catholic king or queen could mean, as it had in Mary's reign, an attempt to return England to Roman Catholicism). Of Shakespeare's ten history plays, eight were concerned with the Wars of the Roses, which were a vivid example of what happened when the king's title was in dispute.

As Shakespeare portrays him, Henry V is a popular and successful king who has descended by right and proper succession from his father. However, even Henry is not free from the guilty responsibility which also descended to him from his father:

> Not today, O Lord,
> Oh, not today, think not upon the fault
> My father made in compassing the crown!
>
> (IV.1.285–7)

His desperation can be judged by the use of three negatives ('not today', 'Oh, not today', 'think not') in the first one and a half lines: it is as if he were willing God not to remember his guilt. It is, of course, a hopeless argument for he still holds on to all the things that his father won for him illegitimately: they go before, and he comes limping after with his guilt.

Of course, many of Shakespeare's contemporaries would be aware of the sequel to Henry V; indeed many in his audience would have seen it enacted by Shakespeare's own company. Even if they hadn't, they would know by the end of the play, because the Chorus in the Epilogue makes the point clearly:

> Henry the Sixth, in infant bands crowned King
> Of France and England, did this King succeed,
> Whose state so many had the managing
> That they lost France, and made his England bleed:
> Which oft our stage hath shown;
>
> (V.Epilogue.9–13)

It is not insignificant that, in the play, Henry V is twice compared with Alexander – once explicitly by Fluellen (IV.7.12–48), and once by implication when the Archbishop refers to Henry's untying of the mythical Gordian Knot (I.1.46–7). (This was the knot that Alexander had been able to deal with only by slicing through it.) Alexander's achievements were brilliant but short-lived, and his empire collapsed into warring factions almost as soon as he died. A contemporary understanding of *Henry V* would involve a clear sense of the similar brevity of Henry's life and the ephemerality of his achievements, and of the link between that ephemerality and Henry's uncertain claim to the throne: 'Small time, but in that small most greatly lived/This Star of England. Fortune made his sword' (V.Epilogue.5–6).

The whole Epilogue, though very brief, is a celebration of heroic achievement and inevitable loss, and the political and moral knowledge of the audience which makes both the achievement and the loss understandable. It is also, however, a most extraordinary account of Henry's triumphs. Think for a moment about Henry's pride-denying piety and of how he spends much of the play giving to God all the credit for his achievements. **In the light of this, what is extraordinary about the Chorus's account?**

D i s c u s s i o n

It is the line 'Fortune made his sword'. It is this stress on 'Fortune', on luck, rather than divine intervention, which makes it such a peculiar conclusion to a play much concerned with justification and divine approval. This final assertion seems to contradict much of what Henry had striven so hard to establish throughout the play. ∎

4 *The contrary Chorus*

Surprising as this is, it is not the only example of the Chorus contradicting the rest of the play or its characters' hopes. Look at the last line spoken by Henry: 'And may our oaths well kept and prosperous be!' (V.2.366). It is a noble hope but one that, as the Chorus's Epilogue makes quite clear, is completely unfulfilled. Henry's treaty will not be kept and the oaths will be broken.

So far in this discussion of *Henry V* we have assumed that the Chorus simply introduces, amplifies or explains the rest of the play. But is this really the case? We have seen how the Epilogue casts a very dark shadow over the achievements recorded in V.2 and in particular shows how Henry's hopes expressed in the last line of the play are unfulfilled. Are there other examples of the Chorus functioning in a way contrary to the thrust of the play proper? Take a look at the Chorus's introduction to Act II. **Can you find any statements that are not confirmed by the rest of the play?**

D i s c u s s i o n

Now all the youth of England are on fire
…
        and honour's thought
Reigns solely in the breast of every man.
(II.Chorus.1, 3–4)

Yet, in IV.3.17–18 Westmorland wishes for 'But one ten thousand of those men in England/That do no work today', implying that 'all the youth of England' is a rather misleading description. The claim that only honour resides 'in the breast of every man' is clearly undercut by the first Eastcheap scene that follows directly after the Chorus. It is, of course, surprising that II.1 is set in Eastcheap, because the Chorus told us that 'Unto Southampton do we shift our scene' (42). ∎

The latter could simply be a fault in the text, or one of the rough places to be found in all texts that are variously acted, but it would be difficult to explain the first two contradictions in this way. Perhaps we ought to leave a question mark over this and look at the Act III Chorus. **Can you find any contradictions here?**

Discussion

What about lines 19–24? Is it not again telling us something that, if we considered the play, we would know not to be true? Quite apart from Westmorland's observations, we have the Archbishop who, in I.2.215–17 advises the king to divide his power into four and take just one quarter into France, so it cannot be that England is guarded only by 'grandsires, babies, and old women'. What about these lines?

> With linstock now the devilish cannon touches,
> And down goes all before them.
>
> (III.Chorus.33–4)

As we have seen from our studies of the Harfleur scene, all does not go down before either the cannon or Henry. The battle is much more desperate and its outcome much less certain than the Chorus admits. ■

Let's now look at the Chorus's introduction to Act IV, the Agincourt scenes. **Again, do you detect any differences between the Chorus's presentation of things and what actually occurs in the body of the play?**

Discussion

Here it is not so much a matter of direct contradiction as of the Chorus's emphasizing one thing and the play representing something quite other. The Chorus concentrates on the idea of 'A little touch of Harry in the night' and talks about Henry as the public man, highly visible, cheerful, raising spirits by showing himself widely. The actual scenes before Agincourt are quite different: Henry disguises himself, acts the part of Harry Le Roy, and does very little to raise the spirits of anyone that he meets. Rather than disguising his feelings, in the latter parts of IV.2 he reveals them more fully than at any other time in the play. ■

A number of these mismatches could be explained by the fact that acting texts do get changed. Written versions – particularly those published over twenty years after the first performance – are likely to preserve contradictions and inconsistencies that were introduced by a sequence of performances in different circumstances and probably for different audiences. (From Figures 2.4 and 2.5 in Chapter 2, for example, you may recall differences between the quarto and First Folio editions of *Henry V.*) However, the fact that we so frequently find the Chorus asserting things and declaring things that are reversed or denied by subsequent developments in the play should make us pause. There are simply too many incompatibilities between Chorus and the play proper to be explained purely by chance or ill-luck. There is a pattern of discontinuity between the reality presented by the Chorus and that presented by the rest of the play. Given this, perhaps we should not be too surprised to learn that, for a significant part of its performance history, *Henry V* was presented without this potentially awkward Chorus.

The Chorus and the stage

Shakespeare did not use a Chorus very often in his plays. He has a prologue in *Romeo and Juliet* and *Troilus and Cressida*; he has a prologue and an epilogue in *King Henry IV, Part 2*. Only in *Pericles Prince of Tyre* did he have a Chorus who appeared, as he does in *Henry V*, in a prologue, an epilogue and in an introduction to Acts II–V. In none of these other plays was the Chorus so apologetic, so keen to point out the limitations of the Elizabethan stage, so determined to get the audience to do the imaginative work.

It might be worth taking a moment to establish the persistence of this apologetic, cajoling tone. Please look at the first five of the Chorus's speeches. **In how many can you find some self-conscious comment about the stage or about the audience's need to compensate for its limitations?**

D i s c u s s i o n

I found references to these things in each of the five. This is by no means exhaustive, and you may well have found others, but consider: Prologue (8–14); Act II (31–2, 36–40); Act III (13–18, 25); Act IV (48–53); Act V (3–6, 42–5).

Again and again in these speeches the same note is struck: 'we're in a theatre, with all the physical limitations that implies; we have a small company of actors with limited props; your imagination (guided by me) will have to do most of the work; now, let me tell you what you should see...' But what you are told to see, as we have observed above, is not always what the play actually presents you with. The Chorus, with its invariably up-beat presentation of the story, sounds like an official spokesman, someone hired to present events in a particular and more favourable light. A light which the rest of the play is frequently at pains to darken. ■

As we have seen, *Henry V is* partly a play about politics and power, and about the way in which a central political figure such as a king has to perform a whole series of roles – to become, in fact, an actor playing many parts according to the needs of the time. But, paradoxically, a king needs to appear to be unwavering, to be as fixed and certain as a rock (in Shakespeare's plays wavering kings such as Richard II and Henry VI are always doomed). So he needs a consistent public front. In *Henry V* one of the functions of the Chorus is to provide this, to use the limitations of the stage to justify the attempt to create a consistent and heroic image of Henry. The irony is, of course, that the events then presented on the 'inadequate' stage often contradict, or at least significantly qualify, the Chorus's propaganda. The important thing to recognize here is that, as with Henry and his many roles, the Chorus's attempt to present a particularly optimistic view is also bound up with references to the physical facts of the Elizabethan theatre

and of acting. Acting and power, the theatre and politics, are in *Henry V* –
as they were in life during Shakespeare's time – all bound up together.

I put aside the Epilogue from all the other Chorus speeches. **Can you
see any justification for this? In what ways does the Epilogue differ
from the other speeches given to the Chorus?**

D i s c u s s i o n

The first thing that struck me was that, unlike all the other Choruses, this
was not in blank verse. Most of the other Choruses have a final rhymed
couplet (often used by Shakespeare as a device to indicate the end of a
speech or scene, very useful when most actors would not have had a complete text but only their parts with cues), but the rest is in unrhymed iambic
pentameter. In contrast, the Epilogue has a distinct rhyme scheme: abab,
cdcd, efef, gg. It also has fourteen lines. These two features alone would
classify it as a sonnet, a poetic form with which Shakespeare was well acquainted. Commonly the sonnet is thought of as having two unequal halves
– an octave (the first eight lines) and a sestet (the last six lines). The octave
frequently poses a problem or an idea, and the sestet often moves towards
a resolution of, or reconciliation to, that idea. **Is there such a division in
this sonnet?**

D i s c u s s i o n

I think there is: the octave in this instance deals with what we have seen,
the life of Henry V, while the sestet deals with the aftermath in terms of the
troubled reign of Henry VI. The concluding couplet returns the audience to
that ever-present feature in the play ('our stage') and to its audience ('in
your fair minds'). ∎

There are other differences between the Epilogue and all other appearances of the Chorus. For the first time, the author is mentioned rather than
the actors. On this occasion there is no attempt to propagandize; instead
there is a rather bleak account of Henry's short life and his apparent dependence on fortune. Most extraordinarily, it reverses the usual pattern. Usually
in this play the Chorus proposes a simple, optimistic interpretation that the
dramatic text then overturns. On this occasion it is the text that proposes an
optimistic possibility ('And may our oaths well kept and prosperous be!')
and the Chorus that presents the pessimistic reality ('That they lost France,
and made his England bleed').

The earlier Choruses are all concerned with what is happening or
about to happen. Note that in the first five of the Chorus's speeches there is
an emphasis not just on immediacy but on the huge size and scope of the
subject; given the perspective of the Chorus (that when you are close to
things they appear relatively large), this is only appropriate:

Act I: '*vasty* fields of France', '*mighty* monarchies'

Act II: 'Now *all* the youth of England'

Act III: 'A *city* on th'inconstant billows dancing'

Act IV: '*wide vessel* of the *universe*', '*A largesse universal*'

Act V: 'in their *huge* and proper life', 'London doth *pour* out her
citizens'

86

The Epilogue's temporal perspective is different: it is retrospective, it is looking back at Henry V's life through the reign of Henry VI and all that occurred subsequently. In this perspective the great events dwindle in space and time: 'In little room', 'Small time'. The dramatic imagination that expanded to encompass two great monarchies over six years contracts again at the end of the play to the 'wooden O' and an 'hour-glass' that were mentioned in the Prologue. The form of the Chorus reflects this change of perspective: instead of expansive blank verse we have the confines of a neat sonnet.

5 Conclusion: 'In little room' and in 'Small time'

As you learnt in Chapter 2, going to the theatre in Shakespeare's time was a much riskier, more dangerous and (perhaps because of this) more exciting experience than we are used to in today's theatres.

There would be very little or no scenery and the props, such as they were, would be carried on and off by the actors. As has been suggested before, such resources as were available would have been invested in fine costumes. Court scenes and battle scenes in *Henry V* would no doubt have been brilliant in colour and decoration but would have flowed onto and then off the stage as the scenes changed. There would have been a butterfly brilliance at the end of Act I that, with only the Chorus intervening, would have been transformed into the squalor of Eastcheap at the beginning of Act II.

Since there were no Acts (division into Acts came only when the play was printed), no interval and no scenery to change, performances were much faster than we would feel comfortable with today. All our evidence suggests that even long plays took no more than a couple of hours to perform. For a contemporary audience, a performance of *Henry V* would be a fast, dazzling display of visual and verbal brilliance, as glorious, as risky, as diverse – and as fleeting – as its subject.

Henry V is a play about kingship, and about the political and moral burdens it brings. It is about the need for even a good (perhaps especially for a good) king to play many roles and use many sorts of diction. It is about the need for such a king to create an idealized self that has all the clarity and simplicity that he is bound to lack, and about the inevitable gulf between the appearance of that ideal self and reality. Above all it is about the way in which the idea of an actor, and the idea of the theatre in which he acts, can be used as a metaphor to explore the delicately poised relationship between appearance and reality on which the good king relies. This metaphor is particularly powerful in *Henry V* because of the crossover in Tudor and Jacobean times between politics and the theatre.

The full and final power of this metaphor, however, is only to be realized if we, as readers and as audience, are able to understand the particularly exciting, risky nature of Elizabethan theatre, and are therefore able to appreciate both its remarkable glory and its peculiar ephemerality, its smallness and its greatness:

Small time, but in that small most greatly lived ...

Further reading

Allmand, C. (1992) *Henry V*, Methuen; a scholarly biography of the king, for those who wish to know about the historical Henry.

Gurr, A. (ed.) (1992) introduction, *King Henry V*, Cambridge University Press (The New Cambridge Shakespeare series). The introduction is thorough and stimulating: Gurr is particularly good on the play's performance history.

Quinn, M. (ed.) (1969) *Shakespeare's* Henry V: *A Selection of Critical Essays,* Macmillan (Casebook Series); contains a selection of early critical reactions as well as some classic twentieth-century essays on the play.

Thomson, P. (1983) *Shakespeare's Theatre,* Routledge; a stimulating introduction to the physical, economic and cultural factors that governed the performance of plays in the Tudor and Jacobean theatre.

Reading Othello

by Roger Day

Introduction

Othello has the distinction of being one of Shakespeare's most consistently popular and frequently performed plays. Unlike *Henry V* and *As You Like It*, which have slipped from public popularity from time to time, *Othello* has remained a firm favourite with theatre companies and audiences alike. Its power to grip the imagination and excite intense feeling for the characters is legendary, as John Russell Brown has pointed out: '*Othello* is famous in the theatre for the number of times that members of the audience have felt impelled to call out to warn the characters of dangers or to express their sympathy, horror or hatred' (*Shakespeare in Performance*, 1973, p.296).

A play that inspires direct audience responses of this kind is an obvious choice for discussion of the status of Shakespeare's plays in 'the canon'. What is less obvious, and even more interesting, is the complex set of reasons *why* it is that *Othello* is such a 'popular' play – what makes the characters so remarkable, and productions of the play so controversial. We will address these issues throughout the chapter, and will consider some of the reasons why *Othello* remains a popular play today – what *keeps* it in the canon.

The first known performances of *Othello* took place in 1604, and it is thought that the play was written some time after 1601. As was his usual custom, Shakespeare drew upon existing material by other writers for the plot of his play. His main source for *Othello* was 'The Story of Desdemona of Venice and the Moorish Captain', which appeared in the Italian Giraldi Cinthio's collection of tales entitled *Hecatommithi* (*One Hundred Tales*) published in 1565. We do not know whether Shakespeare read this in the original Italian or not, but he made some significant changes in adapting the story for his play. For example, in the prose tale only Desdemona is given a name: 'the Ensign' (Iago) and 'the Moorish Captain' (Othello) are referred to simply by their titles. The character of Roderigo does not appear at all, and at the end Desdemona is battered to death by the Ensign and the Moorish Captain, who manage to conceal the murder by pulling down the timbers of the ceiling. The murder is only revealed after both the Moor and the Ensign are dead. You will find a full account of these changes in the introduction to most editions of the text. Perhaps the most significant change is that the unnamed captain is raised by Shakespeare to a position of great influence and importance in the state, and invested with genuine nobility of character.

Before you begin to read *Othello*, it is worth pausing to consider the significance of the title. The full title is *The Tragedy of Othello, the Moor of Venice*, and there are three points to note here. First of all, the play is described as a tragedy. An Elizabethan audience would have had no difficulty in recognizing *Othello* as a tragedy since at the time the term signified a play that involved the death of a great or noble person. Although neither Othello nor Desdemona is a monarch, both would have been identified as highly placed persons. Othello tells us on his first entrance: 'I fetch my life and being/From men of royal siege' (I.2.21–2), and Desdemona is the daughter of a Venetian senator. In a later section of this chapter we will consider the nature of Shakespearean tragedy in more detail.

The second point to note is that Othello is described as a Moor. The Moors were Muslim inhabitants of North Africa, mainly Morocco and Algeria. In the eighth century they conquered Spain and were not completely driven out until the middle of the fifteenth century. Othello would therefore not have been born a Christian, which is an important contrast with other Shakespearean monarchs/heroes such as Henry V. Moors were, of course, black skinned, and the term 'blackamoor' (that is, 'black Moor') came to be used derogatively of any black person. Again, we will return to this important issue in detail later, but it is worth saying at the outset that Shakespeare was doing something quite original in making a Moor, a black man, a tragic hero.

The third point is that the play is set in Venice, not England, and we will return to this point too later.

Othello is a 'canonical' play, often performed, partly because it is one of the only Shakespeare plays that invites considered critical responses in relation to race and cultural identity. We consider a range of such critical perspectives in the course of this chapter.

Othello *as a dramatic text*

The opening scenes of the play

One of the reasons that *Othello* is so compelling is the compact nature of the play. The action of the main plot occupies less than two days, from early Saturday morning to early Monday morning, and there is no sub-plot. The fifteen scenes in the two locations of Venice and then the island of Cyprus are quite condensed. Let us look closely at the two opening scenes of the play to establish how Shakespeare uses language to set up character and situation for the events that follow. If you have access to a video or audio cassette of the play in performance, you may find it helpful to watch or listen as you read.

First of all, what is happening in these opening scenes? How would you summarize the action that takes place?

D i s c u s s i o n

Scene 1 begins in the middle of a conversation between two men, Iago and Roderigo, and at first it is quite difficult to grasp what they are talking about. Roderigo is complaining that Iago, to whom he has given money, knows something that he has not passed on. It is not until later in the scene that we discover that this 'something' is Othello's secret marriage to

Desdemona. Iago has evidently been paid money to press Roderigo's suit with Desdemona, and Roderigo says he trusted Iago to look after his interests because Iago claimed to hate Othello. Iago confirms that he does, giving an elaborate account of how Othello has promoted Cassio to be his Lieutenant while he, Iago, has been appointed to the less senior position of 'Ancient' or Ensign. When Roderigo asks why he continues to serve Othello, Iago expounds a philosophic theory or creed of total, ruthless self-interest. He prompts Roderigo to go to Desdemona's father, Brabantio, with the news of the loss of his daughter. Brabantio is furious, thinking that Roderigo is still hoping to be allowed to marry Desdemona, but once convinced that his daughter is already married, he agrees to follow Roderigo to challenge Othello.

Scene 2 starts with Iago playing a quite different role. In his opening conversation with Othello, he attributes his own insulting remarks to Roderigo and warns him that Desdemona's father will seek redress. Othello responds calmly and confidently to this; they are met by Cassio (Othello's new Lieutenant) who summons him on military business to the Duke of Venice. Othello goes into the house, leaving just enough time for Iago to reveal the marriage to Cassio before Brabantio and Roderigo enter. After the start of a brief scuffle in which Iago pretends to treat Roderigo as an opponent, Brabantio accuses Othello of stealing his daughter and threatens legal redress, until the latter points out that he has an appointment with the Duke on military business. They all make their way to the Duke in council for an emergency session in the middle of the night. ■

It is clear from this summary that the play's opening is 'action packed'. The first two scenes propel the audience right into the middle of a tense situation. Of course, a bare summary of events does not tell us much about the dramatic significance of what is happening, and we need to consider further what the opening scenes reveal to us about the speakers and their characters.

What do we learn about the characters of Iago, Roderigo and Othello? What does each of these characters seem to value? What prejudices do they seem to harbour?

Discussion

In the midst of the comings and goings, we learn quite a lot about the characters. To take Iago first, in the exposition of his 'philosophy' he uses for the first time the epithet 'honest', a word that is to recur frequently throughout the play. He despises, he says, 'honest' knaves, that is, those who are knaves but who do not look after their own interests properly. 'Honest' is a patronizing and contemptuous term here. Elsewhere, and with other characters, Iago will make much play of his own 'honesty' – his (supposed) plain speaking, feeling heart and hatred of all pretence. Did you feel, though, that he is 'play-acting' here, and if so, for whom – for Roderigo, or the audience, or even for himself? It may be that he 'play-acts' in all these senses in various degrees as the scene develops.

The exchanges between Iago and Roderigo tell us, by implication, a lot about their relationship. It would seem that Iago knows Roderigo is likely to be taken in by a show of intellectual cynicism because, as is becoming clear, he is rather easily duped. More importantly, Iago's actions suggest a lack of respect for his 'friend' Roderigo. A few moments later, we learn that Iago gladly takes any opportunity (for whatever motive) to get his 'friend' into trouble. In making Roderigo act as his spokesman under Brabantio's window, Iago is not only deliberately working off vindictive feelings against Othello, Desdemona and Brabantio, he is also taking the opportunity to do Roderigo harm.

The unpleasant relationship between Iago and Roderigo brings out an important issue in the play as a whole: that of Iago's motivation. One interpretation of the text might suggest that Iago sees in Othello's and Desdemona's elopement a perfect opportunity to arouse racist prejudice and hysteria, partly for advantage to himself but perhaps also for its own sake. Roderigo describes Othello, insultingly, as 'thick-lips', an allusion to his race, and Iago goes on to exploit racist stereotypes even more crudely. In his speeches to Brabantio he refers to the marriage between Othello and Desdemona as a mating of two animals, describing Othello as a 'black ram' and a 'Barbary horse', and also as 'the devil'. By raising such a hue and cry beneath Brabantio's window, he manages, deliberately, to startle the bemused old man (who has been asleep and hardly knows what is happening) into similarly violent and instinctive racial prejudice. In the next scene Brabantio accuses Othello of having stolen Desdemona by sorcery. He thinks it is unlikely that she could have by her own volition 'Run from her guardage to the sooty bosom/Of such a thing as thou' (I.2.70–1; all

Figure 4.1 Orson Welles as Othello, Michael McLiammoir as Iago in Orson Welles's film *Othello* 1952. United Artists/Kobal Collection.

quotations in this chapter are taken from The New Penguin Shakespeare edition of *Othello*, edited by Kenneth Muir, 1968).

At a first reading we might come to the conclusion that Shakespeare has set up two different and contrasting ways of seeing Othello in the two opening scenes. Initially we learn of Othello only from the lips of Iago and Roderigo and this leads us, perhaps, to build a picture of him in the negative terms they offer. When, therefore, we meet Othello in Scene 2, and especially in the encounter with Brabantio and his followers (when a scuffle begins), we are immediately struck by his immense dignity, authority, self-possession and Olympian calm. We see instantly why he has been raised to such an eminent position in the state. His detractors are immediately reduced to order by the cool irony of his remarks, and before the end of the scene the whole racist atmosphere generated by Iago has dissipated. Racist stereotypes are dispelled when Othello appears as a grave, middle-aged man who (we learn in Scene 3) has invested all his energies in his career, and who strikes everyone who knows him (including Iago, we learn later in the play) as transparently noble. ∎

Now let us turn to a very different perspective on the opening scenes – one that considers social/historical and theatrical context.

The social context for Othello

It is always helpful to think about the social and historical context of a play if we want to draw conclusions about the play or the playwright being 'canonical'. Michael D. Bristol is known for his pioneering work on the social function of carnival and theatre. He has considered the opening scenes of *Othello* within this framework, and has offered a reading of the play that focuses more on the cultural context than on the text itself.

As you read the extract below, think about the function of the 'charivari' that Bristol defines, and ask yourself what such information adds to a purely text-based reading of the play.

> If certain history plays can be read as rites of 'uncrowning' then *Othello* might be read as a rite of 'unmarrying'. The specific organizing principle operative here is the social custom, common throughout early modern Europe, of charivari. The abusive language, the noisy clamour under Brabantio's window, and the menace of violence in the opening scene of the play link the improvisations of Iago with the codes of carnivalesque disturbance or charivari organized in protest over the marriage of the play's central characters … Despite the sympathy that Othello and Desdemona seem intended to arouse in the audience, the play as a whole is organized around the abjection and violent punishment of its central figures.
>
> Charivari was a practice of noisy festive abuse in which a community enacted its specific objection to inappropriate marriages and more generally exercised a widespread surveillance of sexuality.
>
> ('Charivari and … *Othello*', 1990, p.3)

Bristol gives the general commotion of the opening scene a name (charivari) and with it a set of cultural and social foundations. This 'sets the scene' for the impact of the play on its intended audience and helps us to remember that the play was written in a given period in history and within a given framework for social interaction. The scene no longer stands out as a series of actions and reactions from the characters Shakespeare created, but rather as a fictional representation of a common social practice. This should add to our understanding of the play in a very important way. It should emphasize that the characters are not 'real', not there to be analysed in their own right, but are rather fictional creations, which outlive their author in so far as we can make sense of them, and perhaps even identify with them, today. The characters are types, stock figures which themselves tell us a great deal about Shakespeare's social context. In helping us to see the scene as a representative whole rather than focusing on individual characters, Bristol's reading may give us a better understanding of why the newly-weds may be interrupted on their wedding night, why the other characters react as strongly as they do, and why such a play might be so consistently popular, through many generations. ∎

The different views of gender relations and race relations that the play investigates are also put into social context by Bristol. Charivari scenes were very much like carnival sideshows or dramatic spectacles, designed to draw attention not only to the individuals involved but also to social stereotypes about sexuality. A man would play the role of the bride, and another man would play the bridegroom. Costumes would emphasize and exaggerate 'feminine' sexuality in the bride, whilst comic vulnerability would be emphasized in the bridegroom, who would be portrayed as a kind of 'clown' or 'bumpkin'. In Bristol's words, 'heterosexual desire is staged here as an absurdly mutual attraction between a beautiful woman and a funny monster'. Bristol argues that a third character was crucial to the charivari: the 'ringleader' or master of ceremonies, whose task it was to 'unmask a transgressive marriage' – to point out the problems with the union and to do his best to undermine it, partly by stirring up emotions about the marriage.

The sight of men in women's costumes was a 'normal' part of the theatrical event of the time. Similarly, 'racist' attitudes towards Moors (and indeed towards Jews, as represented in *The Merchant of Venice*), would have been considered 'normal'. An audience in the sixteenth century would probably have been amused by the sight of a white actor in blackface, rather than questioning the perspective this implied.

However, even if we accept that terms and values were different in Shakespeare's day, the treatment of female characters within the play and the attitude towards Othello's race are problematic for modern audiences.

How might Bristol's consideration of the social context of the play add to our perception of the treatment of Othello and Desdemona?

Modern audiences are often struck by the 'racism' and 'sexism' of the play – the way Othello is described and treated by other characters and the depiction of Desdemona in stereotypical terms as a 'pure' and 'passive' victim. If we consider the play in its social context, we can see that such terms are inappropriate. Although the characters of Othello and Desdemona are those of a black man and a woman respectively, existing in a world that is frightened of the potential power of black people and women and therefore punishes them, audiences of the time would not have recognized either 'racism' or 'sexism'. Shakespeare's play reveals the attitudes towards race and gender that were current in his day. ■

When Bristol describes the 'absurd' attraction between a 'beautiful woman and a funny monster', we may think of the function of charivari, but we may also think of the ageless repetition of similar themes in fairy tales and fiction from *Beauty and the Beast* onwards. It is precisely the emphasis on race and gender within the play that keeps it 'current' and makes it a popular choice for contemporary study and performance, often in experimental productions that set out to 're-view' the attitudes of the play in a modern context.

Who would you identify as the third main character, the 'ringleader', in the play?

Iago is the 'ringleader' of the charivari in *Othello*. In fact, he serves a similar function throughout the play. Iago is a manipulator, not only of grand scenes (as in the charivari) but also of more subtle events and ideas. It is Iago who fuels the tension of the play, and his main tool is not a weapon as such, nor a powerful position, but rather his command over language, as he hints, whispers and slanders. ■

Before we can even begin to understand Iago's role, we must consider the use of language in the play as a whole. If you have not already done so, you should now read the rest of the play.

Poetic language in Othello

Shakespeare's writing is full of verbal suggestiveness. As well as establishing the literal sense of a passage (using the notes to the text to help with unfamiliar words and phrases) it is important to stop every now and then to take a close look at *how* he achieves his effects.

The opening scenes of *Othello* contain an amazing variety of poetic language and expression, ranging from magnificently formal, elaborately patterned speeches to fast-moving, idiomatic, 'everyday' dialogue. As we have seen, the language and syntax of Othello's speeches reveal much about his character. The following line is a good example of the calm authority of his 'public' presence: 'Keep up your bright swords, for the dew will rust them' (I.2.59). Othello could simply have said 'put by your weapons', or words to that effect, but, instead, Shakespeare gives him this more poetic line. It is difficult to 'explain' a great line of poetry, but it is enough to say that the effect here is achieved in several ways. The description of the swords being 'bright' may suggest that the torches are causing them to glint in the dark, but the notion of brightness perhaps also suggests that they are 'unused', and that the famous soldier, Othello, is mildly contemptuous of these lesser mortals, whose swords have not been stained.

It is through the measured and elaborate quality of his lines (at this stage of the play) that we develop a sense of what Desdemona later calls Othello's 'clear spirit' (III.4.139). His second speech in Scene 2 provides a good example.

Read the speech aloud several times to obtain a general idea of the sense. What is the language doing here, and what does it suggest about Othello's character?

> Let him do his spite:
> My services, which I have done the signory,
> Shall out-tongue his complaints. 'Tis yet to know –
> Which, when I know that boasting is an honour,
> I shall provulgate – I fetch my life and being
> From men of royal siege, and my demerits
> May speak, unbonneted, to as proud a fortune
> As this that I have reached. For know, Iago,
> But that I love the gentle Desdemona,
> I would not my unhousèd free condition
> Put into circumscription and confine
> For the seas' worth. But look, what lights come yond!
>
> (I.2.17–28)

Discussion

What may impress you about this passage is the way the language works to give us a balanced yet mixed impression of Othello as a man. He 'serves' the state and knows his worth, yet, from modesty, he will not make his deeds known until 'boasting' becomes honourable (which, by definition, it never will). He comes from royal blood and he values his freedom which he is only giving up, willingly, because of his love for Desdemona. The final four lines are deeply memorable. They start with a qualifying clause that leads the reader/listener/viewer in expectation to the main statement about his 'free condition', an idea that is amplified by the expansive notion of the 'seas' worth' and set against the idea of enclosure, so powerfully embodied in the phrase 'circumscription and confine'. ■

Now look at the early part of the first scene of Act IV, up to the point at which Cassio enters, and think back to the opening scenes of the play. Can you see by this comparison an important aspect of the play's construction?

Discussion

The opening scenes lead up to the (unexpected) demonstration of the grand and commanding qualities of Othello's character, revealed not only in action but also in his very presence: his superb, measured and ceremonious eloquence. Act IV, in extreme contrast, shows this Olympian figure reduced, at certain moments, to gibbering incoherence:

> Lie with her? Lie on her? We say lie on her when they belie her. Lie with her! Zounds, that's fulsome! Handkerchief – confession – handkerchief! … It is not words that shakes me thus! Pish! Noses, ears, and lips! Is't possible? – Confess? Handkerchief! O devil!
>
> (IV.1.35–43)

Othello here is a man in a paroxysm of emotional rage. As always in Shakespeare, and particularly in this play, the effect is achieved through *language*. (It is worth noticing too that when Othello has arrived at a firm decision about his course of action, that is, has concluded that he is bound to murder Desdemona, his natural composure returns: the murder is performed in a mechanical, almost ceremonial fashion.) ■

What is characteristic of Act IV is its continual dependence on soliloquy, semi-soliloquy or 'asides'. You should bear in mind that, on the Elizabethan stage, a soliloquy was delivered directly to the audience. In the case of a lengthy formal soliloquy (like Iago's beginning 'And what's he then that says I play the villain', II.3.326–52) this would entail the actor's moving to the front of the apron-stage, thereby leaving the physical world of the other characters. Even an aside would in some sense be directed to the audience. This convention could be a fruitful and flexible tool for the dramatist, as it is in this play.

All through Act IV characters talk ostensibly to others but really, in their bewilderment, to themselves or to the audience or to no-one in particular. Sometimes Othello is listening to Iago all too attentively, or at least responding and over-reacting to the key words that Iago is underlining for his benefit, like 'naked', 'handkerchief' and so on. At other moments, though, his exclamations to Iago are really soliloquies, for instance that poignant cry: 'No, my heart is turned to stone: I strike it, and it hurts my hand' (IV.1.181–2), or even: 'but yet the pity of it, Iago! O, Iago, the pity of it, Iago!' (IV.1.194–5).

Can you think of another example in Act IV of the soliloquy or aside used as a representation of a distracted mind?

Discussion

Look at the striking moment in Act IV, Scene 1 in which Othello is at one and the same time conducting, or trying to conduct, a graceful courtier-like conversation with the Venetian envoy Lodovico and taking part in a savage quarrel with Desdemona, or with himself.

> And sir, tonight
> I do entreat that we may sup together.
> You are welcome, sir, to Cyprus. Goats and monkeys!
>
> (IV.1.263–5)

The effect is harrowing and also, in a pathetic way, comic.

Another memorable example comes in Act IV, Scene 2. Othello has just made his exit after the agonizing and shattering scene in which he has accused Desdemona of being a prostitute. 'How do you, madam? How do you, my good lady?' (l.95), asks Emilia solicitously; to which Desdemona makes the unexpected reply, 'Faith, half asleep' (l.96). What this seems to suggest is that, overwhelmed by the ordeal she has been through, she has escaped into a sort of daydream. Her riddling remarks are not really aimed at Emilia, they are a kind of inward soliloquy:

> EMILIA Good madam, what's the matter with my lord?
> DESDEMONA With who?
> EMILIA Why, with my lord, madam.
> DESDEMONA Who is thy lord?
> (IV.2.97–100)

The same is true of her – we might say, dream-like – instructions to Emilia: 'Lay on my bed my wedding sheets, remember' (l.104). She is already in her own mind rehearsing her murder, and Emilia's comment, 'Here's a change indeed!' (l.105), is very apt. ∎

The use of soliloquy here signals a major change of tone or 'register' in the play. In the bedroom scene to which it looks forward, the move into legendary pathos highlights by contrast how much, in the earlier part of the play, Desdemona is thoroughly in the 'real world': an active and wilful character at the play's opening, who dares to defy her family and social conventions for her love. In the bedroom scene, Desdemona not only sings an old song ('The poor soul sat sighing by a sycamore tree ...', IV.3.38) but herself becomes as it were a figure in a proverb or a song. The scene has an affinity with the one of Ophelia's madness in *Hamlet*, which similarly turns upon fragments of old songs and a death beneath willows. (Ophelia drowns herself in a willow-fringed stream.) It is curious, too, to note Desdemona's words about her mother's maid called Barbary: 'She was in love: and he she loved proved mad/And did forsake her' (IV.3.26–7), which, in a sentence, is the story of Hamlet and Ophelia.

Let us turn now to Act IV, Scene 3 where Emilia chooses to take up Desdemona's commonplace expression 'for all the world' and examine it literally. 'The world's a huge thing: it is a great price for a small vice' (ll.67–8), she says, and she pursues the theme with quite a long flight of imagination and irony. If a wife really could make her husband a monarch by having an affair with another man, surely she would do it? Emilia may be talking like this, partly, simply to take Desdemona's mind off her troubles. But it may also be that she really believes in a certain frank realism towards life – although not the vaunted and vicious 'realism' of her husband Iago. What is striking here is how many echoes the question, 'Wouldst thou do such a deed for all the world?', evokes.

We might link the phrase 'for all the world' to the extraordinary speech of Othello's in Act V:

> Nay, had she been true,
> If heaven would make me such another world
> Of one entire and perfect chrysolite,
> I'd not have sold her for it.
> (V.2.142–5)

Othello's flight of fancy, seeing the world as an inconceivably big jewel, is at once naïve (what could one possibly *do* with such a jewel?) and sublime: evidence of a creative imagination. If we pause to think about it, Othello suggests the idea of 'worlds' to us in other respects too. He imagines himself in terms of vast natural forces. His revenge, he tells Iago,

> Like to the Pontic sea,
> Whose icy current and compulsive course
> Ne'er feels retiring ebb, but keeps due on
> To the Propontic and the Hellespont,
> Even so my bloody thoughts with violent pace
> Shall ne'er look back.
> (III.3.450–5)

This magnificent speech is well described when G. Wilson Knight refers to Othello's 'architectural stateliness of quarried speech' (*The Wheel of Fire*, 1949 edn, p.10). Othello's life experience seems, geographically at least, to have embraced the whole world, including the 'antres vast and deserts idle/Rough quarries, rocks, and hills whose heads touch heaven' (I.3.139–40).

It may be a mistake to try to tie down this sequence of allusions to 'worlds' to a single, precise meaning. What the allusion does is to give the effect of *largeness* to the tragedy, which in other ways is an unusually domestic one, with some resemblance in form to the nineteenth-century 'marriage' novel.

Othello *as tragedy*

Tragedy, at least so far as the Western theatre is concerned, was the invention of the ancient Athenians, and in particular of Aeschylus, Sophocles and Euripides. It had its roots in ritual sacrifice, the tragic hero or heroine corresponding to the sacrificial victim, and in Greece it always retained a certain religious quality. Tragedies were only performed at the city's religious festivals, especially the annual festival of the Dionysia, and citizens were obliged to attend, being fined for failure to do so.

The Greek philosopher Aristotle, in his *Poetics*, gave a famous definition of tragedy. 'Tragedy', he wrote, 'is an imitation of some action that is important, entire, and of a proper magnitude, embellished by language, effecting through pity and terror the purgation of those emotions.' According to Aristotle a tragedy must deal with people of high estate falling into misfortune, doing so because of some *hamartia* or fatal flaw or error of judgement (of which *hubris*, or overweening pride, is one example), and its plot will feature one or more *peripeteia* (or surprising reversal of fortune) and an *anagnorisis* (or final recognition of some gravely unwelcome truth).

Given its sacrificial origins, tragedy is likely to be a solemn affair, but it may also – so at least Friedrich Nietzsche argues in his *The Birth of Tragedy* (1872) – be liberating, an incitement to riot and revel, at once terrifying and exhilarating. This would seem to apply to Shakespeare's tragedies as well as to those of the Greeks, although it is more doubtful whether one could say it of the great 'realistic' tragedies of Henrik Ibsen, like *Rosmersholm* (1886) and *Hedda Gabler* (1890) and his domestic tragedy, *A Doll's House* (1881).

It should be added that the French philosopher Roland Barthes argues that tragedy is a dangerous self-indulgence, encouraging an acceptance of social evils as inescapable:

> Tragedy is only a way of assembling human misfortune, of subsuming it, and thus of justifying it by putting it in the form of necessity, of a kind of wisdom, or of a purification. To reject this regeneration and to seek the technical means of not succumbing perfidiously (nothing is more insidious than tragedy), is today a necessary undertaking.
>
> (Poole, *Tragedy,* 1987, p.10)

The theatre of Aeschylus, Sophocles and Euripides had ceased to be a living tradition more than a millennium before Shakespeare's day, and it is unlikely that he knew much about their plays. He and his fellow Elizabethan dramatists were, on the other hand, considerably influenced by the Roman dramatist and philosopher Seneca (*c.*4 B.C.–A.D. 65). Seneca, like his Athenian predecessors, took his plots from Greek legend, but in a very different manner. His plays use an exaggerated rhetoric, dwell much on bloodthirsty details, and frequently introduce ghosts and magic. They were, moreover, most probably intended for formal declamation rather than for stage performance. Nevertheless, they were a fruitful source of inspiration for the Elizabethan theatre, which achieved a compelling fusion of high poetic rhetoric and Aristotelian 'pity and terror' with Senecan stage-horrors, song, wit and comedy.

There was, traditionally, a hierarchy of literary genres, in which the highest rank belonged to epic, followed by tragedy, with other genres such as comedy, satire etc. placed in descending order below. Perhaps because of this hierarchical approach, Shakespeare's tragedies (*Hamlet, King Lear, Macbeth* and *Othello*) have widely – although not universally – been regarded as his supreme achievement. However, it is important to remember that Shakespeare's is not the only kind of tragedy. Shakespeare's tragic theatre is poles apart from the 'classic' theatre of France, in which all violent action takes place offstage and the idea of mixing the 'nobility' of tragedy with comic subplots and wit-combats (like the curious little duel of wit between Desdemona and Iago in *Othello*) would have been unthinkable.

A writer for the Elizabethan and Jacobean theatre would have been aware of a wide range of conventions and customary assumptions. Shakespeare freely exploited these, although, as he came to maturity as a dramatist, he would also often undermine them or override them. Muriel Bradbrook describes certain popular conventions of character:

> Jacobeans evolved stock subsidiary characters, such as the cheated tool villain, the bluff soldier and the pathetic child. The tool villain's rôle depended upon the narrative rather than upon his character. It was usual to have several villains who were played off against one another, but the minor villains were simply there to cause this imbroglio, and consequently they exist only as counters of the intrigue. For there was

no attempt to make the minor characters 'human'. First and second gentlemen were used as channels for conveying information to the audience; there was no effort to disguise the fact by making one of them into a comic clergyman and the other into a maiden aunt.

(*Elizabethan Tragedy*, 1980 edn, pp.54–5)

It is instructive to trace the complex elaboration given by Shakespeare in *Othello* to such stock figures as the 'cheated tool villain' (Roderigo) and the 'bluff soldier' (Iago). Commonly, in Elizabethan and Jacobean drama, characters do not change and develop, and here again Shakespeare is the exception. Othello is certainly a different man in the middle scenes of the play from the one he is at the beginning, although it may be felt that the change is not fundamental and that eventually, although too late, he returns to his old self.

It was, in fact, a charge levelled at Othello by the critic F.R. Leavis that he was incapable of learning from experience. In a well-known essay on the play first published in 1937, Leavis says that when Othello discovers how he has been tricked

> his reaction is an intolerably intensified form of the common 'I could kick myself':
>
> > Whip me, ye devils,
> > From the possession of this heavenly sight!
> > Blow me about in winds! Roast me in sulphur!
> > Wash me in steep-down gulfs of liquid fire!
> > O Desdemona! Desdemona! dead!
> > Oh! Oh! Oh!
>
> But he remains the same Othello; he has discovered his mistake, but there is no tragic self-discovery. The speech closing with the lines just quoted is that beginning
>
> > Behold, I have a weapon,
>
> one of the finest examples in the play of the self-dramatizing trick. The noble Othello is now seen as tragically pathetic, and he sees himself as pathetic too:
>
> > Man but a rush against Othello's breast,
> > And he retires. Where shall Othello go?
>
> He is ruined, but he is the same Othello in whose essential make-up the tragedy lay: the tragedy doesn't involve the idea of the hero's learning through suffering. The fact that Othello tends to sentimentalize should be the reverse of a reason for our sentimentalizing too.

('Diabolic intellect', in *The Common Pursuit*, 1962 edn, pp.150–1)

Leavis is far from saying that *Othello* is not really a tragedy, but he pictures the nature of the tragedy quite differently from other critics. His account is a subtle one, but it could be objected against on the grounds that it applies psychology to Othello as if he were a character in a novel or, indeed, a 'real person', rather than a figure in the highly convention-bound genre of Jacobean tragedy.

In a book in which he analyses social contexts and concerns in the fictional worlds of Shakespeare's tragedies, David Margolies has described

Othello as a 'problem tragedy' (*Monsters of the Deep*, 1992, p.158). He highlights the differences between the seeming inevitability of the destruction and death that are common to other Shakespearean tragedies such as *Hamlet* and *King Lear* and the unnecessary destruction of *Othello*. He points out that *Othello* does not fit the usual structure of Shakespeare's tragedies, but is a tragedy nonetheless. Perhaps, he argues, *Othello* is even more tragic, given the sense that all the suffering could so easily have been avoided, or at least curtailed.

Many other critics have commented on the extremity of emotion and rage in *Othello*, noting that the play's structure can be rather neatly divided in two. The first half sets up the play, with the seeds of jealousy being planted in Othello's imagination as he is presented with a range of potential threats to his control over both his state and his wife. In the second half, the jealousy explodes out of all proportion to 'real' events within the world of the play, with disastrous consequences for all. For instance, Jan Kott argues: 'If we strip Othello of romantic varnish ... the tragedy of jealousy and the tragedy of betrayed confidence become a dispute between Othello and Iago; a dispute on the nature of the world' (*Shakespeare our Contemporary*, 1967 edn, p.87). Kott sums up the two characters in terms of their opposing viewpoints as expressed throughout the play: Iago's view is that the world is vile, consisting of fools and villains; while Othello's view is of a world that exists in love and loyalty, where people are beautiful and noble. It is precisely because Othello is drawn into Iago's view of the world (because Iago is such an accomplished stage-manager, so adept at hiding the strings as he pulls them) that the tragedy of Othello develops such unwieldy proportions. Iago's negative view of the world is successfully imposed on the other characters, not by argumentation, but by making all the evil he sees within himself come to pass for the characters around him.

Understanding Iago

Although Shakespeare's play is entitled *Othello*, it would not be absurd if someone claimed that Iago rather than Othello was the central character; in fact, the play has sometimes been produced upon this assumption. Iago has more lines than Othello. There are some important surprises in the characterization of Othello, but there are even more surprises in that of Iago, and it can hardly be said even by the end of the play that we completely 'know' him. Moreover, it would be hard to deny that the entire action of the play derives from him. The succession of events and the dramatic action begins, as we saw earlier, not with Desdemona's elopement with Othello, but with Iago's decision to exploit this elopement for all the possible harm he may do with it. Iago plans harm to his General, Othello, and – as an incidental bonus – he also plans to revenge himself upon his crony Roderigo, and to injure Desdemona. In this first effort at general ill-doing, however, he fails. Othello's and Desdemona's qualities of character, and Othello's high position in the state (reinforced by the fact he is required that very instant to lead the Venetian forces against the Turks) turn the tables on Iago's plans completely. Undeterred, Iago at once devises a new scheme. He will inject jealousy into Othello's and Desdemona's relationship, manipulating various other characters, including Roderigo, Cassio, Emilia and Bianca, for the purpose. He manages to exploit the personal weaknesses and vulnerabilities of Othello and Desdemona: Othello's guilelessness and credulity; Desdemona's inexperience; and the social pressures threatening any 'mixed' marriage. Iago can be said to dominate the play, in the sense that he instigates or manipulates most of the play's action.

Let us take another look at Act IV. It is in this Act that the play reaches its climax (as opposed to its *dénouement*, or unravelling of the plot, which occurs in Act V) and it is here that the elaborate plot stage-managed by Iago comes to fruition. It is also a part of the play in which the minor characters – Emilia, Roderigo, Cassio and Bianca – carry much of the weight of the action, and in which we are made aware of how much they, just as much as Othello, are Iago's puppets and are simply performing a 'script' he has written for them. (It should be added that this is not altogether true of Emilia. We sense that she is growing restive under Iago's management and is on the verge of making her own decisions. Consider, for instance, the long speech of hers (starting IV.3.83) about the wrongs done to wives with which the Act ends and to which we will return later.)

Look again at the second scene of Act IV. How would you describe the actions of Iago, Roderigo and Cassio, and how do we respond to Othello's plight?

Discussion

What seems most striking is the sheer resourcefulness of Iago's duplicity. Having successfully led Othello to a state of emotional distress he sees it as an ideal moment to exploit one of his favourite impersonations: the world-weary, fact-facing, hard-bitten cynic. He taunts Othello with not being a 'man' ('Good sir, be a man', IV.1.65), and with taking to heart such a commonplace of adult existence as being cuckolded. Iago manages to make this 'honest' manliness and cynicism seem utterly odious, and the effect is deliberately enhanced in this Act by the commonplace 'average man' cheapness of Cassio and Roderigo. It is not surprising to find Roderigo acting cheaply, as well as absurdly (it is both cheap and absurd on his part to demand that Iago should ask Desdemona for his jewels back). It is, perhaps, more surprising to see Cassio (a character of whom we probably have not so far come to take a view) treating Bianca so callously. Is there not an implicit contrast with the generous-minded Othello and how he treats his wife in the early scenes of the play? Consider too the moment when Othello, trying to learn his lesson from his tutor Iago, says, 'I will be found most cunning in my patience,/But – dost thou hear? – most bloody' (IV.1.90–1). This from the least *cunning* character Shakespeare ever created is surely a moment of great pathos? ∎

It is worth thinking a little more about the fact that Iago, as well as being a supreme play-actor and 'ringleader', with a dozen different roles in his repertoire, reveals himself also as a masterly stage-manager. Can you think of any examples of this in Act IV?

One example you might cite is the brilliantly conceived part of the first scene in which Iago (who knows exactly what behaviour to extract from Cassio, even down to his laugh) contrives to have Cassio talk to him about Bianca in his usual jeering manner, knowing that Othello, who is eavesdropping, will interpret every grimace and laugh as referring to Desdemona. Equally striking, and most painful and moving, is Scene 2, in which as a result Othello accuses Desdemona of being a prostitute and Emilia a brothel-madam or bawd. ■

What kind of man can it possibly be, the spectator or reader is very soon wondering, who is so eager to do evil, so single-minded in his pursuit of it and so brilliantly fertile in ways of achieving it? What makes him like this? What are his motives?

The reason that we find such questions difficult to answer is not that we are given no explanations. On the contrary, Iago himself gives us many explanations. In fact, he gives us far *too many* explanations, so that they cannot conceivably all be correct. Indeed, we have to reckon with the possibility that perhaps none of them is correct. Samuel Taylor Coleridge wrote of the horror of the search for motive in Iago's 'motiveless malignity', meaning that Iago no more knows the reason for his malignity than we do and keeps trying out new ways of explaining it to himself. This is a particularly challenging account of the character, and not an absurd one.

Let us examine some of Iago's essays in self-explanation. In the opening scene (I.1.8–33), he tells Roderigo vehemently that he hates Othello. He says he does so because Othello has cheated him of the promotion he believes he deserves, and has appointed Cassio as his Lieutenant instead. Iago attributes the situation to favouritism and social snobbery. Why, if Iago hates Othello, asks Roderigo, does he continue in his service? Iago replies that he does so to serve his own ends. A man of his superior intellect can afford to despise common virtues like loyalty and sincerity. He would have no respect for himself if he could not conceal his real feelings. The role of such a man as himself is to be (that is, to seem) what he is not.

About this explanation there are several comments we might make. First, Iago is in the paradoxical position of having to justify himself to Roderigo, who suspects him of acting more in Othello's interests then he pretends, by insisting on his hatred of and treachery towards Othello. He is thus clearing himself of one bad motive by claiming another bad one. Must we, therefore, necessarily believe him when he says he hates Othello? Secondly, he backs up this account of his behaviour by a general philosophical theory of cynicism and amorality, ironically calling Heaven to witness that everything he does is purely for his own personal ends. Now, this is well calculated to impress the stupid and unthinking Roderigo, and maybe this is his main reason for adopting this line of talk. However, when Iago imputes bad motives to himself, we do not necessarily have to assume that he is sincere.

In Act I, Scene 3, Iago embroiders on this theme of philosophic amorality, making it sound like a kind of stoicism ('we have reason to cool our raging motions, our carnal stings, our unbitted lusts', ll.326–7). Then, left alone, he takes the audience into his confidence in a soliloquy: 'Thus do I ever make my fool my purse ... ' (ll.377–98). He declares here that he is entirely cynical in his exploitation of Roderigo. As for Othello, he hates him: 'And it is thought abroad that 'twixt my sheets/He's done my office' (ll.381–2). In other words, he suspects Othello of having slept with his wife. He does not say that this is *why* he hates Othello, and he is not even sure that it is true (that is, that Othello has cuckolded him), although he intends to behave as if it were. According to the conventions of the Elizabethan theatre, what a character says directly to the audience is expected to be the 'truth'. However, we have the feeling that in this play even this convention may be being undermined. In this soliloquy, Iago seems to anticipate Coleridge's reading of his character – he does not so much make a straightforward declaration of his motives, as try to invent motives.

Turn now to Iago's (even more elusive) soliloquy in Act II, Scene 1 ('That Cassio loves her, I do well believe't', ll.277–303). Read the soliloquy and try to summarize, in your own words, what Iago is saying. What do you think his motives are?

D i s c u s s i o n

Iago tells the audience that he is sure that Cassio is in love with Desdemona, and that people can at least be made to believe that Desdemona loves Cassio. In fact, this will be false, since – as Iago cannot help admitting, although he hates him – Othello has 'a constant, loving, noble nature' and will be sure to keep Desdemona's love. But, Iago says (and here the soliloquy becomes extremely involved), he (Iago) loves Desdemona also. By this he does not mean that he lusts after her, but that he suspects Othello of cuckolding him with his wife Emilia – a thought that gnaws at him – and he wants to be revenged on Othello by 'loving', that is, seducing, Desdemona. If that is impossible, what will be equally satisfying will be to convince Othello that Desdemona has been seduced by Cassio, which will be a revenge on both of them. (Anyway, he adds in parenthesis, Cassio is another person he suspects of cuckolding him with Emilia.) He feels this is an excellent scheme. He can make Othello positively thank him for deceiving him (a brilliant way of triumphing over him), and in the end he will be able to drive Othello to madness. He concludes that this is the right plan, although it will not be clear to him in every detail until he puts it into action.

When trying to identify Iago's motives, we may read this soliloquy as a clear-cut exposition of his state of mind and intentions (and that is what the soliloquy convention would lead us to do). However, we may also be tempted to read it differently – as if Iago were making it all up as he goes along. What he says about 'love' and about his feelings for Desdemona is so obscure and paradoxical that we have the feeling that he only half understands it himself. Furthermore, does he really suspect Cassio of sleeping with his wife Emilia? Does he *really* suspect Othello of doing so? Or is sexual jealousy just a sort of pretext, a disguise for a profound resentment against humanity and a rooted infatuation with evil? We receive at the least a strong impression, from the remark about Othello's 'constant, loving, noble nature', that Iago's trouble is not so much jealousy, as he pretends, as envy: envy of any kind of human beauty. ■

These perhaps are Iago's most revealing soliloquies – revealing, that is to say, more than he intends. He has another long soliloquy in Act II, Scene 3 (ll.326–52), but this time we feel that he is more in command of himself, and in giving 'everything' away he is actually not revealing so much. With superb effrontery and diabolical irony ('And what's he then that says I play the villain', l.326), he is simply giving a masterly performance of the stage villain. At all events, it is a brilliant speech, and you should study it closely, paying special attention to lines 340–3: 'Divinity of hell!/When devils will the blackest sins put on,/They do suggest at first with heavenly shows/As I do now', wherein Iago reveals a great deal about his character.

So far we have considered one interpretation of Iago and his soliloquies – a very alarming one, crediting him with an extreme wickedness, for which, being profoundly intelligent, he is struggling to find the right explanation or justification. This is by no means everyone's view of him, though, and for a quite different picture we can turn to a remarkable essay ('Honest in Othello') by William Empson. Empson examines the play from the point of view of determining what Shakespeare intends by harping so continually on the word 'honest' (see the next section for a further consideration of this point). Empson seems to picture Iago as, in a way, a disinterested intellectual, whose 'honesty', in the sense of hatred of pretence, is in many ways a genuine virtue: 'a good deal of the "motive-hunting" of the soliloquies must, I think, be seen as part of Iago's "honesty"; he is quite open to his own motives or preferences and interested to find out what they are' (*The Structure of Complex Words*, 1977 edn, p.223). The audience, says Empson, is made to observe in the opening scene a 'thwarted sense of superiority in Iago' and is 'expected to feel a good deal of sympathy for it' (ibid., p.232). 'While Desdemona is waiting for Othello's ship, which may have been lost in the tempest, he puts on an elaborate piece of clowning to distract her', out of kindness, Empson seems to be implying, and Iago is resentful that 'she takes his real opinion of love and women for a piece of hearty and good-natured fun' (ibid., p.224). He feels that his honesty is not valued as it should be. Thus, according to Empson, Iago has 'real' opinions, which he sincerely holds and wishes other people to share. In much of Iago's talk with Roderigo (for instance, 'If thou dost, I shall never love thee after. Why, thou silly gentleman! ... Drown thyself! Drown cats and blind puppies', I.3.303–4, 332–3), Iago is 'a wise uncle, obviously honest in the cheerful sense, and for some time this is our main impression of him' (ibid., p.223).

Discussing the passage in Act II, Scene 1 in which Iago scornfully observes Othello kissing Desdemona and exclaims in an aside, 'O, you are well tuned now!/But I'll set down the pegs that make this music,/As honest as I am', ll.193–5), Empson credits Iago with a genuine belief that he is the kind of man who can see through romantic nonsense:

> Othello's affair is a passing lust which has become a nuisance, and Iago can get it out of the way.
>   It may well be objected that this is far too mild a picture of Iago's plot, and indeed he himself is clearly impressed by its wickedness; at

the end of the first act he calls it a 'monstrous birth' and invokes Hell
to assist it. But after this handsome theatrical effect the second act
begins placidly, in a long scene which includes the 'As honest as I am'
passage, and at the end of this scene we find that Iago still imagines
that he will only

> Make the Moor thank me, love me, and reward me
> For making him egregiously an ass

– to be sure, the next lines say he will practise on Othello 'even to
madness', but even this can be fitted into the picture of the clown who
makes 'fools' of other people; it certainly does not envisage the
holocaust of the end of the play. Thinking in terms of character, it is
clear that Iago has not yet decided how far he will go.

(Ibid., p.224)

Empson, clearly, wants to keep the word 'evil' out of the discussion. He
seems, in fact, to regard Iago as almost as much a victim of circumstances
as Othello and Desdemona, in the sense that he is carried much further
than he ever intended.

There are many other possible views of Iago, but the two discussed
above make such a clear-cut contrast that it is worth adjudicating between
them. It may be helpful to consider the views expressed by Kott in the
following extract from *Shakespeare our Contemporary*.

> Iago has always caused more difficulties to commentators than any
> other Shakespearean character. For the romantics he was simply the
> genius of evil. But even Mephistopheles must have his own reasons for
> what he does. Especially in the theatre. Iago hates Othello, just as he
> hates everybody. Commentators observed long ago that there is
> something disinterested in his hate. Iago hates first, and only then
> seems to invent reasons for his hate. Coleridge's description hits the
> nail on the head: 'the motive-hunting of a motivelessness malignity.'
> Thwarted ambition, jealousy of his wife, of Desdemona, of all women
> and all men: his hate constantly looks for nourishment to feed itself on
> and is never satisfied …
>
> There are two other excellent descriptions of Iago. Carlyle called
> him 'an inarticulate poet', Hazlitt 'an amateur of tragedy in real life'.
> Iago is not satisfied with devising the tragedy; he wants to play it
> through, distributes parts all round, and takes part in it himself.
> Iago is a diabolical stage manager …
> Iago believes in will-power. One can make everything of oneself,
> and of other people.

(1967 edn, pp.85–7)

**What views of Iago's character does Kott compare? How do these
views compare with Empson's? What other interpretation of Iago's
role in the play (referred to earlier in this chapter) does Kott's
reading remind you of?**

Discussion

In comparing the views of Coleridge, Thomas Carlyle and William Hazlitt,
Kott draws on 'canonical' critical sources to support his own interpretation

of Iago as a 'diabolical stage manager' who manipulates and becomes embroiled in the tragedy he devises. These views offer a complete contrast to Empson's. Rather than seeing the character of Iago as a wise, honest man who is misunderstood, all these critics, including Kott, interpret Iago as a manipulator, a character who deliberately creates ill feeling and suspicion among all the other characters. Iago's role is similar to that of the 'ringleader' or 'master of ceremonies' in the account of charivari described earlier. Iago as 'stage-manager' interacts with all the characters and with the audience. He reaches out to us, asking us to consider his motives, taking our attention away from the relationship between Othello and Desdemona by continually 'upstaging them', encouraging readers and viewers of the play to focus instead on himself, to see how he pulls the strings that set the rest of the play in motion. ■

It may be worth broadening out Empson's focus on the word 'honest' in relation to Iago and thinking briefly about its use in the play as a whole.

The word 'honest' in Othello

The word 'honest', or 'honesty', is used repeatedly throughout the play, almost to the point of obsession. If you look the word up in the *Oxford English Dictionary* you will find that there is an interesting gender distinction. In general use, of persons, it gives the word as meaning 'of good moral character, Virtuous, upright', but *for women* it gives the specific meaning of 'chaste'. It records an interesting example of this from Shakespeare's *The Merry Wives of Windsor* which, being dated 1598, was first performed about five years before *Othello*: 'Wives may be merry, yet honest too' (IV.2.103). In this context, the word clearly means that a wife may be good company and yet remain faithful to her husband. Bearing this distinction in mind, let us now look at the way the word is used in *Othello*.

Think back to your reading of the play as a whole. Can you give examples of how Shakespeare employs the two usages of the word 'honesty' in a deliberate way?

D i s c u s s i o n

If you count the number of times 'honest' or 'honesty' is spoken by the main characters in the play, you will find that the tally is: Othello nineteen times; Iago sixteen times; Cassio, Emilia and Desdemona three times each. Iago is the first to use the term when telling Roderigo his view of masters and servants, dismissing those who are faithful with the contemptuous phrase, 'Whip me such honest knaves' (I.1.49). This makes it especially ironic that the next usage is by Othello, describing Iago (his Ancient and therefore inferior) to the duke as 'A man he is of honesty and trust' (I.3.282). From the outset, therefore, the term is inverted and devalued.

As a result, when Othello repeatedly uses it in Act III, Scene 3, the word begins to sound like a parody of itself. By this time, 'honest' is also being used in the gender-specific sense. When Othello, who is visibly disturbed, replies to Iago: 'No, not much moved. I do not think but Desdemona's honest' (III.3.222–3), he uses the word to mean 'faithful'. (The suggestion of jealousy and the word 'cuckold', that is, a betrayed husband, have been introduced by Iago earlier in the scene.) At this point, because it is correctly applied, the word 'honest' stabilizes for a moment in value before being plunged back into ironic loss of meaning by Othello's frenzied description of Iago to Emilia as 'thy husband, honest, honest Iago' (V.2.153). ■

Shakespeare early establishes the unreliable currency of the word in the play and is then free to build on this in a variety of contexts.

Othello, the general and the husband

By comparison with those of Iago, we are much clearer about Othello's character and motivation, which is not to say that they are not complex. We should take a moment to consider what we learn about Othello in the play, and how he is presented. **Could you summarize what you know about Othello's character from the opening scenes of the play?**

D i s c u s s i o n

Othello gives us a lot of information about himself: he is of royal descent and values his freedom (I.2.21–8); he is self-possessed and confident that, in front of her father, his standing and his innocence will defend his action in marrying Desdemona ('My parts, my title, and my perfect soul/Shall manifest me rightly', I.2.31–2). When he appears before the Venetian Senate, we learn that he considers himself a plain-speaking, professional soldier who has devoted most of his life to his profession, having been rescued from slavery in the course of his life of adventure. In recounting this life to Brabantio, he caused Desdemona to fall in love with and marry him, but even this does not distract him from his soldierly duties when called to act against the Turks. Iago attests in a soliloquy that his General is 'of a constant, loving, noble nature' (II.1.280). The picture we have so far seems consistent. Othello is conscious of being an 'outsider' because of his race, colour and birth but feels accepted by the Venetian establishment because of his personal qualities and abilities. ■

Where do we receive a hint that maybe he is not as stable as he appears? Look at Act II, Scene 3.

D i s c u s s i o n

Othello reveals his instability when he is brought from bed to quell the riot engineered by Iago. He warns the assembled revellers:

> Now, by heaven,
> My blood begins my safer guides to rule,
> And passion, having my best judgement collied,
> Assays to lead the way.
>
> (II.3.198–201)

'Collied', as the commentary at the back of the New Penguin edition of the play tells you, means 'blackened'. Othello is saying here that, once his temper, or blood, is roused, it takes over from his better judgement and becomes the instigator of his actions. This is an important self-insight (although a fleeting one, which he later forgets) for it shows us the possibility of a quite different man from the calm, dignified General in Venice. It also indicates that he is probably unsophisticated intellectually, given to action rather than introspection. ■

It is this that Iago is able to make use of when, in Act III, Scene 3, he asks, supposedly innocently, whether Cassio had known of Othello's courtship of Desdemona (ll.93–4). In the dialogue that follows, Othello makes it clear that he does not take half measures. He vows that if he should find that Desdemona had been disloyal, he would 'whistle her off' (l.259), a metaphor taken from falconry meaning that he would set her free to fend for herself. We also learn that, although he is sure of his military abilities and status, he is less confident about himself as a man because of his race, his lack of polish and his age ('I am declined/Into the vale of years', ll.262–3). This lack of confidence accelerates the growth of his suspicions. Fed by Iago's lies, these quickly turn into a blind passion for revenge, which he himself (in a passage of extended similes: 'Like to the Pontic sea …, ll.450–9) vows will not be diverted – it is a case of all or nothing.

From the start of Act IV, Scene 4, Othello is a changed man. When he overhears Cassio's conversation with Iago and then Bianca, he is fired further to kill Desdemona in bed by smothering her. From then the die is cast, in spite of Desdemona's protestations of innocence. She knows the signs of extreme anger in Othello and tells him she fears he is 'fatal then/When your eyes roll so' (V.2.37–8).

Robert Hapgood has done an extensive comparative study of critics' views of Othello's character as part of a bibliographical survey of the play. Hapgood refers to the work of F.R. Leavis, who was known as a pioneer of 'practical' literary criticism. Leavis advocated focusing on the text itself, rather than considering a social or performance context. He offered a reading of *Othello* that emphasized the concepts of dignity and heroism as expressed in the language and characterizations within the text ('Diabolic intellect and noble hero', in *The Common Pursuit*, 1952). Hapgood puts the Leavis approach into social and critical context:

> When considering the three main characters and their relationships, most critics since Leavis have played down Iago's role in the tragedy (even though he has more lines than Othello). They have been more inclined to locate the cause of the tragedy within Othello's personality and within his relationship with Desdemona …
>
> However the individual characters may be interpreted, certain of the relationships that recur among them firmly delineate the unique 'world' Shakespeare envisaged for this tragedy. One of its features is *displacement*, signalized when Shakespeare chose his subtitle: 'The Moor of Venice'. His hero is a black man among whites, a soldier in society … his heroine is a very domestic girl who elopes with a very exotic stranger …
>
> One focus of their very intense relationships involves questions of *control*. All the leading characters are strong-willed. None of them knows when to stop. When at the beginning Othello and Desdemona

dominate, they feel 'free' and sure of themselves, wonderfully poised and self-controlled. Their self-possession will be lost, utterly … as their inner and domestic lives are thrown into chaos. As Iago more and more takes control, he more and more defines the world of the play … Eventually, the chaos extends so far that Iago himself loses control, and chance and circumstance increasingly take charge.

('Othello', in *Shakespeare: A Bibliographical Guide*, 1990, pp.228–31)

The theme of displacement is a crucial factor in coming to an understanding of Othello's character. He is a general who is not a 'native' of the land he must govern; his 'outsider' status (Hapgood uses the loaded term 'exotic') burdens him with doubts, making him feel anxious about his position in Venetian society. This makes him oversensitive to the possibility that he might lose his power, or control, at any time. In this way, Othello can be seen not only as an individual but also as a type – as an 'outsider' who has gained entry into a culture but who (like many 'outsiders', in many different contexts) remains concerned and aware of the possibility of being rejected, excluded, cast back out.

In all the accounts of Othello's character and cultural status, it is important to note that the character is described, not 'the man'. In recognizing this we will avoid falling into the trap of relating to Othello, the fictional character, as if he was a 'real person'. We can learn a great deal about 'real people' by studying plays. Indeed, plays in performance help to translate ideas about human nature into three dimensions, into memorable and interactive illustrations, by which we may learn about ourselves (this was the social function of medieval morality plays). However, study of the characters in *Othello* is not intended to 'teach' us about individual people – nor even about Shakespeare himself, whom we cannot too closely connect to any of the characters he created. Rather, study of characters in drama helps us to see general tendencies in human interaction – tendencies that shift and develop from generation to generation and culture to culture.

That said, it is very interesting to consider Othello's two main roles – as general and as husband. Each of these roles includes sets of assumptions and expected behaviours, often in conflict with one other. For instance, had Othello not been such a proud man, so concerned with matters of state, prestige and authority, he might have been a better husband. Conversely, had he loved his wife less (or had he seen her for herself, rather than as Iago 'framed' her), he need not have been duped into believing ill of her, and his attention might have been much more constructively focused on the larger political situation, outside his marriage. Perhaps the greatest 'tragedy' of *Othello* is Desdemona's, for she is the character who suffers because of her husband's inability to distinguish between the true facts and the backstage artifice, constructed and manipulated by Iago.

Signifying race and gender

The term 'signalized' is used by Hapgood to refer to the power of the subtitle of the play to suggest an alternative world – to designate not just the name of the city, but also a host of visual and imaginative associations associated with Venice, with Italy generally, and even more generally, with a vague and liberating idea of the play as taking place 'somewhere else', that is, not in England. The designation of the play's setting in Venice also 'signalizes' otherness, or 'outsider' status, for the character Othello.

However, there is a much more precise use of the term 'sign' in the study of drama, theatre and performance. Semiotics is the study of sign systems: the ruby slippers in *The Wizard of Oz* are 'signs' with many different meanings and associations (as is argued in one of the companion books to this volume: *Literature and Gender* edited by Lizbeth Goodman). The slippers that appear on the cover of that book can be 'read', almost like a literary text can be 'read', for different layers of meaning. So can the masks that appear on the cover of this book. For example, the masks are taken from the 1994 production of Aphra Behn's *The Rover* (discussed in the next chapter), but they function on the cover of this book as a visual shorthand for 'drama', 'plays' and the study of performance.

Whilst we cannot engage in detail here with any of the more complex and rich strategies that scholars have developed for dealing with semiotics in theatre, we want to consider two particular concerns of the play: race and gender, both of which can be analysed in terms of the visual sign systems used to designate them in performance.

The most obvious 'sign' of racial difference in the play is emphasized in performance when we see Othello played by a black actor. Conversely,

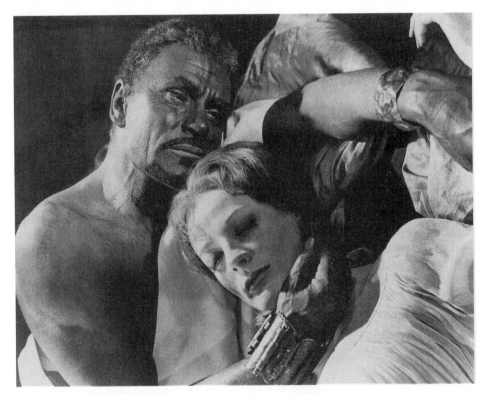

Figure 4.2 Laurence Olivier and Maggie Smith in *Othello*, National Theatre, London 1964. Photo: Angus McBean. Mander and Mitchenson Theatre Collection.

for many years black stage make-up or 'blackface' was used as a way of designating 'blackness' when the part of Othello was played by white actors, including Laurence Olivier. This was considered acceptable within the conventions of theatre, comedy and music hall entertainment, but today 'reads' as racist. Modern views of what is acceptable in portrayal of black characters, or, indeed, of female characters, are influenced to a great extent by modern critical perspectives on issues such as racism and sexism. As new critical perspectives take hold, contemporary audiences may, conversely, learn to accept certain aspects of the plays that Elizabethan audiences, or Victorian audiences, found offensive. Values shift from age to age. For every age, the treatment of Othello's blackness must be carefully handled, as it is potentially so controversial.

The visual sign system used in the play to designate the gender role that Desdemona seems to represent is her handkerchief. Desdemona is the least well developed of the three central characters: her lines rarely reveal her thoughts or ideas about herself – as Othello's do – but rather her perceptions of what the men do and say. Desdemona is an interesting character throughout the play, but her interest to modern readers and audiences arises in two ways. At first, she is intriguing precisely because she is wilful, proclaiming and displaying her love and sexual desire for Othello, despite all social conventions. Then, as the theme of sexual jealousy develops through the interaction of Othello and Iago, Desdemona fades as an individual character, becoming instead a stock figure for the wronged wife – pure, loyal, undeservedly punished.

In Act IV, Scene 3, Emilia launches into a lengthy and striking speech about the wrongs done to wives (ll.83–102), speaking up aggressively in defence of their rights. Interestingly, this speech did not appear in the first published text of *Othello*, the Quarto, of 1622; it is first found in print in the Folio edition of 1623. Lisa Jardine, commenting on this, makes the important point that

> Without this speech, the scene in which Desdemona sings the 'willow song' – the song of a lover abandoned by her beloved, who takes the blame for the breakdown in the relationship – becomes a stylised, emblematic representation of female passivity and culpability. With Emilia's assertive counterpoint the scene becomes one which struggles with female and male responsibility and its limitations and negotiations.
>
> ('Canon to left of them', in *War of the Words*, 1994, p.103)

Some critics have indeed made much of what they see as the feminist implications of the speech. Kiernan Ryan has commented that

> This startling passage invites us to recognise that the true sexual tragedy springs from Othello's thraldom to the male version of marital jealousy and the patriarchal logic of dominion and possession of which such jealousy is the outcome ... The whole scene derails what would otherwise remain the unrivalled male view of events. Its egalitarian female perspective defines and brackets the play as a specifically masculine tragedy.
>
> (*Shakespeare*, 1995 edn, p.91)

Jardine does not agree with Ryan's interpretation. In her view, 'any feminist ought to be dismayed at the suggestion that the single speech on behalf of women is placed in the mouth of the very character who is neither listened to nor believed until after Desdemona's murder' ('Canon to left of them', in *War of the Words*, 1994, p.105). Nevertheless, as Jardine says, the inclusion of the speech does open up explicitly the whole question of 'how historically a wife's behaviour was perceived in relation to her husband's treatment of her (whether or not that treatment was reasonable)' (ibid.).

A study of Desdemona's character is quite as interesting, quite as resonant, as a study of either Othello's or Iago's character. Desdemona is the character about whom the others argue, around whom they plot and plan and whisper and desire, and who, ultimately, falls victim to the competition between men in the play.

Reading Desdemona's handkerchief

The following is a brief summary of the handkerchief's 'role' in the play: the one prop that was crucial to Desdemona's downfall.

III.3.284–. Othello complains of a headache and Desdemona offers to bind his head up with her handkerchief, but he tells her it is too small and she absent-mindedly drops it. Emilia finds it, remarking that it was Desdemona's first gift from Othello, and that Iago has often asked her to steal it for him (presumably as some sort of sexual fetish or token). Desdemona loves it, says Emilia, and in private even talks to it. She decides to have it copied ('taken out'), which will be a harmless way of satisfying Iago. (It tells us something about her relationship with Iago at this stage of things that she is ready to be complaisant over his infidelities.) Iago, however, spots the handkerchief and seizes it, and, in a soliloquy, informs the audience that he is going to drop it in Cassio's lodgings, in the hope that Cassio will keep and use it and be seen to do so by Othello, arousing his jealousy.

430–. Iago advances his plot by telling Othello that he has seen a handkerchief, embroidered with strawberries, in Cassio's hand (he was wiping his beard with it) and he seems to remember that it was one that belonged to Desdemona. (The little invented detail of Cassio's wiping his beard with it – a contemptuous kind of familiarity – is particularly well calculated to upset Othello.)

III.4.51–. Othello, attempting to catch Desdemona out, pretends to have a cold and asks her to lend him her handkerchief, which of course she is unable to do. He then tells her – apparently quite genuinely – about its magic properties, a powerful imaginative description. Desdemona says, with a flash of temper, that she wishes to God she had never seen it, and they have a furious quarrel.

176–. Cassio, who has found the handkerchief in his lodgings, asks Bianca to make a copy of it. (Why? you might ask yourself. Is it simply because he likes its design, or because he too wants a physical token of Desdemona?)

IV.1.10–. Iago cunningly brings the handkerchief into his conversation with Othello, enflaming his obsession with it so successfully that he has a paroxysm (a 'fit').

148–. Bianca angrily returns the handkerchief to Cassio, refusing to copy it. Othello is eavesdropping on this and believes, as he is intended to, that Cassio had given the handkerchief to Bianca.

V.1.10–. Othello, preparing to murder Desdemona, charges her with giving the handkerchief to Cassio. She denies it, and tells Othello that Cassio will bear her out, only to learn that Iago has stabbed him. The handkerchief is the final insult, which seems to send Othello over the edge.

212–. Having murdered Desdemona, Othello defends his action and tells the story of the handkerchief, and Emilia explains how it all 'really' happened – for which Iago kills her.

Of course, this summary only provides a rudimentary guide to the significance of the handkerchief. However, it is enough to illustrate that even a small prop such as a handkerchief can have tremendous significance, not only in itself but also for what it signifies in relation to the rest of the play. Whilst Othello's blackness is a visual and symbolic 'sign' or 'signifier' that can be discussed in terms of its social and theatrical implications, the significance of the handkerchief is more difficult to define. It could be 'read' in many different ways, for instance with reference to Othello's and Iago's psychological fixation on Desdemona, linked to this one miniature 'sign' representing her. Although there is not space here to analyse the handkerchief and its function in any detail, it is important to note that a good deal has been written about this. Indeed, the phrase 'Desdemona's handkerchief' is often quoted out of context. It has become a kind of stock phrase for discussion of important clues or symbols that have gone astray and taken meanings and associations not normally connected with what they are deemed to represent.

It is particularly interesting that Desdemona's handkerchief seems to 'speak' or communicate so much – and to send so many misleading signals – as Desdemona herself has comparatively little to say in her own defence. As we have already noted, she is a strong character who knows her own mind and desires; she is unconventionally free with her love, and nonconformist in her choice of husband. But does this justify the severity of the attacks against her? Surely not. The audiences of the play in Shakespeare's day were encouraged by the familiar form of tragedy (wherein the good often suffer, and even die – and where women are often mistreated by men) to take Desdemona's suffering for granted, to accept it as part of the dramatic form, even while they were encouraged by the brutish behaviour of the men to sympathize with the heroine. So too readers and audiences today will be moved by Desdemona's plight, although advances in feminist consciousness now also encourage us to question the need to punish women for the wrongdoings of men. Within the social and theatrical conventions of Elizabethan England, the character of Desdemona was more or less guaranteed to suffer to some degree. The boy actor playing the part would have been expected to play up the vulnerability of the character, as well as to hint at 'her' sexual side. The handkerchief is a very convenient device within this theatrical dynamic: a 'feminine' prop, and one that could signify the feminine nature of the character in both its pure white unsoiled origins and its sexual associations. In some sense, we can see the development of Desdemona's situation in the play in the development of the handkerchief's significance. Whilst

Desdemona speaks her mind freely in the opening of the play and acts to please herself, she later plays the role of wife, gradually beginning to act less freely and react instead to the actions and accusations of men. As she does so, the handkerchief seems to take on a life of its own. The handkerchief functions, at one level, like a character introduced to take the blame that Othello and Iago are quick to attach to its owner but are very slow to admit of themselves. Although the action of the play is dominated by the male characters, we can see that the 'signifier' of the handkerchief has a place within the visual and symbolic framework of the play, and also has an impact on character development, and on our understanding of the characters' interactions and reactions.

Modern interpretations of the intersecting concerns of race, cultural identity and sexuality

At one level race is 'signified' within the play in a very subtle way: Othello's sense of cultural identity shifts as the play develops. Jyotsna Singh ('Othello's identity', in *Women, "Race," and Writing*, 1994) makes the point that, for all that Othello has won such a highly regarded position in Venice, since he remains an 'outsider' he is forced to construct for himself a 'white' – that is to say, for him, inauthentic – identity. Here, Singh identifies a very important strand in the representation of race in the play. Othello's cultural status cannot be secured by means of his marriage. This earns him the right to remain in Venice, but not to be seen as a rightful member of that society, much less a respected ruler within it. Yet Othello is a general – it is only his race that lowers his status in the eyes of the white men, the 'insiders', and their ringleader, Iago. Othello must therefore invent an identity for himself in order to fit in. Since he cannot overcome the prejudice of his contemporaries, he can only try to flaunt his disregard of it, by engaging in battles for status and power with the other men. In so doing, he loses hold of what he has – the love of Desdemona – and concentrates instead on what he lacks – the respect of white men. He effectively puts on a 'mask' of whiteness, as he becomes further and further embroiled in the effort to become an 'insider'. The mask he puts on is one of cultural identity – he takes on the values of the world of the play, and he is lowered to Iago's base level when he listens to his slanders.

In considering Othello as an 'outsider', we also consider (if only by association) the 'insiders' with whom he wants to align himself. In the world of the play, the 'insider' Othello binds himself to is, obviously, Desdemona. She is more than his wife, lover and friend. She is also his ticket to 'belonging', which is one of the two factors that most enrage Iago and the other male 'insiders' (the other factor is his race). Modern re-readings of the play can be quite exciting, in that they allow us to consider the intersecting factors of Othello's race, his status as 'an outsider' and his sexual relationship with Desdemona – all issues of major concern and interest in contemporary societies and cultural studies.

Ryan and Terry Eagleton have both commented on the tragedy of *Othello* in relation to the subversive potential of the play. Ryan argues that *Othello* is one of the most moving of Shakespeare's tragedies, because

The destruction of Othello and Desdemona lays bare the barbarity of a culture whose preconceptions about race and gender cannot allow a love like theirs to survive and flourish. The modern significance and value of the play are rooted in this revelation. In loving and marrying each other, Othello and Desdemona instinctively act according to principles of racial equality and sexual freedom which are far from generally accepted and practised in our own day, let alone in Shakespeare's. As a result they find unleashed on them, through Iago, the fury of a society whose foundations are rocked by the mere fact of their relationship.

(*Shakespeare*, 1995 edn, p.86)

Here, Ryan reminds us that Desdemona, as well as Othello, is positioned at the very centre of the play. More importantly, Ryan identifies a power inherent in the free thinking of Othello and Desdemona at the play's opening. When they marry despite social censure, both characters identify themselves as wilful and independent. Because this is the case, the very ease with which Iago is able to manipulate Othello, largely through base and irrational jealousy, shows the tragedy of their fates to be more intense. The central characters, Othello and Desdemona, are positioned high on the scale of heroism and righteousness, and so Othello's fall is all the more troubling, and Desdemona's suffering at his hands all the more tragic. Yet the play's subversive potential remains. If we continue to read the play, and to produce it, we may begin to see the play, not necessarily as 'literature' or even 'drama', but as a moving and powerful parable for what happens when jealousy gets the better of love, when prejudice gets the better of independent thought. In this reading, *Othello* becomes a play that can challenge assumptions about race relations and gender relations: a subversive play, which may serve a useful social function if it is 'canonized' and re-canonized by repeated re-interpretation through performance.

Eagleton has argued that '*Othello* is not a play about sexual deviancy, but about the deviancy of sex' (*William Shakespeare*, 1986, p.69). He argues, in other words, that the central tension in the play is not to do with sex itself (the sexual intimacy shared by Othello and Desdemona), but rather with social conventions and prejudices regarding sex. Desdemona clearly enjoys sex – an admission that was considered unacceptable (for women and therefore for female characters) in Shakespeare's day. Furthermore, she enjoys sex with a black man, and an 'outsider'. All kinds of stereotypical ideas and social prejudices are thus called into question by the marriage.

Karen Newman has explored the connection between race, cultural identity and sexuality in critical responses to the play through the ages. **Read the extract from Newman's article below and try to identify the two main points she makes. Does Newman's argument develop any ideas we have already encountered in this chapter?**

In *Othello*, the black Moor and the fair Desdemona are united in a marriage which all the other characters view as unthinkable. Shakespeare uses their assumption to generate the plot itself – Iago's ploy to string Roderigo along is his assurance that Desdemona could not, contrary to nature, long love a black man. Even his manipulation of Othello depends on the Moor's own prejudices against his blackness and belief that the fair Desdemona would prefer the white Cassio.

('"And wash the Ethiop white"', in *Shakespeare Reproduced*, 1987, p.144)

D i s c u s s i o n

Newman identifies the view of Othello's marriage to Desdemona as 'inappropriate' (a point made by Bristol in regard to charivari) on grounds of race and culture. She relates the character of Othello to his role as an 'outsider' (a role implied by Hapgood when he uses the term 'displacement'). Her argument also informs the views of Ryan and Eagleton cited above. Of course, the reference to 'nature' (the assumption that there is a 'natural' order, which designates same-race marriages as more 'natural' than mixed-race marriages) is not Newman's, but is rather a reflection of the assumptions common to the average theatre audience in Shakespeare's day. ■

Jardine looks at the issue of race in *Othello* from a different angle – from her perspective as a teacher. She poses the question of whether black as opposed to white readers and audiences engage differently with the play:

> It was as a result of taking four different paperback editions of *Othello* home and reading through their lengthy introductions to prepare my lecture that it dawned on me (but only slowly) that in every one of the editions we were looking at the twentieth century editor makes the tacit assumption that the reader of the play-text is white.
>
> What I mean is the following. All the introductions to modern editions of *Othello* are reasonably sophisticated in their treatment of race in the play. They devote considerable space to presenting available evidence on the presence (or rather, for the most part, the absence) of Africans and Arabs in England in the late sixteenth and early seventeenth centuries. They assemble contemporary comment on race and attitudes to 'aliens' so as to give an idea of the extent of racial prejudice. They mark the distance between our own more or less enlightened attitudes and the way an infrequent encounter like the embassy from Barbary led by Abd el-Ouahed ben Messaoud 'troubled' the court in 1600, while their dress, customs and behaviour 'caused a scandal' in London. Nevertheless, at the end of such learned discussion, each editor positions us, the readers of the edition, with the Venetians. Sensitive as the discussion of race tends increasingly to be, the readers who carefully resist Elizabethan stereotypical responses are unhesitatingly white, while the play's hero, Othello, is 'other'.

('Canon to the left of them', in *War of the Words*, 1994, pp.98–9)

You will find support for Jardine's observation if you consult the New Penguin edition of the play, even if it is only by implication. That is, you might expect an introduction to a play in which the main character is black at least to ask whether the colour of your skin alters your perception of the play. This question is not usually posed. Jardine considers the reason for the racial bias in studying Shakespeare, and goes on to point out that some of her students were not even aware that they *had* been excluded, because they were so used to it:

For no Afro-Caribbean or Asian student had registered (as far as I have been able to establish) that they were not addressed by their editor. They were, after all, entirely used to the idea that the books they picked up in the classroom were designed for students other than themselves. I was simply voicing concern over something they had learned to live with, something which in some real sense *defined* their participation in our educational system – participants, but not participants on precisely the same terms as 'ordinary' or 'traditional' students.

(Ibid., pp.100–1)

Othello *in performance*

In this part of the chapter, we consider briefly the performance history of *Othello*. As will become clear, it is a play that has been produced in extraordinarily various ways. You might ask yourself as you work through the text whether the number and variety of performances prove that a play *is* 'canonical'. Or is it the other way round: is a play performed frequently because it is already part of the canon? Or does it come to the same thing and, if it does, what does this tell us about the relationship between popularity and canonical status?

Early productions of Othello *in England*

The actors playing in the earliest productions of *Othello* had the supreme advantage of having the author present to indicate how they should interpret the text. Perhaps the most important thing for us to bear in mind is that Desdemona and all the female roles would have been played by young men. As Marvin Rosenberg comments: 'They were not, as they sound, *little* boys; many were well past boyhood, and in legal documents of the time were sometimes called young men. Some were mature men; two who played women's parts in 1635 were at least twenty-four, perhaps as old as twenty-eight' (*The Masks of Othello*, 1961, p.9). We know how effective the performances must have been because when the company played at Oxford in 1610 one spectator reported that Desdemona 'moved us especially in her death when, as she lay on her bed, her face itself implored the pity of the audience' (Tillotson, 'Othello', 1933, p.494, quoted in Sanders' New Cambridge edition of the play).

When you come to the next chapter in this book, which takes Behn's *The Rover* as its text, you will be able to see an interesting link with *Othello* and how it was played in the Restoration years (*c*.1660 when Charles II assumed the restored throne of England). The main point to bear in mind is that, after the years of the Puritans, attitudes changed radically towards morality, especially sexual morality, and this is a key theme in *The Rover* and other 'Restoration comedies', as this type of play is called. Interestingly, Behn quoted performances of *Othello* (as among 'the best Plays I know') to defend herself against a charge of prurience in her writing. From this we might deduce that Restoration performances made the most of the sensual, erotic aspects of the play (just as, later, the Victorians were to remove or

119

bowdlerize them). In addition, convincing as the male actors playing Desdemona might have been, the 'real thing' – a woman playing the female role – was even better when emphasizing this side of the play. Elizabeth Howe, in her book *The First English Actresses*, cites *Othello* as the first text that we can be sure contained a performance by a woman:

> Some time during the last months of 1660, a professional English actress appeared in a play on the English public stage for the first time … [it] is usually assumed to be 8 December 1660, when it is known that a woman played Desdemona in a production of *Othello* by Thomas Killigrew's King's Company.
>
> (1992, p.19)

Othello *in France and Italy*

Production of Shakespeare's plays in continental Europe posed several problems. Voltaire, in his *Philosophical Letters*, observed:

> He it was who created the English theatre. His was a fecund genius, full of vigour, ranging from simple naturalness to the sublime, without the least glimmer of taste or the slightest knowledge of the rules. I am going to tell you something rash, but true: the greatness of Shakespeare has been the ruin of the English stage. There are such beautiful scenes, such grand and terrible passages scattered throughout those monstrous farces of his called tragedies, that these plays have always been put on with great success …
>
> You know that in the tragedy of the Moor of Venice, a most moving play, a husband strangles his wife on the stage, and that when the deed is done she cries out that her murder is most unjust … You will be surprised, however, to hear that this boorishness was imitated in the reign of Charles II, the reign of manners, the golden age of the fine arts.
>
> (1961 edn, pp.85–6)

Consequently, to be acceptable to a French audience, Shakespeare's plays had to undergo considerable modification. In the eighteenth century, around the time of the French Revolution, this was undertaken by Jean-François Ducis who, in 1793, turned his attention to *Othello*, adapting it to French taste of the time. Robert Speiaght describes the adaptations:

> The handkerchief became a diamond bracelet. The rôle of Brabantio was enlarged, and that of Iago diminished. Desdemona died by stabbing; to put a pillow to criminal use was an affront to French propriety. Even so, the play was a hazardous challenge; and at the climax of the fifth act a voice was heard from the audience. 'It's a Moor who has done that; it's not a Frenchman.' At later performances Ducis bowed to popular demand. Brabantio and the Doge arrived in time to stay Othello's avenging arm, and the play ended happily. Not until 1800 was the original ending restored.
>
> (*Shakespeare on the Stage*, 1973, p.90)

The audience intervention recorded here points to a cultural and racial stereotyping, perhaps providing support for the view expressed earlier that the play takes its meaning from cultural interpretation and performance, as well as from the text itself. Although an accurate translation of the play was available, French actors continued to prefer the version by Ducis well into the nineteenth century.

Of course, there are many productions of Shakespeare's work produced in continental Europe today, and it would be seriously misleading to suggest that the few productions mentioned in this section are in any way representative of international perspectives on Shakespeare. Still, focus on one last European (Italian) production highlights the issue of social/cultural representation. The most celebrated production in Italy in the nineteenth century featured an actor called Salvini (1829–1915). Speiaght quotes from an account of this production by the novelist Henry James:

> For Henry James this was still 'the portrait of an African by an Italian'. He noted the 'quick suspicion and passionate rage', but also the 'frank tenderness', the 'easy expenditure of force', the 'passion beginning in noble repose and spending itself in black insanity', the 'visible and audible beauty beyond praise'. He noted Salvini's 'tiger-like spring to reach Iago from his kneeling posture by Desdemona', but he emphasized that for all its 'tremendous force' the performance was 'magnificently quiet, and from beginning to end had not a touch of rant or crudity'.
>   ... He [Salvini] modelled his Othello on a Moor he had seen in Gibraltar with a majestic walk, Roman face, slightly projecting lower lip, slender moustache, and a copper to coffee complexion. Salvini added a little hair to his chin.

> (Ibid., p.100)

What does James think of the play and the actors as 'representative' of Shakespeare?

Discussion

James distances himself from Salvini in his criticisms. It is not James who draws on stereotyped conceptions of 'Africans' or 'Moors' but the actor. These conceptions were not unique to Salvini, nor to Italian culture more generally. Indeed, such stereotypical assumptions were common well into the nineteenth century. That a white actor could approach a black character by modelling him on one real person (a black man) adding 'hair to his chin' is as absurd as a male actor modelling his interpretation of a female on one real woman. No white male actor today would dare to 'model' his portrayal of a white male character on *any arbitrary* white man – or exclusively on himself. ■

So, we begin to see that part of the problem of the handling of both race and gender in *Othello* is contained in our very ways of looking at these issues *as* problems. Let us clarify this point with an example. A white man is seen to represent only himself (not all white men), and many detailed studies analyse the depiction of white male characters as individuals – Hamlet, Macbeth, even Iago. Yet both Othello and Desdemona are analysed in more limited terms – not as *characters* but as *black* and *female* characters respectively.

If we keep this distinction in mind, we can reconsider the various accounts of international productions offered above. We may begin to see that what we make of these accounts will be affected to some extent by our own national and racial identities or 'positions' – what we see and interpret depends on where we are sitting, literally and metaphorically. Here we return to Jardine's ideas about the bias inherent in the situation of the student faced with a Shakespearean canon (textual, critical and performative) that *assumes* whiteness – and we might also argue maleness and Englishness – as a starting-point.

We now move on to consider another 'position' from which Othello has been variously interpreted – the North American context.

Othello *in the United States*

When we consider the history of production of *Othello* in the United States, we touch on issues of race in a very rich context. The story is a fascinating one, which can only be sketched here, drawing particularly on the work of Robert Speaight. As Speaight explains, by the middle of the eighteenth century Shakespeare was being performed in New York, and troupes of actors would tour the country putting on productions. *Othello*, for example, was produced in Williamsburg in 1750 as part of the celebrations following the renewal of a treaty with the Cherokee Indians. It was obviously a most affecting performance, because, according to Speaight, 'the Emperor and Empress of the tribe sent their attendants to stop the killing on the stage' (*Shakespeare on the Stage*, 1973, p.71).

It was the racial issues in *Othello* that ensured it became a popular play in the United States, where race was such an important subject. In Speaight's words:

> As early as 1821 a group of negro actors in New York, with James
> Hewlett at their head, performed *Othello* ... in an improvised
> playhouse at the corner of Bleeker and Mercer Streets ... the venture
> was short-lived. The players were ordered before a magistrate, who,
> from fear of civic disturbances, exacted from them a promise never to
> act Shakespeare again. Near by was the African Free School, founded
> in 1787, and out of this – according to popular report – came Ira
> Aldridge, the most famous figure in negro theatre history. The
> grandson of a Senegalese chieftain, he was born about 1807, either in
> New York or Maryland, and was sent to the University of Glasgow to
> complete his education. Starting his theatrical career as a call-boy, he
> was soon acting in London, touring the provinces, and playing Othello
> in Dublin. Here he was seen by Edmund Kean, who encouraged him
> for a part which he had made so memorably his own. Together, as
> Othello and Iago, they played in England and on the Continent for
> many years.
>
> (Ibid.)

Aldridge's performance is significant because it marked the performance of a black actor in the part of Othello (a novelty for nineteenth-century audiences). In 1930 the famous black singer Paul Robeson performed Othello in London, with a cast including Peggy Ashcroft and Sybil Thorndike, and in the autumn of 1943 it was thought 'safe' to present it on Broadway.

IRA ALDRIDGE, THE AFRICAN TRAGEDIAN, AS "OTHELLO."

Figure 4.3   Ira Aldridge (1804–67) as Othello, *Illustrated London News* 1858. Mary Evans Picture Library.

Figure 4.4 Paul Robeson and Peggy Ashcroft in *Othello*, Savoy Theatre, London 1930. Mander and Mitchenson Theatre Collection.

The signs of racial identity: playing Othello *today*

As we saw in Chapter One, Harold Bloom thinks that Shakespeare is, with Dante, at the very heart of the Western canon. However, Shakespeare is by no means the 'possession' of either Europe or North America and interpretation of *Othello* in other parts of the world can be a particularly contentious issue, especially today. Singh finds a paradox in the fact that 'When Shakespeare's *Othello* – like other Western, canonical works – is read as part of the "civilizing mission" of colonial history, then it tells a story of the empire's African subjects which is generally missing in critical accounts of the play.' She continues:

> It is ironic that a work like *Othello* should have been part of a project
> by which English literary works were to aid in the manufacture of a
> native elite class, who would then be a 'conduit of Western thoughts
> and ideas.' Cultural values, as the colonists perceived them, moved
> downward from a position of power. A number of postcolonial studies
> persuasively show how the British colonial administrators found an ally
> in English literature to support them in maintaining control over the
> natives under the guise of a liberal education. This was achieved by
> representing Western literary knowledge as universal, transhistorical,

and rational and by disguising its hegemonic impulses as a humanizing activity that created a class of persons non-European 'in blood and color, but English in tastes, in opinion, in morals and intellect.'

('Othello's identity', in Women, "Race," and Writing, 1994, pp.292–3)

However, says Singh, 'when Africans see themselves represented in the figure of Shakespeare's Othello ... they quite understandably resist the dichotomy of "civilisation" and "barbarism" in terms of which Othello is judged'. She goes on to describe a modern 'rewriting' of the play:

> In Murray Carlin's revision of *Othello, Not now, sweet Desdemona*, the playwright reminds us that Shakespeare's play as it exists today cannot escape the burden of history: 'This play is not a critical essay on Shakespeare ... my play ... is about the race conflict in the twentieth century.' This race conflict is articulated by a black actor playing Othello who rejects the image of Shakespeare's hero, 'civilized' and Christianized by the Europeans. In the plot of the play, two actors, who are also lovers offstage, are rehearsing for a production of Shakespeare's *Othello* in London. The male lead, known to us as 'Othello,' is a black from Trinidad and the woman, known as 'Desdemona,' is a white, South African heiress. The central question raised by both the playwright and his protagonist is 'Why is Othello a black man?' This ironically refers to the frequent denial of Othello's real race in Western performance history when white actors played the role and usually not as 'a Negro [but] done up – in a romantic, hawk-nosed sort of way, very reassuring to white audiences.' Questioning the cultural validity of this practice, Carlin's black actor wants to disrupt its signification when he suggests to 'Desdemona': 'Suppose I play Othello in white makeup? ... white actors have always played Othello in blackface. Why shouldn't a black actor play him in whiteface?' Mimicry, in this formulation, clearly scrambles and complicates colonial notions of difference where subjects were considered mere imitations of the rulers.

(Ibid., p.293)

Ryan has expressed the view that the play is about Iago's fear and hatred of Othello – feelings founded quite firmly and irrationally on the fact of Othello's race (*Shakespeare*, 1989, pp.88–9). However, we have not yet considered the practical issue of the actor who is cast as Othello – the question of a white actor's 'legitimacy' if he plays the part, as opposed to the considerations involved in casting the part for a black actor.

James R. Andreas has provided a very full account of the implications of staging Othello's 'blackness', in an article in which he argues that 'the play has traumatized African American literature, and indeed Western culture at large, for most of its existence' in that it provides fodder for 'the racist's nightmare of biracial sexual relationships between black men and white women' ('*Othello*', in *Materialist Shakespeare*, 1995, p.181). Andreas goes on to cite many literary texts – novels and stories as well as plays – which have retold the basic story of *Othello*, in various forms. He argues that it is wrong to interpret Iago as 'motiveless', that Iago is clearly motivated by racism and hatred, and that his character is representative of the views of 'western society at large for its predisposition to the periodic, ritual slaughter of marginal and aboriginal groups and all whites – especially women – who consort with them' (ibid., p.185).

Can you find support for Andreas's assertions, either within the play or within the discussions you have read in this chapter?

Discussion

Andreas's view is strongly stated, but it is also supportable (and, as Jardine points out, how we argue may be connected to our own racial, gender and cultural positions). There is a good deal of evidence in the play to suggest that Iago is motivated by what we would now label 'racism'. More to the point, many critics have argued this line, including Ryan and, in a very different context, Newman. In fact, Newman's identification of Othello's role as an 'outsider' in the play supports Andreas's view: Desdemona is punished because she consorts with a black man, an 'outsider'. ∎

Andreas goes on to provide examples to support his argument, not only from the text of the play but also from the play in performance. He illustrates the complexity of the portrayal of racial questions today with reference to what he describes as a 'controversial' production directed by Trevor Nunn at the Young Vic Theatre (London) in 1989. This featured Ian McKellan as an Iago who was a 'monstrous offspring' of miscegenation: 'the invisible theme of racism and the murder it provokes were rendered visible for all to see in this gruesome production' (ibid.).

Let us consider the ideas Andreas has outlined about race in *Othello* in the context of performance. **What would an all-black version of *Othello* be like? How would an all-black cast alter the race relations within the play?**

Discussion

These questions may seem too hypothetical to be answerable, but, in fact, there has been an all-black *Othello* captured on film (sadly, it is not available, except for special viewing at a few selected film libraries). African American film director Liz White produced a small-scale independent film version of the play, which by all accounts captured a great deal of the complexity of mixed-race relations. It is significant that White plays Bianca in the film, her son plays Iago, and his wife plays Desdemona. The relationship between the entire cast was close and supportive – it had to be, as the film was made over a period of several years, on a very low budget. This closeness translated into the film by infusing the race relations depicted with a quite personal and topical note. According to Peter S. Donaldson:

> Shakespeare's *Othello* ... posits a contrast between Europeans and the Moorish (or 'black') general who has married the daughter of a Venetian senator. In Liz White's version, though the 'Venetians' are costumed in Renaissance dress, the ethnic contrast is constructed differently. Yaphet Kotto plays Othello as a young, passionate, and emotionally sensitive African, while the rest of the cast, most of them New Yorkers and lighter in skin colour, sustain a tone of urban American sophistication. Othello, who claims at one point to be 'of

another race, another clime,' only imperfectly understands the social world he has married into and in which he is a respected commander. Yet that world, though not free of skin colour prejudice … is not white, and therefore the contrast between the outsider and his new community is muted. The film everywhere softens the stark black/white conflicts of the text, both in language and in the portrayal of cultural dissonance, and this softening helps to make the stark last act viable as a tragedy. Because Othello is ethnically close to the rest of the cast without really being one of them, the eruption of mistrust and rage is especially poignant: in rejecting Othello, the 'Venetians' are rejecting a part of themselves, a link to their origins. In falling prey to suspicion, Othello too … disavows a shared history.

(*Shakespearean Films*, 1990, p.129)

It is interesting to note that the abstract concept of the 'outsider', discussed earlier, is made concrete by this all-black production, which skilfully succeeds in conveying the 'outsider' status of a black man within a black community. Religious difference might have produced this 'outsider' status, as much as ethnic origin or shade of skin. Racial and gender oppression can be quite subtle. ■

Figure 4.5   Yapet Kotto as Othello, Audrey Dixon as Desdemona in Liz White's film *Othello* 1980. Reproduced by permission of the Estate of Liz White.

You might also be interested to know that, whilst this film was made between 1962 and 1966, it was not given a public showing until 1980, when it premiered at Howard University (the African American University where the black feminist writer Alice Walker was once a student). Critical reviews of the film have been extremely positive but it has still not had a major release. 'Black film', it seems, is still considered 'outside' the mainstream.

Let us consider one last example in this section, this time from live performance. The African American actor James Earl Jones played the part of Othello eight times (in eight different productions). In looking back over his career as Othello, he was able to come to some decisions about what the play means, at least to the actor playing the title role.

As you read Jones's words below, ask yourself whether seeing the play from a black actor's point of view gives it a different 'twist'.

> Othello is usually thought of as a play about jealousy. But it's not that simple .... Othello never reaches the point where you could describe him as obsessed with jealousy. Confused, yes; jealous, no. He has one conception of Desdemona: his portrait of the wonderful, lovely lady he married. Then Iago holds up to him the picture of another creature: a deceiving wanton. There's no way that Othello can put these two images together in a single woman. So he goes mad. His confusion drives him insane.
>
> ... What we must always remember is that *Othello* is the tragedy of a great man ...
>
> The Moors were a proud, highly educated people, with a tradition of learning and intellectual achievement that placed them ahead of many European societies. They were anything but savages or barbarians, and their strength is conveyed through the commanding presence of the general we meet in the opening acts of the play.
>
> ('Foreword', *Othello*, 1991, p.xiii)

Discussion

Although this account may not add a great deal to our understanding of the play, it does add a 'new twist' in the sense that it encourages us – for the first time in this chapter – to consider what it would be like to portray Othello, to play the part and imagine yourself into the role. Jones finds a strength of character and a nobility to draw upon (and he finds a similar strength in Desdemona as his comments later in the same essay reveal). He does so by tracing a history for the character of Othello, identifying his Moorish background as a mark of culture, rather than a weakness or ghettoizing factor. What Jones finds for his Othello is very similar to what African American activists and authors have searched out for generations now: a sense of history, of 'roots' and of indomitability of spirit. ∎

This account by a black actor adds to our understanding of the play at another level as well: in presenting his views of Othello's character, Jones reveals (if we read between the lines) that he finds the part challenging and rewarding – that it has a personal significance for him. Arguing with the character of Iago within the play may be a constructive way of arguing with white culture. Playing Othello, producing *Othello*, may be a way of engaging with debates about race and gender in society, through the theatre. Perhaps this is one reason why the play is still frequently performed, in North America and Britain especially. Perhaps this concentration on race and gender helps to keep the play in the canon.

Figure 4.6 James Earl Jones as Othello,
American Shakespeare Theatre Production, New
York 1982, directed by Peter Coe.
Range/Bettmann/UPI Photo.

Conclusion

Whilst *Henry V* has been treated in this book primarily as an English history play (to do with relationships between men and a definitively 'masculine' sense of cultural identity and power), the tragedy of *Othello* is concerned with relationships between men and women, and it does not take place in England, but in Venice. The implications and imaginative possibilities of this choice of a distant locale for the play have been considered, albeit briefly. You may, therefore, be intrigued to learn that the next play we consider in this book, Behn's *The Rover*, also written by an English playwright, is also set outside England, in Naples. This play too deals with the theme of 'outsiders' and also with gender and race, but it is written by a woman, and in a different age and political context.

However rich the comparison between *Othello* and Behn's play, you may wonder why we chose to include a play by another writer at all in a book that otherwise focuses largely on Shakespeare. To clarify this, before you move on to study Behn's play, it is important to recall a few of the points made about canonization in Chapter One. There, you were encouraged to think about the idea that there might be ways of updating the literary canon, of extending the criteria for inclusion by considering the work of women writers, for instance. You were also asked to consider some of the factors that might affect such an attempt to challenge the existing canon. You might not want to restrict the canon to authors and texts we all tend to associate with ideas of 'great literature'. Instead, you might want to argue for the inclusion of texts that look to more contemporary issues and concerns, and therefore reflect a fuller picture of the value of literature in the modern world. It is for reasons like these that Behn's writing is now frequently included in the reading lists of university literature courses, as well as on the less formal lists of personal favourites, particularly of scholars concerned with the impact of women's writing on the evolution of literature.

The popularity of performances and the topicality of issues raised in a play such as *Othello* may contribute to its continuing status as 'canonical', although the play was first designated part of the canon by virtue of its authorship. In considering the contemporary relevance of the racial and gender issues that *Othello* addresses, we argued that the play is re-canonized for modern audiences by its re-production on different stages, for different audiences, and for different reasons. This aspect of the process of canonization, and indeed of re-canonization, is related to the issue of 'literary value' as well. Whilst the issue of literary value is invoked in the canonization of Shakespeare's plays, it is much more difficult to discuss with reference to a lesser-known author such as Behn. So, to consider the idea of the canon in its fullest potential, we turn now to 'Naples', and to *The Rover.*

Further reading

Adamson, J. (1980) *'Othello' as Tragedy: some Problems of Judgement and Feeling*, Cambridge University Press.

Elliott, M. (1988) *Shakespeare's Invention of Othello: a Study in Early Modern English*, Macmillan.

Jones, E. (1965) *Othello's Countrymen: the African in English Renaissance Drama*, Oxford University Press.

Novy, M.L. (1984) *Love's Argument: Gender Relations in Shakespeare*, University of North Carolina Press.

Orkin, M. (1987) *Shakespeare against Apartheid*, Craig Hall.

Rosenberg, M. (1961) *The Masks of Othello*, University of California Press.

Remaking the canon: Aphra Behn's The Rover

by W.R. Owens

with a section by Lizbeth Goodman

In 1738 *The Gentleman's Magazine* published a lengthy article entitled 'The Apotheosis of Milton'. The author describes how in a dream he is transported to a meeting of the spirits of poets buried in Westminster Abbey who have gathered to discuss whether the great John Milton should be admitted to their company. Writers from Chaucer onwards arrive and are introduced with a commentary on their characters and achievements. Suddenly there is a commotion:

> Observe that lady dressed in the loose *robe de chambre* with her neck and breasts bare: how much fire in her eyes! What a passionate expression in her motions! And how much assurance in her features! Observe what an indignant look she bestows on the President, who is telling her, *that none of her sex has any right to a seat there.* How she throws her eyes about, to see if she can find out any one of the assembly who inclines to take her part. No! Not one stirs. They who are inclined in her favour are overawed, and the rest shake their heads; and now she flings out of the assembly. That extraordinary woman is Aphra Behn.

Aphra Behn was indeed an 'extraordinary woman'. The first English woman to earn her living by her pen, she produced during the 1670s and 1680s a remarkable series of plays, poems, translations and prose fiction, earning recognition as one of the most prolific and successful writers of her age. Yet despite her achievements, as the passage from *The Gentleman's Magazine* indicates, she was not to be admitted into the 'canon' of great authors: there was no place there for a woman. Only a short time after the article quoted above was written, the most popular of her plays, *The Rover*, disappeared from the stage. Written in 1677, it had been performed every season in London between 1677 and 1743, but, with the exception of revivals in 1748, 1757 and 1760, it was not to be seen again for over two hundred years.

Why did this change in Behn's fortune come about? One reason is that oblivion was to be the fate of Restoration dramatists in general, male and female. (The term 'Restoration' is used to refer to the period from 1660 to about 1700, that is, following the restoration of Charles II to the throne.) It perhaps comes as something of a shock to us now to realize just how completely the drama of this period disappeared during the nineteenth century. Indeed, some of it has never been revived. Very few tragedies, and none of the so-called 'heroic plays' produced during the Restoration, are ever performed. The case is different with Restoration comedy, which has seen a marked revival during the twentieth century. Plays such as William Wycherley's *The Country Wife* (1675), George Etherege's *Man of Mode*

Chapter Five

(1676), and William Congreve's *The Way of the World* (1700) are now regarded by critics, theatre directors and audiences as among the very best in the language, sparkling with wit, invention and wonderfully funny characterization.

Where earlier comedy had made much of the antics of low-life characters, Restoration dramatists dealt more exclusively with the follies and affectations of members (or would-be members) of high society. But the frankness of their treatment of sexual relations between women and men, and their general irreverence, not to say profanity, led to attacks from moralistic critics who condemned them as corrupt and corrupting. The backlash had begun well before the end of the seventeenth century with the establishment of public campaigns to 'reform' the stage, but it gathered momentum throughout the eighteenth and nineteenth centuries. By 1841 Lord Macaulay was thundering in the pages of the *Edinburgh Review* that 'this part of our literature is a disgrace to our language and our national character'.

There is no doubt, however, that Behn's reputation suffered additionally simply because she was a woman. Although she earned the respect and friendship of some of the leading male writers of her time, she also had to endure quite vicious attacks on her personal morals. Over the years her name became a byword for depravity, and she was held up as a disgrace to her sex. John Doran's account of her in his history of the English stage (first published in 1864) gives a flavour of the kind of hostility she attracted. According to Doran, Behn was:

> the most shameless woman who ever took pen in hand, to corrupt the public ... She might have been an honour to womanhood – she was its disgrace. She might have gained glory by her labours – but she chose to reap infamy ... To all other male writers of her day she served as a provocation and an apology. Intellectually, she was qualified to lead them through pure and bright ways; but she was a mere harlot, who danced through uncleanness, and dared them to follow. Remonstrance was useless with this wanton hussy.

Women critics were no less severe. Julia Kavanagh, in her *English Women of Letters* (1863), found Behn's mind 'tainted to the very core ... grossness was congenial to her'. Even those few critics who thought Behn was an important writer, like an anonymous essayist in *The Retrospective Review* (November 1852), felt it necessary to apologize for her 'coarse licentiousness': 'Mrs Behn's dramatic writings cannot now be generally read – at all events they could not be given to the public in a popular form'.

Ever since the middle of the eighteenth century, then, Behn had been condemned in company with other Restoration dramatists, and more specifically as a woman. The only one of her works to have remained in the literary canon was *Oroonoko*, widely regarded as the earliest anti-slavery novel. Towards the end of the Victorian period, however, a number of literary scholars began to take an interest in her. The most important of these was Montague Summers (1880–1948), an eccentric defrocked priest whose intellectual interests ranged from Restoration drama and Gothic novels to witchcraft and demonology. He published a very expensive limited edition of *The Works of Aphra Behn* in six volumes in

1915. In his introduction, Summers defended Behn warmly, declaring that 'long neglected and traduced, she will speedily vindicate for herself, as she is already beginning to do, her rightful claim to a high and honourable place in our glorious literature'.

Summers's confidence that Behn would re-enter the literary canon was not misplaced, though it took another half-century or more to accomplish. In *A Room of One's Own* (1929), Virginia Woolf paid tribute to Behn as the first professional woman writer, and Woolf's friend, Vita Sackville-West, published the first book-length study of Behn's life and writings in 1927. But although a good deal of scholarship was directed towards solving some of the puzzles and contradictions surrounding Behn's biography, it was not until the emergence of the modern feminist movement in the 1960s and 1970s that she was taken up and written about seriously as a major woman writer. There are now two substantial biographies of her by Maureen Duffy (1977) and Angeline Goreau (1980); scholarly and critical articles on the whole range of her literary output are appearing with increasing frequency; and, most important of all, her writings are being made available. *The Rover* was edited by Frederick Link in 1967; it was included in a Penguin Classics selection edited by Janet Todd in 1992 and in a World's Classics selection edited by Jane Spencer in 1995. Professor Todd is also editing a new scholarly edition of the complete works, which will run to eight volumes. Finally, Behn's plays are returning to the stage, with revivals by the Women's Playhouse Trust (1984, 1994) and the Royal Shakespeare Company (1986).

We are going to study Behn's most famous play, *The Rover*, the text of which is reprinted in Part Two of this book. Before turning to this in detail, I will outline Behn's career, placing it in its historical context and including a brief sketch of the Restoration theatre within which Behn worked.

Who was Aphra Behn?

Information about Behn's early life is very scanty indeed. She was almost certainly born in or near Canterbury, the daughter of Bartholomew Johnson, a barber, and Elizabeth Denham. They were married in 1638, and 'Eaffry' (or Aphra) was baptized on 14 December 1640. Elizabeth Denham was employed as a nurse for the children of the wealthy Culpepper family who lived nearby, so it is likely that Aphra spent time with the Culpepper children, perhaps even sharing in their education. Sir Thomas Culpepper (the younger) later described her as his 'foster sister'. During this period Canterbury was full of French- and Dutch-speaking refugees, and it is not difficult to imagine the young Aphra picking up foreign languages and being encouraged by the Culpeppers to develop her early talent as a writer.

Whatever the extent of her own educational opportunities, Behn later complained bitterly about the lack of education offered to women. Most of the leading writers with whom she was to come in contact had been educated in the classics at one of the universities, and were thus able to translate from Latin and Greek. Behn particularly regretted that she never learned Latin, which, despite increasing numbers of translations and a gradual shift towards English for scholarly writing, remained the language of learned discourse from which women were effectively barred.

Figure 5.1 Aphra Behn, portrait possibly by Sir Peter
Lely. Collection of Arthur D. Schlechter.

The first twenty years of Behn's life were a period of enormous political
upheaval. Civil War broke out between King and Parliament, and in 1649,
having been defeated, Charles I was tried and executed. For the next
eleven years England was a Republic governed by Parliament, then by
Oliver Cromwell and the army. The monarchy and the House of Lords were
abolished; the Church of England ceased to be the state church; and a
relaxation of press censorship, together with an unprecedented degree of
free speech, led to the emergence of a variety of radical political and
religious groups. However, many of Behn's childhood friends were
Royalists, and she remained a lifelong and staunch supporter of the Stuart
monarchs. In 1659 her 'foster brother' Sir Thomas Culpepper was involved
in plotting a rebellion in support of the exiled Charles II. That plot failed;
but by 1660 Charles had been restored to the throne and England was a
monarchy once again.

In 1663 Behn's life took an unusual and exciting new turn when she sailed with her family to Surinam, on the coast of South America. Surinam (situated between Brazil and Venezuela) was at that time an English colony, and during her brief stay there Behn met the African slave leader whose story subsequently formed the basis of her most famous novel, *Oroonoko*.

It is thought that, shortly after her return to England in 1664, she married Johan Behn, a merchant of German or Dutch extraction. Little is known about the marriage, which did not last more than a few years.

By 1666, possibly through the agency of Culpepper or other friends, Behn had come to the notice of the King and was presented at Court. This opened up a second amazing development in her career, because she was recruited as a government spy. England at this time was at war with the Dutch, and the government feared that disaffected Republicans, some of whom were in exile in Holland, were plotting an uprising to be supported by a Dutch invasion. Behn was sent to Antwerp in July 1666 and throughout the summer and autumn sent reports, partly in code, by nearly every post. In September she passed on a warning of a Dutch plan to sail up the Thames (which indeed happened in June 1667), but no notice was taken. Nor was any notice taken of her increasingly desperate pleas for money to cover her expenses. In the end she had to borrow money to pay off her debts and return home. For more than a year she petitioned the Court for funds to repay her loan, but none were forthcoming and eventually she was imprisoned for debt. How, or by whom, her debts were paid off is unclear, but by 1669 she was out of prison and had begun to write plays for a living.

Women writers in the seventeenth century

It is almost impossible to over-emphasize just how momentous a decision it was for a woman in the seventeenth century to enter the fiercely competitive arena of the professional theatre and to write for the public. Nothing could have flouted more openly the prevailing ideology about the role of women in society, based as it was on the assumption that women were inferior to men in every respect. In the words of the Anglican Homily on Marriage, one of the series of Homilies from which clergymen were ordered by law to read every Sunday in church from 1562 onwards:

> the woman is a weak creature not endued [endowed] with like
> strength and constancy of mind; therefore, they be the sooner
> disquieted, and they be the more prone to all weak affections and
> dispositions of mind, more than men be.

These sentiments were echoed by countless moralists throughout the seventeenth century. Having been assigned a subordinate status, it was demanded of women that they be chaste, obedient, pious and silent. Chastity assumed a particular importance, being linked to the whole economic and social structure. Angeline Goreau, in *Reconstructing Aphra* (1980), puts it like this:

> The principle of chastity was reinforced by the patriarchal,
> primogenital [first-born] system of inheritance and by the idea, then

law, that men had absolute property in women. Since the aristocracy's chief means of consolidating and perpetuating its power was through marriage, the 'honour' of its ladies acquired a property value … A deflowered heiress could be disinherited, since her maidenhead was an essential part of her dowry and she had deprived her father of the possibility of 'selling' her to a husband whose family line she would carry on.

(p.37)

Women from poorer backgrounds may have had more freedom in choosing a marriage partner, but to a very large extent all women were defined not by their occupations, but by their matrimonial, or 'sexual' status. Richard Allestree, author of a popular conduct manual, *The Ladies Calling* (1673), declared that 'the principal and distinct scenes in which a woman can be supposed to be an actor, are these three: virginity, marriage and widowhood'. In *The Mental World of Stuart Women* (1987), Sara Heller Mendelson explains how this led to a 'fundamental asymmetry' in the way in which women and men were perceived:

> Matrimonial status or sexual activity was a relatively minor addendum to a man's occupation, whereas it designated the core of a woman's being. This asymmetry was closely connected with women's dependent status in marriage and their primary role as childbearers and childrearers. Moreover, just as matrimonial or sexual categories defined each stage of a woman's life-cycle, attitudes to female sexuality in a wider sense determined a code of behaviour that applied to all women regardless of age, marital status or social rank … The feminine ideal of 'modesty', the outward expression of female chastity, defined the strictures governing women's limited education, their dress and conversation, their lack of independent choice of a marriage partner, their appropriate sphere of activity, and much else besides.

(p.10)

For a woman to dare to write for the public stage, or to publish her work, was to move outside the 'appropriate sphere of activity' in two ways: first, because knowledge was the prerogative of men, and secondly, because by doing so she would be violating feminine 'modesty' in that she would be moving from the private 'domestic' sphere into the public, masculine world. In Goreau's words, 'To publish one's work … was to make oneself "public": to expose oneself to "the world"' (*Reconstructing Aphra*, 1980, p.150).

This notion that men and women had separate spheres of activity was very powerful in the seventeenth century, and it is clear that the prescription was acknowledged by many women as well as men. It can never have been entirely pervasive, however, and the unprecedented political and ideological ferment of the Civil Wars opened up many questions about the grounds of political and religious authority. During the wars large numbers of women participated in public affairs in new ways. Some ran estates and businesses while their husbands, fathers or brothers were away. More significantly, the breakdown of censorship and the explosion of political and religious debate which ensued in the 1640s and 1650s enabled many women to publish their ideas for the first time.

Although censorship was reimposed at the Restoration the opportunities opened up during the 1640s and 1650s could not be reversed wholesale. Women continued to write and publish in ever increasing numbers, and with more works being translated from the classical languages it was beginning to be possible for them to enter into educated discourse with men. Religious nonconformity, though at times savagely repressed, provided opportunities for women to take on more conspicuous roles, particularly in groups like the Quakers where women were allowed to preach and pray in public. It also seems to be the case that the changed moral climate of the Restoration brought about new social freedoms for some women, which we will look at more closely later.

All these factors help to explain why, despite all the obstacles, someone like Aphra Behn was able to contemplate a career as a professional writer. She was not, it is important to note, the first English woman to have written a play. As early as 1613 Lady Elizabeth Cary's *The Tragedy of Miriam* had been published. During the 1650s Margaret Cavendish, Duchess of Newcastle, had written two volumes of plays, published in 1662 and 1668, but these were intended for private reading, not for the stage. In 1663 a translation of Corneille's *Pompey* by Katherine Philips was performed to great acclaim in Dublin and London. Perhaps emboldened by this success, a young woman named Elizabeth Polwhele wrote two plays, one of which seems to have been performed in the early 1660s, though neither was published. In 1669 a play by another woman, Frances Boothby, was produced and subsequently published. Almost nothing is known of either Polwhele or Boothby, and they seem not to have continued writing for the stage. By contrast, Aphra Behn went on to become one of the most prolific writers of her time.

Restoration theatres

It is not difficult to explain why an aspiring writer, needing to earn money, should have turned to drama. With the restoration of the monarchy in 1660 had come the re-opening of the professional theatres, closed since the early 1640s. Two veteran Royalist dramatists who had accompanied Charles into exile were given patents to set up companies and build theatres in London. Thomas Killigrew formed the King's Company, which in 1663 moved into the new Theatre Royal in Bridges Street, off Drury Lane. Killigrew's company attracted most of the experienced actors and also secured rights to most of the older plays from the early seventeenth century. By contrast, Sir William Davenant, who formed the Duke's Company, had to set up a wholly new company. After his death in 1668 his widow, Lady Davenant, took over as manager until 1673 when her son Charles was old enough to assume this responsibility. In 1671 the Duke's Company moved to a new, purpose-built theatre at Dorset Garden (near the Thames, just south of Fleet Street), designed by Sir Christopher Wren and splendidly equipped with all the most up-to-date stage machinery.

These new Restoration theatres were very different from the play-houses of Shakespeare's time. They were not particularly large by modern

Figure 5.2 Duke's Theatre, Dorset Garden, London, engraving by W. Dolle, from
Elkanah Settle, *The Empress of Morocco*, 1673; the play with this title was
presented at Dorset Garden in 1673. Photo: Mansell Collection.

standards. Dorset Garden, where most of Behn's plays were performed,
was about 140 feet long by just under 60 feet wide. Nevertheless, as
illustrations by W. Dolle show, it was an impressive building (Figures 5.2
and 5.3). The stage area was lavishly embellished, with particularly ornate
decorations above the proscenium opening. Figure 5.3 is perhaps slightly
confusing, in that it does not convey the fact that the stage extended from

Figure 5.3   Stage set for the river scene in *The Empress of Morocco*, 1673, engraving by W. Dolle, from Elkanah Settle, *The Empress of Morocco*, 1673, reproduced by permission of the British Library Board.

behind the proscenium arch about 20 feet into the pit (as the whole of the central seating area was then called). Actors entered through doors on both sides above which were balconies which could be hung with curtains to represent windows. These doors and balconies are just visible on each side of the illustration. It is important to note that most of the acting took place on the forestage in close proximity to the audience. The area behind the proscenium arch was used for scenery. Spectators in the pit were seated on benches, and around the three sides of the pit were tiers of more expensive boxes. At the rear of the theatre were two galleries, which held the cheapest seats. What struck contemporary observers most was the development of elaborate changeable scenery and other stage 'machines' – trapdoors, devices for raising people and objects, and so on. Painted backdrops and 'flats' or side wings could be slid onto the stage in grooves and arranged so as to create an illusion of depth perspective, and could be changed at the end of scenes to create new pictorial representations of place. Both the stage and the auditorium were lit by candles. Costumes became ever more striking and 'authentic' – Charles II even lent his coronation robes for use in a couple of plays! Finally, increasing use was made of music and dance to add to the entertainment.

Fewer people than in Shakespeare's time attended the theatre regularly because charges for admission were quite high in relation to income. Consequently, play runs were very short. Even the most successful new play would only run for eight or ten consecutive performances, and many runs were considerably shorter. It was important for the playwright that a new play ran for at least three nights, for the custom was that the profits on the third night were given to the author. The social composition of the Restoration audience has been much debated. Earlier scholars tended to emphasize the close connection of the audience with the court, claiming that audiences were dominated by the nobility, court wits and assorted hangers-on. Clearly royal patronage was extremely important, particularly while the re-opened theatres were becoming established. Nevertheless, recent scholarship has tended to suggest that the audience was more socially mixed than had been thought, with ordinary citizens well represented. There can be no doubt, however, that the audience was distinctly more élite than in the Elizabethan period, and the success or failure of a play would largely have been determined by whether it appealed to fashionable aristocratic taste. Women formed a significant part of the audience, high-born ladies as well as citizens' wives. Whatever the social mix, the Restoration audience was noisy and disorderly. Prostitutes wearing masks would ply their trade; quarrels would break out in the pit; aristocrats would carry on loud conversations in the boxes during performances.

Of all the changes in the public theatre from Shakespeare's time, perhaps the most significant was the introduction of professional actresses. Formerly in England women's parts were played by boys. But on 8 December 1660, a woman played Desdemona in a production of *Othello* by the King's Company. Both this company and the Duke's Company set about recruiting and training actresses, and in April 1662 the King decreed that henceforth women's parts should be played by women. As can be imagined, the introduction of women to the stage offered rich new possibilities to dramatists. Indeed the whole new genre of Restoration comedy, which turned so completely on promiscuity as its major theme, was to some extent only made possible by the inclusion of women actors.

As Elizabeth Howe shows in *The First English Actresses* (1992), the introduction of women was an enormous commercial success for the Restoration theatre, and the best actresses rapidly became 'stars'. But Howe concludes that 'the Restoration actress was exploited sexually on and off the stage, promoting gratuitous titillation in the drama and prostitution behind the scenes' (p.171). The assumption was made that actresses must also be part-time prostitutes and, Howe notes, this 'rapidly became a self-fulfilling prophecy' (p.32). The sexuality of the actresses was exploited in various ways by dramatists. For example, it is not a coincidence that for the first time rape becomes a regular feature of tragedies, and the threat of rape a recurring theme in comedies. As Howe suggests, this provided an excuse for exposing female bodies. Another favourite device was the so-called 'breeches part', in which a woman dressed up in men's clothes. Although such transvestism could be put to most striking and beautiful dramatic effect, there is evidence that its popularity with Restoration audiences may have had something to do with the fact that it permitted (or required) actresses to show off hips and legs usually covered by skirts.

Behn's early career as a dramatist

Behn's first play, a romantic tragicomedy entitled *The Forced Marriage*, was produced by the Duke's Company on 20 September 1670. The prologue boldly declared the author to be a woman, and made it clear that by writing for the public she was quite consciously invading a male domain. Despite – or maybe because of – this audacity, the play was a hit. It ran for six nights, which was very good indeed for a new play by an unknown author. As the title suggests, it deals with a topic that was to preoccupy Behn throughout her career: the harmful effects of the contemporary system of arranged marriages.

The success of *The Forced Marriage* encouraged Behn to follow it six months later with another romantic tragicomedy, *The Amorous Prince*, which again was well received. With her third play, however, a comedy of intrigue entitled *The Dutch Lover*, performed at the new Dorset Garden theatre in February 1673, Behn faltered, and the critics pounced. The play had weaknesses of construction, and suffered further from a poor production. But more significantly, the critics evidently decided to sabotage it on the grounds that its author was a woman. In a defensive 'Epistle to the Reader' in the published text, Behn rounded on her detractors:

> Indeed that day 'twas acted first, there comes me into the pit a long, lither, phlegmatic, white, ill-favoured, wretched fop ... This thing, I tell ye, opening that which serves it for a mouth, out issued such a noise as this to those that sat about it: that they were to expect a woeful play, God damn him, for it was a woman's. Now ... if I thought there were a man of any tolerable parts, who could upon mature deliberation distinguish well his right hand from his left ... yet had this prejudice upon him, I would take a little pains to make him know how much he errs. For, waiving the examination why women, having equal education with men, were not as capable of knowledge ... as they, I'll only say ... that plays have no great room for that which is men's great

141

advantage over women, that is, learning. We all well know that the immortal Shakespeare's plays (who was not guilty of much more of this [i.e. education] than often falls to women's share) have better pleased the world than Jonson's works ... and for our modern [dramatists], except our most unimitable Laureat [John Dryden], I dare to say I know of none that write at such a formidable rate but that a woman may well hope to reach their greatest heights.

I'd like you to write down in a few words what Behn's argument is here. How would you describe her tone?

Discussion

Clearly Behn believed the best form of defence was attack! She is scathingly sarcastic about her critic ('lither' means withered or impotent; 'phlegmatic' means dull or sluggish). She puts forward a double argument: first that it is their unjust exclusion from education, and not any lack of ability, that has held women back; and secondly 'learning', as the example of Shakespeare proves (by contrast with the educated Ben Jonson), is not essential for the writing of successful plays. ■

After the publication of this defiant feminist manifesto, Behn produced no more plays for three years. In 1676 she returned with *Abdelazar*, a heroic tragedy, and another comedy, *The Town Fop*. Six months later *The Rover* was produced, followed early in 1678 by *Sir Patient Fancy*.

Her productivity and box-office success in the 1670s led to increasingly frequent and virulent attacks. As we shall see, she was accused of plagiarism in *The Rover*. More often the charge was of immorality, whether in her personal life or in her plays. In the 'Preface to the Reader' in *Sir Patient Fancy*, she complained that she was being singled out for criticism on this score simply because she was a woman. Male playwrights could live the most scandalous lives, and write the most bawdy plays, and people would flock to see them: 'but from a woman it was unnatural'.

Restoration drama

As her comments indicate, Behn was certainly not exceptional in dealing with sex in the theatre. The later 1670s were particularly noted for the emergence of 'sex comedies' which were more daring than anything in the 1660s. This was a relatively short-lived phenomenon, however, and the early 1680s saw the beginning of a swing against sexual explicitness. The reaction seems to have been particularly strong among women who attended the theatre. The formation of a Society for the Reformation of Manners represented an attempt not only to reform the stage but to bring about moral change in society. Even more influential was a sweeping assault on Restoration comedy, *A Short View of the Immorality and Profaneness of the English Stage* (1698), by the Anglican clergyman Jeremy Collier. For all the outcry, however, the character of Restoration drama did not change fundamentally for several more decades.

These changes in the nature of drama in the second half of the seventeenth century are bound up with wider cultural developments in society. To understand Behn's plays we need to see them in the context of what has been termed the 'sexual revolution' of the 1660s and 70s. As Goreau has argued:

> Charles II's return to the throne effected an abrupt and deliberate reversal of the Puritan ethic. His need to distinguish himself in every way from his predecessors – added to his natural inclination – created an atmosphere in which promiscuity, systematic frivolity, and extravagance were adhered to as a social norm almost as dogmatically as the more severe of the Puritan party had adhered to godliness ... Adultery was part of the calling of a gentleman, as essential to his place in society as fluency in French, a wig, or a sword at his side. The King set the tone by openly keeping several mistresses, carrying on numerous chance affairs, and bestowing titles, estates, and fortunes on his women and bastards ... The movement primarily affected the fashionable society of London – the court and aristocratic circles, the playhouse, the taverns, coffeehouses, and ordinaries – but as these were both the most visible and the most influential groups, they seemed to dominate the rest.
>
> (*Reconstructing Aphra*, 1980, pp.165–6)

Gathered around the King was a dazzling group of young wits and writers including, most famous of all, John Wilmot, Earl of Rochester. In their writings, especially in obscene poems which were passed around in manuscript, they boasted of their sexual conquests, pouring scorn on the idea of constancy in love and, above all, on marriage. Goreau quotes a passage from Rochester's poem, 'A Ramble in St. James's Park', which catches the tone of this new cynical libertinism:

> Much wine had passed, with grave discourse
> Of who fucks who, and who does worse
> (Such as you usually do hear
> From those that diet at the Bear),
> When I, who still take care to see
> Drunkenness relieved by lechery,
> Went out into St. James's Park
> To cool my head and fire my heart.
> But though St. James has th' honour on 't,
> 'Tis consecrate to prick and cunt.
> There, by a most incestuous birth,
> Strange woods spring from the teeming earth ...
> And nightly now beneath their shade
> Are buggeries, rapes, and incests made.
> Unto this all-sin-sheltering grove
> Whores of the bulk and the alcove,
> Great ladies, chambermaids, and drudges,
> The ragpicker, and heiress trudges.
> Carmen, divines, great lords, and tailors,
> Prentices, poets, pimps, and jailers,
> Footmen, fine fops do here arrive,
> And here promiscuously they swive [copulate].

Figure 5.4   John Wilmot, second Earl of Rochester (1647–80), after Jacob Huysmans, *c.*1665–70. National Portrait Gallery, London.

(The 'Bear' referred to here was an eating-house near the Theatre Royal in Drury Lane, a favourite meeting-place of literary wits and theatre people. 'Whores of the bulk and alcove' refers to prostitutes of the lowest and the highest class, a 'bulk' being a shopfront and an 'alcove' a recess in a bedroom for a bed of state.)

Although this new sexual freedom celebrated by Rochester applied in theory to both sexes, in practice it was a highly dangerous game for women to play. It was widely accepted that a woman's beauty did not last for long, and for women who did not become wives the only alternative was to become a mistress, from which it was a short step to becoming a whore. Although the wits urged women to throw off old-fashioned ideas about modesty and chastity, they also, illogically, heaped abuse on women who did. Women known to be sexually active – even the King's mistresses – were the targets of vicious satires by male poets.

Behn, a friend of Rochester's and a great admirer of his wit and skill as a poet, was a bold proponent of the ideal of sexual freedom, for both women and men. Like the male wits and libertines, she wrote frankly about sexual love. For example, one of her most famous poems, 'The Disappointment', gives a comic account of male impotence from a woman's point of view; and she opens a play in a bedroom with a couple arising from lovemaking. Particularly striking is her forthright acknowledgement of female sexual desire. This is evident in a charming song first published in 1672 and included in her third play, *The Dutch Lover* (1673), where it is sung by a maid to her mistress while she undresses for bed:

> Amyntas bid me to a grove,
> Where all the trees did shade us,
> The sun itself, though it had strove
> Yet could not have betrayed us.
> The place secure from human eyes
> No other fear allows,
> But when the wind doth gently rise
> To kiss the yielding boughs.
>
> Down there we sat upon the moss,
> And did begin to play
> A thousand wanton tricks, to pass
> The heat of all the day.
> A many kisses he did give,
> And I returned the same:
> Which made me willing to receive
> That which I dare not name.
>
> His charming eyes no aid required
> To tell their amorous tale;
> On her that was already fired,
> 'Twas easy to prevail.
> He did but kiss and clasp me round,
> Whilst those his thoughts expressed,
> And laid me softly on the ground;
> Oh! who can guess the rest?

In her own love life Behn seems to have been attracted towards rakish Restoration gallants. The most fully documented case concerns a passionate love affair with John Hoyle, a free-thinking, fast-living, bisexual young lawyer, memorably described by a scandalized contemporary as 'an atheist, a sodomite professed, a corrupter of youth, and a blasphemer of Christ'. From what we know of Hoyle's life, this was, if anything, an understatement. Three years after Behn's death, in 1692, he was stabbed to death in a drunken fight. Their liaison was known to contemporaries, and no doubt provided much ammunition for those who accused Behn of loose morals.

By the end of the 1670s, despite her detractors, Behn had established herself as one of the leading playwrights of the time. The King frequently attended her plays, and *The Rover* was a particular favourite at court. After the initial euphoria of his return to the throne, however, Charles II was faced with increasing political opposition. His reputation as the 'Merry Monarch' came about because of his numerous and well-known affairs with actresses and duchesses, but ironically it was his failure to produce a legitimate heir to the throne that brought about the most serious crisis of his reign. In 1678 rumours began to spread of a 'Popish Plot' to replace Charles with his Roman Catholic brother James, Duke of York. An atmosphere approaching mass hysteria developed rapidly, in which wild accusations were made, suspects were rounded up, and people were executed. In the absence of a legitimate son born to Charles, James was in fact the rightful successor, but repeated attempts were made in Parliament to bring in a Bill to exclude him from the succession. Political opinion in the nation was deeply divided; indeed it was during this period that political parties in the modern sense began to be born. One party, known as Whigs, wanted to exclude James, and pressed Charles to declare his illegitimate son, the Protestant Duke of Monmouth, as his heir. A second party, nicknamed Tories, supported Charles's determination not to give way to demands that he alter the royal succession in this way. Matters eventually cooled down (partly because Charles simply dissolved Parliament) and James II succeeded Charles in 1685.

Behn intervened vigorously in these heated political debates. She was a resolute supporter of the Tory position, and between 1681 and 1682 produced no fewer than five plays designed in one way or another to discredit the Whigs. These went down well with audiences, who were mainly Tory in sympathy. A few months later, however, when she openly castigated the Duke of Monmouth, Behn got into trouble. Charles was fond of Monmouth, despite the fact that he had been taken up by the Whigs, and greatly resented attacks on him. On the King's orders Behn and the actress who spoke the offending lines were arrested by the Lord Chamberlain and held in custody.

It does not seem that Behn was actually imprisoned on this occasion, but the experience must have been alarming. She produced no more works for the stage for four years, though this may also have been partly because the theatre generally had gone into a decline, with falling audiences and a consequent resort by management to cheaper old plays rather than new ones. In 1686, however, Behn returned with *The Lucky Chance*, a comedy, followed in 1687 by a farce, *The Emperor of the Moon*, which was to become one of her longest-running plays. *The Lucky Chance* was a great success, but once again attracted fierce criticism for its bawdiness, and especially because it was the work of a woman. This criticism drew from Behn one of her longest and most passionately argued claims for equal treatment as a woman writer. In a preface to the published text she accused her critics of being jealous of her success, and of persuading the ladies in particular to condemn her for immodesty. Men could write the most indecent things, and get away with it, but a woman was instantly at fault. She denied that *The Lucky Chance* was worse than any other play:

When it happens that I challenge any one to point me out the least expression of [indecency] ... they cry, *That Mr. Leigh opens his night gown, when he comes into the bride-chamber*; if he do, which is a jest of his own making, and which I never saw, I hope he has his clothes on underneath? And if so, where is the indecency? ... Is that any more than you see in the most celebrated of your plays [such] as the *City Politics*, the *Lady Mayoress*, and the *Old Lawyer's Wife*, who goes with a man she never saw before, and comes out again the joyfullest woman alive, for having made her husband a cuckold with such dexterity, and yet I see nothing unnatural nor obscene, 'tis proper for the characters ... Had I a day or two's time ... I would sum up all your beloved plays, and all the things in them that are passed with such silence by, because written by men: such masculine strokes in me must not be allowed ... Had the plays I have writ come forth under any man's name, and never known to have been mine, I appeal to all unbiased judges of sense, if they had not said that person had made as many good comedies, as any one man that has writ in our age; but a devil on't the woman damns the poet ... All I ask is the privilege for my masculine part the poet in me (if any such you will allow me) to tread in those successful paths my predecessors have so long thrived in, to take those measures that both the ancient and modern writers have set me, and by which they have pleased the world so well. If I must not, because of my sex, have this freedom, but that you will usurp all to yourselves, I lay down my quill, and you shall hear no more of me, no not so much as to make comparisons, because I will be kinder to my brothers of the pen then they have been to a defenceless woman; for I am not content to write for a third day only. I value fame as much as if I had been born a hero; and if you rob me of that, I can retire from the ungrateful world, and scorn its fickle favours.

This is, I think you will agree, a most remarkable speech of Behn's. I'd like you to read it again and then write down her argument in your own words.

Discussion

Behn is arguing, first of all, that contemporary plays are not so indecent as is being claimed: the actions depicted are true to the characters and the plots. What she is objecting to is denigration of her own plays just because they are written by a woman. She demands the right, as a woman, to participate equally with men in literary production – hitherto an exclusively male preserve. If writing is to be defined as male, she claims a 'masculine part', and demands the opportunity not just to write for money, but to seek fame and her rightful place in the public literary tradition (or 'canon'). If men are going to continue to 'usurp all' to themselves, and deny women the right to participate, she will lay down her 'quill' and retire. ■

It is a brilliant and powerful speech, but what I think it shows indirectly is that Behn, for all the attacks on her, was very lucky. She was fortunate to have been writing at that particular time, when Restoration comedy was offering the opportunity for a woman, if bold enough, to shine. The new

147

theatre set out very deliberately to affront many of the traditional religious and social values, and Behn was able to take advantage of this ethos to defy the old taboos on women taking on masculine roles such as dramatist, and to go on to subvert male attitudes in her plays. In this sense Behn was a victor, not a victim.

Behn's later work

The final years of Behn's life do not seem to have been happy. She became ill, and when she stopped writing plays her main source of income dried up leaving her once again in debt. Despite these troubles, in a final surge of creative energy she turned to prose fiction, producing some of the works for which she is now best known. This was quite an innovatory step, for prose fiction of a 'realistic' kind (as opposed to romance) was not yet an established literary form. Her first effort was the three-part *Love Letters between a Nobleman and his Sister* (1682–87). The inspiration for this was a real-life contemporary scandal: the elopement of Lord Grey with his sister-in-law, Lady Henrietta Berkeley. Behn offers a fictionalized account of their growing sexual passion for each other, leading to their elopement and, eventually, sexual fulfilment. As Goreau remarks (*Reconstructing Aphra*, 1980, p.275), the story was just the sort to appeal to Behn: 'romance, parental disobedience, defiance of social codes, political intrigue, incest, disguise, escape, betrayal'. It proved extremely popular (going through over sixteen editions before the end of the eighteenth century), and on the strength of it Behn produced several more novellas and short stories.

Her most famous work of prose fiction was *Oroonoko: or, The Royal Slave* (1688), based on her visit to Surinam twenty years earlier. The hero, Oroonoko, is a noble, well-educated African, who is in love with the beautiful Imoinda. His grandfather, the King, has designs on Imoinda, and has her brought to his harem. Enraged to hear that she loves Oroonoko he sells her into slavery. Oroonoko is captured by an English slaver and sold in Surinam, where he discovers Imoinda. He leads the other slaves in a revolt, but they are hunted down and induced to surrender. Oroonoko is cruelly flogged, and determines to exact revenge, even though he knows it will cost him his life. Fearing to leave Imoinda to the mercy of the white slave-owners, he decides, with her willing agreement, to kill her. Discovered near her body, he is captured and, before he can take his own life, is savagely put to death.

Oroonoko is a remarkable work of art. Its popularity and influence was enhanced by a highly successful stage adaptation by Thomas Southerne in 1696 which was performed throughout the eighteenth century. A translation of the novel into French in 1745 went through no fewer than seven separate editions. As the movement to abolish the slave trade got under way in the late eighteenth century, *Oroonoko* was celebrated as the first anti-slavery novel.

Behn died less than a year after the publication of her famous novel, on 16 April 1689, and was buried four days later in Westminster Abbey – a striking tribute to the success of her career against all odds. The inscription on the black marble stone that marks her grave is remarkable for its lack of reference to a husband, father or other relation. Below her name and the date of her death is a simple two-line epitaph:

> Here lies a proof that wit can never be
> Defence enough against mortality.

Reading The Rover

Source and setting

Before we study *The Rover* in detail, it is worth noting one or two points about its source and setting. Turn now to the text of the play, reprinted in Part Two of this book, and look at the title-page, the list of 'Characters' (p.264), and the 'Postscript' (p.326). You should also consult the notes to these sections of the play (pp.328–34), which will help you with unfamiliar words. **What do you understand Behn to be saying in the 'Postscript'?**

D i s c u s s i o n

In the Postscript, Behn is responding to criticism that *The Rover* was not her own work. She admits that it is loosely adapted from Thomas Killigrew's comedy, *Thomaso: or, The Wanderer*, written in 1654 and first published in 1664. The accusation of plagiarism is not to be taken too seriously. The practice of borrowing from and freely adapting earlier plays was endemic at the time. In her Postscript Behn shrugs off the charge, and it would seem likely that she had Killigrew's consent for the rewriting. (Killigrew was, after all, Master of the Revels at the time – too important a person for Behn to have wanted to offend.) ■

Spread over two parts of five acts each, *Thomaso* is a vast, rambling affair, full of lengthy speeches and interminable plots. Although probably intended only for reading, it is not without interest, and it is easy to see why an experienced and skilful playwright might have been attracted to it as a basis for a new play. It is set during the 1650s following the Civil Wars in England which had ended with the execution of Charles I in 1649. His son, Charles II, attempted to regain the throne, but was decisively defeated by Oliver Cromwell and the Parliamentary forces at the Battle of Worcester in 1651. Many Royalists, or 'Cavaliers' as they were known at the time, left England to accompany Charles into exile in Europe. *Thomaso* concerns one such group, and recounts their activities during a visit to Madrid.

If I list some of the main characters in *Thomaso*, you can see how this compares with the cast list of *The Rover*:

Men

DON PEDRO, a noble Spaniard
DON JOHAN *and* DON CARLO, his friends
THOMASO, the Wanderer
EDWARDO *and* FERDINANDO, English gentlemen, his friends
PHILLIPPO, paramour to Lucetta
SANCHO, her bravo
Two bravoes of Angellica's

Women

SERULINA, a beauteous virgin, sister of Don Pedro
ANGELLICA BIANCA, a beautiful courtesan
ANNA, her bawd
LUCETTA, a famous courtesan
CALLIS, waiting woman to Serulina
KECRA, servant to Lucetta

Although many of the characters, some of the scenes, and even bits of dialogue in *The Rover* are taken from *Thomaso*, the two plays are quite different in tone, style, theatrical pace, and approach to the subject-matter. Killigrew's central character, the rakish Thomaso, is treated rather indulgently. He spends much of the play in the arms of a succession of prostitutes or courtesans, of whom the most memorable is the beautiful Angellica Bianca, before finally reforming his ways and settling down to a redeeming marriage with the virginal Serulina. Serulina is being forced to marry someone else, against her will, and is threatened with rape on two occasions by Edwardo, who is himself tricked and robbed by Lucetta. In revenge he has her face cut – an example of the dark and violent atmosphere of *Thomaso*.

A central problem with Killigrew's play is the inconsistency in the character of Thomaso, who simultaneously must be libertine and true lover. Behn solves this by inventing a new character, Belvile, the faithful lover whose devotion to Florinda (Serulina) contrasts with the promiscuity of Willmore (Thomaso). She also invents the witty Hellena who eventually manoeuvres Willmore to the altar. Edwardo and Ferdinando in *Thomaso* become, respectively, Blunt and Frederick in *The Rover*, with Valeria being created by Behn to make up a third pair of lovers. Angellica has a similar role in both plays and, as Behn points out in her Postscript, is the only character from the main plot of *Thomaso* whose name has not been changed. As we shall discover, however, there are significant differences in the way Behn presents the beautiful courtesan.

A further important change introduced by Behn is the setting. The action of *Thomaso* takes place in Madrid, with the Spanish Inquisition as a backdrop, whereas *The Rover* is set in Naples, at Carnival time. Throughout Roman Catholic Europe, particularly in Italy, Carnival was the greatest popular festival of the year. Beginning in January and leading up to the forty-day period of abstinence during Lent, it involved much feasting and merry-making, including boisterous street processions. Carnival costumes and masks allowed people to roam freely in disguise, with women sometimes dressing as men and vice versa. As might be expected in such an atmosphere, there was a good deal of sexual licence.

A final point to note about the setting of *The Rover* is that Naples during this period was part of the Spanish Empire, and was therefore ruled by a Spanish Viceroy. There are thus three main groups of characters: the English (the three Cavaliers, Willmore, Belvile and Frederick, with their companion Blunt); the Spaniards (Don Pedro, Don Antonio, Florinda, Hellena and Valeria); and the Italians (Angellica, Moretta, Stephano, Philippo and Lucetta).

Act I, Scene 1

I would now like you to read and make some notes on the first scene of *The Rover*. What would you say the play is going to be about? How would you describe the characters of Florinda and Hellena? What strikes you about the picture of contemporary marriage that emerges?

Discussion

Judging by this lively opening scene, I would say that the play is going to be about love and marriage from a woman's point of view. Drama almost always arises from conflict, and in this instance the conflict is between the young women, who want freedom to marry for love, and patriarchal authority, here represented by their brother in the absence of their father, which insists that marriage is a financial transaction arranged by men in which women have no say.

What is striking in the scene is first of all the determination of both sisters not to be ruled by their father or brother. Florinda is less fiery than Hellena, but she is adamant that she will not obey her father's 'unjust commands' to marry Don Vincentio. Hellena for her part is outspokenly resolved not to spend her life in a nunnery. Although she has never been in love, she paints a teasing picture of romantic love as she observes it in Florinda, declaring that when the right man comes along, as Belvile did for Florinda, true love will be recognized immediately. Far from waiting passively for this to happen she is prepared to take the initiative in seeking her man, confident that she can use her physical charms 'to the best advantage'. Florinda, too, takes action at the end of the scene to try to make contact with Belvile. It is noticeable, however, that Florinda is a more restrained character than her sister. Hellena dominates the scene, taking the audience into her confidence in asides, butting in to speak on Florinda's behalf, and brushing aside with comic zest Pedro's attempts to shut her up. Both Florinda and Pedro describe her as 'wild' or 'mad', and she comes across here as a bold, witty and resourceful character, one with whom it is impossible not to sympathize in her ambition to throw off some of the restrictions laid down by her gender.

Another very striking feature of this opening scene is the sheer ferocity of the onslaught on the whole institution of arranged marriages. We are left in no doubt that her father and brother regard Florinda as an object for sale. Florinda pleads with her brother 'not to follow the ill customs of our country and make a slave of his sister'. Hellena rails wittily against forced marriage, which she says would be even worse than life in a nunnery. In an impassioned, but also very funny, exchange with her brother, she declares that it would be preferable to be an adulterer than to have to submit to sex with an ugly, unloved husband, and she too makes a direct comparison between the lot of such a wife and that of a slave. ■

Did you note, though, that for all their commitment to the ideal of a free romantic love, the sisters remain very aware of the power of money? Hellena's remark to Florinda to 'lay aside your hopes of my fortune by my being a devote' is only half-joking: she is referring to the fact that Florinda would stand to gain if their father did not have to lay out a second dowry. She impetuously declares that life with an impoverished Belvile would be preferable to marriage with the rich but revolting old Vincentio, but Florinda recognizes that it is less easy to reject Antonio. In a short blank verse soliloquy (lines 142–5) she admits the force of Antonio's claim to her hand, given that he combines both 'youth *and* fortune' (my emphasis).

Finally, it is also worth pausing to note that although the title might have led us to expect a focus on a man, Behn chooses to open *The Rover* with women holding centre stage, voicing their concerns, and initiating the action. In her book *The Prostituted Muse* (1988), Jacqueline Pearson has shown that in this period women dramatists were much more likely than men to open plays with women characters. This is of some significance in a culture that allowed women no public voice, and ceaselessly enjoined them to be silent and submissive in private – while at the same time blaming them for talkativeness. As Pearson puts it, by giving women the first word 'we are introduced to the dramatic world through their eyes, and they are defined not as object but as subject, not as the "Other" but as human beings who can set the standard for their society' (p.64).

This opening scene, then, has set up some important issues, and has put one of the main plot lines in motion: Hellena's search for a husband. It is played out in a private, domestic setting, but Carnival provides the perfect means of escaping from patriarchal control, and the scene ends with the sisters donning their masks and preparing to go out on a 'ramble' through the streets.

Love, sex and marriage in The Rover

If you have not already done so, you should now read through the remainder of the play. As I expect you will have found with the opening scene, the language is not particularly difficult, and my notes on the text are provided to help explain unfamiliar words and phrases. You will find that the plot becomes quite intricate, with lots of misunderstandings, disguises and mistaken identities: this is why it is classified as a 'comedy of intrigue'. The carnival setting means that much of the action is outdoors, and it allows for rapid movement, with different groups on stage at the same time. But although there are many complications, there are really only three main plot lines. The first concerns the attempts of Florinda and Belvile to thwart the opposition of her father and brother to their marriage. The second is

Hellena's pursuit of Willmore, in which she faces competition from Angellica, the courtesan who has fallen in love with him. The third is a kind of low-comedy sub-plot, in which Blunt is robbed of his money by the prostitute Lucetta.

While you are reading, you should make notes about anything that strikes you as significant. As well as following the action, and thinking about how the various characters are presented, you should also jot down any thoughts about how the play might be *performed*. For example, in the opening scene, try to visualize what the set might look like, and what the characters might be *doing* as they speak. If you agree that the two women have different personalities, how might this be signalled to an audience? You should pay particular attention to clues in the text about how the play should be performed. I am thinking, for example, of stage directions that indicate changes of costume and physical actions, scene changes, asides and soliloquies, characters being overheard, and disguises. Then, too, you should think about the language spoken by the various characters, and how Behn moves between prose and verse. Sometimes you will find that verse is used for emotional heightening, and sometimes (as in Willmore's case) for purposes of manoeuvre.

In a later section, Lizbeth Goodman is going to focus in detail on performance aspects of *The Rover*. Before then, I want to discuss two questions: what the play has to say about love, sex and marriage, and to what extent it may be described as a 'feminist' play. Obviously Behn was not a feminist in the modern sense; by 'feminist' here I mean simply being aware of the unjust ways in which women as a group are treated, wanting to remedy this injustice, and holding out a vision of a society that allows women as well as men a degree of autonomy and self-determination. So a seventeenth-century play like *The Rover* might be described as 'feminist' in this broad sense if, for example, it portrayed women characters in a strong and positive light, having them initiate action and articulate issues of concern to women.

It will be obvious from reading the play that its major concerns are about sexual relations between women and men. Almost all the characters offer some comment on these matters, and the whole development of the dramatic action is designed to explore this large theme. We have already discussed how the opening scene raises these issues very much from a woman's point of view. Act I, Scene 2 offers a rather different set of perspectives.

Look again at the first few speeches of this scene, up to the entrance of Willmore. How would you describe the attitude of these male characters to love and sex?

Discussion

I would say that Frederick takes a deeply cynical and narrow view of love: he describes it as a 'judgment', refers to Florinda as 'that damned virtuous [i.e. chaste] woman', and clearly wants only one thing from women: 'dogs eat me if they were not as troublesome to me i'th morning as they were welcome o'er night'. The comic booby Blunt has a similar attitude, which he expresses more crudely. Belvile, by contrast, is devoted to Florinda,

153

whom he despairs of being able to marry, and is mocked by both Frederick and Blunt for his constancy to one woman. ■

The three men, it seems to me, are very different characters, and this could be brought out in production in various ways. Did you feel, as I do, that Blunt is a wonderful comic creation? You will have noticed that he is given a different social background from the Cavaliers. He is a country squire from Essex who has managed not to get embroiled with the Civil Wars ('I thank my stars I had more grace than to forfeit my estate by cavaliering') and is now taking a 'grand tour' through Europe. The Cavaliers regard him as a bit of an idiot, and despise his stinginess with money. It is important to remember that he is marked out as a fool from the start of the play, and that it is his stupidity and self-deception that lead to his farcical humiliation at the hands of Lucetta. Although in his rage he gives voice to some quite horrifyingly misogynistic sentiments, it is worth asking whether his words can be given much credence, or whether his tirades against women make him look even more ridiculous because he is so easily duped by them.

Belvile, the idealized romantic lover, is totally committed to his beloved Florinda, and their chaste and faithful relationship provides an effective contrast to the libertine ethos espoused by Willmore and Hellena. Even when, under disguise, Florinda tries to tempt him, he remains faithful to his vows. Neither is a particularly witty nor interesting character, but their attempts to behave virtuously in the world of *The Rover* are the source of much of the play's comedy. Although they always act with honourable motives, they seem fated to bring disaster upon themselves: Belvile is arrested in mistake for Willmore when he is trying to help Antonio, while Florinda's attempts to make contact with Belvile place her at the mercy of Willmore and Blunt.

The play's most extensive exploration of love and sex comes in the presentation of the Willmore, Hellena and Angellica triangle, and it is this that I want to focus on. First let us consider Hellena. You will remember that when she first sets eyes on Willmore she is immediately attracted to him, describing him as 'a handsome proper fellow'. Under cover of her gipsy disguise she flirts with him, and before going off arranges to meet him again that afternoon.

Look again at the initial exchanges between Hellena and Willmore, I.2.117–218. Do you think they are presented as equals and, if so, in what ways? The allusion to Jeptha's daughter (line 157) is at first sight puzzling. What do you think its meaning might be? (The note refers you to the story in Judges 11: 29–40.)

Discussion

In the Old Testament story, Jeptha promises God that he will sacrifice the first creature to meet him on his homecoming from battle if he is granted victory over the Ammonites. When his only daughter comes out to meet him Jeptha carries out his vow and sacrifices her. But before he does so he allows her to go off into the mountains for two months to lament the fact that she is to die a virgin. It may strike us as an appalling story, but presumably the point is that in being denied the opportunity to marry and produce children, Jeptha's daughter dies without fulfilling her 'natural' purpose as a woman. Willmore, however, jestingly uses the text to claim biblical authority for seducing Hellena, thus saving her from the fate of dying a virgin. Hellena likewise finds it 'a good text, if well handled', by which I think she is referring to her own plan to avoid the fate of Jeptha's daughter, that is to take active steps to lose her virginity, but very much on her own terms.

What comes across in this whole exchange is how well matched Willmore and Hellena are. Each of them can bandy biblical texts, make light of religious vows, and engage in witty banter. And they are both quite frank about their sexual desires. Willmore has just come on shore after a long sea voyage, and is impatient to be taken to Hellena's lodgings. She likewise has been cooped up in a nunnery, and admits to never having had a lover or been in love, but is certainly 'inclined' that way, fears that Willmore will 'prevail' with her 'tender heart', and warns 'when I begin, I fancy I shall love like anything'. As the play develops, all sorts of little points reinforce this impression that they were 'made for each other'. For example, both of them are frequently described as 'mad' by other characters, a term suggesting a shared propensity to break free from social conventions. They have a similar way of speaking, both being fond of phrases like 'hang me'. Indeed it is their witty talk that most attracts them to each other. Willmore remembers Hellena's 'wit and humour' (I.2.277–8), and feels the need to 'fortify myself against her tongue' (II.1.8); she relates how he 'had charms in every word' (IV.2.231). They themselves recognize that they are of 'one humour' (III.1.160; V.1.431), and Blunt addresses Hellena near the end of the play as 'my little rover' (V.1.510). ∎

Hellena's exchanges with Willmore strike me as among the very best things in the play. I am thinking, for example, of the intricate comedy of the three-way confrontation between Willmore, Hellena and Angellica in IV.2, where each character in turn gains and then loses the upper hand. Or again, of the great final tussle near the end of Act V, where Hellena, for all the libertine rhetoric about the oppressiveness of marriage which she shares with Willmore, nevertheless recognizes the practicalities of her position as a woman, and refuses to have sex with him before he marries her: 'what shall I get? A cradle full of noise and mischief, with a pack of repentance at my back' (V.1.417–18).

Now let us turn to Angellica, who I am sure you will agree is one of the most fascinating characters in the play. **I'd like you to make notes on the stage devices by which she is presented to us in Act II. What do you think the significance of the three paintings might be?**

Discussion

In marked contrast to the introduction of Hellena and Florinda, who are very much presented in their own persons, and speaking for themselves, Angellica is presented to us first by way of conversation about her between male characters. We hear that she is a legendary beauty, who hires herself out by the month. Then in the next scene we find the men grouped outside her house waiting, not for her in person, but for her picture to appear: 'the shadow of the fair substance', which can be enjoyed freely, as Willmore remarks. When the three pictures of her are hung up the men gather round, gazing and talking. Blunt, who has earlier been mocked by the others for his inability to recognize a whore, here wants nothing to do with an expensive courtesan: 'Come, let's be gone; I'm sure we're no chapmen [i.e. traders] for this commodity'. The paintings symbolize Angellica's status as an object of male desire, and what Blunt in his coarse way emphasizes is the equation of sex with commerce. The purpose of the paintings, after all, is to advertise the fact that she is a 'commodity' to be purchased by the highest bidder. ∎

It is perhaps worth pausing here to note that the men on stage are not the only ones gazing at the portrait of Angellica. When, according to the stage direction, 'Willmore gazes on the picture', we as the audience will also be focusing our gaze on the painted representation of Angellica's sexual availability. Just as Willmore's curiosity is fired, so we are curious to see this great beauty, and to that extent we identify with Willmore at this point.

Having gazed at the pictures, the Englishmen go off stage, and while they are gone Angellica appears on the balcony veiled behind a silk curtain. We learn that she is expecting to be bought by either Don Pedro or Don Antonio, and, after a song, she displays herself in person to them. When she withdraws, Willmore returns and steals one of the paintings. Notice that he quite explicitly sees it as a substitute object for Angellica's real body: 'This posture's loose and negligent;/The sight on't would beget a warm desire/In souls whom impotence and age had chilled' (II.1.198–200).

This action seems to be a very calculated gesture on Willmore's part – at the same time an expression of real, or pretended, admiration *and* cleverly designed as a piece of disrespect for the proud Angellica, who will certainly be intrigued by this insolent fellow. Elin Diamond, however, in a fascinating article, '*Gestus* and signature in Aphra Behn's *The Rover*' (1989), sees much more in it. She links the painted representation of Angellica with the changing nature of 'representation' in Restoration theatre, the introduction of painted scenery and interiors, which, she argues, encouraged looking rather than imagining:

> Restoration spectators, unlike their Elizabethan counterparts, were no longer compelled to imagine the features of bed-chambers, parks, or battlefields. Like Richard Flecknoe [author of 'A Short Discourse of the English Stage' (1664)], they could rely on scenes and machines as 'excellent helps of imagination, and most grateful deceptions of the sight … Graceful and becoming Ornaments of the Stage [transport] you easily without lassitude from one place to another, or rather by a kinde of delightful Magick, whilst you sit still, does bring the place to you'. Assuming that Flecknoe's reaction is typical, and there is evidence that it is, Restoration stagecraft seems to have created a spectator-fetishist, one who takes pleasure in ornaments that deceive the sight, whose disavowal of material reality produces a desire for the 'delightful Magick' of exotic and enticing representations.

> (pp.521–2)

Diamond sees the paintings of Angellica as analogous to the painted scenes of the theatres, arguing that in stealing the painting Willmore is, in a sense, 'consuming' the female image in the way that male theatre spectators did.

Further, just as Angellica is a 'commodity' to be bought and sold, so, of course, the Restoration theatre was a place where attractive actresses were picked up by rich aristocrats, including the King himself. Nell Gwyn is the best known of these, but there were many more. In this sense, Diamond argues, *the theatre* is 'selling' both Angellica and the actress playing Angellica:

> When Angellica sings behind her balcony curtain for her Italian [*sic*] admirers, and draws the curtain to reveal a bit of beautiful flesh, then closes it while monetary arrangements are discussed, she performs the titillating masquerade required by her purchasers *and* by her spectators. This is mastery's masquerade, not to demonstrate freedom, but to flaunt the charms that guarantee and uphold male power.
>
> (p.532)

Diamond's reading of this episode is certainly suggestive and thought-provoking. I wonder, however, how far it can incorporate what seems to me to be an equally important fact about the presentation of Angellica, which is that she feels herself to be in a powerful position: 'their wonder feeds my vanity, and he that wishes but to buy gives me more pride than he that gives my price can make my pleasure' (lines 111–13). It could be argued that Angellica has *encouraged* the men to treat her as an 'object': the paintings were displayed on her orders, and in full knowledge of the effect they would have. Her reputation as a fabulously expensive courtesan allows her a degree of independence and power over men.

The question then arises as to why the proud Angellica yields herself freely to the penniless Willmore. Look carefully at the arguments he uses in II.2 and pick out the main points in their exchange.

Discussion

The exchanges between Willmore and Angellica in II.2. take the form of an intellectual duel. They immediately argue over the rights and wrongs of her profession. Willmore attacks her for charging money for love which, he says, should not be 'meanly bartered for' (lines 11–12). Moretta will have no truck with this doctrine and roundly berates Willmore when he jestingly tries to bargain for 'a pistole's worth of this vain gay thing' (line 32). The subsequent discussion between Willmore and Angellica is undertaken in blank verse (one of the longest such passages in the play), giving it a heightened emotional power.

The argument of Willmore's first verse speech is intricate and, in its way, very cunningly organized. He first of all claims to be a gentleman who, as such, would not stoop to selling his body, and he condemns her for doing so. Nevertheless, he won't deny he is attracted to her, and would pay her price if he were able. But the knowledge that she would sordidly take money from him is sufficient to cure his desire for her. Then comes a brilliantly calculated couplet – given added emphasis by the stage directions to hold her, look on her, pause, and sigh – 'By heav'n, bright creature, I would not for the world/Thy fame were half so fair as is thy face' (lines 65–6): that is, it is just as well she does not have a better reputation because then he might not be able to stop himself falling in love with her. By saying this, of course, Willmore is cleverly managing to plant in her mind the idea that he just might. Her aside reveals that he has achieved the desired effect: 'His words go through me to the very soul' (line 67). He proceeds to claim that what he is feeling must only be lust: had it been true love he would be flinging himself at her feet, whereas in fact he can bear to be scorned and denied her favours. His whole technique here is to say and do things that are outwardly insulting but, on reflection, flattering.

Angellica's response is to throw the accusation of being mercenary back at him. If he were looking for a wife he would be more concerned with her fortune than with her beauty or virtue. He disarmingly agrees, and offers no defence of this 'barbarous custom' (though as we shall later discover, in IV.2, he is not in fact uninterested to discover that Hellena is worth a lot of money). She proudly declares that no amount of money could buy her *love*, and offers herself to him freely, as a lover. Willmore's asides confirm to us that he has only been feigning contempt, and he is clearly taken aback by her offer. Neither of them know quite how to react in a situation of genuine emotion: they both get angry and perhaps misunderstand each other. He pretends, at least, to believe that she is trying to trick him, provoking her to turn away with pride. But when he claims that he is capable of being vanquished by the power of love, her resistance crumbles completely, though she recognizes that she is losing her freedom as a result. The haste with which he swears love while sweeping her off to the bedroom makes it clear to us that, after all, for him it is only a game. ■

This is, I imagine you will agree, a complex and fascinating scene. It is not absolutely clear how far Willmore is experiencing anything beyond physical lust, or whether at any point he is being wholly serious. There are moments when he seems to feel a flicker of genuine emotion, and finds himself attracted to Angellica – an unexpected and unwelcome feeling. But it is also possible that he is cynically manipulating her throughout. How we respond to the scene will depend very much on how it is played, and on the casting. If Willmore was portrayed as a more attractive character than Angellica, an audience might well simply enjoy seeing him get his way. I think that Behn, though giving Willmore's power to attract its full weight, nevertheless also encourages us to sympathize with Angellica, and that this should come across in performance. She is torn between the claims of a romantic love, which she for the first time is entering into freely, and the pragmatic reality that for a woman in her position the only possibility of economic survival, and of satisfaction for her pride, lies in her ability to sell her body. Knowing what we know of Willmore, we can't help but feel that in opting for romantic passion she has made a disastrous choice.

It is worth dwelling just for a moment on why Behn presents Angellica, a high-class prostitute, with such sympathy. Dramatic representations of prostitutes in earlier drama could often be very moralistic in tone. Here, for example, is a piece from John Marston's play, *The Dutch Courtesan* (1605), in which the hero compares his virginal wife-to-be with a prostitute whom he has just cast off:

158

O Heaven,
What difference is in women and their life!
What man, but worthy name of man, would leave
The modest pleasures of a lawful bed,
The holy union of two equal hearts,
Mutually holding either dear as health,
The undoubted issues, joys of chaste sheets,
The unfeigned embrace of sober ignorance,
To twine th'unhealthful loins of common loves,
The prostituted impudence of things
Senseless like those by cataracts of Nile,
Their use so vile takes away sense! How vile
To love a creature made of blood and hell,
Whose use makes weak, whose company doth shame,
Whose bed doth beggar, issue doth defame!

Nancy Copeland, who quotes this passage in her article '"Once a whore and ever"?' (1992), notes that Killigrew's *Thomaso* preserves this absolute distinction between virgin and prostitute. Thomaso's rejection of Angellica in favour of Serulina is presented in the play as a mark of his maturity. Copeland also draws attention to the significant fact that Killigrew's Angellica is deeply ashamed of her status as a prostitute, begging Thomaso to forgive her for her faults and wishing that her tears 'could make me as pure a virgin as I am now a perfect lover'. By contrast, Behn's Angellica at no stage expresses remorse or repentance for her loss of virginity; indeed her ruling passion is pride, especially pride at being at the top of her profession, in a class by herself.

It is worth exploring a little further the ways in which Angellica is presented in *The Rover* as a sympathetic character, and her relationship to the other women characters in the play. **Think about points that encourage us to sympathize with Angellica's plight, and jot these down. Then note some ways in which Angellica may be linked to, or may seem to resemble, both Hellena and Florinda. Finally, consider possible ways in which Angellica might be linked to Behn herself.**

Discussion

It seems to me that Behn goes to some lengths to make us understand and sympathize with Angellica's plight, presenting her as a woman facing problems all women face. For example, the play reveals clearly the very limited choices open to women, and their lack of control over their lives, as they are bought and sold into marriage. In such a corrupt, materialistic society, where men are eager to avail themselves of the sexual services provided by prostitutes or courtesans, it is difficult to blame the individuals, like Angellica, who provide these services. The play thus forces us to ask whether what Angellica does is any worse than what happens to women forced into mercenary and loveless marriages.

But perhaps the feature of Angellica that most compels our sympathy is her readiness to choose a different kind of love: one entered into freely, not sold as a commodity. It is, of course, a telling irony that she, a courtesan whose sexual favours are paid for, should be the character through whom Behn makes this point. Together with Willmore in the wooing scene, she expresses her contempt for mercenary marriage and, by implication, for a society in which human relationships are reduced to economic exchange.

What of Angellica's relationship to other women characters in the play? The most obvious comparison is with Hellena, her rival for Willmore, and there are several intriguing links and parallels between the two women. Both of them express 'libertine' sentiments, acknowledging and acting upon their sexual desires. There is also an important financial connection. Both women have come into the possession of money from the same source. The old man who formerly kept Angellica is also the uncle who has left Hellena 'two hundred thousand crowns' (IV.2.185). This means that the gold Willmore receives from Angellica (III.1.99) – which presumably explains the change of costume from the 'buff' soldier's coat when he enters in IV.2.87 (stage direction) 'finely dressed' – comes from the same source as the fortune he will earn by marrying the heiress Hellena. Both women also engage in battles of wit with Willmore, taking on a 'masculine' assertiveness as they do so. Both, too, advertise their charms to him, Angellica by means of her picture, Hellena by revealing her face to him (III.1.174). It is also perhaps significant that even Florinda in a sense 'advertises' herself to Belvile by means of her portrait in a locket (III.1.246).

Figure 5.5 Angellica pursuing Willmore with a pistol, engraving by G. Van der Gucht, used as the frontispiece of an edition of *The Rover*, 1735, W. Feales.

What, finally, of the links between Angellica and Behn herself? Several critics have commented on the odd coincidence that they share the same initials: could this indicate an identification at some level between Behn and her fictional character? As I mentioned earlier, Angellica's is the only name from the main plot of *Thomaso* that Behn did not change. Perhaps one link, whether conscious or not, is that, like Angellica, Behn as a woman writer is selling her wares – 'exposing' herself publicly for money. ■

Whatever you think of the last point, it seems clear that Behn, in her treatment of Angellica, has moved away from the stereotypical presentation of a courtesan. Far from being condemned, Angellica is treated with compassion and understanding, though the final scene in which she pursues Willmore round the stage with a pistol could be played with a good deal of comedy. Her generosity of spirit contrasts sharply with that of

Willmore. Tempted to avenge herself for his infidelity by shooting him, in the end she forgives him.

This leads us to consider the character of Willmore himself. **Looking back over your notes, and thinking about his actions in the course of the play, how would you describe his personality?**

D i s c u s s i o n

I guess that the first thing you will have commented on is Willmore's insatiable sexual appetite: no woman is safe from his advances. The very mention of Angellica has him longing 'for my arms full of soft, white, kind woman' (II.1.13–14) and, as we have seen, he persuades her to fall for him. When he subsequently sees Hellena's face he is in raptures and swears devotion, but later that same night he drunkenly assaults Florinda, and then proposes to visit Angellica again. He is incorrigible to the end of the play. Even when Florinda is generously forgiving him, his thoughts are lecherous (see V.1.140). ∎

All this is to say that Willmore is a rake, and to that extent he is a stock figure in Restoration comedy. (The word 'rake' is an abbreviation of 'rake-hell', used commonly in the seventeenth century to describe someone who is utterly immoral, boldly debauched and dissolute.) However it is important to be clear about what kind of rake he is. In a useful article, 'The extravagant rake in Restoration comedy' (1972), Robert Jordan draws a distinction between two major types of rake, which he terms the 'judicious' and the 'extravagant'. Both of them flout the conventional social and moral codes of good behaviour, but whereas the 'judicious' rake is smooth, polished and self-controlled, the 'extravagant' rake lives life with a frenetic intensity, is promiscuous, crazily impulsive, reckless, impudent, frivolous, vain, self-assured and given to exaggerated claims or boasts. Most of all, he stands out sharply from his companions, who usually treat him as a quite unique phenomenon and regard his mad exploits with a mixture of astonishment and affection. He is not a fool, despite his wildness, but he is undoubtedly a comic figure: 'One not only laughs with him in his verbal sallies, one also laughs at him in his extravagances'.

It will be seen, I think, that Jordan's account of the 'extravagant rake' fits Willmore like a glove. It is quite clear that he is in a different class from Frederick, Belvile and Blunt, who frequently refer to him as a 'mad fellow'. His remorseless pursuit of women, his boastfulness, his impulsiveness and his generally 'over the top' behaviour all mark him out. He is also something of a buffoon, with a genius for misinterpreting what is going on – to the extreme irritation of his friends (see, for example, IV.2.113).

So how are we to respond to such a character? From one point of view Willmore might seem a decidedly unattractive proposition. It could be said that he cynically exploits Angellica; he is only prevented from raping a young woman (Florinda) by the arrival of his friends; and it is not at all clear that he would be marrying Hellena were it not for her money. Can we really warm to such a character, or laugh indulgently at his escapades? If not, if we find his behaviour horrifying, how do we explain the fact that Hellena continues to be attracted to him?

Jordan, for his part, emphasizes the entertainment value of the 'extravagant rake' figure. According to him, 'the sheer comicality of these rakes is one of the strongest influences towards the throwing of a mellow glow over their misdemeanours'. He cites as evidence for this Hellena's excuse for Willmore: 'Now if I should be hanged I can't be angry with him, he dissembles so heartily' (III.1.130–1), remarking that 'the adverb "heartily" is one that could be applied to any action of the extravagant rake'. Other characters seem to have a soft spot for Willmore: even Belvile, though he criticizes him quite harshly at times, admits that he does not want to see the 'rogue' killed (III.6.54).

More significantly, perhaps, Jordan draws attention to the fact that quite a number of Restoration comedies featuring extravagant rakes are set at a time of carnival or other public celebration, when a relaxation of the tensions and restraints of normal social behaviour is licensed. He sees the extravagant rake as personifying this carnival role:

> To experience him in the safe confines of the play is to experience the
> spirit of carnival. He is a one-man *mardi gras* and provides the
> appropriate therapeutic release for the audience irrespective of
> whether or not he is put in a carnival setting. In him the customary
> restraints are thrown off with a wild exuberance and an unashamed
> joy, and if he does finally dwindle into a husband this could be said to
> mark the passing of carnival and the acceptance of responsibility.
>
> (pp.87–8)

The 'release' provided by the extravagant rake, Jordan notes, was not just from sexual restraint, but also from the inhibitions of 'decorum' – the rules of 'polite' social behaviour which were so important a feature of fashionable Restoration society.

Jordan's argument is interesting and valuable, it seems to me, in that it forces us to think about the whole question of the purpose or function of comedy as a genre, an issue that Kate Clarke will discuss in the next chapter. But perhaps you felt, as I do, that an appeal to genre to excuse such behaviour does not remove our sense of unease about some of Willmore's actions. It somehow does not seem possible to regard scenes of near-rape as a joyous expression of the spirit of carnival. However well Jordan's thesis may fit some other Restoration comedies, it does not seem adequate as an account of the rather more complex and disturbing play Behn has written. That is to say, it tends to reduce a powerful social satire to a mere romp.

By describing *The Rover* as 'a powerful social satire' I am, of course, claiming that Behn is offering a serious criticism of contemporary social and sexual conventions. In particular, she is opening up the whole question of the sexual 'double standard' by which 'rakish' behaviour in men seems to be tolerated, and is certainly no bar to their marrying well, whereas for women to engage in sex outside marriage is to wreck irretrievably any chance of respectable marriage. Not surprisingly issues like these, and whether Behn's own views can be described as 'feminist', have lain at the heart of much recent criticism of her work, and it is to these that we now turn.

The Rover: *a feminist play?*

The modern feminist revival of interest in Behn may be said to have begun with Virginia Woolf. In a famous passage in *A Room of One's Own* (1929), she declared that 'All women together ought to let flowers fall upon the tomb of Aphra Behn ... for it was she who earned them the right to speak their minds'. Cheri Davis Langdell, in her article 'Aphra Behn and sexual politics' (1985), goes even further. For her, Behn is 'the first feminist writer, the first woman writer conscious politically and sexually of the potentially revolutionary or subversive character of a woman's act of contributing to a literary tradition not intrinsically her own' (p.114).

Recently, however, questions have been raised about how far Behn can be described as a feminist, and in particular whether her plays can without qualification be presented as feminist works. Katherine Rogers, in her book *Feminism in Eighteenth-Century England* (1982), finds little evidence of feminism in Behn's plays, arguing that *The Rover* reveals 'a more masculine set of values' than comparable works by male dramatists of the period. Rogers admits that Behn forthrightly defends women and women writers in her published prefaces and in prologues and epilogues to her plays, but argues that these feminist principles are 'in no way integrated into her creative works':

> Willmore, the Rover, presented as the most attractive male in the play, is a bully, a drunkard, and an unabashed exploiter of women. But Behn suggests no criticism of his behaviour, and rewards him with Hellena, the most desirable of the women, who brings him a fortune of 300,000 crowns ... Even though Hellena has sprightliness and wit, she is far from Willmore's equal. She teases him only very mildly, and not to establish any rights – only to attract and catch him. He thinks of her seriously only after he learns she can bring him a fortune ... Though Behn does assert the right of women, as well as men, to win the people they love, she seems to accept men's emotional domination as natural and proper ... Willmore is the embodiment of the rake who uses women without the slightest consideration for their rights and feelings, who sees nothing in a woman but her body and makes every effort to enjoy it without offering her any return. Behn seems to accept without criticism this callous world in which the strong dominate the weak and her own sex is consequently victimised.
>
> (pp.98–9)

From your own reading and study of *The Rover*, how would you answer Rogers' claim that it reveals a 'masculine set of values' and that feminist principles are in no way integrated into it?

Discussion

Here are my points:

1   Far from being found only in prefaces, prologues and epilogues, Behn's criticism of the oppressive restrictions placed on women is a central concern of *The Rover*, as we saw in our discussion of the critique of forced marriage in the first scene.

2   In *The Rover* Behn gives women characters a striking degree of power and independence. This is most obviously true of the forceful, witty heroine, Hellena, who takes the initiative and acts with much boldness and energy in her pursuit of Willmore; but it is also true of most of the other women. Faced with male authority, and threatened with male violence and rape, most of them nevertheless manage to achieve what they want.

3   In *The Rover* Behn holds up as an ideal a sexual equality between women and men. She recognizes women's physical desires and their right to satisfy these. But although she rejects the sexual double standard, she shows clearly how it operates. For all his promiscuity, Willmore is able to marry a respectable, virgin heiress. Angellica, by contrast, having lost her reputation is unable to re-enter 'respectable' society.

4   Behn presents Angellica, the courtesan, as a sympathetic figure who, fatally for a woman in her position, has given her 'virgin heart' to a man. Paradoxically, perhaps, she is in a far more vulnerable position than Hellena, as well as being less tough-minded. Wanting for the first time in her life to believe that love could be separated from financial considerations, her passionate outburst of anger at her betrayal by Willmore casts a shadow over the final scene of the play in which the lovers are paired off.

5   Finally, Behn's treatment of the near-rape scenes seems profoundly feminist. In these scenes she shows how the seemingly hearty, rakish libertinism of the men – which on one level can be very attractive – can easily degenerate into violence and rape. Her insight into the psychology of rape comes out not only in Blunt's misogynistic rage against women in general (IV.5.1–16) but in giving Willmore the classic rapist's defence, that the woman is to blame for provoking him: 'a judge were he young and vigorous, and saw those eyes of thine, would know 'twas they gave the first blow, the first provocation' (III.5.38–9). ■

These are only some of the points that could be made in response to Rogers, and you may have thought of others. Equally, you may have wanted to argue against, or at least qualify, the idea of Behn as a feminist, or *The Rover* as a feminist play. If so, you would not be alone. Indeed the trend of some recent feminist analysis of Behn's work has been to question her status as a straightforward feminist champion, asking how this can be reconciled with her 'conservative' royalist politics, and finding her a more complex and paradoxical figure than the legend would suggest. For these critics, Behn's feminism lies less in her assertion of women's rights, or her presentation of powerful and active women characters, as in her demonstration of the extent of patriarchal control over women's lives.

To end this section I will give you extracts from some recent critical accounts of *The Rover*, picking out one or two points for further discussion, but also leaving you to think about how far these arguments fit with your own view of the play.

The question of Behn's 'feminism' is tackled in Jacqueline Pearson's book, *The Prostituted Muse* (1988). Her response is in marked contrast to that of Rogers, but are there any points here you might want to query?

> Behn ... depicts personal relationships as political struggles for power which, at least in the early and middle plays, are unusually often won by women. Her typical dramatic pattern shows a wild, witty heroine actively intriguing to win the man she has chosen. In these plays the domination and control of the women and the relative passivity of the men are striking. The most brilliant example is the first part of *The Rover* ... Hellena ... plays a brilliant game of disguise and deception while Willmore is a passive centre of the intrigues of the women rather than, as they are, an active mover. Moreover, he is increasingly subject to criticism or mockery ... In contrast to the passive, ineffectual or drunken Willmore, the play's women have unusual power and independence. Even the sentimental Florinda, who comes closest to a stereotype of female passivity (she is threatened with rape three times and needs to be rescued by a man!), is prepared to fight actively to gain the man she loves and escape the 'confinement' of forced marriage. Hellena too insists on her 'freedom' to do as she chooses, not even coerced by the man she loves ... At every turn she stresses her own rights to self-determination: 'I don't intend every he that likes me shall have me, but he that I like' (III.1.35). She assumes an air of irresponsibility, parodying Willmore's own rakishness – 'I profess myself the gay, the kind, and the inconstant' (III.1.166) – and this carefree style wins him when Angellica Bianca's emotional intensity fails. She finally accepts him, and is promised a relationship without coercion: 'I am of a nation that are of opinion a woman's honour is not worth guarding when she has a mind to part with it' (V.1.487–8).
>
> The extreme example of women's manipulating independence and men's passivity, though, comes in a subplot. Blunt is tricked by the 'jilting wench' Lucetta, who makes an assignation with him but instead of sleeping with him robs him and has him thrown into a drain ... Lucetta is, unconventionally, not punished but escapes scot-free, an extreme example of the power of women and the powerlessness of men in this play. The play celebrates this female power, though even in this cheerful and vivid play it has a dark side. One woman's victory is another's defeat, and if Hellena wins Willmore, Angellica Bianca must lose him. Moreover, Lucetta's victory over Blunt leaves him so angry at women that he attempts to rape Florinda, an act explicitly defined as a result of thwarted power and 'deliberated malice' (IV.5.44) rather than thwarted lust ... The play creates extreme images of female power (Hellena's disguises, the pistol with which Angellica Bianca threatens Willmore, Lucetta's trickery) and powerlessness (Florinda's being in almost constant danger of rape).
>
> (pp.152–4)

Perhaps you feel, as I do, that Pearson is overstating her argument in places. Willmore is hardly so entirely passive as she suggests, and it is exaggerating to imply that Lucetta's activities are 'celebrated'. Is she really so powerful? To what extent is she working with (or for) Phillipo and Sancho?

Another critic, Nancy Cotton, argues in her article 'Aphra Behn and the pattern hero' (1991) that *The Rover* is basically a romantic comedy 'glamorising the days of royalist exile', with Willmore unambiguously portrayed as an attractive, dashing figure: 'good-natured and fun-loving ... a man always ready to enjoy women, wine and swordplay. His penniless condition is a sign of his virtue; like many a real-life cavalier, he lost his estate in the service of his prince'. If this was how the character was played it would help explain why *The Rover* was so popular at court and with Royalist audiences. According to this reading, 'the butt of the play, Ned Blunt' is set up as a foil to enhance the hero:

> Like Willmore, Blunt becomes involved with a prostitute, but, while Willmore attracts a beautiful, wealthy courtesan who dotes on him and gives him money, Blunt is tricked and robbed by a whore ... the play implies not that whoring is foolish, but that Blunt is simply not the man that Willmore is, that he just can't measure up. Blunt's humiliation enhances rather than undercuts the hero.
>
> (p.215)

By contrast, Jones DeRitter in 'The gypsy, *The Rover*, and the wanderer' (1986) sees Willmore as the prime focus of Behn's satire, arguing that 'the most powerful criticism of Behn's title character is suggested by the parallels between Blunt and Willmore':

> Willmore's attempt to rape Florinda occurs immediately after Blunt's misadventure with Lucetta: when Florinda discovers that the intruder in her garden is not Belvile, her description of Willmore as 'a filthy beast' (III.5.28) reminds the audience of Blunt, who has just fallen through a trap door into a sewer ... Lucetta's cozening of Blunt reflects Willmore's cozening of Angellica; the assault and robbery on the one hand, and the rape of emotions on the other, make both Angellica and Blunt into revenge-minded victims ... Willmore is damned not only by his association with Blunt, but also by Behn's sympathetic treatment of the women he assaults. Behn's distinctive treatment of sexual violence and Belvile's furious response to Willmore's behaviour ... drive a wedge between Behn's audience and her title character.
>
> (p.87)

The final extract is from an essay by Heidi Hutner, 'Revisioning the female body' (1993). This is much the longest and most complex extract, and you may need to read it a couple of times to follow Hutner's argument.

> Both Angellica and Hellena dress as males to assert their wills. Angellica wants to seek revenge upon Willmore by her own hand, so she dresses as a man and attempts to kill him with a pistol; the weapon is symbolic of her attempt to usurp phallic control. Significantly, Angellica does not succeed in killing him, and she is led back into her role as courtesan by Pedro [*sic*]. Hellena does – temporarily – win her Rover at the end of part I by imitating his language and behaviour. Yet, when Hellena attempts to obtain the object of her desire by dressing as a male page who will lead the Rover away from Angellica, Willmore discovers the phallic disguise and turns it against her ... The (male) costume, therefore, is not

empowering for Hellena or Angellica in this royalist satire. Willmore's attacks upon the multiplicity of female identities – the masks of the gypsy and the male page – force Hellena and Angellica into traditional roles as disempowered objects of male desire (the wife and the prostitute) ...

Florinda is Behn's revision of Killigrew's Serulina ... What makes Florinda markedly different from Serulina is her choice of a lover. The virgin Serulina is also virtuous, but her lover is not; her goodness is supposed to reform him. Belvile, in contrast, is Florinda's equal, not her opposite. Behn's revision implies that if women are to be virtuous, men must be virtuous too. Florinda is stereotypically good – unappropriative, passive – but so is Belvile.

However, despite Florinda's passive sexual nature and her choice of Belvile because of his genuinely good character (as opposed to Hellena's and Angellica's passionate desire for and self-destructive choice of the untrustworthy Willmore), she ... is subject to a series of attempted rapes, first by Willmore, then by Blunt and Frederick, and finally by a group of men, including her own brother, Pedro ...

Blunt is angry because he has been stripped of his masculine garb; Lucetta – a lower-class petty thief and prostitute – has pretended to seduce him to steal his belongings. Lucetta has stripped him of his clothes/costume, reversing the traditional seduction (like that of Angellica Bianca by the Rover) in which the woman, as the object of desire, is seduced and abandoned. The masked and innocent Florinda, seeking shelter, enters Blunt's lair while trying to escape her brother. Blunt, who is tellingly another good friend of Belvile's, blames all women for his being duped; he sees women as one mass body to be taken, beaten, or abducted as a man desires, although he later accepts the class distinction between a woman of quality and a whore. He wants to 'pull off their false faces', just as his mask has been removed (V.1.516) ... In effect, Behn suggests that Blunt finds it necessary to master a woman because he cannot master himself. In order for the duped Blunt to regain his manly authority, he attacks a woman – any woman. Punning on the image of the highly priced portrait of Angellica, which none of the cavaliers can afford, Blunt then says he will strip Florinda 'stark naked' and hang her out his window 'by the heels, with a paper of scurvy verses fastened to [her] breast, in praise of damnable women' (IV.5.47–8). For Blunt, whore and virgin are interchangeable in the market of the patrilineal masquerade – they are 'as much one as t'other' (IV.5.36). Behn comically disrupts the masculinist discourse of the masquerade, however, by putting it in the mouth of Blunt, the powerless fool with the 'old rusty sword' (IV.5.6), whom the banished cavaliers associate with only for his money.

Despite Florinda's traditionally feminine passive nature, she is ultimately subject to the same verbal and physical abuse and condemnation by the masculinist ideology of her culture as Hellena and Angellica – the desiring women who love a rake. Confronted by the would-be rapists in Act V, including Florinda's brother, who preys unknowingly upon his sister, the circling wolves ironically decide to let the man with the 'longest sword carr[y] her' (V.1.86–7). As it turns out, her brother, 'Pedro, being as a Spaniard, ha[s] the longest' phallus/sword, and he wins Florinda (V.1.88, stage direction). Willmore suggests that Pedro allow the 'lady [to] ... choose her man', however (V.1.108–9). The mask allows Florinda to appear to make this decision at least because Pedro does not realize the effect of what he has done when he says, 'I am better bred than not to leave her choice free' (V.1.110). Yet, significantly, what Pedro offers his sister is no free choice at all: Pedro does not know who Florinda is when he makes this offer; as far as he is aware, he merely allows a nameless and faceless whore/woman to choose her own rapist. Thus Florinda's less aggressive and, hence, more morally correct character (according to the patrilineal economy that constrains and confines her), ultimately affords her no freedom or protection from men's violation and abuse. In this manner, Behn demonstrates that in a patriarchal economy virgin and whore are equally subject to male domination.

(pp.108–11)

I'd like you to say, in two or three sentences, what Hutner's overall point is. Then, can you think of any objections that could be made against her argument?

Discussion

Hutner seems to be arguing that women in *The Rover* cannot win, whether they attempt to challenge male power by adopting a 'masculine' assertiveness, like Angellica and Hellena, or remain passively virtuous and 'feminine', like Florinda. What *The Rover* demonstrates most of all is the power of patriarchy to control and abuse women.

A number of objections occur to me. One concerns the opening paragraph, where Hutner builds much on Angellica dressing as a man. In fact all the stage direction says is that she is led in by a boy, 'in a masquing habit and a vizard', and Willmore immediately mistakes her for Hellena. A second objection is that Florinda's passivity is exaggerated – though not so bold as Hellena, she is certainly not entirely passive (for example, her setting up of the meeting with Belvile). Finally, it is not easy to see how Hutner's reading could be made to work on stage. For example, unless the part of Hellena has been cast very oddly indeed, the audience will be strongly behind her, and it is difficult to see how, at the end of the play, when she has in fact captured Willmore, the actress could bring us round to thinking of her as nothing more than the 'disempowered object of male desire'. ■

This last point brings us back again to the whole issue of performance. Lizbeth Goodman is going to say more about this, but before she does so I will give a brief account of *The Rover's* fortunes on stage.

A history of productions of The Rover

When *The Rover* opened in March 1677 at the Dorset Garden theatre the main parts were taken by some of the most famous actors of the time. Willmore was played by William Smith, one of the leading actors in the Duke's Company, and himself, appropriately, a veteran Cavalier and well-known supporter of the Stuart cause. Hellena was played by Elizabeth Barry, generally regarded as the most accomplished of the early English actresses. She was for several years the mistress of the Earl of Rochester, and bore his daughter in December 1677. Thomas Betterton and his wife Mary played Belvile and Florinda. Mary Betterton, one of the first women to go on the stage, was very popular with audiences, and went on to become a noted teacher of young actresses. Thomas Betterton was by common consent the greatest actor and theatre manager of the age, legendary for the trouble he took in preparing himself for roles. Anne Quin, who played Angellica, had been associated with the King's Company from the early 1660s. Less is known about her career, partly because she seems to have left the stage for about ten years after her marriage, but she was particularly noted for her striking beauty. Finally, the part of Blunt was taken by Cave Underhill, the most celebrated comedian of his time. A contemporary thought that Underhill had no rivals in his 'dry, heavy, downright way in low comedy', and he continued to perform the role until 1710.

Altogether it was a magnificent cast, whose combined talents must have contributed greatly to the play's immediate success. The production was a great favourite of Charles II, who regularly came to performances, and even arranged a special private performance at Whitehall in February 1680. The play continued to be popular with London audiences until the middle of the eighteenth century, with most of the famous actors of the time taking the lead roles.

One question that immediately arises is why *The Rover* and other plays like it survived so long, given the moralistic reaction against Restoration comedy which, as we have seen, got under way in the late seventeenth century. A partial answer is to be found in the promptbook for an early eighteenth-century production, discovered and published by Edward A. Langhans. The chief function of the promptbook was to record entrances and exits, but cuts and other alterations to the text were also marked. A close study of these changes indicates an extensive clean-up operation, with most of the swearing, libertine wit and sexual references removed or toned down considerably. For example, in the first scene the phrases 'a belch or two, loud as a musket' and 'expects you in his foul sheets' are cut from Hellena's speech, and her speech saying that marriage to Don Vincentio would be worse than adultery is completely cut. Later on, Blunt's speech on emerging from the sewer (III.4) is omitted entirely, and extensive cuts are made to his speeches threatening Florinda with violent rape (IV.5). Many of Willmore's more outrageous speeches are cut: for example, his dismissals of female chastity (IV.2.360–3), and of marriage (V.1.411–12), and expressions like 'damned' or 'By Heaven' are removed throughout.

This process of toning down Behn's Restoration frankness no doubt continued in productions up to the 1760s, after which *The Rover* disappeared from the stage altogether. In 1790 an adaptation entitled *Love in Many Masks* was put on at Drury Lane. This was the work of John Philip Kemble, the famous actor-manager, who himself played Willmore. Kemble produced over fifty such adaptations of earlier plays, including many by Shakespeare, freely rearranging and rewriting the originals. *Love in Many Masks* followed the structure of *The Rover*, but cut out all the 'objectionable' passages. Its genteel flavour may be judged by what happens to the sardonic final couplet. Willmore's 'Lead on; no other dangers they can dread,/Who venture in the storms o'th' marriage bed' became, in Kemble's version,

Henceforth no other pleasures can I know,
Than those of fond fidelity to you;
Your pow'r my captive heart in chains shall bind,
Sweet as the graces of your face and mind: –
Blest in my friends, and doubly blest in love,
My joy's complete indeed – if you approve.

The first major restaging of a play by Behn in the twentieth century was a production of *The Lucky Chance* by the Women's Playhouse Trust in 1984. Its success was followed up by the Royal Shakespeare Company (RSC) staging of *The Rover* in 1986. Oddly enough this revival of *The Rover* was, like Kemble's, in an extensively altered version. The play was presented in the inaugural season of the new Swan Theatre at Stratford-upon-Avon, and transferred to the Mermaid Theatre in London where it remained in the RSC repertory for a further two years. This RSC *Rover* was directed by John Barton. The text was published with a commentary by Simon Trussler, and in a 'Director's Note', Barton described his alterations:

> This is an adapted text. The original adaptation was made before rehearsals began, but it was much altered in the course of rehearsal. About 550 lines have been cut and some 350 added.
>
> Many of the new lines are taken from an earlier source play which Aphra Behn herself used extensively when she wrote *The Rover*. This is *Thomaso, or The Wanderer* by Thomas Killigrew, published in 1664. Aphra Behn took over many of its situations, characters and lines, sometimes word for word. Though *The Rover* is a far better play, it is hazy and loose in places, and *Thomaso* has the edge at specific moments.
>
> The alterations I have made are partly to streamline our version and help to clarify a confusing plot. The most obvious change is the turning of Belvile into a black soldier of fortune, and the setting of the play in a Spanish colony rather than in Spain [*sic*]. I have however, deliberately avoided naming a specific location. The most obvious addition is that Valeria is introduced earlier in the action. Aphra Behn seems to regard her as an important engine of the plot, but does not have her speak until well into the play. The scene between Blunt and Lucetta is now closer to *Thomaso* than *The Rover*, Angellica's part has been expanded in the first half, as have the parts of Sebastian, Biskey and Sancho. And there are a number of substantial transpositions, particularly in the first four scenes.
>
> (p.20)

Barton's attitude to Behn's text strikes me as extremely patronizing, not to say arrogant. Clearly he thought that poor Aphra Behn needed quite a lot of help from him to 'steamline' her 'confusing' play. As his note suggests, this help went far beyond the minor cuts and alterations often made in productions of plays. In addition to substantial cuts and transpositions, whole swathes of new lines were added, some taken from Killigrew and some freshly written, presumably by Barton himself. Certain characters were considerably altered. For example, Lucetta, a lively, rapacious prostitute in Behn's play, becomes a sorrowful black slave who only reluctantly engages in prostitution; Valeria becomes a sister of Florinda and

170

Hellena, and her part is greatly expanded by giving her some of their lines as well as new ones; Belvile becomes a black soldier of fortune, and a passage is added to explain how such a character ended up in England fighting for King Charles (a deeply unconvincing explanation, it must be said).

The part of Willmore was played by Jeremy Irons, and that of Hellena by Imogen Stubbs. These well-known RSC stars clearly shared Barton's view of Behn's play as can be seen from interviews published in *This Golden Round* (1989), edited by Ronnie Mulryne and Margaret Shewring. Irons described it as 'a very fragile little ship' which had been greatly strengthened by Barton's direction and the changes introduced during rehearsals: 'Sometimes we found ourselves reverting to Behn's own work. It is a very complicated little machine, that play – even if it stutters in places … One of the principal achievements of the final version was the strengthening of the part of Angellica' (p.106). Stubbs, too, had a very low opinion of Behn's original work:

> I don't think people would have enjoyed the original version before John Barton adapted it. The way we did it, it was a people's play … a 'Carry on up the Rover' production ... We changed the original script a lot, and most of it was made up between the lines. People playing the original script can't understand how we got it to work and to be so successful. Most of the energy and invention were put in by the company. It played almost as a Brian Rix farce. People objected because they thought it was meant to be very feminist – but it isn't. And it wouldn't have been.
>
> (p.110)

In fact, very few reviewers 'objected' to this production. On the contrary, most of them praised it as a highly entertaining show. As the *Punch* reviewer put it (23 July 1986): 'John Barton gives us a joyous Restoration romp … Jeremy Irons leads for the men in a performance of marvellous bravura, a pirate king let loose to buckle his swash through streets where public signboards announce the availability of the most famous local courtesan'. The production was a spectacular affair, with colourful carnival costumes, live music, indoor fireworks, elaborately choreographed sword-fights, and a good deal of gratuitous female undressing on stage. The near-rape scenes were by all accounts very funny, and in general much emphasis was placed on the sexual appetites of the women. As Callis puts it in a speech written for Barton's version: 'tis true, all men are stark mad for wenches, so is it true … that we wenches are as inly stark as men'.

However entertaining it might have been, Barton's *Rover* had evidently very little to do with the play Behn wrote. Jessica Munns, in a devastating critique, 'Barton and Behn's *The Rover*' (1988), objects, I think rightly, to Barton's clumsy attempt to 'improve' Behn's work. In Munns's view, Barton's alterations simplify or ignore the complexities of *The Rover*, robbing it of its power to disturb, as well as entertain.

> His alterations substitute an easy and uncontroversial modern approval of female sexual liberation and aggression for a more complex and alien attempt to balance male and female needs which are not seen as

the same. The colonial material is simply intrusive: fashionable but irrelevant. In seeking recognition of Behn's relevance for today, Barton obscures the points at which we can find genuine parallels between Behn's texts and our social contexts. Just as importantly, he obscures the points at which Behn's values and moral patterns are not our own. A bland and rather smug sympathy for the under-dog smooths down the tougher edges of the work and encourages an ahistorical and fundamentally apolitical approach to dramas from the past. In essence, it turns out, seventeenth-century folk were just like us – only not so fortunate. Although clad in funny costumes and speaking in quaint English, all they really wanted was racial, social and sexual equality. Changes in economic and social relations are irrelevant. The past, especially the Restoration past, merely signals opportunities for characters to talk dirtily to each other; beyond that it can be read off entirely in our own terms and in the light of our own wants and needs. What we can find in the past is sameness not difference. In productions like this one nothing in the text becomes contestable, least of all the sexual, emotional and social relationships of men and women.

(p.19)

Munns emphasizes that she is not arguing for the 'sanctity of a text', or denying the right of directors, or other writers, to make creative use of earlier works.

When Brecht rewrote Gay's *Beggar's Opera* or Shakespeare's *Coriolanus*, Edward Bond reworked *Lear*, or when Charles Marowitz radically rearranges Shakespeare's texts, new works are created which feed intellectually and creatively from the base texts. New texts are produced which derive modern relevance, with which one may or may not agree, from their reference points. There is no assumption that this is what Shakespeare or Gay was trying and failing to say; there is, instead, a more radical dialogue with the past which is as much based on a sense of difference as sameness. Such texts are neither patronizing nor anachronistic, while Barton's version of *The Rover* is both.

(p.19)

The most recent production of *The Rover* was staged in October 1994 by the Women's Playhouse Trust (WPT) in association with the Open University (OU). It took place in the enormous space of the Jacob Street Film Studios in London, with a cast of young actors directed by Jules Wright. Although this production made a welcome return to Behn's original text, Wright, like Barton before her, made a conscious effort to play up themes of empire and race. She also laid much stress on the theme of male violence against women, thus suggesting a link between race and gender oppression.

It was a bold and imaginative production, certainly one that took a very clear directorial line. A rather Oriental setting was created with colour and texture: the dominant colour was terracotta; the floor was covered with sand; a tabla player sat in a corner providing a rhythmic accompaniment to the action; the part of Angellica was played by a Kathakali dancer, Maya

Krishna Rao; and movement around the stage space included the use of bicycles and rickshaws. The imperial connection was reinforced by the costumes. The Cavaliers, together with Blunt, were dressed in white linen suits and hats, thus suggesting a colonial setting in the early twentieth century. Other parts – the Spanish and Italian characters – were played by black actresses and actors, again, presumably, to heighten the colonial theme.

In my view, however, and that of several critics, this production was not wholly successful. One of the basic problems, commented on by several reviewers, was the seeming lack of recognition that the play was supposed to be a *comedy*. Not even Blunt – whose clownish speech with its characteristic ''Adsheartlikins' refrain marks him out as the country booby – could raise a laugh. Indeed no distinction was made between the male characters: they were uniformly unattractive. Thus Belvile, who in the text is clearly presented as an honest, upright, constant lover, came across here as no better than any of the other louts. The swordfights of the original were transformed into vicious knifings, and the near-rape scenes were horrifyingly brutal, with much physical throwing of the women to the ground and forcing of their legs apart.

However, just as particular readings of a text may be contested, or qualified, so too there will be differing judgements on the success of any given staging of a play. In the final section of this chapter, Lizbeth Goodman will present a different view of the WPT production, and will describe the process that led to the production taking the form it did. More generally, she will take up the whole question of performance, and how close attention to performance issues can help us towards a more complete understanding of a play as it is brought to life for different audiences and in different cultural contexts. But before that, I would like to return briefly to the theme of the 'canon': how works get put into the canon, and how they are kept there.

Frank Kermode, in his book *Forms of Attention* (1985), has described the process by which Botticelli was restored to the canon of great painters after centuries of neglect, and proposes a theory about canon formation and preservation which I think has a certain applicability to the case of Aphra Behn. According to Kermode's theory, three things are needed: 'opinion', 'knowledge' and 'interpretation'. Towards the end of the nineteenth century a group of artists and amateur writers about art, who for various reasons wanted a certain kind of early Renaissance art, 're-discovered' Botticelli and enthusiastically championed his work. There was much that this group got wrong, but their *opinion* had the result of bringing Botticelli back to prominence, at which point *knowledge*, in the form of painstaking research by specialist art-historians, took over. According to Kermode, this still would not have been enough to *keep* Botticelli in the canon. What keeps a work of art alive from one generation to another is *interpretation*, the process by which critics offer up to it the homage of fresh commentary – though in the knowledge that such commentary is ephemeral, and will be replaced by further commentary. All such commentary, or 'interpretation', varies endlessly, because each generation has different needs, and asks different questions, and the canonical work proves that it is canonical precisely because it generates and sustains this never-ceasing process of interpretation.

Kermode's argument is extremely persuasive, and certainly applies equally to canon formation in literary studies. The case of John Donne, also briefly discussed by Kermode, is a perfect example. Donne, a famous poet in his own time (the early seventeenth century), for various reasons fell out of favour with the arbiters of taste and his work virtually disappeared until the end of the nineteenth century. Just as in the case of Botticelli, 'opinion', this time in the form of critical discussion by the poet T.S. Eliot, restored him to prominence. Eliot needed an earlier poet to prove a new theory about the development of English poetry and about the 'right' direction for modern poetry, including Eliot's own. Very soon professional scholars and academics supplied much 'knowledge' about Donne, and the ensuing process of 'interpretation' has maintained a central place for the poet's work on every English Literature syllabus.

I trust that you will by now have begun to see how this theory of Kermode's applies to Behn. Like Botticelli and Donne, Behn fell into a neglect that lasted for centuries. Just as in their cases, the process of rehabilitation began when she came to be needed by early feminists such as Virginia Woolf who wanted to uncover the existence of a tradition of women's writing. The *opinion* of early feminist enthusiasts led in turn to the production of scholarly *knowledge* about Behn, in the form of learned books, editions and articles. By this means Behn, I think it may safely be claimed, is on her way to entering the literary canon.

And this brings me back to the chequered history of recent productions of *The Rover*. I cannot help feeling that by radically altering the text, or by moving so quickly to startlingly experimental stage interpretations, directors are giving Behn's play the kind of treatment which would be perfectly understandable, even justifiable, in the case of a work – such as *Othello* – which is already firmly lodged in the canon, but which is quite inappropriate in the case of *The Rover*. An audience going to see a new production of *Othello* will be aware of a whole history of stage-performances of this 'classic' play and others by its famous author. If the director then gives it an original, or clever, or even shocking stage interpretation, this is merely what the audience might expect to happen, and they will proceed to make comparisons, decide how far the new approach may have been illuminating, and all without any concern about the *status* of *Othello*. By contrast, in the case of a play like *The Rover*, where no such history of earlier performances exists, and where the work is not yet solidly in the canon, and indeed has never been seen in a 'straight' production by a modern audience, it seems, or so I would argue, that a different approach may be called for: one designed to present and establish as clearly and sympathetically as possible the play Behn actually wrote. I need hardly say that I am not calling for a bland or 'neutral' production, or even necessarily one played in seventeenth-century costume. It is no use pretending that we can remove ourselves from the present and somehow recreate or achieve an 'authentic' performance of a work from the past entirely as it would have been seen over three hundred years ago. Equally, in my view, it is no use trying to ignore the fact that we are dealing with a text written in a very different historical, literary and theatrical context.

What we can do is attempt to stay as close as we can to the spirit of the very particular work Behn wrote. For example, a modern production might try to replicate the sense of intimacy with the audience which is embedded in the text with its numerous asides, but is also suggested by what we know of the physical space of the Restoration theatre, where actors played in very close proximity to the audience. The aim of such a production would be to try to be faithful to as many features of the original text as possible – including, not least, the supremely important fact that it was written as a comedy. The advantage of such a production would be to help a modern audience get a sense of the particular kind of playwright Behn was, and how her works compare with those of better known contemporaries. Once *The Rover* is firmly established in the canon, the work of generating new interpretations may begin.

The Rover *in performance*

by Lizbeth Goodman

Several times in this chapter, Bob Owens has pointed forward to this section as the place where the performance elements of *The Rover* will be discussed. There is space here only to address briefly a few selected ideas and issues.

Background

There have so far been only two major British productions of *The Rover* (both referred to by Bob Owens above) – the 1987 RSC production directed by John Barton and an experimental modern version directed by Jules Wright for the WPT in 1994. This second production was a collaboration between the WPT and the OU/BBC. Tony Coe, an OU/BBC drama producer, worked very closely with Jules Wright in the planning stages and production process of the WPT production, which was recorded for video. The same rehearsal period led to both the live performance at Jacob Street Film Studios in south London and the video version. The video was recorded out of sequence like a film, during the day (with no audience), and the play was performed live to audiences in the evenings.

Bob Owens edited the new version of the text that was used for this production (and which is included in Part Two of this book), and gave an introductory talk to the company about the play, its history, the social context of its first performances, and the language Behn employed. I was the academic consultant and conducted an interview with Jules Wright and Tony Coe. An OU/BBC video crew recorded the performances and the interview.

I have provided these production credits to show that many people have a stake in any production. Those involved in this production cannot be objective about it, but that is not to say that we cannot be critical. As you will have gleaned from his brief discussion of the production, Bob

Owens was not entirely pleased with the final results. Before explaining why I felt differently about the final result, I wish to make four points:

1   this book has, so far, dealt primarily with Shakespeare;
2   because Shakespeare is so thoroughly 'canonized', many people are familiar with the names and basic storylines of his plays; this partial knowledge (and attendant respect) is picked up in part through cultural osmosis – that is, through living in a social context which routinely sends out many and varied messages about Shakespeare's work, venerates the 'Bard', tells us that his work is 'great', 'important' and also 'enjoyable';
3   any 'new' text, by any other author, may strike us as unusual in this context;
4   it is more difficult for us to consider texts that have no familiar visual images, in whatever medium.

With these points in mind, you will realize that studying Behn's *The Rover* provides you with new challenges, both intellectual and imaginative.

Reading a play is a very different activity from watching it in performance. The two can enrich each other, but the text of any play is not the same 'text' when it is performed. There are many reasons why we might enjoy reading the play, or watching any given play in performance. There is no one 'right' way to read, or to perform, or to respond to the play. Debate is healthy, and the most useful question is not 'Do you like it?', but rather 'What do you learn from the play?', or 'What does the play encourage you to think about?' Let us address those later questions with regard to the WPT production, considering it as one interpretation of Behn's play.

So far in this book you have encountered discussion of performance only with regard to film versions of Shakespeare, or critics' analyses of stage productions. In this section we will look at the 'inside story' of the WPT production – an account of the decisions that were made, the ideas that influenced each stage choice, and the process that led to the productions (both the live performance and the video version). This account will situate the performance, explain the difference between the live performance and the video performance, and also address the issue of canonicity.

Decisions

When *The Rover* was chosen as a set text for a new Open University course (A210 *Approaching Literature*), we found that there was no video version of the performance which we could provide for our students. So we decided to produce our own version of the play and to video it. Our first problem was money. We did not have sufficient funds to mount our own full production of the play, and we needed to look for outside collaboration. We approached the Women's Playhouse Trust, well known for their innovative work on plays by women of the past. Jules Wright was enthusiastic about the possibility of collaborating with us, and about directing the play, not because she 'liked it' as a piece of writing, but rather because she found it challenging: 'I was engaged by *The Rover* in the first instance, not because it was her most popular play (I wouldn't have taken it on, on that basis), but because having read it, I felt there was material which had not been covered in previous productions. It became a challenge in that respect.'

We decided that the text of the play would not be cut because we believed that it would be most valuable to offer a full version on video to students and scholars. This was a very important decision, which affected every aspect of the play in performance. *The Rover* is a long and complicated play, with many characters and locations, plots and subplots. This makes it, in my opinion, a very rich text to read, but also an unwieldy text for performance. Jules Wright agreed: 'It's a well-written play, but also an over-written play. I think there are moments we could have cut, but we have done the full text, which I feel is appropriate because viewers can make a judgement about the quality of the writing.'

Though we did not cut the text of the play, we had to scale down the production in terms of the number of actors. As is often the case with modern versions of plays from previous periods, it was necessary to think of doubling and tripling the roles, so that fewer actors would cover all the parts. (Doubling is not a modern strategy, of course: Shakespeare doubled parts in many of his plays, for many reasons.) We doubled parts for two reasons: on one level, it was a financial decision – most modern plays are written for fewer actors for the very reason that the theatre today is not well funded, and it is therefore necessary to work with small companies. The second reason was artistic.

Having taken the decision to produce the play with a small cast, some artistic decisions had to be made. This is where Jules Wright's vision took over. While doubling roles is a decision prompted by economics, it can only be successfully achieved if the artistic reasons are valid. So it was necessary to address a number of related issues: for instance, were there good reasons to double particular parts? Jules Wright decided that there were: Valeria and Lucetta could be played by the same actor, for instance, and the doubling would make a point about the relationship between these two women (both of whom are 'bid for' by men). Similarly, several of the servant roles could be played by the same actor, making the point that these were 'type' roles to begin with, intrinsically class-based. But the decision to cut down on the cast meant that the play would be altered by the choice of interpretation. The most important change was to do with gender. In tripling the servant roles, it became clear that the male actor who played the rickshaw driver, Philippo, and Sancho, could also play Callis (a woman in Behn's play). The story of the play is not altered by making Callis a man, nor are the lines of the text changed substantially (though personal pronouns had to change: 'she' became 'he'), but the subtext or 'meaning' is certainly affected. Another question had to be answered as well: should the play be produced as a costume drama set in seventeenth-century England? If it were, the doubling and tripling of parts might have seemed strange.

Having broken one convention (by reducing the cast), the question of canonicity as a continuum arose – how far is it possible to be 'faithful' to the original play without making artistic decisions and setting an agenda? This collaborative production had to be guided by academic concerns about teaching, as well as by artistic concerns about producing the play and the video version, and social concerns about entertaining and pleasing audiences and critics. The problem was considered from many different angles: notes and reviews of the RSC version were discussed. The first production had, by all accounts, been 'popular', comic and lighthearted. This seemed to us to fulfil the very important role of popularizing Behn's work – a crucial part of canonization – but also to have underplayed Behn's own radical politics. We wanted a version that would show the more serious side of the play – the power politics of the story, as well as (though not instead of) the more comic moments: 'There's a very dark underbelly to the play. There are two near rapes, and those weren't dealt with in any real way in the previous [RSC] production' (Tony Coe). Jules Wright agreed:

> I would compare this play to contemporary films such as *Pulp Fiction*. You have direct violence and that's expressed in a concrete way, and that expression of violence and action will be overturned seconds later with a very witty line. When you have these juxtapositions, you really make an audience think. If as a director you don't take these contrasts on, then I don't think you do justice to the play, I don't think you tell the story the writer wrote. When you watch our production on video, you don't listen to the seventeenth-century language, but rather to the ideas. So, while some reviewers were critical of this production, they all said, to paraphrase, that 'of course, this is the most serious play Behn wrote, and the way in which she deals with rape really makes you address your position as a male or female' … I've seen other reviews of other productions of the play, and I don't think anyone noticed that there were rapes in it before.

The decision to focus on gender relations in real terms, and to portray the rapes as violence directed against women (not as slapstick), may be uncomfortable to watch. By contrast, the RSC production may have been more entertaining. Neither option is better, but each has its own function. The WPT production was to be more politically challenging. We also hoped that by bringing out an aspect of the play which others had played down, this production would throw new light on Behn's writing, and on the issues of concern in her day.

Another objective of the WPT production was to consider the racial and cultural implications of the play. After discussing the various factors affecting gender and power relations in contemporary London, the WPT decided on a multi-racial production which carefully layered national and cultural identities. A multi-racial cast was chosen: white men as the colonizers, black women and black men interacting with each other (as colonizers and colonized), all thrown into relief by the casting of an Indian woman as Angellica. The reasons for this casting were artistically and politically driven: designed to address the unequal status of all the characters in Behn's play (set in Naples in the seventeenth century) by reinterpreting the characters as people who might be encountered in any ex-colony in the 1990s. The casting of an Indian woman emphasized the danger of stereotyping this character: she would seem to be 'an outsider' both to the British and the Spanish, and so her presence added another dimension to the 'world' of the play.

Reading images

There is space here only for the most cursory discussion of the way in which this production worked. Basically, the playing space was a 14,000 square foot warehouse (once a film studio), surrounded by a saffron-coloured cyclorama (reflective backdrop). The floor was covered in sand, and the space was transformed into a 'theatre' by installing red Victorian chairs around all sides. The 'in-the-round' format meant that the audience were, effectively, watching each other as well as the actors, and they became active participants in the play. While the play was rehearsed in a small church hall – where each movement took the actors only a few feet – the live performance in this vast space demanded that each movement for the actors covered hundreds of feet. So rickshaws and bicycles were introduced, partly to keep the actors and the action moving along, and partly to make the production feel less tied to any one time-frame or culture. The actors wore masks in the carnival scenes, as in Behn's original. This sometimes made the acoustics awkward for the audience: the size of the space demanded a loudspeaker system for amplification, and this combined with the masking of characters meant that it was sometimes difficult to tell which character was speaking (an unavoidable logistic problem which was resolved in the video version, where the recorded soundtrack could be 'matched' to the visual recording in the editing process).

I have selected a range of images from the WPT production. The first set of images (Figures 5.6, 5.7 and 5.8) shows the large size of the playing space. The distance between the camera and the characters is obvious in each shot. **But what can you say about your relationship to each of these images, as a viewer? Where are you, and where is the camera?**

Figure 5.6   (from left) Frederick (Morgan Jones), Belvile (Dougray Scott), Blunt (Daniel Craig). Photo: Trevor White.

Figure 5.7 (from left) Frederick (Morgan Jones), Belvile (Dougray Scott), Blunt (Daniel Craig). Photo: Trevor White.

Figure 5.8 (from left) Belvile (Dougray Scott), Willmore (Andy Serkis), Frederick (Morgan Jones). Photo: Trevor White.

These are photo stills taken while we were recording the video. As well as seeing the characters, you can see the size of the space in which the actors are working, the distances they cover, and the relationship of the camera and sound crew to the actors. In the first image, Frederick, Belvile and Blunt walk towards the camera (a steadicam, which moves with them, to capture the essence of movement with the frame of the video). In the second shot, we see the same three characters closer up, with the camera and sound technicians behind them and a focus puller (person controlling the picture quality) moving in the foreground. In the third image, we see a close-up of two of these characters, who have now been joined by Willmore. In this third shot, you can no longer see the crew or the background. This close-up therefore functions as a 'director' of your view in the sense that you no longer have the choice of considering the relationship between characters and context. What you see here is what the photographer wants you to see: three characters, looking to the side, reacting to action 'off-camera'. The photographer's focus becomes your focus, whether you like it or not, just as the focus of the video camera becomes your focus. In live performance, you would be able to decide for yourself where you wanted to look: whether at the three characters pictured in the third image, for instance, or at something else. ∎

The next set of images (Figures 5.9, 5.10 and 5.11) illustrates the function of the diagonal in an 'in-the-round' production. When characters stand on a diagonal line across the playing space, they can be viewed by the

Figure 5.9 (from left) Hellena (Cecilia Noble), Willmore (Andy Serkis), Angellica (Maya Krishna Rao). Photo: Trevor White.

Figure 5.10   (from left) Willmore (Andy Serkis), Hellena (Cecilia Noble), Angellica (Maya Krishna Rao). Photo: Trevor White.

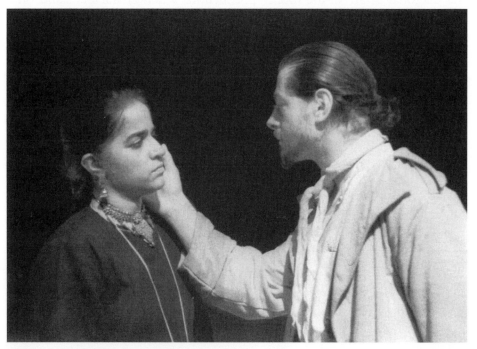

Figure 5.11   (from left) Angellica (Maya Krishna Rao), Willmore (Andy Serkis). Photo: Trevor White.

maximum number of people in the audience, wherever the audience is sitting.

These images also illustrate a power line between the characters: the first image positions Hellena (in male garb) in the centre, about to be touched by Angellica (though this action only becomes apparent when you see the sequence of images). We can see all three characters, though Angellica's back is turned to us. In the second image we see the same grouping, but from a side angle; the focus is on Angellica touching Hellena's face, while Willmore looks on. But in the third image we have a close-up of Willmore touching Angellica's face. For the first time in this sequence we see the expression on Angellica's face, and can tell that she is distant, unresponsive, hesitant, perhaps even hostile. Having seen that expression, we may look again at the previous two images and imagine Angellica's facial expressions as she looks at Hellena and Willmore. In all three shots Angellica is touched or touches – she is less powerful than the man (Willmore), or the 'man' who Hellena pretends to be. But she is more powerful than her servant Moretta, another woman, as Figure 5.12 shows.

Figure 5.12 (from left) Moretta (Judy Browne), Angellica (Maya Krishna Rao). Photo: Trevor White.

In Figure 5.12 the power relationship between the two women –
Moretta as Angellica's servant – is represented by the servant kneeling,
lower in the space (height in an image often represents a power
relationship). Also, Angellica touches the servant's face; she changes from
one who is touched by men, to one with the power to touch.

Figures 5.13 and 5.14 show how characters may find even ground in
terms of status when they both 'ground' themselves, literally. The first
shows Willmore evening out the power relation with Angellica as he moves
to her private area in the centre of the playing space, while in the second,
the same relationship of equality is in evidence between Hellena and
Florinda. This image, from the very opening of the play, shows the women
sharing stories in private, seeming equal, confident and open; it is only as
the men enter their space when Pedro orders that they stand, that the real
power games of the play begin.

Figure 5.13   (from left) Angellica (Maya Krishna Rao),
Willmore (Andy Serkis). Photo: Trevor White.

Figure 5.14   (from left) Florinda (Vicky Licorish),
Hellena (Cecilia Noble). Photo: Trevor White.

Perhaps the most powerful example of power relations occurs in the attempted rape scene with Willmore and Florinda, shown in the next two images (Figures 5.15 and 5.16). In the first image, we get a sense of the space, shadow, and mood of the scene, with Florinda thrown onto the ground violently, but our gaze is above, distant and voyeuristic. The next image positions us with Florinda; we see from her point of view – the towering body and menacing face of her attacker.

Figure 5.15 (from left) Willmore (Andy Serkis), Florinda (Vicky Licorish). Photo: Trevor White.

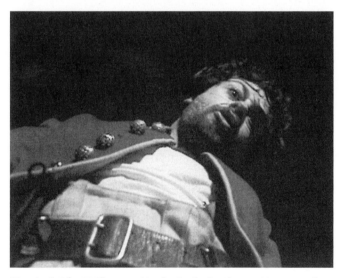

Figure 5.16 Willmore (Andy Serkis). Photo: Trevor White.

In the next set of images (Figures 5.17 to 5.20), Florinda appears again, this time with Hellena and Valeria – all 'women of quality'. In this sequence they wear masks – indeed, the very masks pictured on the cover of this book. **What happens to our relationship to the characters throughout this sequence?**

185

Figure 5.17 (from left) Valeria (Buki Armstrong), Hellena (Cecilia Noble), Florinda (Vicky Licorish). Photo: Trevor White.

Figure 5.18 (from left) Valeria (Buki Armstrong), Hellena (Cecilia Noble), Florinda (Vicky Licorish). Photo: Trevor White.

Figure 5.19 (from left) Valeria (Buki Armstrong), Hellena (Cecilia Noble), Florinda (Vicky Licorish). Photo: Trevor White.

Figure 5.20 (from left) Willmore (Andy Serkis), Hellena (Cecilia Noble). Photo: Trevor White.

Discussion

Throughout this sequence the characters become anonymous through masking. At first the women seem to look at us, the viewers, and Florinda seems to make eye contact with us. But in the next image our eyes are drawn to the hands on the masks, imagining the action of the movement, and in the third image we see the masks rather than the characters' faces. Before our eyes the characters are transformed by their masks into types rather than individuals. We become aware of the style of these masks, which are not like the masks of most 'traditional' Restoration drama. So we may begin to connect these image with a different sense of place, not quite contemporary to us, nor to Behn, but to somewhere else. By the time we look closely at the fourth image, we see the mask as representing all three of the women, and women generally, rather than seeing what is actually before us: Hellena, masked, standing with Willmore. Though we cannot see Hellena's eyes, we assume that she looks where Willmore looks, to the side. Masked faces are far more difficult to read than real human facial expressions. ■

Finally, compare and contrast the two images shown in Figures 5.21 and 5.22, and ask yourself where you are in relation to each, not only physically (for you are positioned with the camera in both), but also emotionally and imaginatively.

Figure 5.21 (from left) Blunt (Daniel Craig), Belvile (Dougray Scott), Frederick (Morgan Jones), Willmore (Andy Serkis). Photo: Trevor White.

Figure 5.22 (from left) Belvile (Dougray Scott), Don Pedro (Hakeem Kae-Kazim), Willmore (Andy Serkis), Frederick (Morgan Jones). Photo: Trevor White.

Discussion

In the first image, the men draw their knives; we look on from a front view, mid-shot. Where we are imaginatively is more difficult to assess. The sight of men with knives is always frightening, and the feeling is enhanced by the context of this image, taken from a play which deals so directly with violence against women by men. But in the second image, we are more likely to share an interpretation as a result of the camera's intervention on our behalf. Willmore is speaking directly to us in this image, through the camera. He makes eye contact and addresses his lines to us. What we witness here is called an 'aside'. As he makes direct contact with the audience, our engagement with him increases. Our role as interpreters and critics is recognized, and whatever we think of the character, or indeed of the actor or the production, we engage with the play more fully when we are recognized as part of the interpretive process. ■

Interpretations and canonicity

To some extent, the process of reading and interpreting plays and other works of literature is always personal. So, the different perspectives on the WPT production (live and video performances) have been constructed in these pages partly as an academic exercise to show two different ways of looking at the same production. This takes us to the heart of our larger debate about the canon: the interpretation of literary texts takes place in a social context. So we can only guess what Behn might have intended her

189

play to do – whether she would have been happier for it to be played as comedy or political drama, for instance, is a matter for conjecture only. But for directors, producers, actors, critics and students considering the play today, our own views and social context will influence our ways of deciding what kind of production best serves the play, at any given point in time, in any community.

From a feminist perspective, I see the play as inherently political. But of course, this may not be the same as 'being true to Behn'. From the perspective of literary scholarship the issues may be different. What makes the play 'true' will be governed in part by a concern with literary value and the essence of the text. Each reader will have a different ideal production of the play. This may change with circumstance: for example, when teaching the play as part of an academic course we may want to emphasize certain stylistic or historical aspects, while we might choose a different tactic if including the play in a course on stage design or acting. If we were directing the play for a mainstream theatre we might work according to one set of priorities, while producing a video involves another set of concerns entirely. All of these approaches lead to a production of the play that Behn wrote, as we interpret it and reinvent it today. Text and context work inevitably in dialogue to create meaning.

It may be most useful to consider the different perspectives offered in this chapter as contributions to a debate about canonicity and interpretation – a debate to which you are invited to contribute as well. All these positions together make up the social context of contemporary performances of *The Rover*, and all inform the larger discussion of the value of Behn's work, and of this play in particular, in relation to the Shakespearean canon, and the larger canon of literature.

It could be argued that *The Rover* is already part of the canon, largely as a result of the work of feminist literary scholars. The different perspectives offered in this chapter open debate about the possible contemporary value of the play. What is true for audiences in 1995 will not be the same as what was 'true' for, or to, Aphra Behn. Perhaps the 'truth' for women in Behn's audiences differed from that of men. What we know for sure is that Behn was provocative, daring, and likely to prefer a presentation which was in some sense confrontational. Her play was radical in its day – it challenged accepted notions of male and female behaviour. So should the play do that today. There is always room for 'realistic' productions of plays, but so too is there room for more experimental productions. Personally, I think Behn would have approved of the WPT production – or at least, she probably would not have objected. What is important, surely, is that the play is read and performed by and for many different students and audiences, actors and directors.

Further reading

Paperback selections of Behn's works currently available are:

Behn, A. (1992) *Oroonoko, The Rover and Other Works*, edited by Janet Todd, Penguin Classics.

Behn, A. (1994) *Oroonoko and Other Writings*, edited by Paul Salzman, Oxford University Press.

Behn, A. (1995) *The Rover and Other Plays*, edited by Jane Spencer, Oxford University Press.

Books with valuable discussions of Behn and her writing are:

Duffy, M. (1977) *The Passionate Shepherdess: Aphra Behn 1640–89*, Cape.

Goreau, A. (1980) *Reconstructing Aphra: A Social Biography of Aphra Behn*, Oxford University Press.

Howe, E. (1992) *The First English Actresses: Women and Drama 1660–1700*, Cambridge University Press.

Hutner, H. (ed.) (1993) *Rereading Aphra Behn: History, Theory, and Criticism*, University Press of Virginia.

Hobby, E. (1988) *Virtue of Necessity: English Women's Writing 1649–88*, Virago.

Hume, R.D. (1976) *The Development of English Drama in the Late Seventeenth Century*, Clarendon Press.

Link, F.M. (1968) *Aphra Behn*, Twayne Publishers.

Mendelson, S.H. (1987) *The Mental World of Stuart Women*, Harvester Press.

Pearson, J. (1988) *The Prostituted Muse: Images of Women and Women Dramatists 1642–1737*, Harvester.

Reading As You Like It

by Kate Clarke

with a section by Lizbeth Goodman

In this chapter we return to Shakespeare, this time to study one of his most popular comedies, *As You Like It*. Despite Shakespeare's status as a literary and dramatic 'genius' – a reputation he has enjoyed since the middle of the eighteenth century – his comedies have, until quite recently, received much less critical attention than his history plays or tragedies. In 1962, a well-known authority on Shakespeare, John Dover Wilson, argued that what he saw as the 'comparative neglect of Shakespeare's comedies is partly due ... to the neglect of comedy in general' (*Shakespeare's Happy Comedies*, p.17). This critical 'neglect' of comedy may be explained in various ways. It may, to some extent, be a consequence of the old idea, deriving from Aristotle, that tragedy as a genre is superior to, and therefore more worthy of study than, comedy. It may be that literary critics are, or have been, uncomfortable with the close association between comedy and popular culture, including its reliance on bawdy language and situations to provoke laughter.

Whatever the reservations of literary critics, Shakespeare's comedies have always been appreciated by theatre-goers. The approach of this chapter will be to read *As You Like It* as a dramatic text (a literary text written for performance), which only fully comes to life in performance. Indeed, it can be argued that each performance of a play *is* a 'text' in its own right. A key concern will be to help you move towards a more active and imaginative exploration of how the play, or parts of it, might be realized on the stage. One of the most important functions of this kind of approach to a play is to appreciate that there is nothing inevitable about the translation from written text to action in performance. There are always choices to be made, and different choices may radically alter the 'text' in the context of performance. As Lizbeth Goodman pointed out in Chapters One and Five, each production and each performance is, in its own way, an interpretation. This is one of the most fundamental distinctions between dramatic literature (plays, evaluated as texts and performances) and other kinds of literature: dramatic text is written to be spoken and so really 'lives' when it is mediated by actors directly to an audience. You will also see that the words on the page are only a small, although immensely important, part of the whole play.

We will use the term 'dramatic function' regularly in our discussion. By this we mean the way in which a particular theme, character or plot develops and functions in terms of the play as a whole. We use this expression instead of 'role' to distinguish it from the written part for the individual actor, particularly in the consideration of character. Thus, when we speak of the dramatic function of female characters in *As You Like It*, for example, we are not necessarily referring to the number of lines or appearances that Rosalind, Celia, Phebe and Audrey have but, rather, to the impact and significance of those lines and appearances in the course of the play. Dramatic function refers to the potential for performance that is inscribed in the text of a play (not to an actual performance, which would be referred to as 'performative function' or 'theatrical function').

Assessing the dramatic function of a character is not a question of describing what kind of character he or she appears to be, or the part played by that character in plot development. Instead, we must ask how these aspects of the character relate to the wider meanings and concerns of the play. For example, Phebe may not have a very large part in the play in terms of lines spoken or the status of her character, but her dramatic function is manifold. As we shall see, she provides the means for a dramatic intensification of comic confusion and plot development when she falls in love with Rosalind disguised as Ganymede.

Later in the chapter we will be considering a number of the dramatic and literary conventions that Shakespeare employs, and in some cases subverts, in *As You Like It*. These include his use of the literature associated with love, especially Petrarchan discourse; his use of soliloquy and pastoral; and his use of comedy as a form. All these terms will be explained when we come to discuss them.

Reading As You Like It: *themes and issues*

Text and performance in Act I

As an introduction to the play, read through Act I. If you have access to a video or audio cassette of the play in performance, you may find it helpful to watch or listen – as well as reading. **How would you describe the 'world(s)' of *As You Like It* as presented in this Act? How do you think Le Beau's two speeches to Orlando at the end of Scene 2 contribute to our understanding of this?**

D i s c u s s i o n

There seem to be two worlds in *As You Like It*, represented by two locations. The first is what we might call the 'real' world: the world of Duke Frederick's court. This world is characterized by discord within families and within the state. In the opening scene we have a younger brother, Orlando, quarrelling violently with his older brother, Oliver. Later in the scene, we learn from Charles the wrestler that the erstwhile ruler, the 'Old Duke', has been driven into exile by his younger brother, Duke Frederick (I.1.93–7; all quotations in this chapter are taken from The New Penguin Shakespeare edition of *As You Like It*, edited by H.J. Oliver, 1968).

The other world is what we might call an 'ideal' world, represented by the Forest of Arden. As we shall discover, courtly rules do not apply in the forest, and the disguised and displaced lovers find 'ideal' love and mend old disagreements, precisely because they leave the 'real' world behind.

Le Beau's words to Orlando imply discontent with the world of the court. Indeed, he is advising Orlando to 'leave this place' (I.2.251). But he also refers to a 'better world than this' which may be found 'Hereafter' (I.2.273). For Rosalind and Celia at the end of the next scene, the forest represents 'liberty' (I.3.136). ■

The situation we are presented with at the opening of the play is one in which the social and political order has been disrupted. The young usurp the authority and inheritance of the old. Moreover, 'the new Duke', disloyal to his brother and to his ruler, enriches himself at the expense of those who are loyal. It is important to appreciate that although the world of the court represents order of a kind, it is of a kind that the play is at pains to discredit. In a sense Duke Frederick's court is a world turned upside down just as much as Arden, for all that it seems (on the surface) to offer a 'real' depiction of order.

If you return to Le Beau's speeches, you will notice that he describes the Duke as 'humorous' (I.2.255). The word refers to the 'humours', the physiological and emotional elements that were thought to make up the individual. Le Beau is suggesting that the Duke is temperamental or unstable.

Look again at Scene 2. How is Duke Frederick presented? What kind of character is he?

Discussion

In Scene 2, the account of Duke Frederick that Charles the wrestler gave in the first scene is verified by Celia and Rosalind. Celia announces her intention to redress the balance. As heir to the usurping Duke, she will deliver the inheritance back to Rosalind (ll.16–22). In the same scene, unravelling the verbal wit of the women's exchanges with Touchstone, we hear in a roundabout way that the Duke loves those without honour. Despite Celia's retort that 'My father's love is enough to honour him' (l.79, which may, in any case, be ironic), Touchstone has added a further testimony to the evidence amassing against Duke Frederick.

Duke Frederick's erratic moods and affections (for Orlando, Rosalind, even for his daughter Celia) are hinted at in the text. When we first see the Duke, his words and his behaviour seem to contradict what we have heard so far. He appears compassionate, expressing 'pity of the challenger's youth' (ll.148–9), seeking and obtaining his daughter's and his niece's good offices to dissuade Orlando from a challenge with the wrestler which, reasonably and empirically, Orlando seems destined to lose. However, before the scene is out, the Duke's fickleness is revealed. Orlando's triumph results in the disclosure of his name, 'youngest son of Sir Rowland de Boys' (l.210–11), which draws from the Duke:

> I would thou hadst been son to some man else.
> The world esteemed thy father honourable,
> But I did find him still mine enemy.
>
> ...
> I would thou hadst told me of another father.
>
> (ll.213–19) ■

195

How does Shakespeare's use of language suggest a change or transformation in Duke Frederick's character here? Can you think of ways in which such a change could be conveyed on the stage?

Discussion

Shakespeare marks a change in Duke Frederick by changing his style of language from prose to verse. The actor playing the Duke is thus provided with a cue for a change in tone. The scale of the change must be conveyed physically and visually too. Perhaps the Duke has been helping Orlando up, and is in close physical contact with him, but now moves away abruptly, putting distance between himself and Orlando? The physical and metaphorical distance is further increased by the Duke's exit.

Alternatively the change could be conveyed more subtly through the bearing of the Duke, perhaps from one that is relaxed and 'loose' to one that is stiff, upright and tense. The actors and director have many possible choices to make. On the stage, even such a small detail as eye contact can have a significant impact, more so perhaps in the intimate setting of the Elizabethan and Jacobean theatres with the audience on three sides. The director of a modern production must decide where the Duke will look when he speaks these words, as well as considering where the non-speaking actors look. Whether the Duke looks Orlando straight in the eye or is 'shifty' will convey different messages about his character. (Lizbeth Goodman will analyse the process of establishing eye contact for the Duke – and its effects – in the last section of this chapter.) ∎

When the actor Andrew Jarvis played Duke Frederick in David Thacker's 1992–3 production for the Royal Shakespeare Company (RSC), he found in this early scene an indication that the Duke is not all bad. For him, this made the conversion of the Duke at the end of the play more credible. Jarvis explains the sudden change in the Duke in the second scene of the play as a kind of vulnerability:

> the behaviour of a man who's just taken over the country – maybe for very good reasons, maybe Duke Senior was terrible, you don't know. He knows he's got to have a strong regime, he's got to be tight on everybody, nobody can be allowed to threaten this very tender new regime. But along with that there is a kind of paranoia that maybe there is a plot – that's what goes on in his mind. Suddenly it grows into this huge insurrection in his mind.

> (Notes on Duke Frederick in the RSC Study Pack for David Thacker's 1992–3 production)

The words spoken by the other characters in this scene also reinforce earlier impressions. Once again, for example, there is a marked contrast between Duke Frederick's conception of what is 'honourable', and the world's conception. Celia remarks on the injustice of the Duke's response to the disclosure of Orlando's name in words that echo and challenge his own: 'Were I my father, coz, would I do this?' (1.219).

Celia's words are, clearly, a direct response to her father's, and reveal her discomfort at being daughter to such a man. They may also be a response to the non-verbal 'text' of Rosalind and Orlando. Rosalind's verbal

Figure 6.1   Andrew Jarvis as Duke Frederick in the RSC production of *As You Like It*, directed by David Thacker, 1992–3. Photo: Alastair Muir.

response to Orlando's disclosure of his identity comes in lines 223–7. In Rosalind's mind, and in her speech, Orlando is allied to her father's cause. The two of them are, momentarily, united in opposition to Duke Frederick and in loyalty to the exiled Duke. This might be emphasized on stage by having Rosalind stand physically close to Orlando, perhaps on the other side of the stage from Duke Frederick and Celia. There are grounds in the text to suggest that soon after Orlando's appearance there is a breach, of sorts, between Rosalind and Celia. It is notable that Celia's attempts to dissociate herself from her father's actions draw no sympathetic response from Rosalind. Some productions make more of this than others. Certainly, from this point until the exit of Rosalind and Celia, there is an uneven battle for Rosalind's attention being waged between Celia and Orlando. At the beginning of Scene 3, however good-natured it is portrayed as being, Celia and Rosalind have what amounts to an argument about Orlando.

What our brief analysis of this second scene has revealed is that body language, gesture, facial expression and the physical relationship between the actors (in terms of the space between them and their stage positions) will all be crucial to the interpretation of the text that is conveyed to the audience. Always there are choices to be made; decisions must be justified by the actors' and director's understanding of the dramatic function of each episode and character in the context of the whole play. If you have not already done so, you should now read the rest of the play.

Love in As You Like It

It has been said that *As You Like It* is 'mainly about love' (French, *Shakespeare's Division of Experience*, 1983, p.111). In the play Shakespeare dramatizes a wide range of different kinds of love and lovers, some of which may present a radical challenge to our understanding. As in other comedies, Shakespeare uses the device of a number of different pairs of lovers. It is interesting to note that Shakespeare draws heavily upon dramatic and literary conventions in his portrayal of the lovers. Indeed, most of the lovers – as diverse a group as they are – conceive of love in literary or idealistic terms.

The pair that represents an ideal of love is Rosalind and Orlando. At one opposite pole to this ideal, we have the airily romantic Silvius's passion for the disdainful Phebe. The representation of Silvius and Phebe and their attitudes is recognizably drawn from Petrarchan discourse, speech based on the work of the fourteenth-century Italian poet Petrarch. For Petrarch, the lover's passion is inflamed by the unobtainability of his desired mistress. The language Silvius uses to describe his love is a reflection of this assumption. At the other extreme we have the socially unequal and lusty passion of Touchstone and Audrey.

In addition, we learn of an earlier liaison of Touchstone with one Jane Smile (II.4.44–9), and there is the 'love at first sight' romance of Celia and Oliver, and the same-sex love of Phebe for Rosalind disguised as Ganymede and of Orlando for Ganymede playing Rosalind. Yet other kinds of love (or its absence) are represented in the relationships of Celia and Rosalind; of Duke Frederick with his daughter and niece, as well as with his exiled brother; of the brothers Orlando and Oliver; and in the master–servant love between Orlando and Adam.

Here we will concentrate mostly upon romantic love. In the play, love is frequently linked with the theme of 'nature and nurture', that is, the balance between the influences of heredity and upbringing on the life of an individual. This link often takes the form of references to the ways in which conceptions of, and attitudes towards, love are shaped by received ideas about it. Most powerfully, such ideas are to be found in literature, so that the play becomes self-referential and self-mocking.

Romantic poetry in As You Like It

The relationship between love and poetry as it is presented in the play shows a 'dependency of thing on thing' (as Shakespeare expresses it in another play, *Measure for Measure*, V.1.62) that is quite remarkable. It is almost as though the one cannot exist without the other. Orlando's love for Rosalind renders him incapable of speech:

> Can I not say 'I thank you'? ...
> What passion hangs these weights upon my tongue?
> I cannot speak to her, yet she urged conference.
> (I.2.238–47)

But it induces the writing of mediocre love poetry. When we see him hanging his verses on trees in Act III, Scene 2, he is playing the part of a conventional lover. Even the words he speaks are redolent with the imagery of the kind of poetry that he has been trying to write:

> Hang there, my verse, in witness of my love,
> And thou, thrice-crownèd queen of night, survey
> With thy chaste eye, from thy pale sphere above,
> Thy huntress' name that my full life doth sway.
> O Rosalind, these trees shall be my books
> And in their barks my thoughts I'll character
> That every eye which in this forest looks
> Shall see thy virtue witnessed everywhere.
> Run, run, Orlando, carve on every tree
> The fair, the chaste, and unexpressive she.
> (III.2.1–10)

The formal pattern of the speech, in metre and in rhyme very close to that of a sonnet, as well as the conventional imagery of the loved one as a 'huntress', 'chaste' and 'fair', emphasize that what Orlando is experiencing of love at this point is largely governed by his expectations, and that these expectations are, in turn, governed by literary expressions of love. Ironically, Orlando's speech is more sophisticated and acceptable as poetry than the clumsily rhymed verses that Rosalind and Celia later find on the trees. This seems to support Touchstone's reply to Audrey's enquiry as to whether love poetry is 'honest in deed and word? Is it a true thing?' 'No, truly', says Touchstone, 'for the truest poetry is the most feigning; and lovers are given to poetry; and what they swear in poetry may be said as lovers they do feign' (III.3.15–19). He concludes that he would have more confidence in Audrey's avowals of being 'honest' (or constant) if she were 'a poet', because then he 'might have some hope thou didst feign' (III.3.22–3) and might therefore be able to induce her to leave her fiancée for him.

The implication is that a 'true' lover cannot write 'true' poetry, so that Orlando's ineptitude in this respect is, paradoxically, positive rather than negative evidence of the value of his love. It is as though he wants to love 'by the book' but the real experience of love prevents this. The paradox is consolidated by the fact that love is the greatest inspiration of poetry. This is self-evident in that the play that we are reading (or watching or listening to) is one such work of art. Even so, it seems that the women who are the objects of such poetry are right to be sceptical about it. Both Celia and Rosalind mark the distinction between Orlando's claims as a poetical lover and his actions: 'O, that's a brave man! He writes brave verses, speaks brave words, swears brave oaths, and breaks them bravely, quite traverse, athwart the heart of his lover' (III.4.36–9). Orlando claims that he would die for love, but in his wooing of Ganymede playing Rosalind he cannot even keep his appointments, much less die.

Phebe too rejects Silvius's poetical declarations of love, but in her case it is largely because her cast of mind is too literal. Silvius is in an ecstasy of Petrarchan love. He loves Phebe for what she represents rather than what she is. She is the scornful and disdainful mistress, all the more desirable because she seems unattainable. Yet, even as she scorns him, Phebe displays another attribute of the conventional Petrarchan mistress, pity: 'I would not be thy executioner./I fly thee, for I would not injure thee' (III.5.8–9). She goes on to refute the Petrarchan fictions with which Silvius is determined to burden her:

> Thou tellest me there is murder in mine eye:
> 'Tis pretty, sure, and very probable,
> That eyes, that are the frail'st and softest things,
> Who shut their coward gates on atomies,
> Should be called tyrants, butchers, murderers!
>
> …
>
> Lie not, to say mine eyes are murderers!
> Now show the wound mine eye hath made in thee.
> (III.5.10–20)

Once again, we see a challenge to the truth of poetry, even though Silvius attempts to defend it, asserting that it is 'the power of fancy' that inflicts 'the wounds invisible/That love's keen arrows make' (III.5.29–31). It is a testimony to the close relationship between love and poetry in this play that the scornful Phebe later turns to poetry to express her own love for Ganymede (see IV.3.40–64).

In contrast, there is nothing romantic, poetic or conventionally 'literary' in the relationship of Touchstone and Audrey. Nevertheless, their experience of what they call love is shown to be just as strong and just as impelling as that of the others. Touchstone, the snob, has met his match in Audrey. Although a 'simple country wench', Audrey has the good sense to know when she is 'on to a good thing'. Touchstone uses his wit to take her from her betrothed, William. His desire for respectability is just more than his desire to possess Audrey, as he tells Jaques: 'As the ox hath his bow, sir, the horse his curb, and the falcon her bells, so man hath his desires; and as pigeons bill, so wedlock would be nibbling' (III.3.72–4). Even before the marriage, he is looking for 'a good excuse for me hereafter to leave my wife' (III.3.84). Audrey uses her wit to insist on marriage so that she may become 'a woman of the world' (V.3.4–5).

In a curious way, all this self-examination about the form and use of art, and of poetry in particular, reaffirms the value of the play itself. In critically examining assumptions about the relationship between art and nature, literature and life, the play can be seen to confirm that they are mutually inclusive rather than exclusive. Such a position is consistent with contemporary Renaissance humanism, which saw in artistic achievement the distinctive and unique achievement of mankind as part of God's creation. Linking this with consideration of love emphasizes the play's focus on identifying the essential features of humanity, and the ways in which these are 'natural' or are cultivated through civilization. Mankind is part of nature but, through art, is also apart from it.

The function of marriage

It is significant that the context for love within the play is marriage. Again, this is connected with the wider theme of nature and civilization, in that marriage can be seen as the civilizing, or control, of natural sexual appetites. Indeed, this was a common Renaissance view of marriage. Shakespeare's audiences would have recognized the mock marriage in Act IV, Scene 1 as a valid and binding pre-contract. Both Rosalind and Celia know what they are doing here. When Rosalind presses Orlando to say when he will marry her, his reply, 'Why, now, as fast as she [Celia disguised as Aliena] can marry us' (l.123), signifies that the marriage is intended to be immediately binding, a present rather than a future promise.

The episode can be very effective on stage. Rosalind is in male disguise; what we see is a marriage of two young men. In many productions, the sexual attraction that the two are shown to feel for one another is a key element of the scene. Clearly, this is at least as much to do with body language and gesture as it is with the written text. When the actors concerned are, in fact, both male (as they would have been in Shakespeare's day) the additional nuances are manifold.

The implausible appearance of a mythical figure, Hymen, God of Marriage, in Act V, Scene 4 is a convenient means to bring the desired resolution and the multiple marriages that the comedy requires. The language of Act V prepares us for this magical resolution in its regular use of repetition and rhythm, creating an atmosphere in which we no longer expect realism (see, for example, V.2.28–39, 80–118; V.4.5–25). Indeed, Rosalind prepares Orlando by telling him that she can 'do strange things' because 'I have, since I was three year old, conversed with a magician, most profound in his art, and yet not damnable'; and she adds 'I am a magician' (V.2.57–9, 68).

The ending of the play, with the appearance of Hymen, functions as a masque. A masque was a particular kind of drama, characterized by a mixture of music and spectacle. Masques, or masque-like dramas, were to become extremely popular at the courts of James I and Charles I. In 1600, with Elizabeth I still on the throne, they were relatively uncommon (although many of the entertainments popular in the Elizabethan period share some of the same features). It is particularly interesting to note that several of Shakespeare's comedies, including *As You Like It*, were performed in aristocratic households as part of marriage celebrations.

The marriages at the end of the play signal a return to community, to society, from the individual freedom that has been enjoyed in Arden. Hymen's song moves the play from the country back to the town: 'Tis Hymen peoples every town', he sings (V.4.140). Just at the point that the 'holiday', or release, threatened to turn into an anarchic society, in which men love other men and women other women, order is restored. The multiple marriages are complemented by other equally fantastic resolutions. The two wicked brothers, Oliver and Duke Frederick, undergo conversion on the road to Arden. The temporary inhabitants of Arden who might be seen to represent the dispossessed, 'the underside of society, made up of women, exiles, outcasts, the poor, the eccentric, and the low in status' (French, *Shakespeare's Division of Experience*, 1983, p.111), had all, in one way or another, been driven there from the margins of a society to which they are now restored.

To digress briefly, it is interesting to compare the kind of resolution that marriage presents in Aphra Behn's *The Rover* and in *As You Like It*. Whereas in Shakespeare's play the resolution is unproblematic, Behn's adoption of the convention offers an implicit challenge to marriage as a social and political instrument, particularly as it relates to the position of women. Thus, Behn, as a woman writer, adopts a patriarchal literary model and subverts it.

Shakespeare subverts the traditional model of marriage in tragedies such as *Othello* by deliberately not offering a happy ending, but it is a characteristic of his comedies that the plays end happily with multiple marriages. What nearly prevents this comic resolution in *As You Like It* is the gendered disguise of the lovers. The use of disguise is a distinctive element of comedy.

Disguise and gender confusion

Shakespeare used the device of disguising the leading female role in a number of comedies. Disguise allows for the compounding of comic confusion, in its potential for mistaken identity and dramatic irony (a situation in which the irony is clear to the audience but not to the characters). In *As You Like It*, Rosalind's disguise is first adopted as a protection because 'Beauty provoketh thieves sooner than gold' (I.3.108), but once in Arden Rosalind's role as Ganymede becomes much more than this. Rosalind and Orlando have already fallen in love before the banishment to Arden takes place, so it would, presumably, have been perfectly possible for Rosalind to reveal her true identity to Orlando and to have gained the required protection from him. Indeed, while Rosalind's lament when she first learns that Orlando is in the forest, 'Alas the day, what shall I do with my doublet and hose?' (III.2.212), is partly a reminder to the audience of the comic possibilities inherent in her disguise, it may also harbour the possibility that she could abandon it. Rosalind acts on impulse and decides to 'speak to him like a saucy lackey, and under that habit play the knave with him' (III.2.287–8). This follows Orlando's defence of love and lovers to Jaques.

The function of the disguise seems, therefore, to be little to do with the needs of the plot. Rather, I will argue, it is closely related to the exploration of gender expectations in respect of love. In addition, it allows an intensification of the tensions set up between appearance and reality, nature and nurture, which are so significant in this play. In his plays, Shakespeare is frequently concerned with the relationship between appearance and reality. In *As You Like It*, and elsewhere, the use of theatrical metaphors as a way of describing the human condition achieves the status of meta-theatre (the way in which a piece of theatre self-consciously examines the nature of theatre). This term has come into the discourse of literary criticism relatively recently. It was coined by Lionel Abel in 1963 'to indicate all modes of theatrical self-consciousness in the drama' (Elam, *Shakespeare's Universe of Discourse*, 1984, p.20). Its most obvious example is the technique of a play within a play in *Hamlet*. The prologue of *Henry V* and the Epilogue of *As You Like It* are also meta-theatrical as, in a more subtle way, is the donning of masks and disguises in *The Rover*. The meta-theatrical aspects of *As You Like It* lead us to question our understanding of 'reality', social or natural, and of gender roles within society. The self-referential nature of this device is directly related to the role of the audience in the context of live performance.

It is notable that, as Ganymede, Rosalind's confidence and self-possession is dramatically increased. In the scenes before they reach Arden, Celia is the dominant character. She urges Rosalind to action and rouses her from a passive acceptance to active revolt. However, when they reach Arden in Act II, Scene 4, the roles are dramatically reversed. Rosalind's male disguise immediately endows her with a desire not only to look masculine but to adopt masculine attributes. Rosalind's first words as Ganymede invoke a male god, Jupiter, in an oath (II.4.1). The choice of the name Ganymede may be significant, in that the story it would recall would have been well known among the educated members of Shakespeare's audience as one that represented homo-erotic love. In the myth, Ganymede was a beautiful young man with whom the god Jupiter fell in love. He was carried up to heaven on the back of an eagle and became a servant to the gods and Jupiter's lover. Rosalind's oath is, therefore, doubly significant. Rosalind goes on to draw attention to the very different stereotypically gendered responses to the situation in which they find themselves: 'I could find it in my heart to disgrace my man's apparel, and to cry like a woman, but I must comfort the weaker vessel, as doublet-and-hose ought to show itself courageous to petticoat: therefore courage, good Aliena' (II.4.4–7).

Masculinity and femininity are seen to be entirely external and superficial, simply a question of 'doublet and hose' or 'petticoat'. The notion of gender as a construction, and especially its relationship with play-acting and dressing-up, is at the heart of the play's presentation of gender.

In view of the social and stage conventions of Shakespeare's day, which reflected the constraints and prescriptions of women's lives, male

Figure 6.2 Peggy Ashcroft as Rosalind, Jane Wenham as Celia, Patrick Wymark as Touchstone and Donald Eccles as Corin in *As You Like It* at the Shakespeare Memorial Theatre, Stratford, directed by Glen Byam Shaw, 1957. Photograph in the Shakespeare Collection, Birmingham Public Library Services.

disguise allows Shakespeare to develop aspects of Rosalind's personality. It also allows the romantic heroine to meet with Orlando alone. In adopting this device, Shakespeare effectively but subtly draws attention to gender-based constraints that influence the lives of men and women and their relationships with one another. In making Rosalind (and other comic heroines, often in marked contrast to their male counterparts in the plays) so witty, sensitive and intelligent, it might also be argued that the play reveals the loss to humanity and society that the subordination of women entails.

In some ways, then, Rosalind's male disguise is a liberation for her. However, I would argue that this liberation is not in the adoption of a guise of masculinity but in the recognition of gender expectations and gendered responses that it permits. Precisely because she is not male, Rosalind's adoption of a pose of masculinity draws attention to its attributes. Even though Rosalind is, on the whole, conscious that she is playing at being a man and chides Celia: 'Dost thou think, though I am caparisoned like a man, I have doublet and hose in my disposition?' (III.2.188–90), there are moments when she parodies masculine attitudes to women. For example, she tells Celia 'Do you not know I am a woman? When I think, I must speak' (III.2.242–3), invoking stereotypical attitudes to women's supposed loquaciousness.

We have noted that Celia's role declines substantially in Arden, so her outburst after the mock marriage in Act IV, Scene 1 is all the more emphatic: 'You have simply misused our sex in your love-prate. We must have your doublet and hose plucked over your head, and show the world what the bird hath done to her own nest' (IV.1.186–9). The implication of

Figure 6.3   Katharine Hepburn as Rosalind and William Prince as Orlando in *As You Like It* at the Theatre Guild, New York, directed by Michael Benthall with scenery and costumes by James Baitly, 1950. Photograph in the Shakespeare Collection, Birmingham Public Library Services.

defilement in the image of 'what the bird hath done to her own nest' is clear and the danger of disguise is brought to the fore. It is not entirely clear what has provoked Celia's outburst. Perhaps it is the pragmatic, wholly unromantic attitude to love and marriage that Rosalind has just been expounding: 'The poor world is almost six thousand years old, and in all this time there was not any man died in his own person, videlicet, in a love-cause' (IV.1.85–8). There is too her hard-nosed assessment of the difference between men's and women's romantic expectations and the reality of love and marriage: 'men are April when they woo, December when they wed; maids are May when they are maids, but the sky changes when they are wives' (IV.1.136–8). Furthermore, she again invokes stereotypical views of women as licentious, claiming that women's 'wit' and wisdom rests in the means and the excuses they devise to cuckold their husbands (IV.1.150–63).

It seems that it is the exposing of the fiction upon which romantic love is based, and by implication the challenging of the gender expectations implicit in the fiction, that Celia finds a threat. Both by her disguise and by what she says, Rosalind undermines what have appeared to be secure assumptions about men and women and their relations with one another. However, in this play, as Catherine Belsey argues, 'the emphasis is on the pleasures rather than the dangers implicit in the transgression of sexual difference' ('Disrupting sexual difference', in *Alternative Shakespeares*, 1985, p.184), and from this viewpoint Celia's misgivings do not carry much weight.

Rosalind's cruelty to Phebe seems to be a further example of a parody of the crudest of male attitudes to women:

> ... down on your knees
> And thank heaven, fasting, for a good man's love!
> For I must tell you friendly in your ear,
> Sell when you can, you are not for all markets.
>
> (III.5.57–60)

It may be significant that Phebe is more inclined to respond to such 'macho' posturing than to the Petrarchan 'prissiness' of Silvius. Ironically, Phebe's attraction to Ganymede can be compared with Silvius's attraction to her, in that both desire the unobtainable.

There are a number of further significant aspects of Rosalind's disguise, which have not yet been mentioned. The first is the fact that her disguise is multiple. It is not just that she is Rosalind disguised as Ganymede. She is Rosalind disguised as Ganymede who then 'plays' Rosalind for Orlando – except, of course, that she really *is* Rosalind, so that her play-acting here is in fact revelation. The sense of a shared secret between the audience and Rosalind, heavily laced as it is with dramatic irony, is an important part of the comic value of these layers of disguise. Another point about the disguise, which is usually lost to us in modern productions, is the additional illusion that would have been involved by the use of a boy actor to play the part of Rosalind in Shakespeare's day. What the early audiences (and the audiences of modern all-male productions, discussed later) would see would be a boy (or in the modern productions, a man) playing a woman who disguises as a man, who pretends to be a woman and then returns to being a woman – but is still, in reality, a boy! This is gender-confusion on a grand scale indeed! It certainly adds another dimension to the consideration of gender in the play and also to the consideration of audience response.

Perhaps the most important aspect of the multi-layered disguise is the focus on gendered expectations and behaviour that is a direct consequence. By drawing attention to the differences between women and men, the play defines what it is to be a woman or a man. But the device of cross-dressing offers the opportunity to undermine that definition. As Belsey has argued, the deliberate gender confusion in this play raises the question, 'Who is speaking?' When Rosalind mocks women, is our response to this different if we know that a male actor speaks the lines? Belsey suggests:

> if we imagine the part played by a male actor it becomes possible to attribute a certain autonomy to the voice of Ganymede … in this limited sense the extra-textual sex of the actor may be seen as significant. Visually and aurally the actor does not insist on the femininity of Rosalind-as-Ganymede, but holds the issue unresolved, releasing for the audience the possibility of glimpsing a disruption of sexual difference.
>
> ('Disrupting sexual difference', in *Alternative Shakespeares*, 1985, p.183)

The question 'Who is speaking?' is quite explicitly left with the audience of *As You Like It* in the Epilogue. It is extremely unusual for an Epilogue to be spoken by a female character, yet Rosalind's 'getting the last word' in this play seems entirely appropriate. One very interesting feature of this speech is that it represents a direct address to the women in Shakespeare's audience. There has been considerable scholarly disagreement about the constitution of Shakespeare's audiences, and such evidence as there is has been interpreted very differently. To summarize, the range of opinion extends from those who believe that Shakespeare's audiences were largely drawn from the artisans, apprentices and lower middle classes of London, through those who believe that the audiences consisted of representatives from all classes, to those who hold the view that the audiences were predominantly aristocratic and well educated (see Andrew Gurr, *Playgoing in Shakespeare's London*, 1987). Within these shades of opinion, views about the representation of women are equally diverse. However, there seems to be general agreement that women did go to the theatres, even if we are not sure that they went to see the plays. There is some evidence that prostitutes, for example, went to find customers. Certainly, there is a good deal of contemporary comment which suggests that the public playhouses were not considered suitable places for respectable women, unlike the audiences of Restoration theatre (discussed in Chapter Five).

Of course, the theatre as a public forum plays a very different role in modern culture. Women today write and perform in many different kinds of play, and research has shown that theatre audiences since the 1980s at least have, for a variety of reasons, tended to include more women than men (see, for example, Lizbeth Goodman's *Contemporary Feminist Theatres,*

1993). A similar gender balance applies to the readers of plays, since a high proportion of undergraduate literature students are women. Both women and men in theatre audiences today will respond to Rosalind's Epilogue. Given that it is a direct address to the audience, it seems appropriate to consider what such responses might be. Will the responses of men and women be different? How might the gender of the actor playing Rosalind influence the response of either men or women?

Re-read the Epilogue. Why does Rosalind speak the Epilogue and what does she say? What does the Epilogue add to our understanding of gender issues?

D i s c u s s i o n

Rosalind begins by seeking audience approbation for the play. However, she soon introduces a reference to illusion or magic: 'My way is to conjure you, and I'll begin with the women' (ll.205–6). This is followed by an attempt directly to relate approval for the play to the attitudes of women towards men, and vice versa:

> I charge you, O women, for the love you bear to men, to like as much of this play as please you; and I charge you, O men, for the love you bear to women – as I perceive by your simpering, none of you hates them – that between you and the women the play may please.
>
> (ll.206–11)

Liking of the play is clearly made a joint effort, and the play's title – *As You Like It* – is related to the recognition of love and its dependence upon gendered expectations, which has been a major theme. Whilst the play has raised the possibility that love transcends gender, the Epilogue seems to assume that sexuality is expressly heterosexual, thus, apparently, heralding a return to clearly defined gender roles. ■

A further important aspect of the Epilogue's function is to draw attention to the dramatic illusion of the play. **Rosalind's final words 'If I were a woman' (l.211) are very puzzling. What can they mean?**

D i s c u s s i o n

This phrase, surely, depends upon the audience's assumption that the actor playing Rosalind is male. Just at the moment when, as Rosalind, the character's true gender identity has been resumed, Shakespeare deliberately draws attention to the fact that, all along, 'she' was a young man. Paradoxically, the shattering of the dramatic illusion reinforces its power. In addition, the Epilogue exposes the audience's acceptance of stage convention, and their willingness to believe a male actor to be a woman. The fiction of gender construction is similarly exposed. As Belsey suggests, 'A male actor *and* a female character is speaking' ('Disrupting sexual difference', in *Alternative Shakespeares*, 1985, p.181). ■

The shock element of gender reversals and disguise adds a layer of intrigue to each performance of the play – one of the many functions of comedy as a form.

Dramatic and literary conventions: soliloquy and pastoral

The use of soliloquy in As You Like It

In earlier chapters of this book, you have been introduced to Shakespeare's use of soliloquy as a dramatic device that helps us to read the text of a play with a greater understanding of its status as a text for performance. There was a very full discussion of soliloquy in the chapter on *Henry V.* You will also recall how, in *Othello*, Iago's soliloquies are the means by which we, the audience, learn about the depths of his deception, while Othello's soliloquies demonstrate the ever-increasing grip that 'the green-eyed monster', jealousy, has over him. Through the soliloquies, we come to know the two men and to appreciate the tragedy that results from their individual characters and their relationship to one another. In *The Rover*, Behn used 'asides' and soliloquies to reveal the characters' true feelings and motives. Shakespeare's use of soliloquy has been tremendously influential in the development of dramatic literature from Behn to the present. Let us now consider an example from *As You Like It.*

Re-read Oliver's soliloquy at the end of the opening scene. What is the function of this soliloquy with regard to both the action of the play and the possibilities for performance?

D i s c u s s i o n

One of the functions of this soliloquy is to reveal Oliver's villainy to the audience, so that we will not, like Charles the wrestler, be taken in by him. Another function is to reveal the root of his villainy – jealousy of Orlando – and further to develop a theme already introduced by Orlando: that of 'nature and nurture'. Orlando has, earlier in the scene, railed against his lack of nurture, or education. Yet he acknowledges 'the something that nature gave me ... my gentility' (ll.16–19). In his soliloquy, Oliver recognizes that there is an innate nobility in Orlando, 'Yet he's gentle, never schooled and yet learned, full of noble device', which makes him 'of all sorts enchantingly beloved' (ll.154–6). ■

This is the only soliloquy in the main body of the play. Apart from this one exception, we are permitted no privileged access to the inner thoughts of any of the characters. Always we are on the outside, very firmly an audience to what occurs. There is no attempt directly to engage our emotions with the predicaments of those who are in often painful confusion on the stage (although we will argue later that the mediation of some of the characters – such as Touchstone and Jaques – between the action and the audience may function in a way that engages the audience's sensibilities and promotes a questioning approach to the experiences portrayed). As you may recognize when we come to discuss the nature of comedy as a genre, the absence of soliloquies is another aspect of the necessary distance required to enable the release of laughter.

There is, however, one other, extremely interesting, soliloquy in *As You Like It*, which occurs at the very end of the play and is, arguably, outside the play proper. This is the Epilogue, in which Rosalind addresses the audience directly. As we have noted, its purpose seems to be explicitly to draw attention to the gender confusion that has been at the heart of the plot, as well to the resulting theatrical illusion. Like other soliloquies, it is revelatory, but in this case it is not so much the character as the illusion of character that is revealed.

Pastoral and political critique in As You Like It

Now let us see how the setting of the play helps to situate the action, both in terms of the language of the text and the performance context. In order to do so, we will need to think about the function of pastoral and Shakespeare's use of the pastoral convention. Pastoral is a name derived from the Latin word for shepherd, *pastor*, to describe a form of literature developed by the ancient Greeks and Romans. This depicted an idealized rural life in which the loves and laments of shepherds and shepherdesses were given prominence. Pastoral was revived during the sixteenth century as part of the Renaissance enthusiasm for all things classical. Its appeal was

> partly to human wishfulness – the desire to conceive of circumstances in which the complexity of human problems could be reduced to its simplest elements: the shepherds and shepherdesses of pastoral are imagined as having no worries ... love and death, and making songs and music about these experiences, are their only preoccupations.
>
> (Wynne-Davies, *Bloomsbury Guide to English Literature*, 1995 edn, p.219)

Sixteenth-century pastoral reached its peak during the 1580s and early 1590s, when courtly writers such as Walter Raleigh, Edmund Spenser and Philip Sidney all wrote influential pastoral works. *As You Like It*, first performed in 1600, was able to rely upon common knowledge of the convention, and to parody it.

A contemporary writer, George Puttenham, in his book *The Arte of English Poesie* (1589), recognized a significant feature of pastoral. The Latin poet, Virgil, devised his 'Eclogues' (short pastoral dialogues), Puttenham contends,

> not of purpose to counterfeit or represent the rustical manner of loves and communication, but under the veil of homely persons and in rude speeches to insinuate and glance at great matters, and such as perchance had not been safe to have been disclosed in any other sort.
>
> (Cited in Loughrey, *The Pastoral Mode*, 1984, p.35)

The suggestion is that the pastoral can enable writers to address 'great matters' which, for reasons of decorum perhaps, it would be unacceptable for them to tackle more directly.

A number of twentieth-century critics (notably, Annabel Patterson in *Pastoral and Ideology*, 1988) have recognized that sixteenth-century pastoral was not pure escapism, but a strategy that facilitated social, moral and political criticism in an age when a more open critique was not possible. The strategy relied more upon the effective discrediting of court life than upon any real suggestion that the shepherd's rural existence represented

Figure 6.4   Micheline Patton as Rosalind, Andrew Keir as Orlando, Michael Martin-Harvey as Touchstone, Moira Robertson as Audrey, Paul Curran as Oliver, Mary Llewellyn as Celia, Ian MacNaughton as Le Beau, Fulton Mackay as Amiens, Douglas Lamond as Duke Senior and Norman Tyrrell as Jaques with, in the foreground, Roddy MacMillan as Silvius and Mandy Noel as Phebe in *As You Like It* at the Glasgow Citizens Theatre, produced by John Casson with scenery by Molly MacEwen, 1951. Photograph in the Shakespeare Collection, Birmingham Public Library Services.

the ideal. The shepherd was presented as a true counsellor, in contrast to the courtly flatterer; the chief value of his country life was its real and metaphorical distance from the court.

It has been suggested by Agnes Latham in her introduction to the Arden edition of the play that aspects of *As You Like It* can be related to a troubled period of Elizabeth's reign. In particular, Latham argues that it can be associated with the discontent of the Earl of Essex and his followers and, subsequent to his failed 'rebellion' (if such it was) in 1599, their exile or execution. You will remember that in Chapter Three Simon Eliot has also related this event to aspects of *Henry V.* In *As You Like It*, however, it is less important to find a direct and specific contemporary parallel than it is to understand that educated members of the audience might have expected to find political critique embedded within pastoral.

Can you think of ways in which the pastoral form might serve a political function in *As You Like It*?

D i s c u s s i o n

I would argue that a political critique is important in the play. The situation presented in the play's opening scenes creates the necessary conditions against which the pastoral elements are firmly established in Act II. The corruption and 'unnaturalness' of Duke Frederick's court and of the city that he governs are, as we have already observed, regularly invoked through-

211

out Act I. In the first scene, Adam contrasts the treatment he receives from Oliver with his treatment in the old days, under 'my old master' (ll.78–9). Although one of the younger generation, Orlando is associated with an older code of chivalry and honour. Rosalind loves him for it, at first perhaps in part because he participates in the values and morals with which she associates her father; Duke Frederick hates him for the same reason. Orlando recognizes this in himself when he regularly claims 'the spirit' of his father lives in him. Adam calls him 'you memory/of old Sir Rowland' (II.3.3–4) but he also realizes that Orlando's virtues 'are sanctified and holy traitors' to him in the new world:

> Know you not, master, to some kind of men
> Their graces serve them but as enemies?
> …
> O, what a world is this, when what is comely
> Envenoms him that bears it!
>
> (II.3.10–15)

This further endorses the view that Duke Frederick's court is a corruption of proper order. Orlando recognizes in Adam's duty and loyalty a remnant of an older and better time:

> O good old man, how well in thee appears
> The constant service of the antique world,
> When service sweat for duty, not for meed!
> Thou art not for the fashion of these times,
> Where none will sweat but for promotion,
> And having that do choke their service up
> Even with the having.
>
> (II.3.56–62)

If we think of the structure of the play as a whole, we could argue that the political ascendancy and succession of Orlando and Rosalind that is promised by their marriage at the end of the play represents continuity with the best aspects of the past, with which Duke Frederick's interregnum had broken. The end of the play sees not so much a new order as a re-establishment of an older, though renewed and refreshed, order. ∎

Re-read Duke Senior's speech at the beginning of Act II, Scene 1. What does it tell us about the virtues of country life? What else does it tell us about?

Discussion

The speech tells us very little about country life, which the Duke purports to extol, but a great deal about the court life from which he is an exile. The new court is 'envious' and life there full of 'peril'. It is characterized by 'painted pomp' (the glossy and self-important surface with which the court and courtiers present themselves), and by false 'counsellors' who persuade a man by 'flattery' to think highly of himself. The emphasis is all on the superficial, almost ritual, nature of the court. The Duke also tells us of the attributes of civilized life that characterize the court: society ('public haunt'), conversation ('tongues'), intellectual and spiritual inspiration ('books' and 'sermons'). We know that he values these because he claims to have found them in the forest: 'And this our life, exempt from public haunt,/Finds tongues in trees, books in the running brooks,/Sermons in stones, and good in everything' (ll.15–18).

The benefits of life in the forest are all seen as relative to life at court. The constant comparison is reassuring – it renders exile bearable. However, the Duke's earlier reference to the 'precious jewel' (l.14) in the toad's head suggests that these benefits are, like that jewel, largely imaginary, and that life in the forest is more of an adversity to the Duke and his followers than he cares to admit. Life in the forest is 'sweet' only in the sense that it contrasts with the bitterness of rejection from court and the uncongenial moral corruption of the new court. 'Sweet are the uses of adversity' (l.12) does not deny that exile is adversity. Amiens' reply endorses this view: 'Happy is your grace/That can translate the stubbornness of fortune/Into so quiet and so sweet a style' (ll.18–20).

The contrast that Shakespeare sets up between the formal world of the court and country life in Arden allows too for an exploration of the 'real' versus the 'ideal', which is an abiding concern of the play. ■

For the Duke and his followers, and for some of the other characters in the play, notably Touchstone and Jaques, the value of the country is the light it sheds on life at court. Conversely, experience of country life is mediated by courtly understanding. The contrast between the 'real' rustics, Corin, Silvius, Phebe and Audrey, and the courtly 'usurpers' is made explicit in their differing attitudes towards country life. Shakespeare mixes pastoral and anti-pastoral in this play. Anti-pastoral can be described as an opposing view, an antithesis of pastoral. In particular, it is a view that the kind of existence represented in pastoral as being an ideal is not, in fact, attractive or desirable. We cannot easily say 'Shakespeare mocks the pastoral' because, paradoxically, the way in which it is mocked seems to endorse its value. Corin's more realistic presentation of the hardships as well as the benefits of rural life discloses a nobility and dignity that are admirable:

> Sir, I am a true labourer: I earn that I eat, get that I wear, owe no man hate, envy no man's happiness, glad of other men's good, content with my harm; and the greatest of my pride is to see my ewes graze and my lambs suck.
> (III.2.69–73)

The 'real' shepherd (the one who lives in Arden, and is not on holiday there) shows us that Arden is not an ideal world. He is 'shepherd to another man,/And do not shear the fleeces that I graze' (II.4.75–6). Moreover, his master is an absentee landlord 'of churlish disposition,/And little recks to find the way to heaven/By doing deeds of hospitality' (II.4.77–9).

If the exiled Duke seems to promote the pastoral ideal, Touchstone and Jaques function as satiric observers of the delusion. Touchstone is sceptical about the charms of country life. When he arrives there with Ganymede and Aliena in Act II, Scene 4, he is not impressed: 'now am I in Arden, the more fool I. When I was at home I was in a better place' (ll.13–14).

Figure 6.5   Michael Gardiner as Jaques in the Cheek by Jowl production of *As You Like It*, directed by Declan Donnellan, 1994–5. Photo: John Haynes.

For Touchstone the court is his milieu, his home. Later, in Act III, Scene 2, his riddling reply to the old shepherd's question 'how like you this shepherd's life' (l.11), endorses his desire to be elsewhere:

> Truly, shepherd, in respect of itself, it is a good life; but in respect that it is a shepherd's life, it is naught. In respect that it is solitary, I like it very well; but in respect that it is private, it is a very vile life. Now in respect it is in the fields, it pleaseth me well; but in respect it is not in the court, it is tedious. As it is a spare life, look you, it fits my humour well; but as there is no more plenty in it, it goes much against my stomach.
>
> (ll.13–20)

Unlike Duke Senior, Touchstone dislikes the country precisely because it is not like the court. Moreover, he regards the court as the benchmark, the reference point, the 'touchstone', against which all other kinds of men and society are to be measured. Even though Corin puts forward a reasoned argument to the effect that the manners of the country are appropriate to the country, Touchstone persists in his belief that country life is ungodly, asserting that Corin will be damned for her part in it. Although this is light-hearted, the contrast between civilization and nature that is implicit is an important theme in the play, and one that is intrinsic to the comic structure. It informs the wider underlying debate about the tension between the individual and society – a debate that is communicated through so many of the dramatic and thematic mechanisms employed, such as disguise. The inter-weaving of these different elements gives the play a cohesion and style.

The individual and society

Before we meet Jaques we already know that he is not entirely happy with the pastoral existence because he is avoiding the company of his fellows (Act II, Scene 1). He sees, in Touchstone, someone else with a critical perspective. When Jaques reports his first meeting with Touchstone there is in his words a suggestion that the Duke and his followers have in some way abdicated their responsibilities. Time is passing them by. Jaques tells us and his on-stage audience that, drawing a 'dial' (a watch) from his pocket, Touchstone moralized:

> Thus we may see ... how the world wags:
> 'Tis but an hour ago since it was nine,
> And after one hour more 'twill be eleven,
> And so from hour to hour, we ripe, and ripe,
> And then from hour to hour we rot, and rot,
> And thereby hangs a tale.
> (II.7.23–8)

Despite the apparent irrelevance of time in the forest, mortality remains an imperative: 'And so from hour to hour we rot, and rot.' Jaques picks up this theme again later in the scene (II.7.140–7). That the world of Arden is not, in fact, outside time in any meaningful sense is also emphasized during the courtship of Ganymede playing Rosalind and Orlando, with the latter's inadequacies as a lover often directly associated with his inability to keep appointments.

Like Touchstone, Jaques offers an anti-pastoral challenge to Arden. He insists upon exposing the delusion of his fellows, claiming that, as outsiders, their domination over nature in the forest (for example, by hunting the deer) is a kind of tyranny. In Act II, Scene 1, the First Lord reports to Duke Senior Jaques' view that 'you do more usurp/Than doth your brother that hath banished you' (ll.27–8). When Jaques speaks, all listen and expect to hear wisdom, but Jaques mocks their expectations, delivering little but contempt and cynicism. In Act II, Scene 5, he summarizes his own function in the verse that he adds to Amiens' song. His 'Ducdame' (l.51), 'a Greek invocation, to call fools into a circle' (l.56), aptly demonstrates his tendency to observe and comment upon society without participating in it. Indeed, his function as an observer is partly anchored in his status as a character 'on the margins'. In the world of the play this is not a happy condition. Orlando recognizes him as 'either a fool or a cipher' (III.2.282), and Rosalind exposes the bitterness that he finds in experience and the means by which he has found it: 'A traveller! By my faith, you have great reason to be sad. I fear you have sold your own lands to see other men's; then, to have seen much and to have nothing is to have rich eyes and poor hands' (IV.1.19–22).

The suggestion is that Jaques has lost his integrity. His search for individual experience, through travel, has ultimately impoverished him so that one kind of liberty has led to a loss of economic independence. Shakespeare's audience would also have recognized – in Jaques' disposition of land to fund his dissolute life – a lack of regard for the community for whom Jaques ought to have felt some responsibility. It is a measure of the transforming power of Arden that he of all characters can be said to have his integrity restored to him at the end of the play. Of all those who at the beginning of the play claim that they 'would not change' (II.1.18) their pastoral existence, only Jaques stays.

On the other hand, it is not surprising at all that it is Jaques who chooses to stay behind. His preference is for solitariness and his view of humanity runs counter to the movement of the play, which, I shall argue, is towards recognition of community.

Re-read Orlando's speech in Act II, Scene 7, lines 107–20. How do you think the language here contributes to a recognition of the value of community in the play?

Discussion

Orlando's rough intrusion into the pastoral idyll serves to remind us (as readers and audience) and Duke Senior's company (within the world of the play) of the human society that they have abandoned. Orlando's words, with the repetition of 'If ever', become an invocation, almost as though they are a litany for the breaking of a spell:

> But whate'er you are
> That in this desert inaccessible,
> Under the shade of melancholy boughs,
> Lose and neglect the creeping hours of time:
> If ever you have looked on better days;
> If ever been where bells have knolled to church;
> If ever sat at any good man's feast;
> If ever from your eyelids wiped a tear,
> And know what 'tis to pity and be pitied,
> Let gentleness my strong enforcement be,
> In the which hope I blush, and hide my sword.
>
> (II.7.110–20)

Here the forest is imaged as a hostile environment, a 'desert'. The fact that it is 'inaccessible' to the benefits of society is what makes it so, for Orlando. Even the trees, or 'boughs', are sad ('melancholy'). Notice the way that the language and imagery develop in this passage to evoke the mood. The shadows cast by the trees are fittingly related to 'the creeping hours of time'. Orlando sees this pastoral existence in terms of loss and neglect (l.113), which are explicitly contrasted with the attributes of society. These are firmly anchored in a sense of the importance of community: 'church', 'feast' and the fellow-feeling that is seen to be the mark of humanity 'to pity and be pitied'. The Duke, in repeating the terms in which Orlando defines 'better days', accepts these terms (see ll.121–7). ■

Re-read Act II, Scene 7, lines 128–67. How does this sequence develop some of the themes we have already discussed?

Discussion

Orlando has departed to fetch the exhausted Adam. Orlando's arrival in Arden has served the function of introducing the outside world (and a touch of reality) to the pastoral idyll. Duke Senior's words in lines 136–9 demonstrate that, for him, this has reawakened a sense of the society that is conspicuously lacking in Arden. The references to 'theatre', 'pageants' and 'the scene/Wherein we play' suggest an awareness of role-playing as a feature of society. There is, perhaps, an implication that in their withdrawal the Duke and his followers are not 'playing their parts' (we might link this with the concept of meta-theatre).These words seem to represent an expansion of the play, a movement from introspection and passivity towards recognition of mutual needs and responsibilities and actions. ■

Let us now consider Jaques' famous speech 'All the world's a stage' (II.7.140–67). **How does the theatrical context inform our understanding of Jaques' speech and of his character?**

Discussion

In terms of the verse pattern, Jaques shares the first line of his speech with the last line of the Duke's. The clue to the actor playing Jaques is to pick up the cue quickly. Jaques jumps in straight away, but he has completely missed the point. Duke Senior has recognized that fellow-feeling is an important aspect of what it is to be human – 'Thou seest we are not all alone unhappy' (l.137) – but Jaques picks up the theatrical images and develops them in a way that is wholly inappropriate. He launches into a moralizing diatribe about the seven ages of man. Jaques' pessimistic view of human life, which sees human existence as lonely, futile and ridiculous, is absolutely devoid of the spirit which infuses Orlando and which has moved the Duke. When viewed in the wider context of the play's concern with gender issues, there may also be something about the exclusively (and somewhat stereotypical) male vision of humanity offered by Jaques (schoolboy, soldier, lover, justice, pantaloon) that functions to highlight its inadequacy. It is significant that Jaques, as well as being anti-pastoral, is also anti-love. His decision to remain in Arden at the end of the play is made necessary, to some extent, by the fact that he remains unpartnered.

Earlier, in Act II, Scene 2, we heard something of Jaques' pessimism in the First Lord's report of the injured deer and the moralizing that this provoked from Jaques. When the other deer ignore their injured companion, it is no more than Jaques expects; he sees in this an analogy to human society:

> 'Ay', quoth Jaques,
> 'Sweep on, you fat and greasy citizens,
> 'Tis just the fashion! Wherefore do you look
> Upon that poor and broken bankrupt there?'
> Thus most invectively he pierceth through
> The body of country, city, court.
>
> (II.1.54–9)

For Jaques, life is essentially the same whether it is at court or in the country. This view is governed by a pessimistic attitude to human nature in which the imperative for self-preservation dominates. It is an anti-social view of humanity and, as such, it seems entirely appropriate that Jaques excludes himself from the return to community that the end of the play heralds.

Before Jaques' speech, his outlook has already been challenged by Orlando's words, which may be a deliberate allusion and contrast to Jaques' view as expressed in Act II, Scene 1. Orlando says: 'like a doe, I go to find my fawn/And give it food' (II.7.129–30). At the end of Jaques' speech, the challenge to what it portends is reinforced when Orlando brings on stage the ailing and aged Adam. ∎

Re-read to the end of Act II, Scene 7. What is the dramatic function of this ending to the scene?

Discussion

The end of the scene maintains a balance between the tensions that have been present throughout. On the one hand, what we see on stage is a communal meal, with entertainment. Duke Senior has extended the hand of friendship to Orlando and Adam as fellow human beings, irrespective of who they are: 'I will not trouble you/As yet to question you about your fortunes' (ll.172–3). The atmosphere is harmonious and friendly. There is music. On the other hand, the words of the song that Amiens sings tell of 'man's ingratitude' (l.177) being more difficult to bear than the 'winter wind' (l.175). The winter sky

> dost not bite so nigh
> As benefits forgot.
> …
> Thy sting is not so sharp
> As friend remembered not.
>
> (ll.186–9)

The refrain seeks to persuade the listeners that the life apart, in Arden, is preferable: 'Most friendship is feigning, most loving mere folly … This life is most jolly' (ll.192–3). Whilst this reinforces the sense of bitterness in human experience, the Duke's final speech recalls love and loyalty, expressed through the references to Sir Rowland (l.195) and the loyalty of

Adam, 'Good old man' (l.201). The feeling of communal goodwill achieved here is reinforced by the visual image of the three men leaving the stage linked in companionship and mutual support, with the final words: 'Support him by the arm. Give me your hand,/And let me all your fortunes understand' (ll.203–4). ∎

From your study of *Henry V* and *Othello*, you will recognize that this balancing of one view with another is characteristically Shakespearean. It is central to the way in which the structure, themes, the use and abuse of literary convention and the language of the play operate together.

We have seen that life in Arden is not presented uncritically. It provides a catalyst for the country and court, nature and nurture tensions that inform the themes and the action of the play. Nevertheless, it is clear from the way in which the plot devices move the action so quickly into Arden – with all of the necessary banishments having been speedily, some would say clumsily, expedited by the end of Act I, for example – that Shakespeare is interested in Arden (or what it represents) for itself too. Whilst I have argued that the idealization of Arden represents an unhealthy withdrawal from society, the play raises questions about the nature of society through the experiences that the characters undergo in exile from it.

Comedy and its function in As You Like It

So far we have examined the text and social context of the play with reference to its comic moments, but without defining the term 'comedy'. The form has a long and fascinating history. One of the most widely accepted interpretations of comedy and its function, from classical times through Freud to our own post-modern times, might be said to be a recognition of its value in releasing tension. It has often been observed, for example, that people laugh at moments that seem wholly inappropriate. In everyday life, we can all think of occasions when a nervous or even tragic situation has provoked laughter. Embarrassment, apprehension, grief and even fear can induce laughter.

This is partly because laughter is a way of psychologically distancing ourselves from a situation. In order to laugh at something or someone, we have, metaphorically, to stand back and see things objectively. Thus, laughter can become a way of postponing or evading, emotionally, a problem for which we are not yet ready. It can be seen as a kind of automatic self-defence mechanism. The release that the laugh offers is both emotional and physical.

How can we relate this psychological interpretation of laughter to comic drama? Freud thought that the reason we laugh at comic situations on stage is because of the release of nervous energy when we realize that the misfortune we see coming does not directly affect us. It has also been argued that the release that the comic form embodies can be not only personal but communal, extending into society itself. From its earliest origins in classical Greece, comedy was integral to social and religious dramatic festivals, which represented temporary release from the everyday world in the form of holidays.

The structure of Shakespearean comedy

The work of C.L. Barber has been influential in exploring the 'festive' aspects of Shakespeare's comedies. Barber's book *Shakespeare's Festive Comedy* (1963) takes the premise that 'Much comedy is festive – all comedy if the word festive is pressed far enough' (p.3). He considers Shakespeare's comic art in relation to the festivities and customs of Elizabethan England. For Barber, 'festive' describes the atmosphere of the comedies, but it also describes their structure and meaning. The structure is, essentially, 'the way this comedy organizes experience'. Barber identifies what he calls a 'saturnalian pattern' in the comedies. It is 'saturnalian' because, like the pagan festivals that celebrated the benefits bestowed by Saturn (or Bacchus), the God of wine, the comedies are deliberately excessive. The pattern 'appears in many variations, all of which involve inversion, statement and counterstatement, and a basic movement which can be summarized in the formula, through release to clarification' (ibid., p.4).

Barber's thesis is that the function of comedy can be closely related to the social function of the feast or holiday, which was embedded within the folklore and customs of Shakespeare's England. He cites the examples of Mayday and Twelfth Night festivities in which 'normal' social conventions and morality were temporarily suspended and figures such as the 'Lord of Misrule' disrupted accepted hierarchical expectations. Barber suggests that this represents a movement 'through release to clarification' (ibid.) which is echoed in the structure and meaning of Shakespeare's plays. The clarification is of man's relationship to nature and to society.

Alvin Kernan has observed that the structure of Shakespearean comedy can be seen as a three-part movement. This movement can be described in a number of ways, which recognize the variety of different levels at which the plays operate. It can be seen as a movement from the familiar through the strange, returning changed to the familiar; from everyday to holiday and back to everyday; from the restraints of society and order, to release and freedom, then back to work and sobriety; or

> from an old society which has become repressive, tyrannous and life-destroying to a revolutionary explosion … leading to a second period of disorder and excess [which] gives way in turn to the third period of the formation of a new society, which, while including all within its feasts and celebrations, is centred on youth and the new generation.
>
> ("Ducdame", in *The Revels History of Drama in English*, 1975, p.308)

How far do you think Kernan's suggestion of a three-part movement describes the structure of *As You Like It*?

D i s c u s s i o n

At the beginning of the play, we learn of Oliver's tyranny over Orlando and of Duke Frederick's autocratic rule. The atmosphere is repressive, but the potential for rebellion is there from the start. We learn of Duke Senior's alternative lifestyle in the Forest of Arden, and how this is so attractive to the youth that 'many young gentlemen flock to him every day, and fleet the time carelessly as they did in the golden world' (I.1.110–12). Similarly, we know of Orlando's intention to take action: 'The spirit of my father grows strong in me, and I will no longer endure it' (I.1.65–6), and of Adam's intention to go with him. By the end of Act I, the atmosphere of tyranny and repression at court has been so well established that we can readily share Celia's opinion that to leave will be to go in 'content/To liberty, and not to banishment' (I.3.135–6).

In sharp contrast to the world of the court is the idealized pastoral existence enjoyed in the forest. Here, despite 'the icy fang/And churlish chiding of the winter's wind' (II.1.6–7), we find a world turned upside down. In the forest, young people can meet and woo without the usual constraints that society imposes. However, excessive liberty is shown to be just as much of a threat to personal and social order as excessive tyranny. When it allows one young man (Orlando) to woo another (Ganymede playing Rosalind) and one young woman (Phebe) to fall in love with another (Rosalind disguised as Ganymede), release becomes disorder.

At the end of the play, the 'wicked' are converted to 'goodness'. Social, sexual and political order is re-established and there is a promise to return to the town and court, with all that represents. The time in Arden has been an interlude, a period for renewal and refreshment. Its temporary nature is essential to its value. ∎

Kernan notes some of the other ways in which the movement of plot may be analysed, for example in terms of

> the loss and rediscovery of identity, the movement from appearance to reality, or the alternation of nurture and nature. But whatever terms are used, the three-part movement is built not on a simple opposition of two opposed values but on a complex interaction of two basic realities, seemingly antithetical but ultimately mutually supporting. At the beginning reason grows too rational and law becomes too legal, which forces an excessive action in the opposite direction of absolute freedom and excessive playfulness, which finally exhausts or thwarts itself and returns, with a sense of relief but renewed, from fresh contact with the springs of life and the powers of nature to the man-ordered, rationally organized world. The process usually ends with dancing, feasting, and multiple marriage.

> ("Ducdame", in *The Revels History of Drama in English*, 1975, pp.308–9)

In *As You Like It*, as in several other plays (such as *A Midsummer Night's Dream*), Shakespeare uses the journey from the city to the woods and back again to demonstrate many of the values that, as Kernan suggests, are not so much antithetical as 'mutually supporting'. It is interesting to note that in Elizabethan usage the word 'wood' also meant 'mad'. This is appropriate because madness is also a kind of liberty, a freedom from convention. Shakespeare regularly associated love with madness. It is also notable that the wood, or forest, in literature or art has become an archetypal image of disorientation, frequently employed to signify a lost or wandering soul. Often such images are connected with humanity's search for meaningful existence and for an understanding of the relationship between man and nature (including God). The wood, as a template for a 'natural' (as distinct from a 'civilized') location, may also be associated with the Garden of Eden.

Figure 6.6   Matilda Ziegler as Celia (left) and Susan Lynch as Rosalind perform before a painted wall mural in the St Pancras Hotel, London, the banishment scene from *As You Like It*, directed by Fiona Shaw and recorded for an Open University/BBC video, produced by Amanda Willett, 1995. Photo: Trevor White.

Whilst the experience of a temporary sojourn in the wood or forest is one of transformation, or what Barber called 'clarification', there is another sense in which the holiday, the brief respite from 'normality', reinforces rather than undermines that reality. In terms of social conventions, *As You Like It* can be seen to endorse the old adage that rules are honoured more in the breach than in the observance; in terms of the archetypal imagery outlined above, the return from the forest may signify an acceptance of the fallen human condition.

You can see that a holiday atmosphere is an essential ingredient of the mood of both *The Rover* and *As You Like It*. In *The Rover*, the women are able to transgress social norms and to don gypsy disguises because there is a carnival that permits this. There is a suspension of normal conventions that allows young women a temporary freedom. In *As You Like It*, this atmosphere is created by the opposing worlds of the court and the Forest of Arden. Orlando indicates the 'outside time' quality of the forest when he tells Rosalind, 'There's no clock in the forest' (III.2.292–3). Rosalind encourages Orlando to woo Ganymede playing Rosalind because 'now I am in a holiday humour, and like enough to consent' (IV.1.61–2). The exiled Duke calls his erstwhile subjects 'co-mates and brothers in exile' (II.1.1), disrupting hierarchical expectations. The disguises of Rosalind and, to a lesser extent, of Celia, also contribute to the freedom from normal constraints that is such an important aspect of the comedy.

Finally, there is also a sense in which the theatrical 'event' that the performance of a play represents is itself a holiday of sorts – at least for the audience; it is not called a 'play' without reason. Samuel Taylor Coleridge spoke of the 'willing suspension of disbelief' that is required of the audience. What he meant by this is that in going to a play we signify, individually and collectively, our willingness to believe that at which, under more 'normal' circumstances, we might well balk. This is the complicity between what happens on stage and the audience which, at its best, when the chemistry is right, can be magical. *As You Like It*, with its layers of disguise and gender confusion, stretches this 'willingness' to its limits, and pushes the audience to consider shattering the illusion. Indeed, as we have seen, the Epilogue seems deliberately to set out to shatter the theatrical illusion entirely, in its direct address to women and men in the audience. Yet – and here is the magic – its effect (in a good production) is the reverse. Acknowledging the nature of theatrical illusion miraculously reinforces, rather than destroys, it.

Some of the ideas about comedy noted above were already familiar to Shakespeare and his contemporaries. In particular, the function of comedy to reflect but greatly exaggerate life, embodied in the notion of excess, was seen as part of the didactic purpose to which comedy could be put. Thomas Elyot (1531), for example, saw the cautionary tales that were presented in the comedies of the Roman authors Terence and Plautus (both of whom are said to have influenced Shakespeare's early comedies) as 'a mirror of man's life … they being thereof warned may prepare themselves to resist or prevent occasion'. Thomas Wilson (1533) claimed that 'the occasion of laughter and the mean that maketh us merry … is the fondness, the filthiness, the deformity and all such evil behaviour as we see to be in the other'. Sidney wrote: 'Comedy is an imitation of the common errors of our life, which he [the dramatist] representeth in the most ridiculous and scornful sort that may be; so as it is impossible that any beholder can be content to be such a one' (see Wilson, *Shakespeare's Happy Comedies*, 1962).

How far does *As You Like It* exemplify Sidney's theory?

D i s c u s s i o n

In *As You Like It* we can see that 'the common errors' of love and lovers are examined and mocked. There are numerous examples of hyperbole, which Sidney identifies as a characteristic of comedy. The contrasting of so many different pairs of lovers in the play is one feature of this exaggeration. In addition, 'the common errors' of love are central to the debate about the distinction between 'real' and romantic love, which is at the heart of Ganymede's lessons in love. We should also note that Shakespearean comedy is more subtle than Sidney's analysis allows. Some of the characters in *As You Like It* are presented sympathetically and are attractive. ■

Comparing *As You Like It* with the plays you have studied already in this book, can you identify any of the key features of comedy?

One response might be that comedies contain active female characters and domestic settings. In *Othello*, for example, Desdemona's dramatic function is largely divorced from what we can learn about her as a character. Her function, it might be argued, is to provide the means for Iago's revenge, a focus for Cassio's courtliness, and the catalyst for Othello's jealousy. Beyond her initial disobedience in marrying Othello without parental consent, she is passive – the object rather than the initiator of action – and offers very little resistance to Othello's accusations. By contrast, in the two comedies you study in this book, *The Rover* and *As You Like It*, women are able to act rather than being acted upon, even though sometimes it is necessary for them to be disguised to do so. This is partly related to the subject-matter – love and marriage – of the two plays. The sphere of comedy is, on one level, more 'domestic'. It is not concerned with the large affairs of state that occupy such a central position in history or tragedy. This marks one of the most significant differences between comedy and the other kinds of drama considered in this book.

Another characteristic of comedy is, as we noted above, the suspension of 'normal' conditions and conventions. ■

Shakespeare's (and Behn's) audiences may have been able to accept the portrayal of active, intelligent women in the comedies precisely because it was implicit that the context for such portrayals was 'a world turned upside down'. At another level, the examination of the very 'political' and 'real' issues of self-identity and gender relations gives the comedies a serious impact – comedy becomes an enjoyable form for presentation of serious ideas.

The detachment we have identified as a special characteristic in our response to comedy has important consequences for characterization. It is important that we do not identify too closely with the characters, or we will not be able to laugh at them. We must recognize them but not empathize too closely with them. The consequence of this imperative is that, on balance, the characters in comedies are more often stereotypical than those in tragedies, with whom it is crucial that we *do* empathize. The fool, the lovers, the wicked brothers, the shepherds – all of these characters are, to some extent, stereotypical stock figures. Nevertheless, it is a tribute to the subtlety of Shakespeare's comic vision that characterization is never entirely stereotypical. There is a psychological truth about Shakespeare's characters and their motivation that rescues them from pure stereotype. In particular, the extent to which we sympathize with the pain and the joy experienced by Shakespeare's comic heroines is remarkable.

Touchstone: foolery and comic function

Touchstone is the 'allowed fool' who acts as a measure of a healthy society, and in the play he contributes to the persistent comparisons between the old and the new. In Act I, Scene 2, his exchange with the young female characters suggests that words have slippery meanings at the new court. There is also an indication that his role as court fool is no longer valued.

Celia warns him, 'you'll be whipped for taxation one of these days' (ll. 80–1) and the exchange that follows is significant:

TOUCHSTONE The more pity that fools may not speak wisely what wise men do foolishly.

CELIA By my troth, thou sayest true: for since the little wit that fools have was silenced, the little foolery that wise men have makes a great show.

(ll.82–6)

Shakespeare's audience would have recognized the privileged position of an allowed fool that is alluded to here and which, Celia suggests, has been curtailed. The role of the fool in aristocratic households and at court was, through mockery and satire, to draw attention to the folly of his betters, thus preventing arrogance and maintaining a sense of proportion. The fact that fooling is discredited at Duke Frederick's court might, therefore, be taken to imply a lack of confidence and security in a society that cannot take criticism.

It is the fool's privileged position that Jaques envies when he declares 'motley's the only wear!' (II.7.34). 'Motley' refers to the traditional costume of a fool – multi-coloured and very distinctive. Jaques also draws attention to the social function that the fool performs:

Invest me in my motley; give me leave
To speak my mind, and I will through and through
Cleanse the foul body of th'infected world,
If they will patiently receive my medicine.

(II.7.58–61)

WILLIAM KEMP DANCING THE MORRIS.
Kemp's "Nine Daies Wonder," 1600.
Jusserand, "*English Novel.*"

Figure 6.7   Actor William Kemp dancing the Morris, detail from the title page of his book, *Kemp's Nine Daies Wonder, performed in a daunce from London to Norwich in 1599*, 1600. Mansell Collection.

The therapeutic and purgative nature of comedy is also invoked. Jaques goes on to deny any charges of personal slander that may be levelled at the fool. The mockery or satire is not personal, he claims, not aimed at individuals but at society in general. This is, in part, a recognition of comedy's characteristic use of stereotypes. Jaques argues that if individuals recognize themselves in a fool's 'fooling', they condemn themselves:

> What woman in the city do I name
> When that I say the city woman bears
> The cost of princes on unworthy shoulders?
> Who can come in and say that I mean her
> When such a one as she, such is her neighbour?
> Or what is he of basest function,
> That says his bravery is not on my cost,
> Thinking that I mean him, but therein suits
> His folly to the mettle of my speech?
> (II.7.74–82)

Here Shakespeare would have raised a laugh at the expense of members of his audience. Jaques addresses the audience directly, and the theatre was a well-known place for city women and gallants to see and to be seen (see Gurr, *Playgoing in Shakespeare's London*, 1987, pp.68–9). The context and the way the joke is expressed would have made it difficult for the audience to take offence. Shakespeare may also have been aiming the speech at some critics of the theatre, who were influenced by the emergence of Puritan ideas and were unable, or perhaps unwilling, to distinguish life from art.

As You Like It in performance

The audience

So far, we have identified some of the choices and acts of interpretation that actors and directors have to make when the written text is translated into performance. One of the most important points that we hope you will take away from this approach to the play is that each production and, to some extent, each performance is a new interpretation of the play. This is part of the excitement of dramatic literature: the text is, we have suggested, in a very literal and real sense recreated each time it is performed. We have also suggested that, in the case of live performances, the audience have a part to play in that recreation.

We have already mentioned the relationship that exists between the audience and the play. We want to extend this to suggest that there are fundamental differences between a modern audience and a seventeenth-century audience, and to consider some of the implications of these differences for our understanding of Shakespeare's plays.

To Shakespeare's audience, the whimsical title of the play, *As You Like It*, and the early introduction of the motif and device of disguise would have provided clear and recognizable signals that the play was a comedy.

The obviously comic figures would have reinforced audience awareness that they were watching a comedy. Audience expectation and response were and are, therefore, primed.

If you doubt the importance or significance of this, consider conversations you have had with friends after seeing a new play, or a programme on television, where such clear signals have been absent. You will recall comments such as 'Was it supposed to be funny?' or 'I thought it was serious until ... '. The extent to which we take our cues from our friends in the audience (even if that audience consists of only two or three people watching television) is very marked. This is recognized both by actors, who will talk of 'good' and 'bad' audiences and often regard 'the audience' as a single entity rather than a group of individuals, and by the producers of television 'sit-coms', who introduce artificial 'canned' laughter as a prompt to the lone home viewer. The sense of community contributes to the shared experience that a live theatre event offers. The audience is not composed of passive observers but active participants; they can influence what happens on stage, often tangibly. This participation is especially noticeable where comedy is concerned because timing will be affected by the actors having to pause for laughter. The sense of community is integral to the experience. Although this participation and sense of community is, as you may have noted, in direct contrast with the distancing device of laughter considered earlier, there is something intrinsically communal and social (rather than individualistic or anti-social) at the heart of comedy.

It follows that it will be more difficult to achieve the necessary sense of community if the work being performed is treated as a museum piece. Gary Taylor's provocative book, *Reinventing Shakespeare* (1990) traces the ways in which successive generations of literary scholars, actors and critics reappropriate and reinvent Shakespeare. In many ways, Taylor and others have argued, this protean aspect of Shakespeare's work is one of the key reasons for its canonization: each generation finds the Shakespeare it seeks. In Chapter Four it was suggested, for instance, that one of the reasons that *Othello* is canonical today is that modern audiences are newly intrigued by representation of issues of gender and race in the theatre: both issues are still topical for theatrical presentation.

Taylor makes the point that Shakespeare's work was originally conceived for a specifically theatrical context. It 'was not designed for printed distribution. The theatre – and particularly Shakespeare's theatre ... presupposes presence, recognition, community and sound' (*Reinventing Shakespeare*, 1990, p.324). Taylor notes that the authorities in Shakespeare's day recognized the potentially subversive influence of the theatre:

> The theatre can enable isolated dispersed individuals to recognize that they form part of a cohesive, and therefore powerful, present group consensus. Groups are less inhibited than individuals. The consciousness of belonging to a crowd tempts and enables an individual to do things that, left alone, s/he would resist – something any censor understands.

(Ibid.)

In other words, the theatre is, potentially, an agent of personal and social change. The thesis that underpins Taylor's book is that changes in society necessarily influence the composition of audiences, reception of plays and, indeed, attitudes towards Shakespeare as the Bard: 'national poet' and 'canonical author'. Although he regards 'the awareness of community' as a constant factor in theatre audiences, Taylor notes that 'typical contemporary auditoriums' such as the RSC's Barbican complex in London, are

> artificially lighted; our attention is focused on 'them', the actors, not on 'us', the spectators. This enforced distinction itself decreases our sense of a shared physical and mental space. The individual seats in which we sit, the darkness, the silence, the restriction of physical movement, the armchair partitions that carefully separate us in tiny cubes of purchased private space – all of these conventions of modern theatregoing do not destroy but do diminish our sense of belonging to a group.
>
> (Ibid., p.325)

The physical spaces in which plays are performed are, indeed, subject to social and cultural fashion, and are partly influenced by current attitudes to the theatre. In Chapters Two and Five, Bob Owens outlined some of the differences between the kinds of theatres in which Shakespeare's and Behn's plays were originally performed, relating these differences in part to the social composition of the audiences. In Chapter Five, Lizbeth Goodman discussed a modern playing space where the audience are very much a part of the playing 'community'. If you have been able to see the opening scenes of *Henry V* with Laurence Olivier in the title role, you will have gained an impression of what it might have been like to watch a play at the Globe Theatre, and you can appreciate that it will have been very different from the present-day experience outlined by Taylor in the extract above.

Because Shakespeare's stage had the audience on three sides, actors and audience inhabited, literally, the same space. We know that, sometimes, members of the audience sat on the stage (this continued to be true during the Restoration). Moreover, the social cohesion of Shakespeare's audience was much more marked than one could expect from most modern audiences, particularly an RSC audience. As Taylor says, modern audiences are often international: 'Shakespeare is the only thing they have in common, and Shakespeare is not enough to unite them' (ibid.).

However, I would argue that the audience watching a comedy in any period are united in at least one important sense: they have privileged access to the action that takes place on stage, which the characters do not have, although the actors do. In this sense, the actors and audience share a knowledge from which the characters are excluded and this is the source of some fine comic moments and dramatic irony. For example, we the audience know that Orlando really is wooing Rosalind and not, as he believes, Ganymede playing Rosalind. When Ganymede playing Rosalind tells Orlando 'I am your Rosalind' (IV.1.58) and enquires 'What would you say to me now, an I were your very, very Rosalind?' (IV.1.62–3), much of the comedy rests in the audience's knowledge that Ganymede *is* Rosalind. Similarly, the audience alone understand Ganymede's reiteration of 'And I for no woman' (V.2.83–7). The gender dynamics inherent in this comic exchange add another dimension to the text of the play.

Production history

Before you read the inside story of a workshop production of the play in the next section of the chapter, I would like to survey a range of twentieth-century productions. In doing so, I want to draw attention to the need to consider many different aspects of production. The design, including costume, set, lighting and the period that is evoked, is an important part of the interpretation of the play that is presented to us. With *As You Like It*, for example, the way in which the Forest of Arden is realized can have a significant impact on the total experience of the play. I also want to consider the implications of productions in different media, such as the stage, television and film.

Let us begin with the 1967 all-male production directed by Clifford Williams for the National Theatre at the Old Vic Theatre, London. Jan Kott, to whose work you have already been introduced in Chapter Four, is cited in the printed programme as an adviser on the production. The choice of Kott as the expert whose views best characterized the production is significant. Kott's influential collection of essays, *Shakespeare our Contemporary*, published in 1965, has had a profound effect upon theatre practice and criticism. As a Pole, Kott's need to find contemporaneity in Shakespeare was partly born of the repressive communist regimes in Eastern Europe, which denied freedom of speech to writers. Finding political and social challenge in Shakespeare's texts became a strategy that enabled actors and directors to comment on their own time and place. In the West, where the so-called permissive society was in full swing, Kott's work was seized upon, partly for the freedom of interpretation that it allowed in areas such as sexual behaviour and gender confusion. Thus, Kott's ideas were central to the 1967 all-male production of *As You Like It*. There has been plenty of controversy about the impact of Kott's ideas. Some find the assumption that Shakespeare can be 'updated' arrogant and see Kott's influence as a distortion of the texts. Others argue that Shakespeare's work must be seen in the context of the time in which he lived and that his work is interesting to us 'precisely because he is not our contemporary' (Elsom, Introduction to *Is Shakespeare Still our Contemporary?*, 1989, p.4).

The arguments for and against the view of Shakespeare as 'our contemporary' are often influenced by political perspectives. For example, there are those who object to the notion of Shakespeare's universality on the grounds that his work embodies an essentially conservative outlook, a view of mankind and society that stresses continuity at the expense of the potential for change.

In 1988, the International Association of Theatre Critics hosted a public seminar in London which asked the question: 'Is Shakespeare still our contemporary?' At the seminar, Richard Wilson was vehement in his defence of the need to interpret Shakespeare, in response to conservative criticism of innovative productions. Wilson argued:

> The attack on interpretation and the defence of something called
> poetry that will speak for itself is based on a complete naivety about
> language. Language has meaning because it refers to a social context
> in which it is spoken. It doesn't speak itself. It has to be constantly
> re-spoken, re-created in different social contexts.

> We should also be aware that every interpretation is, as it were, ideological. Every performance of every production is political in one way or another. There is no innocent interpretation. There is no essential Shakespeare who is free from all modern political bias.
>
> (Elsom, *Is Shakespeare Still our Contemporary?*, 1989, p.177)

Wilson's point recognizes the dynamic nature of performance and raises the question of what happens to a Shakespearean production that is not dynamic but fixed, such as film, television or video. In such cases, the production becomes a record of perceptions of a particular play at a particular time. You have already seen one example of this in your study of different versions of *Henry V.*

At the same seminar, David Thacker suggested: 'We should really think in terms of three historical moments. The first is the time about which Shakespeare was writing, the second is the time when he was writing and the third is the time when we receive the play in performance' (ibid., pp.23–4). Thacker pointed out that even in plays that Shakespeare sets in another time and place such as ancient Britain (*King Lear*) or Imperial Rome (*Julius Caesar*) he 'always seems to imagine that the play is happening now. He always treats his subject in some kind of contemporary idiom' (ibid., p.24).

Another speaker, Peter Brook, said:

> Ever since I started working in the theatre, I have been struck by one extraordinary fact, that the only thing that matters is what is happening at the moment when it is happening ...
>
> Being contemporary does not necessarily mean blindly bringing everything down to the present, nor does being timeless mean just being in a dream, so loftily elevated that the present has no importance. There is a point at which the great myths of the past and our sensation of living in the present, here and now, come together.
>
> (Ibid., p.97)

Many of the debates presented at the seminar centred upon the understanding of 'contemporary' and the premise that it is the task of every performance to make the text accessible to its audience in order that the text can 'live' for them. The productions of *As You Like It* that are considered below have all been influenced by the debate in one way or another.

Penny Gay provides a useful summary of RSC productions over the last forty years in an essay on *As You Like It* in her book *As She Likes It: Shakespeare's Unruly Women*, 1994. Gay opens her essay with an indication of some of the interpretative choices available to productions of *As You Like It*: 'Pretty pastoral or exploration of the dark recesses of the psyche? Or damning indictment of a power-hungry urban society? The conventions of pastoral, which Shakespeare drew on so extensively in *As You Like It*, allow for all these interpretative emphases, and more' (*As She Likes It*, 1994, p.48).

Gay also suggests that this play 'effects, through Rosalind's behaviour, the most thorough deconstruction of patriarchy and its gender roles in the Shakespearean canon', emphasizing the function of Arden as a 'magic space' while acknowledging the temporary nature that the 'carnival licence' allows. 'At the end, all must return to the real world and its social constraints', Gay argues, although she goes on to acknowledge the potential subversion of this apparent re-establishment of social and sexual order by Rosalind's Epilogue (ibid., p.49).

A number of twentieth-century productions have emphasized the transformative aspects of Arden. In the 1967 all-male production already mentioned, Williams's aim was to investigate love 'in an atmosphere of spiritual purity that transcends sexuality. It is for this reason that I employ a male cast ... so that we shall not – entranced by the surface reality – miss the interior truth' (Kennedy, *Looking at Shakespeare*, 1993, p.257).

Dennis Kennedy says of this production:

> the absence of women on the stage impelled a renewed attention to the power of convention in the theatre. Shakespeare's use of boy actors for female roles derived from cultural, social, and religious circumstances deeply rooted in his age, just as our use of actresses for those same roles is rooted in many unexamined contemporary assumptions about realism.
>
> (Ibid., p.258)

In other words, because the character is female it is assumed that a female actor must take the part for it to be realistic.

Figure 6.8   Jeremy Brett as Orlando, Ronald Pickup as Rosalind and Charles Kay as Celia in the National Theatre production of *As You Like It*, directed by Clifford Williams and designed by Ralph Koltai, 1967. Photo: Zoë Dominic.

The design for this production

> transformed Arden into a manmade forest, a dreamspace of modern art
> … On a burnished raked stage, mostly empty for the court scenes …
> White light, and black and white Carnaby Street costumes (often in
> plastics), underscored the artificiality of a psychedelic reverie … It was
> an Arden detached from nature and detached from the comforts of the
> natural, a space age Arden.

> (Ibid., p.258)

Most productions attempt to convey through the design (including costume
and lighting) the distinctive atmosphere of the play's contrasting locations:
the court and the country. In Michael Elliott's 1961 RSC production, an
immense tree, which was at once naturalistic and surreal, dominated the
stage. Together with the costumes, this suggested a Brothers Grimm type of
fairy tale, the tree representing the entire forest and, through it, the 'ideal'
world of romance and possibility.

In Berlin in 1977, Peter Stein directed a promenade production of *As
You Like It* in a vast film studio in which the audience literally accompanied
the actors on the journey from the court to Arden and back again:

> In the first part of play the audience was required to stand in a long
> narrow hall with light blue walls, brightly lit from below … The text
> was rearranged so that all the scenes in the court and near Oliver's
> house were played here … The audience, having shared the
> confinement of the court, shared the journey to the forest … through a
> tunnel of marvels.

> (Ibid., pp.261–2)

As one spectator described it:

> We found ourselves in a dimly lit, green labyrinth, artificial creepers
> hanging from above, water dripping down the walls. As we followed
> the twists and turns of this passage, we passed curious collages pasted
> on the walls, small booth like openings containing, for example, an
> Elizabethan workshop, or, more strikingly, an androgynous man …
> The conception was brilliant: to pass from the formality and brutality of
> the court through an underground labyrinth to the freedom and
> innocence of the forest was like being born anew.

> (Ibid., p.262)

In the 1973 RSC production directed by Buzz Goodbody (one of England's
only high-profile female theatre directors of the time), the sense of Arden as
a place where social responsibility has been abdicated was evoked through
costumes of studied 'hippieness'. The fashion for unisex clothing also had
the effect of blurring the gender identities, with Eileen Atkins's Ganymede a
long-haired youth in flared trousers and a fringed waistcoat. Michael Billington's review suggested that 'she seemed even more seductive as
Ganymede than before' (Gay, *As She Likes It*, 1994, p.67). Billington also
commented on 'Eileen Atkins's minimal attempt to disguise her femininity'
(ibid.). The set design recalled the 1961 RSC production, with the forest
depicted as a man-made, high-tech, tubular structure suspended from the
ceiling.

Figure 6.9   Richard Pasco as Jaques (left) and David Suchet as Orlando in the Forest of Arden in the RSC production of *As You Like It*, directed by Buzz Goodbody, 1973. Photo: Zoë Dominic.

Christine Edzard's 1991 film of the play emphasizes the relationship between the two worlds by having the actors double up parts. For example, Dukes Frederick and Senior are played by the same actor. The court is portrayed as a large multinational corporation with grand, ultra-modern headquarters. This contrasts with the urban deprivation outside its doors into which the exiles and the escapees are placed. The contrast of spaces effectively highlights the status of Arden as a place outside the normal bounds of society. Whilst there is a kind of freedom in this version of Arden, the costs (in terms of the loss of many of the benefits of society) are shown to be unacceptably high. These are not so much exiles as drop-outs.

There is, in all productions, a decision to be made about the extent to which the actor playing Rosalind should 'play' a man when he or she is disguised as Ganymede. As indicated in the consideration of Atkins's portrayal, this decision extends to the choice of costume. As Gay has suggested, some critics appear to have been influenced by the expectations of our own culture as to what constitutes 'ladylike' behaviour, in their response to stage Rosalinds. Thus, in Glen Byam Shaw's 1952 production for the RSC, Margaret Leighton's 'straddle-legged disguise' and 'inelegant posturing' was criticized by Kenneth Pearson in the *Manchester Daily Despatch* (ibid., p.51). Others also felt that 'heavenly Rosalind' was 'almost too well disguised' (ibid., p.50). Some enjoyed Leighton's 'sprightliness' and her 'tomboyish fun and high spirits' but others criticized this as a lack of restraint (ibid.). Gay suggests that such responses represent a view that Rosalind is thought of 'as society's ideal young woman, on the verge of marriage' (ibid., p.49) and she goes on to suggest that 'when an actress presents Rosalind's "singularity" as disruptive of social norms, there is often considerable unease in the ranks of critics' (ibid.).

Attitudes had changed by the time Vanessa Redgrave played Rosalind in the 1961 RSC production. Her performance was praised for being 'immensely natural', 'at once timeless and contemporary' (ibid., pp.54–5). Redgrave's costume was very similar to that which had been worn by Leighton. Yet critical response to this Rosalind was quite different: 'Where Leighton was berated for sitting inelegantly on the ground, Redgrave's naturalness was expressed in her lying on the greensward next to Orlando, chatting animatedly' (ibid., p.55). A critic writing in the *Birmingham Mail* suggested that *As You Like It* 'has had to wait until the 1960s for someone to appreciate that this is what Rosalind is' (ibid., p.55).

Figure 6.10   Ian Bannen as Orlando and Vanessa Redgrave as Rosalind in the RSC production of *As You Like It*, directed by Clifford Williams, 1961. Photograph by Angus McBean by courtesy of the Shakespeare Birthplace Trust.

Samantha Bond, who played Rosalind in David Thacker's 1992–3 production for the RSC, decided that it would be inappropriate for Rosalind to 'try any naff male impersonation' in her portrayal of Ganymede. Instead, she argued 'the reality of the play is that everyone in the forest believes Ganymede is a boy ... All we ask the audience to do is believe that Orlando believes – that's all you have to do' (RSC Study Pack for David

Figure 6.11   Simon Coates as Celia (left) and Adrian Lester as Rosalind/Ganymede in the Cheek by Jowl production of *As You Like It*, directed by Declan Donnellan, 1994–5. Photo: John Haynes.

Thacker's 1992–3 production). Bond suggested that it is only with Phebe that Rosalind really pretends to be a man; she saw this as greatly increasing the sexual tension of the Phebe/Rosalind scenes.

Declan Donnellan's production for Cheek By Jowl first performed in 1992 was revolutionary theatre. There was no attempt to disguise the real gender of the members of the all-male cast who played the women's parts. No wigs were worn and no false breasts. Femaleness was conveyed entirely through behaviour, movement and facial expression. Adrian Lester's Rosalind was shocked, confused and hurt to find that Orlando did not recognize her.

Donnellan has suggested that the production revealed that there is something violent at the heart of *As You Like It*. In the emotional turmoil of Rosalind we glimpse the pain of adolescence and of young love. There was also, in the realization of the Rosalind/Celia relationship, a recognition of the intensity of adolescent female friendship. This Celia was embittered by Rosalind's love for Orlando. To some extent, the exile offers her the opportunity to re-establish their former closeness, so she is not pleased when Orlando arrives in Arden. Jaques was presented in highly stereotyped, 'camp' terms as a gay man, constantly seeking to seduce young men. Donnellan suggests that there is a strong vein of despair in the presence of Jaques in the play, with his bleak pessimism about humanity and the meaninglessness of human existence.

The Cheek by Jowl production allowed the audience to take away some vivid memories. For example, on one occasion, the house lights were brought up before the Epilogue, and the audience had already launched into rapturous applause. Lester, as Rosalind, stepped forward, removing the headband that had been used throughout to signify when he was Rosalind, and using hand gestures signalled to the audience to stop clapping. 'If I were a woman' now became a joke between him and the audience. In the address to the men at lines 211–16, there was a clear homoerotic charge in the offer of this beautiful young actor to kiss them. Similarly, there was a lovely moment when Lester's Ganymede placed Jaques' hand inside 'his' jacket to feel Rosalind's breast, in an effort to persuade Jaques that, in this instance, he is wasting his time. That we, the audience, also 'believed' that there was a breast there to be felt – even though we knew at a conscious level that this was a male actor – is yet another example of the 'willing suspension of disbelief' mentioned earlier in this chapter.

Stephen Greenblatt has argued that Shakespearean comedy 'constantly appeals to the body and in particular to sexuality as the heart of its theatrical magic' (*Shakespearean Negotiation*, 1988, p.86). It has also been observed that the personal magnetism of actors and a 'circulation of erotic energy between actors and audience' is an intrinsic element of theatre-going (Gay, *As She Likes It*, 1994, pp.14–15). We have already considered Brook's view that 'in the theatre ... the only thing that matters is what is happening at the moment it is happening'. John Harrop contrasts this immediacy with the fact that 'we spend most of our time as human beings living in the past or in the future' and suggests that the energy that the actor brings to performance 'is partly rooted in sexual energy and owes some of its chemical attraction to that'. He concludes that there is 'an animal quality about powerful acting' (*Acting*, 1992, pp.111–12).

For Gay, the

uniqueness of Shakespearean comedy is that it operates powerfully on us through the play of a paradox: a conventional (patriarchal) community is revitalized by the incorporation, through the institution of marriage, of the remarkable energies of a charismatic female presence; yet she has spent most of the play flouting patriarchal protocols.

(As She Likes It, 1994, p.178)

Gay suggests that inherent in Shakespeare's comedies is an acknowledgement of 'the potential of women', although she is critical of the way in which the RSC, for example, 'as the national theatre of the national bard' (ibid., p.179) has frequently failed to realize the radical potential for retextualizing the written texts in performance. For Gay 'Rosalind prefigures this, as writer, director, protagonist, and manager of her own play of women in a man's world. And despite "fashion" or decorum, she has the last word' (ibid.).

How does any director or theatre company come to a decision about the 'realization' of Rosalind's potential? To what extent does the language of the play interact with the voice of the actor who speaks it, and the many visual and audio 'signs' of live drama? How is any of this integrated by an audience, either of live theatre or of video productions? In the next section, Lizbeth Goodman discusses the process of mounting a new production for video.

The play in process: from workshop to rehearsal to performance

by Lizbeth Goodman

The aims of this section are two-fold. First, I will try to illustrate the difference between the play as a dramatic text and the play as a text for performance. Secondly, I want to involve your imagination in an active process of engaging with performance possibilities by analysing visual images from particular points of view. Whilst consideration of isolated images cannot replicate the unique experience of attending a live performance, it can help to bring the play to life by offering some idea of the visual side of the theatre experience. This section is intended to help you further into the world of the play by inviting you to imagine yourself in the audience of one production. The general feel of live performance is represented in these pages with photographs, taken 'behind the scenes' as we followed the collaborative process of producing a performance. We traced the stages involved as a director and a set of actors moved from a first reading of the text through exploratory workshops to rehearsal to performance, and then as their live performance was recorded for video. In this way, we were able to follow the development from Shakespeare's text, first to a blueprint for theatrical presentation and then to a performance text, which depends on the audience's interpretation of visual and aural clues for a full appreciation of the play.

I also question the impact of different presentation media: that is, the difference between watching a live performance and a video performance. I analyse the development of the visual images in different productions as clues to different approaches and the performances that result. My aim is to engage with Shakespeare's *As You Like It* from a variety of angles, all of which explore the multi-sensory and multimedia possibilities of the text in performance.

Choosing a focus

The all-male Cheek by Jowl production directed by Declan Donnellan referred to above made a great impact, visually as well as politically. The production raised a number of interesting questions about the potential for gender issues to be explored in modern productions of Shakespeare. In what ways can a man play at being a woman? What does it say about the nature of gender if performance can (seemingly) get beyond such categories? These questions led to the making by the Open University in conjunction with the BBC of a video on *As You Like It*. The video features rehearsed readings, seminar discussion and a series of workshops in which actor-director Fiona Shaw and student actors attempt to engage with the gender and power dynamics inscribed in the language of the play. A range of other approaches offered by directors and academics is also considered. The approaches of Donnellan and Shaw are compared using extracts from the Cheek by Jowl production of the play and extracts from a new production of the banishment scene commissioned for this video and directed by Shaw.

It was hoped that the video would open up possibilities for a range of interpretations of the same lines and help us to come to a more general understanding of the many complex ways in which text and performance interact in any production.

Let us consider the 'inside story' of the making of the video, and Shaw's part in it. Shaw has engaged with *As You Like It* in many ways, over a period of years. Her approach to the play has influenced the ideas set out in these pages, so I want to pause for a moment to reflect on a brief statement about the nature of performance, which she made in interview in 1995. Shaw said that 'the nature of theatre is conflict', referring to the contrast between what we think a character is and might do in a situation, and what actually happens to make the play interesting. This is the conflict between expectation and eventuality, which is expressed in a fluid way through the development of performance action from moment to moment. For instance, Rosalind does not become a stronger character in an instant, she grows though her experiences in the play. We as the audience take part in her growth, as we experience each moment when the character is faced with a conflict, whether in the action of the play or in the development of her character.

Shaw's directorial approach emphasizes the rhythm of Shakespeare's language, the development of meaning from the performance of words in real time and space, with actors whose voices and experiences affect their presentation. She emphasizes the power of the words of the text, and the way that characters take power and convey meaning through words and movement.

Before we consider Shaw's way of directing the play, let us think about one 'playing out' of Shaw's ideas, in her own performance of the part of Rosalind.

Playing Shakespeare/playing gender

The social context of the play in performance will always be affected to some extent by the relationships and working practices of the actors who play the parts. In addition, every performance is influenced by social context in the sense that different audiences 'create' different performance experiences, as the reception of each scene feeds back to the actors on stage and affects their performance in the next scene.

However, social context can be seen to affect the play in a much more immediate way when the approach taken is in any way 'radical' or unusual: when the play is directed in a way that runs counter to public expectation. The all-male productions mentioned earlier spring to mind as obvious examples of productions wherein the conflict between relationships on stage (where the female and male characters are all played by men) and in the audience (composed, like most theatre audiences, of more than fifty per cent women) produce an overall atmosphere of challenge to the status quo. Attending such a performance is an event in itself, something so unique that you are likely to remember it, even if you do not agree with the interpretation. As you sit in the audience you have the sense of being part of theatre history (and new ways of thinking about gender roles) in the making.

It is interesting to ask how a male actor playing Rosalind affects a modern audience's view of the part, and of the play. The answer to such a question will, of course, be complicated. The casting may produce a subversion of expectations, and perhaps also introduce a homoerotic charge to the courtship scenes (although many argue that these scenes are implicitly charged, whoever plays the parts). If you look again at the image of Rosalind and Celia dancing in the Cheek by Jowl production of *As You Like It* (Figure 6.11), you will see how the posture and body language of the two male actors who play the parts seem to fight against the fabric of the dresses they wear. At the same time, if you can imagine the still photograph as part of a moving image, you will also detect a certain sense in which the bodies of these actors, which seem to be in the process of controlled and deliberate movements, may challenge or fight against the rhythm of the music and of the scene. Making gender substitutions can produce powerful effects in staging, and can encourage fresh thought about even the most canonical of plays.

In a much-discussed RSC production of *As You Like It*, directed by Adrian Noble in 1985, Shaw played Celia to Juliet Stevenson's Rosalind. The two actors have since worked closely together on many productions. For the rehearsed reading that forms part of the Open University/BBC video on the play, they exchanged roles briefly (Shaw playing Rosalind to Stevenson's Celia).

Figure 6.12   Fiona Shaw and Juliet Stevenson, rehearsed reading of a scene from *As You Like It*, still photograph from an Open University/BBC video, produced by Amanda Willett, 1995. Photo: Trevor White.

The exchange of roles was a deliberate choice, intended to emphasize the process of interpretation involved in negotiating one character, one role, against another. In the reading, Shaw and Stevenson found energy, and also humour, in the attempt to bring life to their assigned characters, whilst remembering the feeling of playing the opposite role as well.

Shaw had also played Rosalind in another memorable RSC production, directed by Tim Albery and produced at the Old Vic Theatre, London, in 1989.

It is not possible to recreate for you the experience of being in the audience of this production 'live', but we will try to convey the sense of it by quoting an analysis of one image from the production.

> Shaw's Rosalind … was self-possessed, strong but not 'masculine' even when dressed in breeches: she was androgyny powerfully, and somehow erotically, personified.
>
> The photograph from the production [Figure 6.13] illustrates Shaw's erotic androgyny more explicitly than words can: the photo shows Shaw seated, embraced by but not embracing Orlando (Adam Kotz). Both are on the ground, but neither is in a supplicant position. Nor do the two seem equal. Shaw is mud-splattered, Kotz is clean. Shaw is barefoot, Kotz wears shoes. Their hair is the same length, and is combed back in similar styles. Shaw's features are more angular, her pose more possessed. Orlando's expression is more exaggerated, yet Rosalind's (Shaw's) is more engaging.

240

Body language in this isolated pose is indicative of the presentation of gender relationships in the play as a whole. This Orlando embraces Rosalind and (it seems) the idea of her, while she seems to embrace another idea. His eyes are rapturously closed, his smiling mouth wide open. Her eyes are open and directed into the distance, her mouth nearly closed in a grin. Orlando's body is directed at Rosalind's, and hers is angled slightly, with one foot pressed to the ground and the other loose but positioned for movement. In the tangle

Figure 6.13   Fiona Shaw as Rosalind and Adam Kotz as Orlando in *As You Like It* at the Old Vic Theatre, London, directed by Tim Albery, 1989. Photo: Simon Annand.

of arms, his are on top, touching hers, while her right hand touches her own grounded leg, and she curls the fingers of her left hand carelessly, as if unconscious of the overarching embrace.

(Goodman, 'Women's alternative Shakespeares', in Cross-cultural Performances, 1993, p.210)

A photograph cannot capture the power of Shaw's presence in live performance, when the gaze of the audience was 'literally redirected at her, whether she plays woman or man' (ibid., pp.210–11). Shaw's interpretation of Rosalind was compelling in part because it embodied

> a contradiction: a strong person for whom a single gender cannot be read into either costume or gesture … The unique power of Shaw's presence stems from her performance of [aspects or characteristics of] two genders and her ability to project an individual woman out of both. She appears not as a woman dressed as a man but as herself. It is not the costume which makes Shaw's Rosalind into a man; rather it is Shaw's personality which enlivens and supports both parts.

(Ibid., pp.211–12)

In Chapter Four, it was argued that the representation of the female in Shakespeare's theatre has often been attached to visual symbols or 'sign systems', for instance Desdemona's handkerchief. In this chapter, we have observed that the female parts in Shakespeare's day tended to be represented visually through the assignment of 'gendered' costumes to the boy actors playing them, so that costumes and props came to represent gender on stage. Keeping this point in mind, it is interesting to note by way of contrast that 'Shaw's characterization of Rosalind illustrates one way in which performers today may reclaim the power to wear the costume, rather than be subsumed into it. Her costume is not a sign representing her but rather a disguise she uses to subvert expectation' (ibid., p.212).

Similarly, the dress and headband worn by the male actor (Adrian Lester) who plays Rosalind in the Cheek by Jowl production are not 'signs' of gender in and of themselves, but become gendered in a three-part process. In the first part, there is the presentation of a 'conflict' (to borrow Shaw's term) between the actor and the attire considered appropriate for his gender. This leads, secondly, to the challenging of a social expectation (the assumption that only women wear such apparel). Thirdly, this in turn produces a possible reconsideration of the gendered aspects of the clothing in relation to the gendered assumptions attached to the presence of the male actor who wears it.

The conflict is expressed in body language, posture and demeanour, which can be detected even in one isolated image. In this sense, visual images can convey a general picture of the kinds of dynamics involved in live stage performances. What cannot be conveyed through still photographs is any sense of the way lines are delivered (or speech is performed).

As we noted earlier, Shaw's approach to performance is very much concerned with finding the meaning of the play through performance and interpretation of the language. Let us now see how Shaw's approach was followed through in the process of developing a particular production.

The workshops

Preparation for the production involved lengthy discussions about the ways in which Shakespeare's language works on stage. A series of student workshops was developed, with the intent of emphasizing the power games that the characters play, as they exchange insults and accusations, sometimes in the guise of civilized speech. A good example is the exchange between Celia and Rosalind mentioned earlier in the chapter. The two characters argue about Orlando, in what is, at one level, a humorously framed emotional competition for Rosalind's affections. In a workshop on this scene, Shaw asked the student actors to take a coin each time their characters 'won a point' by winning control over the other character's emotions.

Figure 6.14   Fiona Shaw with student actors Anwhen Hughes-Roberts (left) and Suzannah Wise, Open University/BBC video, produced by Amanda Willett, 1995. Photo: Trevor White.

What is most interesting about this workshop exercise is the theatrical pace in Shakespeare's language that it reveals. As the characters take more and more coins in quick succession (someone wins a point on nearly every line), it becomes clear that the emotional warfare underlying the comic argument is much more intense and carefully structured than might seem to be the case on a first reading. As importantly, the repeated action of taking a coin helped to show the student actors just how interactive and *physical* the language of the play is, or can be. It also helped to illustrate the ingrained power relations between the characters by showing, in a real, physical sense, how they treat each other, through the language they use and the attitudes which that language conveys.

Workshop exercises were recorded, and as the 'live' exchanges between student actors were made permanent on video, the process of learning about Shakespeare through performance was also made 'permanent'. This strange but fascinating process of recording rehearsals and readings and theatre games and discussion, at different times, in the process of thinking about the play, and with reference to different scenes and different themes within the play, all contributed to a sense of shared creativity and energy. This is contained within the frame of the video (and maybe suggested by the still photographs included here) and reaches out to include the audience. Whilst video workshop material can never replace live performance, it can help to create a sense of engagement with the performance process.

Performance extracts

Now let us consider a range of photographs taken from later in the video: from a performance of one scene, played by professional actors directed by Shaw. The performance of the banishment scene followed on from the exploratory workshops and further developed ideas about the language of the text and the power lines conveyed through the intersection of spoken language and body language, gesture and movement. For this performance extract, costumes and some theatrical effects (such as smoke) were added and a 'set' was chosen: the derelict St Pancras Hotel in London.

The four images below can be viewed individually and as a sequence. Some are images taken from the video itself (that is, images captured from the moving image of the video and printed as static shots) and others are still production photographs taken during the process of recording the video. As you 'read' the images, ask yourself the following questions.

Can you tell which are images taken from video and which are still photographs? How?

Can you imagine the actual space of the hotel? How might it have been transformed into both a 'court' and a 'forest'?

You will need to consider these general questions as you consider the specific questions printed below each of the images.

Figures 6.15 and 6.16 **Where is the camera? Who or what are the characters looking at?**

Figure 6.17 shows a slightly wider view of Figure 6.16. **Where are the Duke and the First Lord looking? Where is the camera that frames them? Where is the camera that we see within the frame directed (that is, where is the cameraman looking)?**

In Figure 6.18 Rosalind and Celia have moved towards the Duke and the First Lord. **Where is the camera? Where were Rosalind and Celia a moment ago? What does this image allow you to see in addition to the characters and the relevant sections of the performance space or 'set'?**

D i s c u s s i o n

Let us consider the general questions first.

Figures 6.15 and 6.16 are taken from the video, whilst Figures 6.17 and 6.18 are still photographs taken during the process of recording. We can tell

Figure 6.16   Karl Johnson as Duke Frederick and Jack Elliott as the First Lord, Open University/BBC video, produced by Amanda Willett, 1995.

Figure 6.15   Susan Lynch as Rosalind and Matilda Ziegler as Celia, Open University/BBC video, produced by Amanda Willett, 1995.

this because the still photographs include a range of visual material not necessary to the performance – the cameras, the microphones, the crew, the background clutter of a crowded set.

Figure 6.17 Karl Johnson as Duke Frederick, Jack Elliott as the First Lord and a cameraman, Open University/BBC video, produced by Amanda Willett, 1995. Photo: Trevor White.

Figure 6.18 Susan Lynch as Rosalind, Matilda Ziegler as Celia, Karl Johnson as Duke Frederick and Jack Elliott as the First Lord, Open University/BBC video, produced by Amanda Willett, 1995. Photo: Trevor White.

The general space of the hotel is only 'readable' in Figure 6.18. The others are shot closer to the subjects (in what the cameraman called 'two shots' – pictures of two people), so that what you see is the people. Only the image in Figure 6.18 pulls out to a wide shot, to allow you to see 'behind the scenes'. Even in this image, however, you do not receive an accurate sense of the size of the space (which is enormous) or the derelict state of some areas of it. If you watch the video, a sense of space is conveyed through the slightly 'echoey' sound quality. This was something that could have been corrected in editing but was deliberately left in to convey a sense of people dwarfed by their menacing surroundings. In fact, the video makes even more of this idea of the unease of the space, by adding smoke and a sound track of quite atmospheric music. All these components combine to produce the total effect or mood of the video production, but very little of this is conveyed in the images reproduced here.

If you look back to Figure 6.6, you can see how the 'forest' was created in this performance space. In effect, the forest was already there – it is a mural, painted on the wall in one of the alcoves. The female characters stand in front of the alcove in Figure 6.15, but the mural itself is obscured by shadows (so the 'forest' recedes by a trick of light).

Now we will consider the questions specific to each of the images.

Figure 6.15 If you put yourself in the position of the characters in the image, you will see that the camera is located in front of and at an angle to them. They look up and out of the frame, and their facial expressions suggest that they are not pleased to see someone or something. We discover what they are looking at only when we see the next image.

Figure 6.16 The camera is located in front of and at an angle to the characters, and also below them; we look up at an angle. This gives the characters a certain power, conveyed through their positioning in terms of physical space, as they look down on us and also on Rosalind and Celia. The two images taken together tell a story: father/uncle descending the stairs, looking down on the women who are backed up, quite literally, against the wall of his displeasure.

Figure 6.17 Duke Frederick looks down at Rosalind and Celia. But where is the camera that frames the Duke and the First Lord? As we see one camera pointing down at the female characters, we are reminded that there must be another camera, on a similar level in terms of height but located at another angle. In fact, the photographer who took this picture is on a stairway that comes into view in Figure 6.18.

Figure 6.18 Rosalind and Celia have now moved up a level in height (as they challenge the Duke's authority physically and verbally). The camera that took this photograph is located on the lower level, in front of the alcove that functions as the 'forest', where Rosalind and Celia previously stood. This photograph allows you to see the larger context of the performance as a process involving a number of people who never appear 'on screen'. ■

To what extent do these images begin to capture, although only in a fragmentary way, some sense of the ephemeral 'live' aspect of the performance, even as it was recorded on video?

The images function as a sequence to illustrate one set of movements and actions. They cannot create a sense of performance, but they can provide visual clues to the approach taken in any production.

What all these images show, when viewed as a set, is the power of the camera to dictate what we see in a recorded version of live performance. We also receive a sense of the power of the performance space, the ways in which spaces and worlds can be created artificially, partly through cutting off the edges of the image, as in creation of the artificial forest. The theatrical illusion is shattered when the seemingly self-contained world of the court (suggested in the images taken from the video) is opened out by the move to a wide shot. The wide-angle still photograph shows the cameras and microphones and crew, as well as the grand staircase and pillars that symbolize the court.

In addition, we can see how camera-work can create a sense of point of view by lining up the characters' faces and eyes so that they appear to look at each other. The making of eye contact is always an important feature of performance, and the video shows quite clearly that Duke Frederick's eye contact with his daughter is partly what maintains his connection to her and his position of authority over her. We can see too how editing together different shots from the video will affect the audience's viewing and interpretation. If you were free to substitute perhaps a close-up of the Duke's face versus him looking angry, versus him looking away, versus shots only of Rosalind and Celia, in your preferred order, you would quickly obtain the sense of how perspective and interpretation are manipulated by the camera directors and, to a lesser extent, by theatre directors as well. ∎

Touchstone: voyeurism and perspective

As we observed earlier in this chapter, the character of the fool often serves to offer a sense of perspective – another way of looking at things – within the world of the play. Touchstone is the fool of *As You Like It*. He brings the world of the court – the rules of which he respects and protects – into line with those of the forest. His presence in the play serves to highlight the tension between reality and appearance, the court and the forest. In the video production, the decision was taken to make Touchstone an even more important character.

How might this be achieved? Given what you now know about the positioning of cameras, the use of camera angles and the importance of eye contact, how would you, as a director, position Touchstone in relation to the other characters and the audience, in order to make him a powerful character?

One approach would be to position Touchstone even higher in the playing space than Duke Frederick. Having established that the Duke's physical location (higher in the performance space than the female characters) conveys a sense of authority and power, putting Touchstone even higher would enhance his role as the character who stands outside the values of the court, perhaps precisely because he is not taken seriously by the court.

In fact, Shaw's choice of direction positioned Touchstone as the silent witness to the scene we have been analysing. In Figure 6.19 he is looking down on the action as the Duke confronts his daughter and his niece.

Figure 6.19   Aiden McArdle as Touchstone, Open University/BBC video, produced by Amanda Willett, 1995. Photo: Trevor White.

Here, Touchstone sees from an omniscient perspective; he knows more than any of the characters do, has a better view of the scene and is empowered by his very absence from the main action. In looking down from above, Touchstone sees without being seen: he occupies the most powerful position of all. In addition, he is seen in close up. He does not compete with any other characters for our visual attention. Or does he? ∎

What would allow you to occupy a position of equal power to Touchstone's; to engage most directly with the scene; to enter into the world of the play without interrupting the action?

D i s c u s s i o n

In order for us as viewers to engage with the play in an empowered way, we need to attain some of Touchstone's status as silent witness. We need to be recognized as having a connection to the play without this recognition interrupting the action. What we need is eye contact, and we need to establish it with Touchstone. In the final image, then, Touchstone empowers us by looking directly at us, making eye contact with the audience.

Figure 6.20   Aiden McArdle as Touchstone, Open University/BBC video, produced by Amanda Willett, 1995. Photo: Trevor White.

Here, we engage directly with the grounding, unifying character of Touchstone, and through him with the scene as a whole. The character who makes eye contact has the visual equivalent of a soliloquy: a direct contact or communion with the audience, which invites engagement and interest of a unique and personalized kind. ∎

In order to emphasize this kind of power, the video producer and editor chose to include images of Touchstone looking on, at unlikely moments. Just when you think you know who sees who, you are reminded that there are always other perspectives, both within the play and from every possible interpretative angle in the audience.

Further reading

Jardine, L. (1983) *Still Harping on Daughters: Women and Drama in the Age of Shakespeare*, Columbia University Press.

Gay, P. (1994) *As She Likes It: Shakespeare's Unruly Women*, Routledge.

Novy, M. (ed.) (1993) *Cross-cultural Performances*, University of Illinois Press.

Rutter, C. (1988) *Clamorous Voices*, ed. F. Evans, The Women's Press, pp.97–121.

Reviewing the idea of the canon

by Lizbeth Goodman

In Chapter One we considered some of the ways in which the canon of literature is constructed. We looked, for example, at the influence of Englishness and at the power of English as a world language. We also looked at the way in which literature by people of colour, and by women of all ethnic groups, has tended to be excluded until recently. In that chapter a wide range of ideas was put forward, and I'd like to return to one of them now – the idea offered by Arnold Kettle. You may remember his argument that 'Literature is a part of life and can be judged only in its relevance to life. Life is not static but moving and changing' (Kettle, *An Introduction to the English Novel*, 1983 edn, p.12).

This, in my opinion, offers the key to reviewing the canon of plays in contemporary culture. The works we have looked at might be interpreted today in a number of interesting ways that are relevant to our lives. But at the same time we presumably put limits on that interpretation. Don't we demand an interpretation that, in addition to being relevant to us today, is also 'true to the author' so that the spirit of the original play remains in some form?

If so, we have to try to recover that original spirit, and we are likely to do this by taking into account the social processes and historical concerns that shaped the work in the first place. We may feel that there is a tension here between our quest for contemporary relevance and our quest for historical 'truth', as if we can only make play productions relevant to our own concerns if we downplay or mask the play's significance for its original audiences. This tension undoubtedly exists, but it's not very useful or informative to treat our contemporary concerns as if they spring from nowhere; we must acknowledge that most of what we know about literature, and indeed our drive to read and watch plays, and to study drama and performance, is influenced by cultural teaching about the value of ideas. Codes for the making of value-judgements are picked up and developed as we make our way through life, whether or not we ever come to see them as part of an organized process of 'canonization'.

Let's see how such arguments can be applied to the three Shakespeare texts we've studied, and then to *The Rover*. As we do this, we will also be reviewing the differences of approach between one chapter and another.

Reviewing Henry V

The approach in Chapter Three was broadly that of 'dramatic criticism'. Simon Eliot encouraged you to look closely at the text, and he gave a number of exercises that enabled you to analyse the way in which important themes are treated in the play – themes such as the king as actor, the effect of war on soldiers, the link between deals and sexual relations, and so on. Not that Eliot completely disregarded performance but, when he referred to the films of Olivier and Branagh, he was often demonstrating how the directors had played up features that occupy little space in the text, or alternatively had excluded certain lines. This was not to be derisory about the medium of film, but to show a few of the differences between what is possible in the theatre and what is possible on the big screen.

In addition to referring to films, Eliot also mentioned the politics of the period *in which the play is set*, without which you might not have understood the text. But he also made clear that Elizabethan audiences would have related the play to the sometimes tumultuous events of their own time, and to questions about the right of succession to the throne. By working through the exercises, you will also have seen that the play – ostensibly about the exploits of a fifteenth-century king – takes a subtle and often ambivalent approach to the use of power, the question of a just war, and other aspects of the political arena. Nor is it confined to war and politics: it raises issues about the depiction of women, about class and so on.

Thus dramatic criticism, though text-focused, does not have to be arid: it can lead into a wide range of interesting issues. But you may like to compare Chapter Three with the chapters on *Othello* and *As You Like It*, where we focused on theatre and performance studies. Are we therefore implying that a text-based approach is more appropriate to *Henry V* while a performance-based approach is more appropriate to, say, *As You Like It*? I would say not: it is worth examining each work in a range of ways to gain a sense of what the different approaches can yield.

We may well find that certain types of play provide us with certain types of insight. For example, a history play might be thought the least informative about the relative roles of men and women because it would tend to have fewer women (with smaller parts and fewer lines). And one might think that the comedies, on the other hand, would tend to be richer in social and cultural sources on gender, power and politics, but would not always be the most accurate sources for historical (or, indeed, geographical) information.

However, even this distinction can be challenged: *Henry V*, for example, does throw light on gender issues, whereas it is not invariably reliable about history. Shakespeare was distinctly 'economical with the truth' in his use of historical events in *Henry V*. Does this then lead us to conclude that it sheds no light on history? I would say rather that *Henry V* offers us a different *type* of history. Graham Holderness (*Shakespeare Recycled*, 1992) has argued at length that the history plays give insights into the social context of three periods – the period in which the play is set, the Elizabethan period in which Shakespeare wrote, and our own contemporary history in the sense that we can measure the cultural values of our time by looking carefully to see which plays are included in the canon, and why.

Holderness has also explored the text and cultural context of modern productions of *Henry V* on stage and on film, and argues that, as a political play dealing with nationalism and ideas of authority, it raises the question: 'What is most English about the play?' ('What is my nation?', 1991). Holderness challenges the idea that *Henry V* is only an *English* history play, and considers its wider implications as it has been interpreted for a diverse international audience, particularly on film. He comes to the conclusion that perhaps what is most 'English' about *Henry V*, in terms of what he refers to as the play's 'tub-thumping' patriotism, is Shakespeare himself –

the man and the myth. Perhaps, Holderness argues, the play's Englishness for modern audiences is not contained in any allegiance to the historical events chronicled and reinvented in the play, but rather in the cultural tendency to venerate Shakespeare as the Bard, the great 'English' author.

Reviewing Othello

There are many ways of approaching *Othello*. In Chapter Four we discussed the issues of race, gender and 'outsider status', and I want to expand on these here to show that the play takes on new meanings when we choose a new focus.

Karen Newman argues that the social and political values of the play need to be judged against the values that prevailed at the time Shakespeare was writing. She suggests that while Shakespeare was not immune to the racism, sexism and colonialism of his time, his work did challenge those values – was 'in a contestatory relation' to them:

> Shakespeare was certainly subject to the racist, sexist and colonialist discourses of his time, but by making the black Othello a hero, and by making Desdemona's love for Othello, and her transgression of her society's norms for women in choosing him, sympathetic, Shakespeare's play stands in a contestatory relation to the hegemonic ideologies of race and gender in early modern England.
>
> (Newman, '"And wash the Ethiop white"', 1987, p.157)

It may be worth getting to grips with her language since this kind of writing is found elsewhere. 'Hegemonic', for example, derives from 'hegemony', which refers to a process of social domination; in this process, one class or group of society dominates other groups by persuading them that its particular way of seeing society, of describing 'normal reality', is common sense or is in some way 'natural'. (For example, men have hegemonic control in patriarchy, while white people exercise hegemony in a white racist social structure.) So the 'hegemonic ideologies' to which Newman refers are the particular ways of thinking about race and gender (about the place of black people and white people, and women and men) that were widely accepted in the society of Shakespeare's time.

Newman argues that it would not be reasonable to label Shakespeare as either 'racist' or 'sexist' merely on the grounds that (in the sixteenth century) he represented characters which, when viewed from the twentieth century, let down our ideals of the status of people of colour, and of women. Rather, the play keeps enough of a critical distance to suggest that Shakespeare may have been contesting some of the attitudes current in his time. In any case, whatever Shakespeare meant to do (and we will never know for sure), the issues of race, gender and power in the play can take on new meanings when we review them from our own critical perspective.

Further we should note that the play may have served as a source for an author who did challenge the prevailing ideologies on gender and race. *Othello* may well have influenced the creation of *Oroonoko*, Aphra Behn's novel about an 'African Prince' (Margaret Ferguson, 'Transmuting *Othello*', 1993). Written and published in 1688, the year before her death, *Oroonoko* is closely based on Behn's experience of living in the British colony of Surinam when she was a young woman (as Bob Owens pointed out in Chapter Five). Ferguson argues that Behn's fascination with race and sexuality is connected to the idea of 'otherness', in Newman's terms, but not in any romanticized way. Ferguson does not agree with those scholars who say that, because both Shakespeare and Behn lacked higher education, they are linked in some way as 'outsiders'. She argues that lack of education was not necessarily a handicap in writing for the theatre: capturing the imagination of audiences – with action, adventure and bawdy scenes – was as valuable in the theatre of the sixteenth and seventeenth centuries as any claim to 'literary value' would have been.

Reviewing As You Like It

Our decision that the chapter on *As You Like It* would come *after* the chapter on *The Rover* reveals something about our approach to these works. We might have offered the three Shakespeare plays one after the other, with the play by Behn added as an alternative perspective. But we wanted to make the point that study of Behn's play informs study of Shakespeare, as well as vice versa. We looked at Behn's treatment of comedy, gender-roles and power-relations, and cross-dressing and disguise. When you arrived at your reading and study of *As You Like It* in Chapter Six, you had already encountered the form of the stage comedy, and had already practised analysing the use of space and visual images in performances. What, then, did we offer in our discussion of *As You Like It*?

It is easiest to begin by saying what we did not offer: we did not use dramatic criticism to approach the play text in isolation; we did not emphasize the 'textual integrity' or undertake detailed study of the language (though some examples were given). Nor did we offer a strongly politicized reading of the play (though reference was made to feminist interpretation, and to the play as a political critique). Both of these approaches would have been perfectly valid; both would have highlighted aspects of the play in intriguing ways. But as those two approaches had been covered to some extent in the previous chapters, what we offered instead was a treatment of *As You Like It* as a performance: we discussed the text in relation to its performance context and possibilities, focusing on the potential of the words to act as a blueprint for production of the play. If you go back and reread any section of the chapter, you'll see how this is so. While Kate Clarke provides very useful information about the pastoral form, for instance, it is offered by way of explaining the potential for subverting that form in a comic production of the play. Similarly, Clarke's discussion of the Fool character and its function in comedy generally is closely connected to her discussion of the character of Touchstone. This is not only a general point, but also helps translate the potential of the text into visual images of stage performances.

Reviewing The Rover

Since we included *The Rover* precisely to throw the idea of the canon into question, let's think again about that play.

In Chapter Five Bob Owens argued that Behn and her work bear an uneasy relationship to the accepted literary canon, though I argued that her work is already a part of many 'alternative' canons – both for feminist literature courses and for many theatre repertoires. Our views were carefully chosen and contrasted; we did not wish to contradict each other, but we did wish to temper our accounts of the 'official canon' with some indication of the problematic nature of considering individual perspectives and modern challenges to it. In addition, I wanted to stress Behn's work as part of my ideal 'personal canon'.

By studying Behn's work alongside Shakespeare's, we may see what's involved in reinventing a canon for each generation and culture. Many scholars have challenged the canon, sometimes by writing about it and sometimes – if they have the power to shape a literature course – by including new authors such as Behn on students' reading lists. Theatre practitioners including John Barton, Imogen Stubbs, Jeremy Irons and Jules Wright have also contributed to the canonization of *The Rover* and its author – whatever their interpretation of the play, and whether or not they 'like' it. You may or may not be pleased at the inclusion of Behn's work in this volume, and indeed you may have mixed feelings about the study of Shakespeare. But I hope you will grant that consideration of new authors invigorates the study of canonical authors.

In my view, the study of Behn poses a fascinating challenge to the idea of a fixed literary canon. At the same time, it can be argued that she and her work are already part of a new canon that embraces selected work by women, people of colour and working-class authors, as well as (not necessarily instead of) work by well-educated white men.

Reviewing the idea of the canon

Many critics in the past, and even in the present, have tried to make the case that to include new works in the canon (especially if such works are considered 'politically correct') is in some way harmful, dangerous, pernicious. In my view, such an argument misses the point. If work by white men is truly interesting, well written, relevant to readers today, then it will continue to be read, and will remain in the canon. It is only work which doesn't hold up to that test which might possibly be 'replaced'. But feminist critics and cultural critics are not, on the whole, interested in replacing one canon with another, but rather with expanding and enriching the canon so that it includes the widest possible range of work by women and men, of all races, classes, nationalities, writing in a range of styles, for all kinds of reasons. No author or literary work will be removed from the canon simply because of the author's race or sex, nor will any piece be added on those grounds alone. But when literary worth is valued according to the perspectives and interests and ideas of a wide range of people, it is only 'natural' that the canon will change and grow. We may as well acknowledge our own role in that process, as we all learn from and contribute to the diversification of the field of literary study.

Students in the 1990s will routinely encounter work by Toni Morrison, Alice Walker, Derek Walcott, Samuel Beckett, Harold Pinter and Caryl Churchill as well as by Chaucer, Shakespeare, Milton, Byron, Dickens, Austen, the Brontës, Yeats and Woolf. So it should be. Reading a novel by an African-American woman, for instance, may be an experience that takes British students outside their own culture, temporarily at least. Many students will watch the popular Spielberg film of Walker's novel *The Color Purple* before – or perhaps instead of – reading the novel. A great deal will be lost in the translation between media, but there will also be a great deal to be learned from what the director decided to include and exclude, to focus on and to ignore. Just as we might study and appreciate the film version of *The Color Purple* without first studying the novel, and without undertaking a wholesale evaluation of Walker's possible place in the evolving canon, so we can appreciate innovative productions of Behn's *The Rover.* Those who don't engage fully with the WPT/OU/BBC interpretation, or the RSC interpretation, may be inspired to think through and produce interpretations of their own. In so doing, we will all participate in the process of canonization – critical engagement with texts and contexts. In gaining the imaginative interest and attention of audiences today, each production of the play raises the question of Behn's place in the ever-evolving canon of literature.

The same can be said of many alternative critical readings and productions of Shakespeare's plays.

Canonizing plays in performance: reviewing the role of the audience

Finally, let's review some of the unique aspects of plays in performance. These include: the viewer's relationship as active; the listener's power of interpretation; and the difference that the medium can make to the overall reception and perceived 'meaning' of a play (the difference between reading a play text, listening to an audio-recording of a performance, and viewing plays on stage, video, television, film and in multi-media).

It is easiest to review these aspects with reference to Shakespeare himself. In Chapter Two we considered the scanty but intriguing historical evidence about the man. We still need to connect that man with the plays and performances his work produced, and to consider his relation to the idea of the canon.

What does it mean that a man about whom we know so little has become, if Harold Bloom is right, the 'centre' of the Western literary canon? Does it help us to review the idea of the canon if we consider that the plays have, in some sense, 'canonized' themselves through century after century of production and reception?

I think it does. It is, of course, useful to consider the role of the authors in creating any literary text, 'canonical' or not. In the study of prose fiction and poetry, it is often the case that consideration of the author's intentions and ideas and life experiences sheds useful light on the texts (though of course, the texts are still valuable in and of themselves). But the author of a dramatic text is in a different position: while it is interesting to learn about playwrights, and while such information can inform and enrich our reading of any play text, it is not essential to know about the author in order to appreciate a play in performance – when the author is in some sense 'in the background' because the characters are interpreted through the contribution of the director, the actors and others.

I would argue that, with drama, what is at stake is the unique aspect of the play as an event, a cultural enterprise that involves the cast, crew and audience. Many people leave theatres having enjoyed the spectacle of a play, but not necessarily knowing much about its author. Programme notes are often provided, but not always read. It isn't historical or biographical information about authors that we seek when we go to the theatre; it is primarily the event of the performance itself. And when plays are adapted for television, video, film or other media, the position of the author is further obscured. Each textual editor and director effectively rewrites the play, even if only by removing words, interpreting stage directions or inventing visual images and physical movements that become part of the overall 'stage language' of the play in performance. Each camera director limits and controls the view of the spectator. All these factors, as we have seen, enrich the study of plays in performance, but also complicate the question of 'canonicity'.

When we ask about the 'value' of *Othello*, for instance, do we mean the value of the play as originally conceived by its author, about which we must piece together sketchy information to create our own idea of the play? Or do we mean the play as it was first received by Elizabethan audiences, or subsequent audiences? (If that is the case, we must look to the records of theatre history, reviews and scholarship – all of which are also written by individuals with agendas and views of their own.) Or do we mean the printed play text and, if so, which version? (And how do we go about evaluating editorial decisions and their effects on the play?) Or do we mean modern performances that we attend and evaluate ourselves? In that case we are judging the production values and the talent and achievements of a cast and crew as well as the play itself. Or do we mean the general composite notion of 'the play' as 'the thing' composed of all these elements, and also of general ideas created and reflected in film and television and video versions, in references to the play in classrooms and in popular culture?

The problem with evaluating a play as 'canonical' is its uneasy – and therefore fascinating – status in between all these areas. That's what makes it interesting. That's what fires the imagination. Theatre director Peter Brook has written a preface to the work of Polish theatre professor Jan Kott, whose ideas have been referred to several times in this book. Brook sets out to show why 'Shakespeare is a contemporary of Kott, and Kott a contemporary of Shakespeare' (Kott, *Shakespeare our Contemporary*, 1967 edn, p.x), arguing that what makes the study of Shakespeare's plays exciting today is not any measure of 'literary value' but rather the feeling that Shakespeare captured a sense of what it is to be alive, to dream and to act in the world. As the world changes then, each of us becomes contemporary to Shakespeare and Shakespeare to us, to the extent that we engage with the plays and the imagination that created them, and in so far as we review and rethink the plays, and our own ideas, in contemporary critical perspective.

But is Hall implying that Shakespeare is of eternal relevance? From Chapter One you may remember a quotation from Eagleton, who asks whether society could develop in such a way that Shakespeare's works come to seem

> desperately alien, full of styles of thought and feeling which such a society found limited or irrelevant. In such a situation, Shakespeare would be no more valuable than much present-day graffiti.
>
> (*Literary Theory*, 1983, pp.11–12)

Thus by thinking about Shakespeare we have come full circle, back to our earliest questions about 'the canon'. By asking whether Shakespeare will always be seen as a 'great writer', we can call into question the very rules of deciding which works should enter the official canon. If Shakespeare is to remain relevant, interesting and 'valuable', then it will be through a continual process of re-evaluating the works, positioning them next to works by other authors who write in different ages, contexts, languages and cultures – and perhaps for different reasons. This is what we have done in this book, by including Behn as a near contemporary of Shakespeare.

We might say, in conclusion, that what is most fascinating about Shakespeare is the way in which he and his work seem both to encapsulate the idea of an official canon (Shakespeare the Bard of Avon) and to inspire new thinking about the nature of the canon and the values of literature, drama, theatre and performance. Each reader and audience member will make up her or his own mind.

Further reading

Hawkes, T. (1992) *Meaning by Shakespeare*, Routledge.

Smith, B.H. (1988) *Contingencies of Value: Alternative Perspectives for Critical Theory*, Harvard University Press.

Todd, J. (ed.) (1992) Aphra Behn, *Oroonoko, The Rover and Other Works*, Penguin.

Wayne, V. (ed.) (1991) *The Matter of Difference: Materialist Feminist Criticism of Shakespeare*, Harvester Wheatsheaf.

Part Two

The Rover
or
The Banished Cavaliers

Aphra Behn

edited by W.R. Owens

Note on the text

The Rover was first performed by the Duke's Company at their Dorset Garden theatre in March 1677, and the text was published later the same year. This was the only edition published in Behn's lifetime, and thus represents the only authoritative text. There seem to have been three issues, all during 1677, differing only in the title page. The name of the author, 'Mrs. A. Behn', appeared on the title-page of the third issue.

The text that follows is based on the first edition. Spelling, punctuation, and such matters as use of capitals and italics have been modernized and regularized throughout. I have tried to follow the copy text as closely as possible in representing shifts from prose into poetry, but it is sometimes unclear whether certain lines are intended as prose or as verse. Some scene divisions and stage directions have been inserted where none exist in the original. Significant editorial insertions are indicated by use of square brackets.

In preparing the present text I have consulted two modern editions of *The Rover.* One was the text edited by Frederick M. Link for the 'Regents Restoration Drama Series' (1967, University of Nebraska Press). The other was Janet Todd's edition of *Oroonoko, The Rover and Other Works* (1992, Penguin Books).

Prologue

Wits, like physicians, never can agree,
When of a different society.
And Rabell's Drops were never more cried down
By all the learned doctors of the town,
Than a new play whose author is unknown.
Nor can those doctors with more malice sue
(And powerful purses) the dissenting few,
Than those with an insulting pride, do rail
At all who are not of their own cabal.
   If a young poet hit your humour right,   10
You judge him then out of revenge and spite:
So amongst men there are ridiculous elves,
Who monkeys hate for being too like themselves.
So that the reason of the grand debate,
Why wit so oft is damned, when good plays take,
Is, that you censure as you love, or hate.
   Thus like a learned conclave poets sit,
Catholic judges both of sense and wit,
And damn or save, as they themselves think fit.
Yet those who to others' faults are so severe,   20
Are not so perfect but themselves may err.
Some write correct indeed, but then the whole
(Bating their own dull stuff i'th' play) is stole:
As bees do suck from flowers their honeydew,
So they rob others, striving to please you.
   Some write their characters genteel and fine,
But then they do so toil for every line,
That what to you does easy seem, and plain,
Is the hard issue of their labouring brain.
And some th'effects of all their pains we see,   30
Is but to mimic good extempore.
Others by long converse about the town,
Have wit enough to write a lewd lampoon,
But their chief skill lies in a bawdy song.
In short, the only wit that's now in fashion
Is but the gleanings of good conversation.
As for the author of this coming play,
I asked him what he thought fit I should say
In thanks for your good company today:
He called me fool, and said it was well known   40
You came not here for our sakes, but your own.
New plays are stuffed with wits, and with debauches,
That crowd and sweat like cits, in May-Day coaches.

Written by a Person of Quality

Characters

Men

DON ANTONIO, the Viceroy's son
DON PEDRO, a noble Spaniard, his friend
BELVILE, an English Colonel in love with Florinda
WILLMORE, the Rover
FREDERICK, an English gentleman, and friend to Belvile and Blunt
BLUNT, an English country gentleman
STEPHANO, servant to Don Pedro
PHILIPPO, Lucetta's gallant
SANCHO, pimp to Lucetta
BISKEY *and* SEBASTIAN, two bravoes to Angellica
OFFICERS *and* SOLDIERS
DIEGO, page to Don Antonio

Women

FLORINDA, sister to Don Pedro
HELLENA, a gay young woman designed for a nun, and sister to Florinda
VALERIA, a kinswoman to Florinda
ANGELLICA BIANCA, a famous courtesan
MORETTA, her woman
CALLIS, governess to Florinda and Hellena
LUCETTA, a jilting wench

Servants, other masqueraders, men and women

The scene: Naples, in Carnival time

Act I Scene 1

A chamber
Enter Florinda *and* Hellena.

FLORINDA What an impertinent thing is a young girl bred in a nunnery! How full of questions! Prithee no more Hellena; I have told thee more than thou understand'st already.

HELLENA The more's my grief. I would fain know as much as you, which makes me so inquisitive; nor is't enough I know you're a lover, unless you tell me too, who 'tis you sigh for.

FLORINDA When you're a lover, I'll think you fit for a secret of that nature.

HELLENA 'Tis true, I never was a lover yet, but I begin to have a shrewd guess what 'tis to be so, and fancy it very pretty to sigh, and sing, and blush, and wish, and dream and wish, and long and wish to see the man; and when I   10
do, look pale and tremble, just as you did when my brother brought home the fine English colonel to see you. What do you call him? Don Belvile?

FLORINDA Fie, Hellena.

HELLENA That blush betrays you. I am sure 'tis so. Or is it Don Antonio the Viceroy's son? Or perhaps the rich old Don Vincentio, whom my father designs you for a husband? Why do you blush again?

FLORINDA With indignation; and how near soever my father thinks I am to marrying that hated object, I shall let him see I understand better what's due to my beauty, birth and fortune, and more to my soul, than to obey those unjust commands.   20

HELLENA Now hang me, if I don't love thee for that dear disobedience. I love mischief strangely, as most of our sex do, who are come to love nothing else. But tell me dear Florinda, don't you love that fine *Anglese*? For I vow, next to loving him myself, 'twill please me most that you do so, for he is so gay and so handsome.

FLORINDA Hellena, a maid designed for a nun ought not to be so curious in a discourse of love.

HELLENA And dost thou think that ever I'll be a nun? Or at least till I'm so old I'm fit for nothing else? Faith no, sister; and that which makes me long to know whether you love Belvile, is because I hope he has some mad   30
companion or other that will spoil my devotion. Nay, I'm resolved to provide myself this Carnival, if there be e'er a handsome proper fellow of my humour above ground, though I ask first.

FLORINDA Prithee be not so wild.

HELLENA Now you have provided yourself of a man, you take no care for poor me. Prithee tell me, what dost thou see about me that is unfit for love? Have I not a world of youth? A humour gay? A beauty passable? A vigour desirable? Well shaped? Clean limbed? Sweet breathed? And sense enough to know how all these ought to be employed to the best advantage? Yes, I do and will; therefore lay aside your hopes of my fortune by my being a   40
devote, and tell me how you came acquainted with this Belvile, for I perceive you knew him before he came to Naples.

FLORINDA Yes, I knew him at the siege of Pamplona; he was then a colonel of French horse, who, when the town was ransacked, nobly treated my brother and myself, preserving us from all insolences. And I must own, besides great obligations, I have I know not what that pleads kindly for him about my heart, and will suffer no other to enter. —But see, my brother.

Enter Don Pedro, Stephano *with a masquing habit, and* Callis.

PEDRO Good morrow, sister. Pray when saw you your lover Don
Vincentio?

50 FLORINDA I know not, sir—Callis, when was he here?—for I consider it so
little, I know not when it was.

PEDRO I have a command from my father here to tell you you ought not to
despise him, a man of so vast a fortune, and such a passion for you.
—Stephano, my things.   *Puts on his masquing habit*

FLORINDA A passion for me? 'Tis more than e'er I saw, or he had a desire
should be known. I hate Vincentio, sir, and I would not have a man so dear
to me as my brother follow the ill customs of our country and make a slave
of his sister. And, sir, my father's will I'm sure you may divert.

60 PEDRO I know not how dear I am to you, but I wish only to be ranked in
your esteem equal with the English colonel Belvile. Why do you frown and
blush? Is there any guilt belongs to the name of that cavalier?

FLORINDA I'll not deny I value Belvile. When I was exposed to such dangers
as the licensed lust of common soldiers threatened, when rage and conquest
flew through the city, then Belvile, this criminal, for my sake threw himself
into all dangers to save my honour—and will you not allow him my esteem?

PEDRO Yes, pay him what you will in honour, but you must consider Don
Vincentio's fortune, and the jointure he'll make you.

FLORINDA Let him consider my youth, beauty, and fortune, which ought not
to be thrown away on his age and jointure.

70 PEDRO 'Tis true, he's not so young and fine a gentleman as that Belvile. But
what jewels will that cavalier present you with? Those of his eyes and heart?

HELLENA And are not those better than any Don Vincentio has brought from
the Indies?

PEDRO Why, how now! Has your nunnery breeding taught you to understand
the value of hearts and eyes?

HELLENA Better than to believe Vincentio's deserve value from any woman.
He may perhaps increase her bags, but not her family.

PEDRO This is fine! Go! Up to your devotion! You are not designed for the
conversation of lovers.

80 HELLENA (*aside*) Nor saints yet awhile, I hope. —Is't not enough you make a
nun of me, but you must cast my sister away too, exposing her to a worse
confinement than a religious life?

PEDRO The girl's mad! It is a confinement to be carried into the country, to an
ancient villa belonging to the family of the Vincentios these five hundred
years, and have no other prospect than that pleasing one of feeling all her
own that meets her eyes: a fine air, large fields, and gardens where she may
walk and gather flowers!

HELLENA When, by moonlight? For I am sure she dares not encounter with
the heat of the sun; that were a task only for Don Vincentio and his Indian
90 breeding, who loves it in the dog days. And if these be her daily
divertisements, what are those of the night? To lie in a wide moth-eaten
bedchamber, with furniture in fashion in the reign of King Sancho the First;
the bed, that which his forefathers lived and died in.

PEDRO Very well.

HELLENA This apartment, new furbushed and fitted out for the young wife, he
out of freedom makes his dressing room, and being a frugal and a jealous

266

coxcomb, instead of a valet to uncase his feeble carcass, he desires you to do that office—signs of favour I'll assure you, and such as you must not hope for, unless your woman be out of the way.

PEDRO Have you done yet? 100

HELLENA That honour being past, the giant stretches itself, yawns and sighs a belch or two, loud as a musket, throws himself into bed, and expects you in his foul sheets, and e'er you can get yourself undressed, calls you with a snore or two—and are not these fine blessings to a young lady?

PEDRO Have you done yet?

HELLENA And this man you must kiss, nay you must kiss none but him too, and nuzzle through his beard to find his lips. And this you must submit to for threescore years, and all for a jointure.

PEDRO For all your character of Don Vincentio, she is as like to marry him as she was before. 110

HELLENA Marry Don Vincentio! Hang me, such a wedlock would be worse than adultery with another man. I had rather see her in the *Hostel de Dieu*, to waste her youth there in vows, and be a hand-maid to lazars and cripples, than to lose it in such a marriage.

PEDRO [*to* Florinda] You have considered, sister, that Belvile has no fortune to bring to you; banished his country, despised at home, and pitied abroad.

HELLENA What then? The Viceroy's son is better than that old Sir Fifty, Don Vincentio! Don Indian! He thinks he's trading to Gambo still, and would barter himself—that bell and bauble—for your youth and fortune.

PEDRO Callis, take her hence, and lock her up all this Carnival, and at Lent 120 she shall begin her everlasting penance in a monastery.

HELLENA I care not; I had rather be a nun than be obliged to marry as you would have me, if I were designed for it.

PEDRO Do not fear the blessing of that choice. You shall be a nun.

HELLENA (*aside*) Shall I so? You may chance to be mistaken in my way of devotion. A nun! Yes, I am like to make a fine nun! I have an excellent humour for a grate! No, I'll have a saint of my own to pray to shortly, if I like any that dares venture on me.

PEDRO Callis, make it your business to watch this wild cat. As for you Florinda, I've only tried you all this while and urged my father's will; but mine is that 130 you would love Antonio. He is brave and young, and all that can complete the happiness of a gallant maid. This absence of my father will give us opportunity to free you from Vincentio by marrying here, which you must do tomorrow.

FLORINDA Tomorrow!

PEDRO Tomorrow, or 'twill be too late. 'Tis not my friendship to Antonio which makes me urge this, but love to thee, and hatred to Vincentio; therefore resolve upon tomorrow.

FLORINDA Sir, I shall strive to do as shall become your sister.

PEDRO I'll both believe and trust you. Adieu.   *Exeunt* Pedro *and* Stephano.

HELLENA As becomes his sister! That is to be as resolved your way, as he is 140 his.   Hellena *goes to* Callis.

FLORINDA I ne'er till now perceived my ruin near.
   I've no defence against Antonio's love,
   For he has all the advantages of nature,
   The moving arguments of youth and fortune.

HELLENA But hark you, Callis, you will not be so cruel to lock me up indeed, will you?

CALLIS I must obey the commands I have. Besides, do you consider what a life you are going to lead?

150 HELLENA Yes, Callis, that of a nun; and till then I'll be indebted a world of prayers to you if you'll let me now see, what I never did, the divertisements of a Carnival.

CALLIS What, go in masquerade? 'Twill be a fine farewell to the world, I take it. Pray what would you do there?

HELLENA That which all the world does, as I am told: be as mad as the rest, and take all innocent freedoms. —Sister, you'll go too, will you not? Come, prithee, be not sad. We'll outwit twenty brothers, if you'll be ruled by me. Come, put off this dull humour with your clothes, and assume one as gay and as fantastic as the dress my cousin Valeria and I have provided, and let's
160 ramble.

FLORINDA Callis, will you give us leave to go?

CALLIS (*aside*) I have a youthful itch of going myself. —Madam, if I thought your brother might not know it, and I might wait on you; for by my troth I'll not trust young girls alone.

FLORINDA Thou see'st my brother's gone already, and thou shalt attend and watch us.

Enter Stephano.

STEPHANO Madam, the habits are come, and your cousin Valeria is dressed, and stays for you.

170 FLORINDA [*aside*] 'Tis well. I'll write a note, and if I chance to see Belvile, and want an opportunity to speak to him, that shall let him know what I've resolved in favour of him.

HELLENA Come, let's in and dress us.   *Exeunt.*

Act I Scene 2

A long street
Enter Belvile, *melancholy;* Blunt *and* Frederick.

FREDERICK Why, what the devil ails the colonel? In a time when all the world is gay, to look like mere Lent thus? Hadst thou been long enough in Naples to have been in love, I should have sworn some such judgment had befallen thee.

BELVILE No, I have made no new amours since I came to Naples.

FREDERICK You have left none behind you in Paris?

BELVILE Neither.

FREDERICK I cannot divine the cause then, unless the old cause, the want of money.

10 BLUNT And another old cause, the want of a wench. Would not that revive you?

BELVILE You are mistaken, Ned.

BLUNT Nay, 'adsheartlikins, then thou'rt past cure.

FREDERICK I have found it out: thou hast renewed thy acquaintance with the lady that cost thee so many sighs at the siege of Pamplona—pox on't, what d'you call her—her brother's a noble Spaniard, nephew to the dead general—Florinda—aye, Florinda. And will nothing serve thy turn but that damned virtuous woman, whom on my conscience thou lovest in spite too, because thou seest little or no possibility of gaining her?

BELVILE Thou art mistaken; I have interest enough in that lovely virgin's heart to make me proud and vain, were it not abated by the severity of a brother, who, perceiving my happiness—

FREDERICK Has civilly forbid thee the house?

BELVILE 'Tis so, to make way for a powerful rival, the Viceroy's son, who has the advantage of me in being a man of fortune, a Spaniard, and her brother's friend; which gives him liberty to make his court, whilst I have recourse only to letters, and distant looks from her window, which are as soft and kind—'As those which Heaven sends down on penitents'.

BLUNT Heyday! 'Adsheartlikins, simile! By this light the man is quite spoiled! Fred, what the devil are we made of, that we cannot be thus concerned for a wench? 'Adsheartlikins, our Cupids are like the cooks of the camp: they can roast or boil a woman, but they have none of the fine tricks to set 'em off, no hogoes to make the sauce pleasant and the stomach sharp.

FREDERICK I dare swear I have had a hundred as young, kind, and handsome as this Florinda; and dogs eat me if they were not as troublesome to me i'th' morning as they were welcome o'er night.

BLUNT And yet I warrant he would not touch another woman, if he might have her for nothing.

BELVILE That's thy joy, a cheap whore.

BLUNT Why, 'adsheartlikins, I love a frank soul. When did you ever hear of an honest woman that took a man's money? I warrant 'em good ones. But gentlemen, you may be free; you have been kept so poor with Parliaments and Protectors that the little stock you have is not worth preserving. But I thank my stars I had more grace than to forfeit my estate by cavaliering.

BELVILE Methinks only following the court should be sufficient to entitle 'em to that.

BLUNT 'Adsheartlikins, they know I follow it to do it no good, unless they pick a hole in my coat for lending you money now and then, which is a greater crime to my conscience, gentlemen, than to the Commonwealth.

Enter Willmore.

WILLMORE Ha! Dear Belvile! Noble colonel!

BELVILE Willmore! Welcome ashore, my dear rover! What happy wind blew us this good fortune?

WILLMORE Let me salute my dear Fred and then command me. —How is't, honest lad?

FREDERICK Faith, sir, the old compliment, infinitely the better to see my dear mad Willmore again. Prithee why cam'st thou ashore? And where's the Prince?

WILLMORE He's well, and reigns still lord of the watery element. I must aboard again within a day or two, and my business ashore was only to enjoy myself a little this Carnival.

BELVILE Pray know our new friend, sir; he's but bashful, a raw traveller, but honest, stout, and one of us.

WILLMORE That you esteem him gives him an interest here.   *Embraces* Blunt.

BLUNT Your servant, sir.

WILLMORE But well, faith, I'm glad to meet you again in a warm climate, where the kind sun has its god-like power still over the wine and women. Love and mirth are my business in Naples, and if I mistake not the place, here's an excellent market for chapmen of my humour.

BELVILE See, here be those kind merchants of love you look for.

Enter several men in masquing habits, some playing on music, others dancing after; women dressed like courtesans, with papers pinned on their breasts, and baskets of flowers in their hands.

70 BLUNT 'Adsheartlikins, what have we here?

FREDERICK Now the game begins.

WILLMORE Fine pretty creatures! May a stranger have leave to look and love? What's here? 'Roses for every month'? *Reads the papers.*

BLUNT 'Roses for every month'? What means that?

BELVILE They are, or would have you think they're courtesans, who here in Naples are to be hired by the month.

WILLMORE Kind and obliging to inform us, pray where do these roses grow? I would fain plant some of 'em in a bed of mine.

WOMAN Beware such roses, sir.

80 WILLMORE A pox of fear: I'll be baked with thee between a pair of sheets, and that's thy proper still so I might but strew such roses over me, and under me. Fair one, would you would give me leave to gather at your bush this idle month, I would go near to make somebody smell of it all the year after.

BELVILE And thou hast need of such a remedy, for thou stinkest of tar and ropes' ends, like a dock or pest-house.

The woman puts herself into the hands of a man, and exeunt.

WILLMORE Nay, nay, you shall not leave me so.

BELVILE By all means use no violence here.

90 WILLMORE Death! Just as I was going to be damnably in love, to have her led off! I could pluck that rose out of his hand, and even kiss the bed the bush grew in.

FREDERICK No friend to love like a long voyage at sea.

BLUNT Except a nunnery, Fred.

WILLMORE Death! But will they not be kind? Quickly be kind? Thou know'st I'm no tame sigher, but a rampant lion of the forest.

Advances from the farther end of the scenes, two men dressed all over with horns of several sorts, making grimaces at one another, with papers pinned on their backs.

BELVILE Oh the fantastical rogues, how they're dressed! 'Tis a satire against the whole sex.

WILLMORE Is this a fruit that grows in this warm country?

100 BELVILE Yes. 'Tis pretty to see these Italians start, swell, and stab at the word cuckold, and yet stumble at horns on every threshold.

WILLMORE See what's on their back. (*Reads.*) 'Flowers of every night.' Ah, rogue! And more sweet than roses of every month! This is a gardener of Adam's own breeding. *They dance.*

BELVILE What think you of these grave people? Is a wake in Essex half so mad or extravagant?

WILLMORE I like their sober grave way: 'tis a kind of legal authorized fornication, where the men are not chid for't nor the women despised, as amongst our dull English. Even the monsieurs want that part of good manners.

BELVILE But here in Italy, a monsieur is the humblest, best-bred gentleman; 110 duels are so baffled by bravoes that an age shows not one but between a Frenchman and a hangman, who is as much too hard for him on the Piazza as they are for a Dutchman on the New Bridge. But see, another crew.

Enter Florinda, Hellena *and* Valeria, *dressed like gipsies;* Callis *and* Stephano, Lucetta, Philippo *and* Sancho *in masquerade.*

HELLENA Sister, there's your Englishman, and with him a handsome proper fellow. I'll to him, and instead of telling him his fortune, try my own.

WILLMORE Gipsies, on my life. Sure these will prattle if a man cross their hands. (*Goes to* Hellena.) —Dear, pretty, and, I hope, young devil, will you tell an amorous stranger what luck he's like to have?

HELLENA Have a care how you venture with me, sir, lest I pick your pocket, which will more vex your English humour than an Italian fortune will please 120 you.

WILLMORE How the devil cam'st thou to know my country and humour?

HELLENA The first I guess by a certain forward impudence, which does not displease me at this time; and the loss of your money will vex you because I hope you have but very little to lose.

WILLMORE Egad, child, thou'rt i'th' right; it is so little, I dare not offer it thee for a kindness. But cannot you divine what other things of more value I have about me, that I would more willingly part with?

HELLENA Indeed no, that's the business of a witch, and I am but a gipsy yet. Yet without looking in your hand, I have a parlous guess 'tis some foolish 130 heart you mean, an inconstant English heart, as little worth stealing as your purse.

WILLMORE Nay, then thou dost deal with the devil, that's certain. Thou hast guessed as right as if thou hadst been one of that number it has languished for. I find you'll be better acquainted with it, nor can you take it in a better time; for I am come from sea, child, and Venus not being propitious to me in her own element, I have a world of love in store. Would you would be good-natured and take some on't off my hands.

HELLENA Why, I could be inclined that way but for a foolish vow I am going to make—to die a maid. 140

WILLMORE Then thou art damned without redemption, and as I am a good Christian, I ought in charity to divert so wicked a design. Therefore prithee, dear creature, let me know quickly when and where I shall begin to set a helping hand to so good a work.

HELLENA If you should prevail with my tender heart, as I begin to fear you will, for you have horrible loving eyes, there will be difficulty in't that you'll hardly undergo for my sake.

WILLMORE Faith, child, I have been bred in dangers, and wear a sword that has been employed in a worse cause than for a handsome kind woman. Name the danger; let it be anything but a long siege and I'll undertake it. 150

HELLENA Can you storm?

WILLMORE Oh, most furiously.

HELLENA What think you of a nunnery wall? For he that wins me must gain that first.

WILLMORE A nun! Oh, how I love thee for't! There's no sinner like a young saint. Nay, now there's no denying me; the old law had no curse to a woman like dying a maid: witness Jephtha's daughter.

HELLENA A very good text this, if well handled; and I perceive, Father Captain, you would impose no severe penance on her who were inclined to console herself before she took orders.

WILLMORE If she be young and handsome.

HELLENA Aye, there's it. But if she be not—

WILLMORE By this hand, child, I have an implicit faith, and dare venture on thee with all faults. Besides, 'tis more meritorious to leave the world, when thou hast tasted and proved the pleasure on't. Then 'twill be a virtue in thee, which now will be pure ignorance.

HELLENA I perceive, good Father Captain, you design only to make me fit for heaven. But if, on the contrary, you should quite divert me from it, and bring me back to the world again, I should have a new man to seek, I find. And what a grief that will be; for when I begin, I fancy I shall love like anything; I never tried yet.

WILLMORE Egad, and that's kind! Prithee, dear creature, give me credit for a heart, for faith I'm a very honest fellow. Oh, I long to come first to the banquet of love! And such swinging appetite I bring. Oh, I'm impatient. Thy lodging, sweetheart, thy lodging, or I'm a dead man!

HELLENA Why must we be either guilty of fornication or murder if we converse with you men? And is there no difference between leave to love me, and leave to lie with me?

WILLMORE Faith, child, they were made to go together.

LUCETTA (*pointing to* Blunt) Are you sure this is the man?

SANCHO When did I mistake your game?

LUCETTA This is a stranger, I know by his gazing; if he be brisk he'll venture to follow me; and then if I understand my trade, he's mine. He's English too, and they say that's a sort of good-natured loving people, and have generally so kind an opinion of themselves that a woman with any wit may flatter 'em into any sort of fool she pleases.

She often passes by Blunt, *and gazes on him; he struts and cocks, and walks and gazes on her.*

BLUNT 'Tis so, she is taken; I have beauties which my false glass at home did not discover.

FLORINDA [*aside*] This woman watches me so, I shall get no opportunity to discover myself to him, and so miss the intent of my coming. —[*To* Belvile.] But as I was saying, sir, by this line you should be a lover.

Looking in his hand.

BELVILE I thought how right you guessed; all men are in love, or pretend to be so. Come, let me go, I'm weary of this fooling. *Walks away.*

FLORINDA I will not, sir, till you have confessed whether the passion that you have vowed Florinda be true or false. *She holds him; he strives to get from her.*

BELVILE Florinda! *Turns quick towards her.*

FLORINDA Softly.

BELVILE Thou hast named one will fix me here for ever.

FLORINDA She'll be disappointed then, who expects you this night at the garden gate, and if you fail not, as— (*Looks on* Callis, *who observes 'em.*) Let me see the other hand—you will go near to do, she vows to die or make you happy. 200

BELVILE What canst thou mean?

FLORINDA That which I say. Farewell. *Offers to go.*

BELVILE Oh charming sybil, stay, complete that joy which as it is will turn into distraction! Where must I be? At the garden gate? I know it. At night, you say? I'll sooner forfeit heaven than disobey.

Enter Don Pedro *and other masquers, and pass over the stage.*

CALLIS Madam, your brother's here.

FLORINDA Take this to instruct you farther. *Gives him a letter, and goes off.*

FREDERICK Have a care, sir, what you promise; this may be a trap laid by her brother to ruin you. 210

BELVILE Do not disturb my happiness with doubts. *Opens the letter.*

WILLMORE My dear pretty creature, a thousand blessings on thee! Still in this habit, you say? And after dinner at this place?

HELLENA Yes, if you will swear to keep your heart, and not bestow it between this and that.

WILLMORE By all the little gods of love, I swear; I'll leave it with you, and if you run away with it, those deities of justice will revenge me.

Exeunt all the women [except Lucetta].

FREDERICK Do you know the hand?

BELVILE 'Tis Florinda's. All blessings fall upon the virtuous maid. 220

FREDERICK Nay, no idolatry; a sober sacrifice I'll allow you.

BELVILE Oh friends, the welcomest news! The softest letter! Nay, you shall all see it! And could you now be serious, I might be made the happiest man the sun shines on!

WILLMORE The reason of this mighty joy?

BELVILE See how kindly she invites me to deliver her from the threatened violence of her brother. Will you not assist me?

WILLMORE I know not what thou mean'st, but I'll make one at any mischief where a woman's concerned. But she'll be grateful to us for the favour, will she not? 230

BELVILE How mean you?

WILLMORE How should I mean? Thou know'st there's but one way for a woman to oblige me.

BELVILE Do not profane, the maid is nicely virtuous.

WILLMORE Who, pox, then she's fit for nothing but a husband. Let her e'en go, colonel.

FREDERICK Peace, she's the colonel's mistress, sir.

WILLMORE Let her be the devil, if she be thy mistress I'll serve her. Name the way.

240 BELVILE Read here this postscript. *Gives him a letter.*

WILLMORE (*reads*) 'At ten at night, at the garden gate, of which, if I cannot get the key, I will contrive a way over the wall. Come attended with a friend or two.' —Kind heart, if we three cannot weave a string to let her down a garden wall, 'twere pity but the hangman wove one for us all.

FREDERICK Let her alone for that. Your woman's wit, your fair kind woman, will out-trick a broker or a Jew, and contrive like a Jesuit in chains. But see, Ned Blunt is stolen out after the lure of a damsel.

Exeunt Blunt *and* Lucetta.

BELVILE So, he'll scarce find his way home again unless we get him cried by the bellman in the market-place, and 'twould sound prettily: 'A lost English
250 boy of thirty.'

FREDERICK I hope 'tis some common crafty sinner, one that will fit him. It may be she'll sell him for Peru: the rogue's sturdy, and would work well in a mine. At least I hope she'll dress him for our mirth, cheat him of all, then have him well-favouredly banged, and turned out naked at midnight.

WILLMORE Prithee what humour is he of, that you wish him so well?

BELVILE Why, of an English elder brother's humour: educated in a nursery, with a maid to tend him till fifteen, and lies with his grandmother till he's of age; one that knows no pleasure beyond riding to the next fair, or going up to London with his right worshipful father in Parliament-time, wearing gay
260 clothes, or making honourable love to his lady mother's laundry-maid; gets drunk at a hunting-match, and ten to one then gives some proofs of his prowess. A pox upon him, he's our banker, and has all our cash about him; and if he fail, we are all broke.

FREDERICK Oh, let him alone for that matter: he's of a damned stingy quality that will secure our stock. I know not in what danger it were indeed if the jilt should pretend she's in love with him, for 'tis a kind believing coxcomb; otherwise, if he part with more than a piece of eight, geld him—for which offer he may chance to be beaten, if she be a whore of the first rank.

BELVILE Nay, the rogue will not be easily beaten, he's stout enough; perhaps
270 if they talk beyond his capacity, he may chance to exercise his courage upon some of them, else I'm sure they'll find it as difficult to beat as to please him.

WILLMORE 'Tis a lucky devil to light upon so kind a wench!

FREDERICK Thou hadst a great deal of talk with thy little gipsy; couldst thou do no good upon her? For mine was hard-hearted.

WILLMORE Hang her, she was some damned honest person of quality I'm sure, she was so very free and witty. If her face be but answerable to her wit and humour, I would be bound to constancy this month to gain her. In the meantime, have you made no kind acquaintance since you came to town?
280 You do not use to be honest so long, gentlemen.

FREDERICK Faith, love has kept us honest: we have been all fired with a beauty newly come to town, the famous Paduana Angellica Bianca.

WILLMORE What, the mistress of the dead Spanish general?

BELVILE Yes, she's now the only adored beauty of all the youth in Naples, who put on all their charms to appear lovely in her sight: their coaches, liveries, and themselves, all gay, as on a monarch's birthday, to attract the eyes of this fair charmer, while she has the pleasure to behold all languish for her that see her.

FREDERICK 'Tis pretty to see with how much love the men regard her, and how much envy the women. 290

WILLMORE What gallant has she?

BELVILE None, she's exposed to sale, and four days in the week she's yours, for so much a month.

WILLMORE The very thought of it quenches all manner of fire in me. Yet prithee, let's see her.

BELVILE Let's first to dinner, and after that we'll pass the day as you please. But at night ye must all be at my devotion.

WILLMORE I will not fail you. *Exeunt.*

Act II Scene 1

The long street
Enter Belvile *and* Frederick *in masquing habits, and* Willmore *in his own clothes, with a vizard in his hand.*

WILLMORE But why thus disguised and muzzled?

BELVILE Because whatever extravagances we commit in these faces, our own may not be obliged to answer 'em.

WILLMORE I should have changed my eternal buff too; but no matter, my little gipsy would not have found me out then; for if she should change hers, it is impossible I should know her, unless I should hear her prattle. A pox on't, I cannot get her out of my head. Pray Heaven, if ever I do see her again, she prove damnably ugly, that I may fortify myself against her tongue.

BELVILE Have a care of love; for o' my conscience she was not of a quality to give thee any hopes. 10

WILLMORE Pox on 'em, why do they draw a man in then? She has played with my heart so, that 'twill never lie still, till I have met with some kind wench that will play the game out with me. Oh, for my arms full of soft, white, kind woman—such as I fancy Angellica.

BELVILE This is her house, if you were but in a stock to gain admittance. They have not dined yet; I perceive the picture is not out.

Enter Blunt.

WILLMORE I long to see the shadow of the fair substance; a man may gaze on that for nothing.

BLUNT Colonel, thy hand—and thine, Fred. I have been an ass, a deluded fool, a very coxcomb from my birth till this hour, and heartily repent my little faith. 20

BELVILE What the devil's the matter with thee, Ned?

BLUNT Oh, such a mistress, Fred! Such a girl!

WILLMORE Ha! Where?

FREDERICK Aye, where?

BLUNT So fond, so amorous, so toying, and so fine! And all for sheer love, ye rogue! Oh, how she looked and kissed! And soothed my heart from my bosom! I cannot think I was awake, and yet methinks I see and feel her charms still. Fred, try if she have not left the taste of her balmy kisses upon my lips. *Kisses him.* 30

BELVILE Ha! Ha! Ha!

WILLMORE Death, man, where is she?

BLUNT What a dog was I to stay in dull England so long. How have I laughed at the colonel when he sighed for love! But now the little archer has revenged him, and by this one dart I can guess at all his joys, which then I took for fancies, mere dreams and fables. Well, I'm resolved to sell all in Essex and plant here for ever.

BELVILE What a blessing 'tis, thou hast a mistress thou dar'st boast of; for I know thy humour is rather to have a proclaimed clap than a secret amour.

40 WILLMORE Dost know her name?

BLUNT Her name? No, 'adsheartlikins, what care I for names? She's fair, young, brisk and kind, even to ravishment! And what a pox care I for knowing her by any other title?

WILLMORE Didst give her anything?

BLUNT Give her! Ha, ha, ha! Why, she's a person of quality. That's a good one, give her! 'Adsheartlikins, dost think such creatures are to be bought? Or are we provided for such a purchase? Give her, quoth ye? Why, she presented me with this bracelet for the toy of a diamond I used to wear. No, gentlemen, Ned Blunt is not everybody. She expects me again tonight.

50 WILLMORE Egad, that's well; we'll all go.

BLUNT Not a soul! No, gentlemen, you are wits; I am a dull country rogue, I.

FREDERICK Well, sir, for all your person of quality, I shall be very glad to understand your purse be secure; 'tis our whole estate at present, which we are loth to hazard in one bottom. Come, sir, unlade.

BLUNT Take the necessary trifle, useless now to me, that am beloved by such a gentlewoman. 'Adsheartlikins, money! Here, take mine too.

FREDERICK No, keep that to be cozened, that we may laugh.

WILLMORE Cozened? Death! Would I could meet with one that would cozen me of all the love I could spare tonight.

60 FREDERICK Pox, 'tis some common whore, upon my life.

BLUNT A whore? Yes, with such clothes, such jewels, such a house, such furniture, and so attended! A whore!

BELVILE Why yes, sir, they are whores, though they'll neither entertain you with drinking, swearing, or bawdry; are whores in all those gay clothes, and right jewels; are whores with those great houses richly furnished with velvet beds, store of plate, handsome attendance, and fine coaches; are whores, and errant ones.

WILLMORE Pox on't, where do these fine whores live?

BELVILE Where no rogues in office ycleped constables dare give 'em laws,
70 nor the wine-inspired bullies of the town break their windows; yet they are whores though this Essex calf believe 'em persons of quality.

BLUNT 'Adsheartlikins, y'are all fools. There are things about this Essex calf that shall take with the ladies, beyond all your wit and parts. This shape and size, gentlemen, are not to be despised; my waist, too, tolerably long, with other inviting signs that shall be nameless.

WILLMORE Egad, I believe he may have met with some person of quality that may be kind to him.

BELVILE Dost thou perceive any such tempting things about him that should make a fine woman, and of quality, pick him out from all mankind, to throw
80 away her youth and beauty upon; nay, and her dear heart too? No, no,

Angellica has raised the price too high.

WILLMORE May she languish for mankind till she die, and be damned for that one sin alone.

Enter two Bravoes, *and hang up a great picture of Angellica's against the balcony and two little ones at each side of the door.*

BELVILE See there the fair sign to the inn where a man may lodge that's fool enough to give her price. Willmore *gazes on the picture.*

BLUNT 'Adsheartlikins, gentlemen, what's this?

BELVILE A famous courtesan, that's to be sold.

BLUNT How? To be sold? Nay, then I have nothing to say to her. Sold? What impudence is practised in this country; with what order and decency whoring's established here by virtue of the Inquisition! Come, let's be gone; I'm sure we're no chapmen for this commodity. 90

FREDERICK Thou art none I'm sure, unless thou couldst have her in thy bed at a price of a coach in the street.

WILLMORE How wondrous fair she is! A thousand crowns a month? By heaven, as many kingdoms were too little! A plague of this poverty, of which I ne'er complain but when it hinders my approach to beauty, which virtue ne'er could purchase. *Turns from the picture.*

BLUNT What's this? (*Reads.*) 'A thousand crowns a month'! 'Adsheartlikins, here's a sum! Sure 'tis a mistake. —[*To one of the* Bravoes.] Hark you, friend, does she take or give so much by the month? 100

FREDERICK A thousand crowns! Why, 'tis a portion for the Infanta!

BLUNT Hark ye, friends, won't she trust?

BRAVO This is a trade, sir, that cannot live by credit.

Enter Don Pedro *in masquerade, followed by* Stephano.

BELVILE See, here's more company; let's walk off a while.

Exeunt English; Pedro *reads.*

PEDRO Fetch me a thousand crowns. I never wished to buy this beauty at an easier rate. *Passes off.*

Enter ANGELLICA *and* MORETTA *in the balcony, and draw a silk curtain.*

ANGELLICA Prithee, what said those fellows to thee?

BRAVO Madam, the first were admirers of beauty only, but no purchasers; they were merry with your price and picture, laughed at the sum, and so passed off. 110

ANGELLICA No matter, I'm not displeased with their rallying; their wonder feeds my vanity, and he that wishes but to buy gives me more pride than he that gives my price can make my pleasure.

BRAVO Madam, the last I knew through all his disguises to be Don Pedro, nephew to the general, and who was with him in Pamplona.

ANGELLICA Don Pedro? My old gallant's nephew? When his uncle died he left him a vast sum of money; it is he who was so in love with me at Padua, and who used to make the general so jealous.

MORETTA Is this he that used to prance before our window, and take such care to show himself an amorous ass? If I am not mistaken he is the likeliest 120 man to give your price.

ANGELLICA The man is brave and generous, but of a humour so uneasy and inconstant that the victory over his heart is as soon lost as won; a slave that can add little to the triumph of the conqueror. But inconstancy's the sin of all mankind, therefore I'm resolved that nothing but gold shall charm my heart.

MORETTA I'm glad on't; 'tis only interest that women of our profession ought to consider: though I wonder what has kept you from that general disease of our sex so long, I mean that of being in love.

130 ANGELLICA A kind but sullen star under which I had the happiness to be born. Yet I have had no time for love; the bravest and noblest of mankind have purchased my favours at so dear a rate, as if no coin but gold were current with our trade. But here's Don Pedro again; fetch me my lute, for 'tis for him or Don Antonio the Viceroy's son that I have spread my nets.

Enter at one door Don Pedro, Stephano; Don Antonio *and* Diego *at the other door with people following him in masquerade, anticly attired, some with music. They both go up to the picture.*

ANTONIO A thousand crowns! Had not the painter flattered her, I should not think it dear.

PEDRO Flattered her! By heaven he cannot. I have seen the original, nor is there one charm here more than adorns her face and eyes; all this soft and sweet, with a certain languishing air that no artist can represent.

140 ANTONIO What I heard of her beauty before had fired my soul, but this confirmation of it has blown it to a flame.

PEDRO Ha!

DIEGO Sir, I have known you throw away a thousand crowns on a worse face, and though y'are near your marriage, you may venture a little love here; Florinda will not miss it.

PEDRO (*aside*) Ha! Florinda! Sure 'tis Antonio.

ANTONIO Florinda! Name not those distant joys; there's not one thought of her will check my passion here.

150 PEDRO [*aside*] Florinda scorned! And all my hopes defeated of the possession of Angellica. (*A noise of a lute above.* Antonio *gazes up.*) Her injuries, by Heaven, he shall not boast of! *Song to a lute above.*

SONG

I   When Damon first began to love
     He languished in a soft desire,
     And knew not how the gods to move,
     To lessen or increase his fire:
     For Celia in her charming eyes
Wore all love's sweets, and all his cruelties.

II But as beneath a shade he lay,
     Weaving of flowers for Celia's hair,
160 She chanced to lead her flock that way,
     And saw the am'rous shepherd there.
     She gazed around upon the place,
     And saw the grove, resembling night,
     To all the joys of love invite,
Whilst guilty smiles and blushes dressed her face.

At this the bashful youth all transport grew,
And with kind force he taught the virgin how
To yield what all his sighs could never do.

Angellica *throws open the curtains, and bows to* Antonio, *who pulls off his vizard and bows and blows up kisses.* Pedro, *unseen, looks in his face. [The curtains are closed.]*

ANTONIO By heaven, she's charming fair!

PEDRO (*aside*) 'Tis he; the false Antonio! 170

ANTONIO (*to the Bravo*) Friend, where must I pay my offering of love?
    My thousand crowns I mean.

PEDRO That offering I have designed to make.
    And yours will come too late.

ANTONIO Prithee begone, I shall grow angry else,
    And then thou art not safe.

PEDRO My anger may be fatal, sir, as yours,
    And he that enters here may prove this truth.

ANTONIO I know not who thou art, but I am sure thou'rt worth my killing,
for aiming at Angellica. *They draw and fight.* 180

Enter Willmore *and* Blunt, *who draw and part them.*

BLUNT 'Adsheartlikins, here's fine doings.

WILLMORE Tilting for the wench I'm sure. Nay, gad, if that would win her I have as good a sword as the best of ye. Put up, put up, and take another time and place, for this is designed for lovers only. *They all put up.*

PEDRO We are prevented; dare you meet me tomorrow on the Molo?
    For I've a title to a better quarrel,
    That of Florinda in whose credulous heart
    Thou'st made an int'rest, and destroyed my hopes.

ANTONIO Dare!
    I'll meet thee there as early as the day. 190

PEDRO We will come thus disguised, that whosoever chance to get the better, he may escape unknown.

ANTONIO It shall be so. *Exeunt* Pedro *and* Stephano.

—Who should this rival be, unless the English colonel, of whom I've often heard Don Pedro speak? It must be he, and time he were removed, who lays a claim to all my happiness.

Willmore, *having gazed all this while on the picture, pulls down a little one.*

WILLMORE This posture's loose and negligent;
    The sight on't would beget a warm desire
    In souls whom impotence and age had chilled. 200
    This must along with me.

BRAVO What means this rudeness, sir? Restore the picture.

ANTONIO Ha! Rudeness committed to the fair Angellica! —Restore the picture, sir.

WILLMORE Indeed I will not, sir.

ANTONIO By heaven, but you shall.

WILLMORE Nay, do not show your sword; if you do, by this dear beauty, I will show mine too.

ANTONIO What right can you pretend to't?

210 WILLMORE That of possession, which I will maintain. You, perhaps, have a thousand crowns to give for the original.

ANTONIO No matter, sir, you shall restore the picture.

[*The curtains open;*] Angellica *and* Moretta, *above.*

ANGELLICA Oh Moretta, what's the matter?

ANTONIO Or leave your life behind.

WILLMORE Death! You lie; I will do neither.

They fight. The Spaniards join with Antonio, Blunt *laying on like mad.*

ANGELLICA Hold, I command you, if for me you fight.

They leave off and bow.

WILLMORE (*aside*) How heavenly fair she is! Ah, plague of her price.

ANGELLICA You, sir, in buff, you that appear a soldier, that first began this insolence—

220 WILLMORE 'Tis true, I did so, if you call it insolence for a man to preserve himself. I saw your charming picture and was wounded; quite through my soul each pointed beauty ran; and wanting a thousand crowns to procure my remedy, I laid this little picture to my bosom, which, if you cannot allow me, I'll resign.

ANGELLICA No, you may keep the trifle.

ANTONIO You shall first ask me leave, and this.   *Fight again as before.*

Enter Belvile *and* Frederick, *who join with the English.*

ANGELLICA Hold! Will you ruin me? —Biskey! Sebastian! Part 'em!

The Spaniards are beaten off.

MORETTA Oh, madam, we're undone. A pox upon that rude fellow; he's set on to ruin us. We shall never see good days again till all these fighting poor 230 rogues are sent to the galleys.

Enter Belvile, Blunt, Frederick, *and* Willmore *with his shirt bloody.*

BLUNT 'Adsheartlikins, beat me at this sport and I'll ne'er wear sword more.

BELVILE (*to* Willmore) The devil's in thee for a mad fellow; thou art always one at an unlucky adventure. Come, let's be gone whilst we're safe, and remember these are Spaniards, a sort of people that know how to revenge an affront.

FREDERICK You bleed! I hope you are not wounded.

WILLMORE Not much. A plague on your dons; if they fight no better they'll ne'er recover Flanders. What the devil was't to them that I took down the picture?

240 BLUNT Took it! 'Adsheartlikins, we'll have the great one too; 'tis ours by conquest. Prithee help me up and I'll pull it down.

ANGELLICA [*to* Willmore] Stay, sir, and ere you affront me farther let me know how you durst commit this outrage. To you I speak, sir, for you appear a gentleman.

WILLMORE To me, madam? —Gentlemen, your servant.   Belvile *stays him.*

BELVILE Is the devil in thee? Dost know the danger of entering the house of an incensed courtesan?

WILLMORE I thank you for your care, but there are other matters in hand, there are, though we have no great temptation. Death! Let me go!

FREDERICK Yes, to your lodging if you will, but not in here. Damn these gay harlots; by this hand I'll have as sound and handsome a whore for a patacoon. Death, man, she'll murder thee! 250

WILLMORE Oh, fear me not. Shall I not venture where a beauty calls? A lovely charming beauty! For fear of danger! When, by Heaven, there's none so great as to long for her whilst I want money to purchase her.

FREDERICK Therefore 'tis loss of time unless you had the thousand crowns to pay.

WILLMORE It may be she may give a favour; at least I shall have the pleasure of saluting her when I enter, and when I depart.

BELVILE Pox, she'll as soon lie with thee as kiss thee, and sooner stab than do either. You shall not go. 260

ANGELLICA Fear not, sir, all I have to wound with is my eyes.

BLUNT Let him go. 'Adsheartlikins, I believe the gentlewoman means well.

BELVILE Well, take thy fortune; we'll expect you in the next street. Farewell fool, farewell.

WILLMORE 'Bye, colonel.   *Goes in.*

FREDERICK The rogue's stark mad for a wench.   *Exeunt.*

Act II Scene [2]

A fine chamber
Enter Willmore, Angellica, *and* Moretta.

ANGELLICA Insolent sir, how durst you pull down my picture?

WILLMORE Rather, how durst you set it up to tempt poor am'rous mortals with so much excellence, which I find you have but too well consulted by the unmerciful price you set upon't. Is all this heaven of beauty shown to move despair in those that cannot buy? And can you think th'effects of that despair should be less extravagant than I have shown?

ANGELLICA I sent for you to ask my pardon, sir, not to aggravate your crime. I thought I should have seen you at my feet imploring it.

WILLMORE You are deceived. I came to rail at you, and rail such truths, too, as shall let you see the vanity of that pride which taught you how to set such price on sin. For such it is, whilst that which is love's due is meanly bartered for. 10

ANGELLICA Ha! Ha! Ha! Alas good captain, what pity 'tis your edifying doctrine will do no good upon me. Moretta, fetch the gentleman a glass, and let him survey himself to see what charms he has. —(*Aside, in a soft tone.*) And guess my business.

MORETTA He knows himself of old. I believe those breeches and he have been acquainted ever since he was beaten at Worcester.

ANGELLICA Nay, do not abuse the poor creature.

MORETTA Good weather-beaten corporal, will you march off? We have no need of your doctrine, though you have of our charity, but at present we have no scraps; we can afford no kindness for God's sake; in fine, sirrah, the price is too high i'th' mouth for you, therefore troop, I say. 20

WILLMORE Here, good forewoman of the shop, serve me and I'll be gone.

MORETTA Keep it to pay your laundress; your linen stinks of the gun room. For here's no selling by retail.

WILLMORE Thou hast sold plenty of thy stale ware at a cheap rate.

MORETTA Aye, the more silly kind heart I, but this is an age wherein beauty is at higher rates. In fine, you know the price of this.

30 WILLMORE I grant you 'tis here set down, a thousand crowns a month. Pray how much may come to my share for a pistole? Bawd, take your black lead and sum it up, that I may have a pistole's worth of this vain gay thing, and I'll trouble you no more.

MORETTA Pox on him, he'll fret me to death! Abominable fellow, I tell thee we only sell by the whole piece.

WILLMORE 'Tis very hard, the whole cargo or nothing. Faith, madam, my stock will not reach it; I cannot be your chapman. Yet I have countrymen in town, merchants of love like me; I'll see if they'll put in for a share. We cannot lose much by it, and what we have no use for, we'll sell upon the
40 Friday's mart at 'Who gives more?' —I am studying, madam, how to purchase you, though at present I am unprovided of money.

ANGELLICA (*aside*) Sure this from any other man would anger me, nor shall he know the conquest he has made. —Poor angry man, how I despise this railing.

WILLMORE Yes, I am poor. But I'm a gentleman,
And one that scorns this baseness which you practise.
Poor as I am, I would not sell myself,
No, not to gain your charming high-prized person.
Though I admire you strangely for your beauty,
50 Yet I contemn your mind.
And yet I would at any rate enjoy you,
At your own rate; but cannot. See here
The only sum I can command on earth:
I know not where to eat when this is gone.
Yet such a slave I am to love and beauty
This last reserve I'll sacrifice to enjoy you.
Nay, do not frown, I know you're to be bought,
And would be bought by me. By me,
For a mean trifling sum, if I could pay it down.
60 Which happy knowledge I will still repeat,
And lay it to my heart: it has a virtue in't,
And soon will cure those wounds your eyes have made,
And yet, there's something so divinely powerful there—
Nay, I will gaze, to let you see my strength.

Holds her, looks on her, and pauses and sighs.

By heav'n, bright creature, I would not for the world
Thy fame were half so fair as is thy face.

Turns her away from him.

ANGELLICA (*aside*) His words go through me to the very soul.
—If you have nothing else to say to me—

WILLMORE Yes, you shall hear how infamous you are—
70 For which I do not hate thee—
But that secures my heart, and all the flames it feels
Are but so many lusts:

282

I know it by their sudden bold intrusion.
The fire's impatient and betrays, 'tis false.
For had it been the purer flame of love,
I should have pined and languished at your feet,
E'er found the impudence to have discovered it.
I now dare stand your scorn, and your denial.

MORETTA Sure she's bewitched that she can stand thus tamely and hear his saucy railings. —Sirrah, will you be gone?　　　　　　　　80

ANGELLICA (*to* Moretta) How dare you take this liberty? Withdraw. —Pray tell me, sir, are not you guilty of the same mercenary crime? When a lady is proposed to you for a wife, you never ask, how fair, discreet, or virtuous she is; but what's her fortune—which if but small, you cry 'she will not do my business', and basely leave her, though she languish for you. Say, is not this as poor?

WILLMORE It is a barbarous custom, which I will scorn to defend in our sex, and do despise in yours.

ANGELLICA Thou'rt a brave fellow! Put up thy gold, and know,
That were thy fortune large as is thy soul,　　　　　　　　90
Thou shouldst not buy my love,
Couldst thou forget those mean effects of vanity
Which set me out to sale, and, as a lover, prize my yielding joys.
Canst thou believe they'll be entirely thine,
Without considering they were mercenary?

WILLMORE I cannot tell, I must bethink me first.
(*Aside*.) Ha! Death, I'm going to believe her.

ANGELLICA Prithee confirm that faith, or if thou canst not
Flatter me a little, 'twill please me from thy mouth.

WILLMORE (*aside*) Curse on thy charming tongue!　　　　　　　　100
Dost thou return my feigned contempt with so much subtlety?
—Thou'st found the easiest way into my heart,
Though I yet know that all thou say'st is false.　　*Turning from her in rage.*

ANGELLICA By all that's good, 'tis real;
I never loved before, though oft a mistress.
Shall my first vows be slighted?

WILLMORE (*aside*) What can she mean?

ANGELLICA (*in an angry tone*) I find you cannot credit me.

WILLMORE I know you take me for an errant ass,
An ass that may be soothed into belief,　　　　　　　　110
And then be used at pleasure;
But, madam, I have been so often cheated
By perjured, soft, deluding hypocrites,
That I've no faith left for the cozening sex,
Especially for women of your trade.

ANGELLICA The low esteem you have of me perhaps
May bring my heart again:
For I have pride, that yet surmounts my love.

　　　　　　　　　　　　She turns with pride; he holds her.

WILLMORE Throw off this pride, this enemy to bliss,
And show the power of love: 'tis with those arms　　　　　　　　120
I can be only vanquished, made a slave.

283

ANGELLICA Is all my mighty expectation vanished?
    No, I will not hear thee talk; thou hast a charm
    In every word that draws my heart away,
    And all the thousand trophies I designed
    Thou hast undone. Why art thou soft?
    Thy looks are bravely rough, and meant for war.
    Couldst thou not storm on still?
    I then perhaps had been as free as thou.

130 WILLMORE (*aside*) Death, how she throws her fire about my soul!
    —Take heed, fair creature, how you raise my hopes,
    Which once assumed pretends to all dominion:
    There's not a joy thou hast in store
    I shall not then command.
    For which I'll pay you back my soul, my life!
    Come, let's begin th'account this happy minute!

ANGELLICA And will you pay me then the price I ask?

WILLMORE Oh, why dost thou draw me from an awful worship,
    By showing thou art no divinity.
140   Conceal the fiend, and show me all the angel!
    Keep me but ignorant, and I'll be devout
    And pay my vows for ever at this shrine.

                            Kneels and kisses her hand.

ANGELLICA The pay I mean is but thy love for mine.
    Can you give that?

WILLMORE Entirely. Come, let's withdraw where I'll renew my vows, and breathe 'em with such ardour thou shalt not doubt my zeal.

ANGELLICA Thou hast a power too strong to be resisted.

                          Exeunt Willmore *and* Angellica.

MORETTA Now my curse go with you! Is all our project fallen to this? To love the only enemy to our trade? Nay, to love such a shameroon, a very beggar, 150 nay a pirate beggar, whose business is to rifle and be gone; a no-purchase, o-pay tatterdemalion, and English picaroon; a rogue that fights for daily drink, and takes a pride in being loyally lousy? Oh, I could curse now, if I durst. This is the fate of most whores.
    Trophies, which from believing fops we win,
    Are spoils to those who cozen us again.

                                  [*Exit.*]

Act III Scene 1

A street
Enter Florinda, Valeria, Hellena, *in antic different dresses from what they were in before;* Callis *attending.*

FLORINDA I wonder what should make my brother in so ill a humour? I hope he has not found out our ramble this morning.

HELLENA No, if he had, we should have heard on't at both ears, and have been mewed up this afternoon, which I would not for the world should have happened. Hey ho, I'm as sad as a lover's lute.

VALERIA Well, methinks we have learnt this trade of gipsies as readily as if we have been bred upon the road to Loretto: and yet I did so fumble when I told the stranger his fortune that I was afraid I should have told my own and yours by mistake. But methinks Hellena has been very serious ever since.

FLORINDA I would give my garters she were in love, to be revenged upon her for abusing me. How is't, Hellena?

HELLENA Ah, would I had never seen my mad monsieur. And yet, for all your laughing, I am not in love. And yet this small acquaintance, o' my conscience, will never out of my head.

VALERIA Ha! Ha! Ha! I laugh to think how thou art fitted with a lover, a fellow that I warrant loves every new face he sees.

HELLENA Hum, he has not kept his word with me here, and may be taken up. That thought is not very pleasant to me. What the deuce should this be now that I feel?

VALERIA What is't like?

HELLENA Nay, the Lord knows, but if I should be hanged I cannot choose but be angry and afraid, when I think that mad fellow should be in love with anybody but me. What to think of myself I know not: would I could meet with some true damned gipsy, that I might know my fortune.

VALERIA Know it! Why, there's nothing so easy: thou wilt love this wandering inconstant till thou find'st thyself hanged about his neck, and then be as mad to get free again.

FLORINDA Yes, Valeria, we shall see her bestride his baggage horse and follow him to the campaign.

HELLENA So, so, now you are provided for there's no care taken of poor me. But since you have set my heart a-wishing, I am resolved to know for what; I will not die of the pip, so I will not.

FLORINDA Art thou mad to talk so? Who will like thee well enough to have thee, that hears what a mad wench thou art?

HELLENA Like me! I don't intend every he that likes me shall have me, but he that I like. I should have stayed in the nunnery still if I had liked my lady Abbess as well as she liked me. No, I came thence not (as my wise brother imagines) to take an eternal farewell of the world, but to love, and to be beloved; and I will be beloved, or I'll get one of your men, so I will.

VALERIA Am I put into the number of lovers?

HELLENA You? Why, coz, I know thou'rt too good-natured to leave us in any design; thou wouldst venture a cast though thou comest off a loser, especially with such a gamester. I observed your man, and your willing ear incline that way; and if you are not a lover, 'tis an art soon learnt—that I find.   *Sighs.*

FLORINDA I wonder how you learnt to love so easily. I had a thousand charms to meet my eyes and ears e'er I could yield, and 'twas the knowledge of Belvile's merit, not the surprising person, took my soul. Thou art too rash, to give a heart at first sight.

HELLENA Hang your considering lover! I never thought beyond the fancy that 'twas a very pretty, idle, silly kind of pleasure to pass one's time with: to write little soft nonsensical billets, and with great difficulty and danger receive answers in which I shall have my beauty praised, my wit admired (though little or none), and have the vanity and power to know I am desirable. Then I have the more inclination that way because I am to be a nun, and so shall not be suspected to have any such earthly thoughts about me; but when I walk thus—and sigh thus—they'll think my mind's upon my monastery, and cry, 'How happy 'tis she's so resolved.' But not a word of man.

60 FLORINDA What a mad creature's this!

HELLENA I'll warrant, if my brother hears either of you sigh, he cries gravely, 'I fear you have the indiscretion to be in love, but take heed of the honour of our house, and your own unspotted fame'; and so he conjures on till he has laid the soft-winged god in your hearts, or broke the bird's nest. But see, here comes your lover, but where's my inconstant? Let's step aside, and we may learn something.   *Go aside.*

Enter Belvile, Frederick, *and* Blunt.

BELVILE What means this! The picture's taken in.

BLUNT It may be the wench is good-natured, and will be kind gratis. Your friend's a proper handsome fellow.

70 BELVILE I rather think she has cut his throat and is fled. I am mad he should throw himself into dangers. Pox on't, I shall want him, too, at night. Let's knock and ask for him.

HELLENA My heart goes a-pit, a-pat, for fear 'tis my man they talk of.

Knock; Moretta *above.*

MORETTA What would you have?

BELVILE Tell the stranger that entered here about two hours ago that his friends stay here for him.

MORETTA A curse upon him for Moretta—would he were at the devil! But he's coming to you.

Enter Willmore.

HELLENA Aye, aye, 'tis he! Oh, how this vexes me!

80 BELVILE And how and how, dear lad, has fortune smiled? Are we to break her windows? Or raise up altars to her? Ha!

WILLMORE Does not my fortune sit triumphant on my brow? Dost not see the little wanton god there all gay and smiling? Have I not an air about my face and eyes that distinguish me from the crowd of common lovers? By Heaven, Cupid's quiver has not half so many darts as her eyes! Oh, such a *bona roba!* To sleep in her arms is lying *in fresco,* all perfumed air about me.

HELLENA (*aside*) Here's fine encouragement for me to fool on!

WILLMORE Hark'ee, where didst thou purchase that rich Canary we drank today? Tell me that I may adore the spigot, and sacrifice to the butt! The 90 juice was divine: into which I must dip my rosary, and then bless all things hat I would have bold or fortunate.

BELVILE Well sir, let's go take a bottle, and hear the story of your success.

FREDERICK Would not French wine do better?

WILLMORE Damn the hungry balderdash! Cheerful sack has a generous virtue in't inspiring a successful confidence, gives eloquence to the tongue, and vigour to the soul, and has in a few hours completed all my hopes and wishes! There's nothing left to raise a new desire in me. Come, let's be gay and wanton. And, gentlemen, study, study what you want, for here are friends that will supply gentlemen. [*Jingles coins.*] Hark what a charming 100 sound they make! 'Tis he and she gold whilst here, and shall beget new leasures every moment.

BLUNT But hark'ee sir, you are not married are you?

WILLMORE All the honey of matrimony, but none of the sting, friend.

BLUNT 'Adsheartlikins, thou'rt a fortunate rogue!

WILLMORE I am so, sir: let these inform you! Ha, how sweetly they chime! Pox of poverty; it makes a man a slave, makes wit and honour sneak. My soul grew lean and rusty for want of credit.

BLUNT 'Adsheartlikins, this I like well; it looks like my lucky bargain! Oh, how I long for the approach of my squire, that is to conduct me to her house again. Why, here's two provided for! 110

FREDERICK By this light y'are happy men.

BLUNT Fortune is pleased to smile on us, gentlemen, to smile on us.

Enter Sancho *and pulls down* Blunt *by the sleeve; they go aside.*

SANCHO Sir, my lady expects you. She has removed all that might oppose your will and pleasure, and is impatient till you come.

BLUNT Sir, I'll attend you. —Oh, the happiest rogue! I'll take no leave, lest they either dog me, or stay me. *Exit with* Sancho.

BELVILE But then the little gipsy is forgot?

WILLMORE A mischief on thee for putting her into my thoughts! I had quite forgot her else, and this night's debauch had drunk her quite down.

HELLENA Had it so, good captain! *Claps him on the back.* 120

WILLMORE (*aside*) Ha! I hope she did not hear me.

HELLENA What, afraid of such a champion?

WILLMORE Oh, you're a fine lady of your word, are you not? To make a man languish a whole day—

HELLENA In tedious search of me.

WILLMORE Egad, child thou'rt in the right. Hadst thou seen what a melancholy dog I have been ever since I was a lover, how I have walked the streets like a Capuchin with my hands in my sleeves—faith, sweetheart, thou would'st pity me.

HELLENA [*aside*] Now if I should be hanged I can't be angry with him, he 130 dissembles so heartily. —Alas, good captain, what pains you have taken; now were I ungrateful not to reward so true a servant.

WILLMORE Poor soul, that's kindly said; I see thou barest a conscience. Come then, for a beginning show me thy dear face.

HELLENA I'm afraid, my small acquaintance, you have been staying that swinging stomach you boasted of this morning. I then remember my little collation would have gone down with you without the sauce of a handsome face. Is your stomach so queasy now?

WILLMORE Faith, long fasting, child, spoils a man's appetite. Yet if you durst treat, I could so lay about me still— 140

HELLENA And would you fall to, before a priest says grace?

WILLMORE Oh fie, fie, what an old out-of-fashioned thing hast thou named? Thou couldst not dash me more out of countenance shouldst thou show me an ugly face.

Whilst he is seemingly courting Hellena, *enter* Angellica, Moretta, Biskey, *and* Sebastian, *all in masquerade;* Angellica *sees* Willmore *and stares.*

ANGELLICA Heavens, 'tis he! And passionately fond to see another woman!

MORETTA What could you less expect from such a swaggerer?

287

ANGELLICA Expect! As much as I paid him; a heart entire,
    Which I had pride enough to think when'er I gave,
    It would have raised the man above the vulgar,
150   Made him all soul, and that all soft and constant.

HELLENA You see, captain, how willing I am to be friends with you, till time
and ill luck make us lovers; and ask you the question first, rather than put
your modesty to the blush by asking me. For alas, I know you captains are
such strict men, and such severe observers of your vows to chastity, that
'twill be hard to prevail with your tender conscience to marry a young
willing maid.

WILLMORE Do not abuse me, for fear I should take thee at thy word, and
marry thee indeed, which I'm sure will be revenge sufficient.

HELLENA O' my conscience, that will be our destiny, because we are both of
160 one humour: I am as inconstant as you. For I have considered, captain, that
handsome woman has a great deal to do whilst her face is good, for then is
our harvest-time to gather friends; and should I in these days of my youth
catch a fit of foolish constancy, I were undone: 'tis loitering by daylight in
our great journey. Therefore I declare I'll allow but one year for love, one
year for indifference, and one year for hate; and then go hang yourself, for I
profess myself the gay, the kind, and the inconstant. The devil's in't if this
won't please you!

WILLMORE Oh, most damnably. I have a heart with a hole quite through it
too; no prison, mine, to keep a mistress in.

170   ANGELLICA (*aside*) Perjured man! How I believe thee now!

HELLENA Well, I see our business as well as humours are alike: yours to
cozen as many maids as will trust you, and I as many men as have faith. See
if I have not as desperate a lying look as you can have for the heart of you.
(*Pulls off her vizard; he starts.*) How do you like it, captain?

WILLMORE Like it! By heaven, I never saw so much beauty! Oh the charms of
those sprightly black eyes! That strangely fair face full of smiles and dimples!
Those soft round melting cherry lips and small even white teeth! Not to be
expressed, but silently adored! [*She replaces her mask.*] Oh, one look more,
and strike me dumb, or I shall repeat nothing else till I'm mad.

He seems to court her to pull off her vizard, she refuses.

180   ANGELLICA I can endure no more; nor is it fit to interrupt him, for if I do, my
jealousy has so destroyed my reason I shall undo him. Therefore I'll retire,
and you, Sebastian (*to one of her* Bravoes), follow that woman and learn
who 'tis; while you (*to the other* Bravo) tell the fugitive I would speak to
him instantly.   *Exit.*

This while Florinda is *talking to* Belvile, *who stands sullenly*, Frederick
courting Valeria.

VALERIA [*to* Belvile] Prithee, dear stranger, be not so sullen, for though you
have lost your love, you see my friend frankly offers you hers to play with
in the meantime.

BELVILE Faith madam, I am sorry I can't play at her game.

FREDERICK [*to* Valeria] Pray leave your intercession, and mind your own affair.
190   They'll better agree apart: he's a modest sigher in company, but alone no
woman 'scapes him.

FLORINDA [*aside*] Sure he does but rally. Yet if it should be true? I'll tempt him
farther. —Believe me, noble stranger, I'm no common mistress; and for a

little proof on't, wear this jewel. Nay, take it, sir, 'tis right, and bills of exchange may sometimes miscarry.

BELVILE Madam, why am I chose out of all mankind to be the object of your bounty?

VALERIA There's another civil question asked.

FREDERICK [*aside*] Pox of's modesty; it spoils his own markets and hinders mine.   200

FLORINDA Sir, from my window I have often seen you, and women of my quality have so few opportunities for love that we ought to lose none.

FREDERICK [*to Valeria*] Aye, this is something! Here's a woman! When shall I be blessed with so much kindness from your fair mouth? —(*Aside to* Belvile.) Take the jewel, fool!

BELVILE You tempt me strangely, madam, every way—

FLORINDA (*aside*) So, if I find him false, my whole repose is gone.

BELVILE And but for a vow I've made to a very fair lady, this goodness had subdued me.

FREDERICK [*aside to* Belvile] Pox on't, be kind, in pity to me be kind. For I am   210
to thrive here but as you treat her friend.

HELLENA Tell me what you did in yonder house, and I'll unmask.

WILLMORE Yonder house? Oh, I went to a—to—why, there's a friend of mine lives there.

HELLENA What, a she or a he friend?

WILLMORE A man, upon honour, a man. A she friend? No, no, madam, you have done my business, I thank you.

HELLENA And was't your man friend that had more darts in's eyes than Cupid carries in's whole budget of arrows?

WILLMORE So—   220

HELLENA 'Ah such a *bona roba*! To be in her arms is lying *in fresco*, all perfumed air about me.' Was this your man friend too?

WILLMORE So—

HELLENA That gave you the he and the she gold, that begets young pleasures?

WILLMORE Well, well, madam, then you can see there are ladies in the world that will not be cruel. There are, madam, there are.

HELLENA And there be men too, as fine, wild, inconstant fellows as yourself. There be, captain, there be, if you go to that now. Therefore, I'm resolved—

WILLMORE Oh!

HELLENA To see your face no more—   230

WILLMORE Oh!

HELLENA Till tomorrow.

WILLMORE Egad, you frighted me.

HELLENA Nor then neither, unless you'll swear never to see that lady more.

WILLMORE See her! Why, never to think of womankind again.

HELLENA Kneel and swear.   *Kneels, she gives him her hand.*

WILLMORE I do, never to think, to see, to love, nor lie, with any but thyself.

HELLENA Kiss the book.

WILLMORE Oh, most religiously.   *Kisses her hand.*

240 HELLENA Now what a wicked creature am I, to damn a proper fellow.

CALLIS (*to* Florinda) Madam, I'll stay no longer, 'tis e'en dark.

FLORINDA [*to* Belvile] However, sir, I'll leave this with you, that when I'm gone you may repent the opportunity you have lost by your modesty.

Gives him the jewel, which is her picture, and exit. He gazes after her.

WILLMORE [*to* Hellena] 'Twill be an age till tomorrow, and till then I will most impatiently expect you. Adieu, my dear pretty angel.

Exeunt all the women.

BELVILE Ha! Florinda's picture! 'Twas she herself. What a dull dog was I! I would have given the world for one minute's discourse with her.

FREDERICK This comes of your modesty! Ah, pox o' your vow; 'twas ten to one but we had lost the jewel by't.

250 BELVILE Willmore, the blessed'st opportunity lost! Florinda, friends, Florinda!

WILLMORE Ah, rogue! Such black eyes! Such a face! Such a mouth! Such teeth! And so much wit!

BELVILE All, all, and a thousand charms besides.

WILLMORE Why, dost thou know her?

BELVILE Know her! Aye, aye, and a pox take me with all my heart for being so modest.

WILLMORE But hark'ee, friend of mine, are you my rival? And have I been only beating the bush all this while?

BELVILE I understand thee not. I'm mad! See here— *Shows the picture.*

260 WILLMORE Ha! Whose picture's this? 'Tis a fine wench!

FREDERICK The colonel's mistress, sir.

WILLMORE Oh, oh here. (*Gives the picture back.*) I thought it had been another prize. Come, come, a bottle will set thee right again.

BELVILE I am content to try, and by that time 'twill be late enough for our design.

WILLMORE Agreed.
Love does all day the soul's great empire keep,
But wine at night lulls the soft god asleep.

Exeunt.

Act III Scene 2

Lucetta's house.
Enter Blunt *and* Lucetta *with a light.*

LUCETTA Now we are safe and free; no fears of the coming home of my old jealous husband, which made me a little thoughtful when you came in first. But now love is all the business of my soul.

BLUNT I am transported! —(*Aside.*) Pox on't, that I had but some fine things to say to her, such as lovers use. I was a fool not to learn of Fred a little by heart before I came. Something I must say. —'Adsheartlikins, sweet soul, I am not used to compliment, but I'm an honest gentleman, and thy humble servant.

LUCETTA I have nothing to pay for so great a favour, but such a love as cannot but be great, since at first sight of that sweet face and shape it made me your absolute captive.

BLUNT (*aside*) Kind heart, how prettily she talks! Egad, I'll show her husband a Spanish trick: send him out of the world and marry her. She's damnably in love with me, and will ne'er mind settlements, and so there's that saved.

LUCETTA Well, sir, I'll go and undress me, and be with you instantly.

BLUNT Make haste then, for 'adsheartlikins, dear soul, thou canst not guess at the pain of a longing lover, when his joys are drawn within the compass of a few minutes.

LUCETTA You speak my sense, and I'll make haste to prove it.   *Exit.*

BLUNT 'Tis a rare girl, and this one night's enjoyment with her will be worth   20
all the days I ever passed in Essex. Would she would go with me into England; though to say truth there's plenty of whores already. But a pox on 'em, they are such mercenary prodigal whores that they want such a one as this, that's free and generous, to give 'em good examples. Why, what a house she has, how rich and fine!

Enter Sancho.

SANCHO Sir, my lady has sent me to conduct you to her chamber.

BLUNT Sir, I shall be proud to follow. —(*Aside.*) Here's one of her servants too; 'adsheartlikins, by this garb and gravity he might be a Justice of Peace in Essex, and is but a pimp here.   *Exeunt.*

Act III [Scene 3]

The scene changes to a chamber with an alcove bed in it, a table, etc.;
Lucetta *in bed.*
Enter Sancho, *and* Blunt, *who takes the candle of* Sancho *at the door.*

SANCHO Sir, my commission reaches no farther.   [*Exit* Sancho.]

BLUNT Sir, I'll excuse your compliment. What, in bed, my sweet mistress?

LUCETTA You see, I still outdo you in kindness.

BLUNT And thou shalt see what haste I'll make to quit scores. Oh, the luckiest rogue!   *He undresses himself.*

LUCETTA Should you be false or cruel now—

BLUNT False! 'Adsheartlikins, what dost thou take me for, a Jew? An insensible heathen? A pox of thy old jealous husband; an he were dead, egad, sweet soul, it should be none of my fault if I did not marry thee.

LUCETTA It never should be mine.   10

LUNT Good soul! I'm the fortunatest dog!

LUCETTA Are you not undressed yet?

BLUNT As much as my impatience will permit.

                    Goes towards the bed in his shirt, drawers, etc.

LUCETTA Hold, sir, put out the light; it may betray us else.

BLUNT Anything; I need no other light, but that of thine eyes! —(*Aside.*) 'Adsheartlikins, there I think I had it. (*Puts out the candle; the bed descends; he gropes about to find it.*) Why, why, where am I got? What, not yet? Where are you, sweetest? —Ah, the rogue's silent now. A pretty love-trick this; how she'll laugh at me anon! —You need not, my dear rogue, you need not! I'm all on fire already; come, come, now call me, in pity. —Sure I'm enchanted!   20
have been round the chamber, and can find neither woman nor bed. I locked the door, I'm sure she cannot go that way, or if she could, the bed

could not. —Enough, enough, my pretty wanton, do not carry the jest too far. (*Lights on a trap, and is let down.*) Ha! Betrayed! Dogs! Rogues! Pimps! Help! Help!

Enter Lucetta, Philippo, *and* Sancho *with a light.*

PHILIPPO Ha! Ha! Ha! He's dispatched finely.

LUCETTA Now, sir, had I been coy, we had missed of this booty.

PHILIPPO Nay, when I saw 'twas a substantial fool, I was mollified; but when you dote upon a serenading coxcomb, upon a face, fine clothes, and a lute, it makes me rage.

LUCETTA You know I was never guilty of that folly, my dear Philippo, but with yourself. But come, let's see what we have got by this.

PHILIPPO A rich coat; sword and hat; these breeches, too, are well lined! See here, a gold watch! A purse —Ha! Gold! At least two hundred pistoles! A bunch of diamond rings and one with the family arms! A gold box, with a medal of his king, and his lady mother's picture! These were sacred relics, believe me! See, the waistband of his breeches have a mine of gold—old Queen Bess's! We have a quarrel to her ever since eighty-eight, and may therefore justify the theft: the Inquisition might have committed it.

LUCETTA See, a bracelet of bowed gold! These his sisters tied about his arm at parting. But well, for all this, I fear his being a stranger may make a noise and hinder our trade with them hereafter.

PHILIPPO That's our security; he is not only a stranger to us, but to the country too. The common shore into which he is descended, thou know'st, conducts him into another street, which this light will hinder him from ever finding again. He knows neither your name, nor that of the street where your house is; nay, nor the way to his own lodgings.

LUCETTA And art not thou an unmerciful rogue, not to afford him one night for all this? I should not have been such a Jew.

PHILIPPO Blame me not, Lucetta, to keep as much of thee as I can to myself. Come, that thought makes me wanton; let's to bed! —Sancho, lock up these.
> This is the fleece which fools do bear,
> Designed for witty men to shear.

Exeunt.

Act III [Scene 4]

The scene changes, and discovers Blunt, *creeping out of a common shore; his face, etc., all dirty.*

BLUNT (*climbing up*) Oh Lord! I am got out at last, and, which is a miracle, without a clue. And now to damning and cursing! But if that would ease me, where shall I begin? With my fortune, myself, or the quean that cozened me? What a dog was I to believe in woman! Oh, coxcomb! Ignorant, conceited coxcomb! To fancy she could be enamoured with my person! At first sight enamoured! Oh, I'm a cursed puppy! 'Tis plain, fool was writ upon my forehead! She perceived it—saw the Essex calf there. For what allurements could there be in this countenance, which I can endure because I'm acquainted with it. Oh, dull silly dog, to be thus soothed into a cozening! Had I been drunk, I might fondly have credited the young quean; but as I as in my right wits, to be thus cheated, confirms it: I am a dull believing English country fop. But my comrades! Death and the devil, there's the worst of all! Then a ballad will be sung tomorrow on the Prado, to a lousy tune of the enchanted squire and the annihilated damsel. But Fred—that rogue—and the colonel will abuse me beyond all Christian patience. Had she left me my clothes, I have a bill of exchange at home would have saved my credit. But now all hope is taken from me. Well, I'll home, if I can find the way, with this consolation: that I am not the first kind believing coxcomb; but there are, gallants, many such good natures amongst ye.

> And though you've better arts to hide your follies,   20
> 'Adsheartlikins, y'are all as errant cullies.

Exit.

Act III [Scene 5]

The garden in the night
Enter Florinda *in an undress, with a key and a little box.*

FLORINDA Well, thus far I'm in my way to happiness. I have got myself free from Callis; my brother too, I find by yonder light, is got into his cabinet, and thinks not of me; I have, by good fortune, got the key of the garden back door. I'll open it to prevent Belvile's knocking—a little noise will now alarm my brother. Now am I as fearful as a young thief. (*Unlocks the door.*) Hark! What noise is that? Oh, 'twas the wind that played amongst the boughs. Belvile stays long, methinks; it's time. Stay, for fear of a surprise, I'll hide these jewels in yonder jessamine.   *She goes to lay down the box.*

Enter Willmore, *drunk.*

WILLMORE What the devil is become of these fellows, Belvile and Frederick? They promised to stay at the next corner for me, but who the devil knows   10 the corner of a full moon? Now whereabouts am I? Ha, what have we here? A garden! A very convenient place to sleep in. Ha! What has God sent us here? A female! By this light, a woman! I'm a dog if it be not a very wench!

FLORINDA He's come! Ha! Who's there?

WILLMORE Sweet soul, let me salute thy shoe-string.

FLORINDA [*aside*] 'Tis not my Belvile. Good heavens, I know him not! —Who are you, and from whence come you?

WILLMORE Prithee, prithee, child, not so many hard questions! Let it suffice I am here, child. Come, come kiss me.

FLORINDA Good gods! What luck is mine?   20

WILLMORE Only good luck, child, parlous good luck. Come hither. —'Tis a delicate shining wench. By this hand, she's perfumed, and smells like any nosegay. —Prithee, dear soul, let's not play the fool, and lose time—precious time. For as God shall save me, I'm as honest a fellow as breathes, though I'm a little disguised at present. Come, I say. Why, thou mayst be free with me: I'll be very secret. I'll not boast who 'twas obliged me, not I—for hang me if I know thy name.

FLORINDA Heavens! What a filthy beast is this!

WILLMORE I am so, and thou ought'st the sooner to lie with me for that reason. For look you child, there will be no sin in't, because 'twas neither   30 designed nor premeditated: 'tis pure accident on both sides. That's a certain thing now. Indeed, should I make love to you, and you vow fidelity, and swear and lie till you believed and yielded—that were to make it wilful fornication, the crying sin of the nation. Thou art therefore, as thou art a good Christian, obliged in conscience to deny me nothing. Now, come, be kind without any more idle prating.

FLORINDA Oh I am ruined! Wicked man, unhand me!

WILLMORE Wicked? Egad child, a judge were he young and vigorous, and saw those eyes of thine, would know 'twas they gave the first blow, the first provocation. Come, prithee, let's lose no time, I say. This is a fine convenient place.

40

FLORINDA Sir, let me go, I conjure you, or I'll call out.

WILLMORE Aye, aye, you were best to call witness to see how finely you treat me. Do!

FLORINDA I'll cry murder, rape, or anything, if you do not instantly let me go!

WILLMORE A rape! Come, come, you lie, you baggage, you lie. What, I'll warrant you would fain have the world believe now that you are not so forward as I. No, not you. Why at this time of night was your cobweb door set open, dear spider, but to catch flies? Ha! Come, or I shall be damnably angry. Why, what a coil is here!

50

FLORINDA Sir, can you think—

WILLMORE That you would do't for nothing? Oh, oh I find what you would be at. Look here, here's a pistole for you. Here's a work indeed! Here, take it I say!

FLORINDA For heaven's sake, sir, as you're a gentleman—

WILLMORE So now, now, she would be wheedling me for more! —What, you will not take it then? You are resolved you will not? Come, come, take it, or I'll put it up again, for look ye, I never give more. Why, how now mistress, are you so high i'th' mouth a pistole won't down with you? Ha! Why, what a work's here! In good time! Come, no struggling to be gone. But an y'are good at a dumb wrestle, I'm for ye, look ye, I'm for ye.

60

She struggles with him.

Enter Belvile *and* Frederick.

BELVILE The door is open. A pox of this mad fellow, I'm angry that we've lost him. I durst have sworn he had followed us.

FREDERICK But you were so hasty, colonel, to be gone.

FLORINDA Help! Help! Murder! Help! Oh, I am ruined!

BELVILE Ha! Sure that's Florinda's voice! (*Comes up to them.*) A man! —Villain, let go that lady!

A noise. Willmore *turns and draws;* Frederick *interposes.*

FLORINDA Belvile! Heavens! My brother too is coming, and 'twill be impossible to escape. Belvile, I conjure you to walk under my chamber window, from whence I'll give you some instructions what to do. This rude man has undone us. *Exit.*

70

WILLMORE Belvile!

Enter Pedro, Stephano, *and other servants, with lights.*

PEDRO I'm betrayed! Run, Stephano, and see if Florinda be safe.

Exit Stephano.

They fight, and Pedro's party beats them out.

So, whoe'er they be, all is not well. I'll to Florinda's chamber.

Going out, meets Stephano.

STEPHANO You need not, sir: the poor lady's fast asleep and thinks no harm. I would not awake her, sir, for fear of frighting her with your danger.

PEDRO I'm glad she's there. —Rascals, how came the garden door open?

STEPHANO That question comes too late, sir; some of my fellow servants masquerading, I'll warrant.

PEDRO Masquerading! A lewd custom to debauch our youth! There's something more in this than I imagine.   *Exeunt.*   80

Act III [Scene 6]

Scene changes to the street
Enter Belvile *in rage,* Frederick *holding him, and* Willmore *melancholy.*

WILLMORE Why, how the devil should I know Florinda?

BELVILE Ah, plague of your ignorance! If it had not been Florinda, must you be a beast? A brute? A senseless swine?

WILLMORE Well, sir, you see I am endued with patience; I can bear. Though egad, y'are very free with me, methinks. I was in good hopes the quarrel would have been on my side, for so uncivilly interrupting me.

BELVILE Peace, brute, whilst thou'rt safe. Oh, I'm distracted!

WILLMORE Nay, nay, I'm an unlucky dog, that's certain.

BELVILE Ah, curse upon the star that ruled my birth, or whatsoever other influence that makes me still so wretched.   10

WILLMORE Thou break'st my heart with these complaints. There is no star in fault, no influence but sack, the cursed sack I drunk.

FREDERICK Why, how the devil came you so drunk?

WILLMORE Why, how the devil came you so sober?

BELVILE A curse upon his thin skull, he was always beforehand that way.

FREDERICK Prithee, dear colonel, forgive him; he's sorry for his fault.

BELVILE He's always so after he has done a mischief. A plague on all such brutes!

WILLMORE By this light, I took her for an errant harlot.

BELVILE Damn your debauched opinion! Tell me, sot, hadst thou so much sense   20
and light about thee to distinguish her woman, and couldst not see something about her face and person to strike an awful reverence into thy soul?

WILLMORE Faith no, I considered her as mere a woman as I could wish.

BELVILE 'Sdeath, I have no patience. Draw, or I'll kill you!

WILLMORE Let that alone till tomorrow, and if I set not all right again, use your pleasure.

BELVILE Tomorrow! Damn it,
    The spiteful light will lead me to no happiness.
    Tomorrow is Antonio's, and perhaps
    Guides him to my undoing. Oh, that I could meet   30
    This rival, this powerful fortunate!

WILLMORE What then?

BELVILE Let thy own reason, or my rage, instruct thee.

WILLMORE I shall be finely informed then, no doubt. Hear me, colonel, hear me; show me the man and I'll do his business.

BELVILE I know him no more than thou, or if I did I should not need thy aid.

295

WILLMORE This you say is Angellica's house; I promised the kind baggage to lie with her tonight. *Offers to go in.*

Enter Antonio *and his* Page. Antonio *knocks [with] the hilt of his sword.*

ANTONIO You paid the thousand crowns I directed?

40 PAGE To the lady's old woman, sir, I did.

WILLMORE Who the devil have we here?

BELVILE I'll now plant myself under Florinda's window, and if I find no comfort there, I'll die. *Exeunt Belvile and Frederick.*

Enter Moretta.

MORETTA Page!

PAGE Here's my lord.

WILLMORE How is this? A picaroon going to board my frigate? Here's one chase-gun for you.

Drawing his sword, jostles Antonio *who turns and draws. They fight;* Antonio *falls.*

MORETTA Oh, bless us! We're all undone! *Runs in and shuts the door.*

PAGE Help! Murder!

50 Belvile *returns at the noise of fighting.*

BELVILE Ha! The mad rogue's engaged in some unlucky adventure again.

Enter two or three masqueraders.

MASQUERADER Ha! A man killed!

WILLMORE How, a man killed? Then I'll go home to sleep.

Puts up and reels out. Exeunt masqueraders another way.

BELVILE Who should it be? Pray heaven the rogue is safe, for all my quarrel to him.

As Belvile is *groping about, enter an* Officer *and six* Soldiers.

SOLDIER Who's there?

OFFICER So, here's one dispatched. Secure the murderer.

BELVILE Do not mistake my charity for murder! I came to his assistance!

Soldiers seize on Belvile.

OFFICER That shall be tried, sir. St Jago! Swords drawn in the Carnival time!

Goes to Antonio.

60 ANTONIO Thy hand, prithee.

OFFICER Ha! Don Antonio! Look well to the villain there. —How is it, sir?

ANTONIO I'm hurt.

BELVILE Has my humanity made me a criminal?

OFFICER Away with him!

BELVILE What a curst chance is this! *Exeunt Soldiers with* Belvile.

ANTONIO [aside] This is the man, that has set upon me twice. —(*To the Officer.*) Carry him to my apartment, till you have farther orders from me.

Exit Antonio, *led.*

Act IV Scene 1

A fine room
Discovers Belvile *as by dark alone.*

BELVILE When shall I be weary of railing on Fortune, who is resolved never to turn with smiles upon me? Two such defeats in one night none but the devil and that mad rogue could have contrived to have plagued me with. I am here a prisoner, but where, heaven knows. And if there be murder done, I can soon decide the fate of a stranger in a nation without mercy. Yet this is nothing to the torture my soul bows with, when I think of losing my fair, my dear Florinda. Hark, my door opens. A light! A man—and seems of quality! Armed too! Now shall I die like a dog, without defence.

Enter Antonio *in a nightgown, with a light; his arm in a scarf, and a sword under his arm; he sets the candle on the table.*

ANTONIO Sir, I come to know what injuries I have done you, that could provoke you to so mean an action as to attack me basely without allowing time for my defence?   10

BELVILE Sir, for a man in my circumstances to plead innocence would look like fear. But view me well, and you will find no marks of coward on me, nor anything that betrays that brutality you accuse me with.

ANTONIO In vain, sir, you impose upon my sense.
    You are not only he who drew on me last night,
    But yesterday before the same house, that of Angellica.
    Yet there is something in your face and mien
    That makes me wish I were mistaken.

BELVILE I own I fought today in the defence of a friend of mine, with whom   20
you, if you're the same, and your party were first engaged.
    Perhaps you think this crime enough to kill me,
    But if you do, I cannot fear you'll do it basely.

ANTONIO No, sir, I'll make you fit for a defence with this.

                              Gives him the sword.

BELVILE This gallantry surprises me, nor know I how to use this present, sir, against a man so brave.

ANTONIO You shall not need;
    For know, I come to snatch you from a danger
    That is decreed against you:
    Perhaps your life, or long imprisonment;   30
    And 'twas with so much courage you offended,
    I cannot see you punished.

BELVILE How shall I pay this generosity?

ANTONIO It had been safer to have killed another
    Than have attempted me.
    To show your danger, sir, I'll let you know my quality:
    And 'tis the Viceroy's son, whom you have wounded.

BELVILE The Viceroy's son!
    (*Aside.*) Death and confusion! Was this plague reserved
    To complete all the rest? Obliged by him,   40
    The man of all the world I would destroy!

ANTONIO You seem disordered, sir.

BELVILE Yes, trust me, sir, I am, and 'tis with pain
That man receives such bounties
Who wants the power to pay 'em back again.

ANTONIO To gallant spirits 'tis indeed uneasy,
But you may quickly overpay me, sir.

BELVILE (*aside*) Then I am well. Kind Heaven, but set us even,
That I may fight with him and keep my honour safe.
50 —Oh, I'm impatient, sir, to be discounting
The mighty debt I owe you. Command me quickly.

ANTONIO I have a quarrel with a rival, sir,
About the maid we love.

BELVILE (*aside*) Death, 'tis Florinda he means!
That thought destroys my reason,
And I shall kill him.

ANTONIO My rival, sir,
Is one has all the virtues man can boast of—

BELVILE (*aside*) Death! Who should this be?

60 ANTONIO He challenged me to meet him on the Molo
As soon as day appeared, but last night's quarrel
Has made my arm unfit to guide a sword.

BELVILE I apprehend you, sir, you'd have me kill the man
That lays a claim to the maid you speak of.
I'll do't. I'll fly to do't!

ANTONIO Sir, do you know her?

BELVILE No, sir, but 'tis enough she is admired by you.

ANTONIO Sir, I shall rob you of the glory on't,
For you must fight under my name and dress.

70 BELVILE That opinion must be strangely obliging that makes
You think I can personate the brave Antonio,
Whom I can but strive to imitate.

ANTONIO You say too much to my advantage.
Come, sir, the day appears that calls you forth.
Within, sir, is the habit.

Exit Antonio.

BELVILE Fantastic Fortune, thou deceitful light,
That cheats the wearied traveller by night,
Though on a precipice each step you tread,
I am resolved to follow where you lead.

Exit.

Act IV Scene [2]

The Molo
Enter Florinda *and* Callis *in masques, with* Stephano.

FLORINDA (*aside*) I'm dying with my fears, Belvile's not coming as I expected
under my window
Makes me believe that all those fears are true.
—Canst thou not tell with whom my brother fights?

STEPHANO No, madam, they were both in masquerade. I was by when they challenged one another, and they had decided the quarrel then, but were prevented by some cavaliers which made 'em put it off till now. But I am sure 'tis about you they fight.

FLORINDA (*aside*) Nay, then 'tis with Belvile, for what other lover have I that dares fight for me, except Antonio, and he is too much in favour with my brother. If it be he, for whom shall I direct my prayers to heaven?   10

STEPHANO Madam, I must leave you, for if my master see me, I shall be hanged for being your conductor. I escaped narrowly for the excuse I made for you last night i'th' garden.

FLORINDA And I'll reward thee for't. Prithee, no more.   *Exit* Stephano.

Enter Don Pedro *in his masquing habit.*

PEDRO Antonio's late today; the place will fill, and we may be prevented.

Walks about.

FLORINDA (*aside*) Antonio? Sure I heard amiss.

PEDRO But who will not excuse a happy lover
    When soft fair arms confine the yielding neck,
    And the kind whisper languishingly breathes   20
    'Must you begone so soon?'
    Sure I had dwelt for ever on her bosom—
    But stay he's here.

Enter Belvile *dressed in* Antonio's *clothes.*

FLORINDA [*aside*] 'Tis not Belvile; half my fears are vanished.

PEDRO Antonio!

BELVILE (*aside*) This must be he.
    —You're early, sir; I do not use to be outdone this way.

PEDRO The wretched, sir, are watchful, and 'tis enough
    You've the advantage of me in Angellica.

BELVILE (*aside*) Angellica! Or I've mistook my man, or else Antonio!   30
    Can he forget his interest in Florinda
    And fight for common prize?

PEDRO Come, sir, you know our terms.

BELVILE (*aside*) By heaven, not I.
    —No talking; I am ready, sir.

Offers to fight; Florinda *runs in.*

FLORINDA (*to* Belvile) Oh, hold! Whoe'er you be, I do conjure you hold! If you strike here I die!

PEDRO Florinda!

BELVILE Florinda imploring for my rival!

PEDRO Away; this kindness is unseasonable.   40

Puts her by; they fight; she runs in just as Belvile *disarms* Pedro.

FLORINDA Who are you, sir, that dares deny my prayers?

BELVILE Thy prayers destroy him, if thou wouldst preserve him,
    Do that thou'rt unacquainted with, and curse him.

She holds him.

FLORINDA By all you hold most dear, by her you love,
I do conjure you, touch him not.

BELVILE By her I love?
See, I obey, and at your feet resign
The useless trophy of my victory.

Lays his sword at her feet.

PEDRO Antonio, you've done enough to prove you love Florinda.

50 BELVILE Love Florinda! Does Heaven love adoration, prayer,
Or penitence? Love her? Here, sir, your sword again.

Snatches up the sword and gives it him.

Upon this truth I'll fight my life away.

PEDRO No, you've redeemed my sister, and my friendship.

He gives him Florinda, *and pulls off his vizard to show his face, and puts it on again.*

BELVILE Don Pedro!

PEDRO Can you resign your claims to other women,
And give your heart entirely to Florinda?

BELVILE Entire, as dying saints' confessions are!
I can delay my happiness no longer:
This minute let me make Florinda mine.

60 PEDRO This minute let it be. No time so proper:
This night my father will arrive from Rome,
And possibly may hinder what we purpose.

FLORINDA Oh Heavens! This minute?

Enter masqueraders and pass over.

BELVILE Oh, do not ruin me!

PEDRO The place begins to fill, and that we may not be observed, do you
walk off to St Peter's church, where I will meet you and conclude your
happiness.

BELVILE I'll meet you there. —(*Aside.*) If there be no more saints' churches in
Naples.

70 FLORINDA Oh stay, sir, and recall your hasty doom!
Alas I have not yet prepared my heart
To entertain so strange a guest.

PEDRO Away; this silly modesty is assumed too late.

BELVILE Heaven, madam, what do you do?

FLORINDA Do! Despise the man that lays a tyrant's claim
To what he ought to conquer by submission.

BELVILE You do not know me. Move a little this way.

Draws her aside.

FLORINDA Yes, you may force me even to the altar,
But not the holy man that offers there
80 Shall force me to be thine.

Pedro talks to Callis *this while.*

BELVILE Oh do not lose so blest an opportunity!

300

(Pulls off his vizard.)

See, 'tis your Belvile, not Antonio,
Whom your mistaken scorn and anger ruins.

FLORINDA Belvile!
Where was my soul it could not meet thy voice,
And take this knowledge in.

As they are talking, enter Willmore *finely dressed, and* Frederick.

WILLMORE No intelligence? No news of Belvile yet? Well, I am the
most unlucky rascal in nature. Ha! Am I deceived, or is it he? Look Fred!
'Tis he, my dear Belvile!

Runs and embraces him. Belvile's vizard falls out on's hand.

BELVILE Hell and confusion seize thee!   90

PEDRO Ha! Belvile! I beg your pardon, sir.   *Takes Florinda from him.*

BELVILE Nay, touch her not. She's mine by conquest, sir;
I won her by my sword.

WILLMORE Didst thou so? And egad, child, we'll keep her by the sword.

Draws on Pedro; Belvile *goes between.*

BELVILE Stand off!
Thou'rt so profanely lewd, so curst by heaven,
All quarrels thou espousest must be fatal.

WILLMORE Nay, an you be so hot, my valour's coy,
And shall be courted when you want it next.

Puts up his sword.

BELVILE (*to* Pedro) You know I ought to claim a victor's right,   100
But you're the brother to divine Florinda,
To whom I'm such a slave. To purchase her
I durst not hurt the man she holds so dear.

PEDRO 'Twas by Antonio's, not by Belvile's sword
This question should have been decided, sir.
I must confess much to your bravery's due,
Both now and when I met you last in arms;
But I am nicely punctual in my word,
As men of honour ought, and beg your pardon:
For this mistake another time shall clear.   110

Aside to Florinda *as they are going out.*

—This was some plot between you and Belvile,
But I'll prevent you.

[*Exeunt* Pedro *and* Florinda.]

Belvile *looks after her and begins to walk up and down in rage.*

WILLMORE Do not be modest now and lose the woman. But if we shall fetch
her back so—

BELVILE Do not speak to me!

WILLMORE Not speak to you? Egad, I'll speak to you, and will be answered
too.

BELVILE Will you, sir?—

WILLMORE I know I've done some mischief, but I'm so dull a puppy that I'm
120   the son of a whore if I know how or where. Prithee inform my
understanding.

BELVILE Leave me I say, and leave me instantly!

WILLMORE I will not leave you in this humour, nor till I know my crime.

BELVILE Death, I'll tell you, sir.

> *Draws and runs at* Willmore; *he runs out,* Belvile *after him;* Frederick
> *interposes.*

Enter Angellica, Moretta *and* Sebastian.

ANGELLICA Ha! Sebastian, is not that Willmore? Haste! Haste and bring him
back.   [*Exit* Sebastian.]

FREDERICK [*aside*] The colonel's mad: I never saw him thus before. I'll after
'em lest he do some mischief, for I am sure Willmore will not draw on him.

> *Exit.*

ANGELLICA I am all rage! My first desires defeated!
130   For one for aught he knows that has no
        Other merit than her quality,
        Her being Don Pedro's sister. He loves her!
        I know 'tis so. Dull, dull, insensible,
        He will not see me now, though oft invited,
        And broke his word last night—false perjured man!
        He that but yesterday fought for my favours,
        And would have made his life a sacrifice
        To've gained one night with me,
        Must now be hired and courted to my arms.

140 MORETTA I told you what would come on't, but Moretta's an old doting fool.
Why did you give him five hundred crowns, but to set himself out for other
lovers? You should have kept him poor, if you had meant to have had any
good from him.

ANGELLICA Oh, name not such mean trifles!
        Had I given him all my youth has earned from sin,
        I had not lost a thought nor sigh upon't.
        But I have given him my eternal rest,
        My whole repose, my future joys, my heart!
        My virgin heart, Moretta! Oh 'tis gone!

150 MORETTA Curse on him, here he comes;
        How fine she has made him too.

Enter Willmore *and* Sebastian; Angellica *turns and walks away.*

WILLMORE How now, turned shadow?
        Fly when I pursue, and follow when I fly?

> *Sings.*

Stay, gentle shadow of my dove,
    And tell me e'er I go,
Whether the substance may not prove
    A fleeting thing like you.

> *As she turns she looks on him.*

There's a soft kind look remaining yet.

ANGELLICA Well, sir, you may be gay: all happiness, all joys pursue you still. Fortune's your slave, and gives you every hour choice of new hearts and 160 beauties, till you are cloyed with the repeated bliss which others vainly languish for.

But know, false man, that I shall be revenged.

Turns away in rage.

WILLMORE So, gad, there are of those faint-hearted lovers, whom such a sharp lesson next their hearts would make as impotent as fourscore. Pox o' this whining; my business is to laugh and love. A pox on't, I hate your sullen lover: a man shall lose as much time to put you in humour now as would serve to gain a new woman.

ANGELLICA I scorn to cool that fire I cannot raise,
Or do the drudgery of your virtuous mistress. 170

WILLMORE A virtuous mistress? Death, what a thing thou hast found out for me! Why, what the devil should I do with a virtuous woman, a sort of ill-natured creatures that take a pride to torment a lover. Virtue is but an infirmity in woman, a disease that renders even the handsome ungrateful; whilst the ill-favoured, for want of solicitations and address, only fancy themselves so. I have lain with a woman of quality, who has all the while been railing at whores.

ANGELLICA I will not answer for your mistress's virtue,
Though she be young enough to know no guilt;
And I could wish you would persuade my heart
'Twas the two hundred thousand crowns you courted. 180

WILLMORE Two hundred thousand crowns! What story's this? What trick? What woman, ha?

ANGELLICA How strange you make it. Have you forgot the creature you entertained on the piazza last night?

WILLMORE (*aside*) Ha! My gipsy worth two hundred thousand crowns! Oh, how I long to be with her! Pox, I knew she was of quality.

ANGELLICA False man! I see my ruin in thy face.
How many vows you breathed upon my bosom
Never to be unjust. Have you forgot so soon?

WILLMORE Faith no, I was just coming to repeat 'em. But here's a humour 190 indeed would make a man a saint. —(*Aside.*) Would she be angry enough to leave me, and command me not to wait on her.

Enter Hellena *dressed in man's clothes.*

HELLENA This must be Angellica! I know it by her mumping matron here. Aye, aye, 'tis she! My mad captain's with her too, for all his swearing. How this unconstant humour makes me love him! —Pray, good grave gentlewoman, is not this Angellica?

MORETTA My too young sir, it is —[*Aside.*] I hope 'tis one from Don Antonio.

Goes to Angellica.

HELLENA (*aside*) Well, something I'll do to vex him for this.

ANGELLICA I will not speak with him. Am I in humour to receive a lover?

WILLMORE Not speak with him? Why, I'll be gone, and wait your idler 200 minutes. Can I show less obedience to the thing I love so fondly?

Offers to go.

ANGELLICA A fine excuse, this! Stay—

303

WILLMORE And hinder your advantage? Should I repay your bounties so ungratefully?

ANGELLICA [*to* Hellena] Come hither, boy.
 —[*To* Willmore.] That I may let you see
 How much above the advantages you name
 I prize one minute's joy with you.

WILLMORE (*impatient to be gone*) Oh, you destroy me with this endearment.
 —[*Aside.*] Death! How shall I get away?—Madam, 'twill not be fit I should be seen with you. Besides, it will not be convenient. And I've a friend—that's dangerously sick.

ANGELLICA I see you're impatient. Yet you shall stay.

WILLMORE [*aside*] And miss my assignation with my gipsy.

              Walks about impatiently.

Moretta *brings* Hellena, *who addresses herself to* Angellica.

HELLENA Madam,
 You'll hardly pardon my intrusion
 When you shall know my business,
 And I'm too young to tell my tale with art;
 But there must be a wondrous store of goodness
 Where so much beauty dwells.

ANGELLICA A pretty advocate, whoever sent thee.
 Prithee proceed. —Nay, sir, you shall not go.

         To Willmore, *who is stealing off.*

WILLMORE (*aside*) Then I shall lose my dear gipsy for ever.
 Pox on't, she stays me out of spite.

HELLENA I am related to a lady, madam,
 Young, rich, and nobly born, but has the fate
 To be in love with a young English gentleman.
 Strangely she loves him, at first sight she loved him,
 But did adore him when she heard him speak;
 For he, she said, had charms in every word,
 That failed not to surprise, to wound and conquer.

WILLMORE (*aside*) Ha! Egad, I hope this concerns me.

ANGELLICA (*aside*) 'Tis my false man he means. Would he were gone:
 This praise will raise his pride, and ruin me.
 (*To* Willmore.) —Well,
 Since you are so impatient to be gone
 I will release you, sir.

WILLMORE (*aside*) Nay, then I'm sure 'twas me he spoke of: this cannot be the efects of kindness in her.
 —No, madam, I've considered better on't,
 And will not give you cause of jealousy.

ANGELLICA But, sir, I've business, that—

WILLMORE This shall not do; I know 'tis but to try me.

ANGELLICA Well, to your story, boy. —(*Aside.*) Though 'twill undo me.

HELLENA With this addition to his other beauties,
 He won her unresisting tender heart.
 He vowed, and sighed, and swore he loved her dearly;

And she believed the cunning flatterer,
And thought herself the happiest maid alive.　　　　　　　　250
Today was the appointed time by both
To consummate their bliss:
The virgin, altar, and the priest were dressed;
And whilst she languished for th'expected bridegroom,
She heard he paid his broken vows to you.

WILLMORE (*aside*) So, this is some dear rogue that's in love with me, and this way lets me know it; or, if it be not me, he means someone whose place I may supply.

ANGELLICA Now I perceive
The cause of thy impatience to be gone,　　　　　　　　260
And all the business of this glorious dress.

WILLMORE Damn the young prater; I know not what he means.

HELLENA Madam,
In your fair eyes I read too much concern
To tell my farther business.

ANGELLICA Prithee, sweet youth, talk on; thou mayest perhaps
Raise here a storm that may undo my passion,
And then I'll grant thee anything.

HELLENA Madam, 'tis to entreat you (oh unreasonable)
You would not see this stranger;　　　　　　　　270
For if you do, she vows you are undone,
Though Nature never made a man so excellent,
And sure he 'ad been a god, but for inconstancy.

WILLMORE (*aside*) Ah, rogue, how finely he's instructed! 'Tis plain, some woman that has seen me *en passant*.

ANGELLICA Oh, I shall burst with jealousy! Do you know the man you speak of?

HELLENA Yes, madam, he used to be in buff and scarlet.

ANGELLICA (*to* Willmore) Thou, false as hell, what canst thou say to this?

WILLMORE By heaven——　　　　　　　　280

ANGELLICA Hold, do not damn thyself——

HELLENA Nor hope to be believed.　　　　　*He walks about; they follow.*

ANGELLICA Oh perjured man!
Is't thus you pay my generous passion back?

HELLENA Why would you, sir, abuse my lady's faith?

ANGELLICA And use me so inhumanely.

HELLENA A maid so young, so innocent——

WILLMORE Ah, young devil!

ANGELLICA Dost thou not know thy life is in my power?

HELLENA Or think my lady cannot be revenged?　　　　　　　　290

WILLMORE (*aside*) So, so, the storm comes finely on.

ANGELLICA Now thou art silent, guilt has struck thee dumb.
Oh, hadst thou still been so, I'd lived in safety.

　　　　　　　　　　　　　She turns away and weeps.

WILLMORE (*aside to* Hellena) Sweetheart, the lady's name and house—quickly! I'm impatient to be with her.

Looks towards Angellica *to watch her turning, and as he comes towards them he meets her.*

HELLENA (*aside*) So, now is he for another woman.

WILLMORE The impudent'st young thing in nature; I cannot persuade him out of his error, madam.

ANGELLICA I know he's in the right; yet thou'st a tongue
    That would persuade him to deny his faith.

In rage walks away.

WILLMORE (*said softly to* Hellena) Her name, her name, dear boy!

HELLENA Have you forgot it, sir?

WILLMORE (*aside*) Oh, I perceive he's not to know I am a stranger to his lady.
—Yes, yes, I do know—but I have forgot the— (Angellica *turns.*) —By heaven, such early confidence I never saw.

ANGELLICA Did I not charge you with this mistress, sir?
    Which you denied, though I beheld your perjury.
    This little generosity of thine has rendered back my heart.

Walks away.

WILLMORE (*to* Hellena) So, you have made sweet work here, my little mischief.
    Look your lady be kind and good-natured now, or
    I shall have but a cursed bargain on't.

Angellica turns towards them.

    —The rogue's bred up to mischief;
    Art thou so great a fool to credit him?

ANGELLICA Yes, I do, and you in vain impose upon me.
    Come hither, boy. Is not this he you spake of?

HELLENA I think it is. I cannot swear, but I vow he has just such another lying lover's look.   Hellena *looks in his face; he gazes on her.*

WILLMORE (*aside*) Ha! Do not I know that face? By heaven my little gipsy! What a dull dog was I: had I but looked that way I'd known her. Are all my hopes of a new woman banished? Egad, if I do not fit thee for this, hang me. —[*To* Angellica.] Madam, I have found out the plot.

HELLENA [*aside*] Oh Lord, what does he say? Am I discovered now?

WILLMORE Do you see this young spark here?

HELLENA [*aside*] He'll tell her who I am.

WILLMORE Who do you think this is?

HELLENA [*aside*] Aye, aye he does know me. —Nay, dear captain, I am undone if you discover me.

WILLMORE Nay, nay, no cogging; she shall know what a precious mistress I have.

HELLENA Will you be such a devil?

WILLMORE Nay, nay, I'll teach you to spoil sport you will not make.—This small ambassador comes not from a person of quality as you imagine and he says, but from a very errant gipsy: the talking'st, prating'st, canting'st little animal thou ever saw'st.

ANGELLICA What news you tell me, that's the thing I mean.

306

HELLENA (*aside*) Would I were well off the place! If ever I go
a-captain-hunting again—

WILLMORE Mean that thing? That gipsy thing? Thou mayest as well be jealous
of thy monkey or parrot as of her. A German motion were worth a dozen of   340
her, and a dream were a better enjoyment—a creature of a constitution fitter
for heaven than man.

HELLENA (*aside*) Though I am sure he lies, yet this vexes me.

ANGELLICA You are mistaken: she's a Spanish woman made up of no such
dull materials.

WILLMORE Materials? Egad, an she be made of any that will either dispense or
admit of love, I'll be bound to continence.

HELLENA (*aside to him*) Unreasonable man, do you think so?

WILLMORE You may return, my little brazen head, and tell your lady that till
she be handsome enough to be beloved, or I dull enough to be religious,   350
there will be small hopes of me.

ANGELLICA Did you not promise, then, to marry her?

WILLMORE Not I, by heaven.

ANGELLICA You cannot undeceive my fears and torments, till you have vowed
you will not marry her.

HELLENA (*aside*) If he swears that, he'll be revenged on me indeed for all my
rogueries.

ANGELLICA I know what arguments you'll bring against me: fortune, and
honour.

WILLMORE Honour! I tell you, I hate it in your sex; and those that fancy   360
themselves possessed of that foppery are the most impertinently
troublesome of all womankind, and will transgress nine commandments to
keep one. And to satisfy your jealousy, I swear—

HELLENA (*aside to him*) Oh, no swearing, dear captain.

WILLMORE If it were possible I should ever be inclined to marry, it should be
some kind young sinner, one that has generosity enough to give a favour
handsomely to one that can ask it discreetly, one that has wit enough to
manage an intrigue of love. Oh, how civil such a wench is, to a man that
does her the honour to marry her.

ANGELLICA By Heaven, there's no faith in anything he says.   370

Enter Sebastian.

SEBASTIAN Madam, Don Antonio—

ANGELLICA Come hither.

HELLENA [*aside*] Ha! Antonio! He may be coming hither, and he'll certainly
discover me. I'll therefore retire without a ceremony.   *Exit* Hellena.

ANGELLICA I'll see him. Get my coach ready.

SEBASTIAN It waits you, madam.

WILLMORE [*aside*] This is lucky. —What, madam, now I may be gone and
leave you to the enjoyment of my rival?

ANGELLICA Dull man, that canst not see how ill, how poor,
    That false dissimulation looks. Begone,   380
    And never let me see thy cozening face again,
    Lest I relapse and kill thee.

WILLMORE Yes, you can spare me now. Farewell, till you're in better humour.
—[*Aside.*] I'm glad of this release. Now for my gipsy:
> For though to worse we change, yet still we find
> New joys, new charms, in a new miss that's kind.

Exit Willmore.

ANGELLICA He's gone, and in this ague of my soul
> The shivering fit returns.
> Oh, with what willing haste he took his leave,
390   As if the longed-for minute were arrived
> Of some blest assignation.
> In vain I have consulted all my charms,
> In vain this beauty prized, in vain believed
> My eyes could kindle any lasting fires;
> I had forgot my name, my infamy,
> And the reproach that honour lays on those
> That dare pretend a sober passion here.
> Nice reputation, though it leave behind
> More virtues than inhabit where that dwells;
400   Yet that once gone, those virtues shine no more.
> Then since I am not fit to be beloved,
> I am resolved to think on a revenge
> On him that soothed me thus to my undoing.

Exeunt.

Act IV Scene 3

A street
Enter Florinda *and* Valeria *in habits different from what they have been seen in.*

FLORINDA We're happily escaped, and yet I tremble still.

VALERIA A lover, and fear? Why, I am but half an one, and yet I have courage for any attempt. Would Hellena were here: I would fain have had her as deep in this mischief as we; she'll fare but ill else, I doubt.

FLORINDA She pretended a visit to the Augustine nuns, but I believe some other design carried her out; pray heaven we light on her. Prithee, what didst do with Callis?

VALERIA When I saw no reason would do good on her, I followed her into the wardrobe, and as she was looking for something in a great chest, I
10   toppled her in by the heels, snatched the key of the apartment where you were confined, locked her in, and left her bawling for help.

FLORINDA 'Tis well you resolve to follow my fortunes, for thou darest never appear at home again after such an action.

VALERIA That's according as the young stranger and I shall agree. But to our business. I delivered your letter, your note to Belvile, when I got out under pretence of going to mass. I found him at his lodging, and believe me it came seasonably, for never was man in so desperate a condition. I told him of your resolution of making your escape today, if your brother would be absent long enough to permit you; if not, to die rather than be Antonio's.

20   FLORINDA Thou should'st have told him I was confined to my chamber upon my brother's suspicion that the business on the Molo was a plot laid between him and I.

VALERIA I said all this, and told him your brother was now gone to his devotion; and he resolves to visit every church till he find him, and not only undeceive him in that, but caress him so as shall delay his return home.

FLORINDA Oh heavens! He's here, and Belvile with him too.

They put on their vizards.

Enter Don Pedro, Belvile, Willmore; Belvile *and* Don Pedro *seeming in serious discourse.*

VALERIA Walk boldly by them, and I'll come at a distance, lest he suspect us.

She walks by them, and looks back on them.

WILLMORE Ha! A woman, and of an excellent mien!

PEDRO She throws a kind look back on you.

WILLMORE Death, 'tis a likely wench, and that kind look shall not be cast away. I'll follow her.   30

BELVILE Prithee do not.

WILLMORE Do not? By heavens, to the Antipodes, with such an invitation.

She goes out, and Willmore *follows her.*

BELVILE 'Tis a mad fellow for a wench.

Enter Frederick.

FREDERICK Oh colonel, such news!

BELVILE Prithee what?

FREDERICK News that will make you laugh in spite of Fortune.

BELVILE What, Blunt has had some damned trick put upon him? Cheated, banged or clapped?

FREDERICK Cheated, sir, rarely cheated of all but his shirt and drawers; the   40
unconscionable whore too turned him out before consummation, so that traversing the streets at midnight, the Watch found him in this *fresco*, and conducted him home. By heaven, 'tis such a sight, and yet I durst as well been hanged as laugh at him, or pity him: he beats all that do but ask him a question, and is in such a humour.

PEDRO Who is't has met with this ill usage, sir?

BELVILE A friend of ours whom you must see for mirth's sake. —(*Aside.*) I'll employ him to give Florinda time for an escape.

PEDRO What is he?

BELVILE A young countryman of ours, one that has been educated at so   50
plentiful a rate he yet ne'er knew the want of money; and 'twill be a great jest to see how simply he'll look without it. For my part I'll lend him none: and the rogue know not how to put on a borrowing face, and ask first, I'll let him see how good 'tis to play our parts whilst I play his. Prithee, Fred, do you go home and keep him in that posture till we come.   *Exeunt.*

FLORINDA I am followed still. Ha! My brother too advancing this way! Good heavens defend me from being seen by him!   *She goes off.*

WILLMORE Ah, there she sails! She looks back as she were willing to be boarded; I'll warrant her prize.   *He goes out,* Valeria *following.*

Enter Hellena, *just as he goes out, with a* Page.

HELLENA Ha, is not that my captain that has a woman in chase? 'Tis not   60
Angellica. —Boy, follow those people at a distance, and bring me an

account where they go in. (*Exit* Page.) —I'll find his haunts, and plague him everywhere. Ha! My brother!

Belvile, Willmore *and* Pedro *cross the stage;* Hellena *runs off.*

Act IV [Scene 4]

Scene changes to another street. Enter Florinda.

FLORINDA What shall I do? My brother now pursues me. Will no kind power protect me from his tyranny? Ha! Here's a door open; I'll venture in, since nothing can be worse than to fall into his hands. My life and honour are at stake, and my necessity has no choice.   *She goes in.*

Enter Valeria *and* Hellena's Page, *peeping after* Florinda.

PAGE Here she went in; I shall remember this house.   *Exit* Page.

VALERIA This is Belvile's lodging; she's gone in as readily as if she knew it. Ha! Here's that mad fellow again; I dare not venture in. I'll watch my opportunity.   *Goes aside.*

Enter Willmore, *gazing about him.*

WILLMORE I have lost her hereabouts. Pox on't, she must not 'scape me so.

     Goes out.

Act IV [Scene 5]

Scene changes to Blunt's *chamber, discovers him sitting on a couch in his shirt and drawers, reading.*

BLUNT So, now my mind's a little at peace, since I have resolved revenge. A pox on this tailor, though, for not bringing home the clothes I bespoke. And a pox of all poor cavaliers: a man can never keep a spare suit for 'em, and I shall have these rogues come in and find me naked, and then I'm undone. But I'm resolved to arm myself: the rascals shall not insult over me too much. (*Puts on an old rusty sword, and buff belt.*) Now, how like a morris dancer I am equipped! A fine ladylike whore to cheat me thus, without affording me a kindness for my money! A pox light on her, I shall never be reconciled to the sex more; she has made me as faithless as a physician, as

10   uncharitable as a churchman, and as ill-natured as a poet. Oh, how I'll use all womankind hereafter! What would I give to have one of 'em within my reach now! Any mortal thing in petticoats, kind Fortune, send me, and I'll forgive thy last night's malice. —Here's a cursed book too—a warning to all young travellers—that can instruct me how to prevent such mischiefs now 'tis too late. Well, 'tis a rare convenient thing to read a little now and then, as well as hawk and hunt.   *Sits down again and reads.*

Enter to him Florinda.

FLORINDA This house is haunted, sure, 'tis well furnished and no living thing inhabits it. Ha! A man! Heavens, how he's attired! Sure 'tis some rope dancer, or fencing master. I tremble now for fear, and yet I must venture now to

20   speak to him. —Sir, if I may not interrupt your meditations—

     He starts up and gazes.

BLUNT Ha, what's here? Are my wishes granted? And is not that a she creature? 'Adsheartlikins, 'tis! —What wretched thing art thou, ha?

FLORINDA Charitable sir, you've told yourself already what I am; a very wretched maid, forced by a strange unlucky accident to seek a safety here, and must be ruined, if you do not grant it.

BLUNT Ruined! Is there any ruin so inevitable as that which now threatens thee? Dost thou know, miserable woman, into what den of mischiefs thou art fallen? What abyss of confusion, ha? Dost not see something in my looks that frights thy guilty soul, and makes thee wish to change that shape of woman for any humble animal, or devil? For those were safer for thee, and less mischievous.   30

FLORINDA Alas, what mean you, sir? I must confess, your looks have something in 'em makes me fear, but I beseech you, as you seem a gentleman, pity a harmless virgin that takes your house for sanctuary.

BLUNT Talk on, talk on, and weep too, till my faith return. Do, flatter me out of my senses again. A harmless virgin with a pox—as much one as t'other, 'adsheartlikins. Why, what the devil, can I not be safe in my house for you, not in my chamber? Nay, even being naked too cannot secure me? This is an impudence greater than has invaded me yet. Come, no resistance.

Pulls her rudely.

FLORINDA Dare you be so cruel?   40

BLUNT Cruel? 'Adsheartlikins, as a galley slave, or a Spanish whore. Cruel? Yes, I will kiss and beat thee all over; kiss, and see thee all over; thou shalt lie with me too, not that I care for the enjoyment, but to let thee see I have ta'en deliberated malice to thee, and will be revenged on one whore for the sins of another. I will smile and deceive thee, flatter thee, and beat thee; kiss and swear, and lie to thee; embrace thee and rob thee, as she did me; fawn on thee, and strip thee stark naked; then hang thee out at my window by the heels, with a paper of scurvy verses fastened to thy breast, in praise of damnable women. Come, come along.

FLORINDA Alas, sir, must I be sacrificed for the crimes of the most infamous of my sex? I never understood the sins you name.   50

BLUNT Do, persuade the fool you love him, or that one of you can be just or honest; tell me I was not an easy coxcomb or any strange impossible tale: it will be believed sooner than thy false showers or protestations. A generation of damned hypocrites! To flatter my very clothes from my back! Dissembling witches! Are these the returns you make an honest gentleman, that trusts, believes, and loves you? But if I be not even with you —Come along, or I shall—   *Pulls her again.*

Enter Frederick.

FREDERICK Ha! What's here to do?

BLUNT 'Adsheartlikins, Fred, I am glad thou art come to be a witness of my dire revenge.   60

FREDERICK What's this, a person of quality too, who is upon the ramble to supply the defects of some grave impotent husband?

BLUNT No, this has another pretence: some very unfortunate accident brought her hither, to save a life pursued by I know not who, or why, and forced to take sanctuary here at fool's haven. 'Adsheartlikins, to me of all mankind for protection? Is the ass to be cajoled again, think ye? No, young one, no prayers or tears shall mitigate my rage; therefore prepare for both my pleasures of enjoyment and revenge, for I am resolved to make up my loss here on thy body: I'll take it out in kindness and in beating.   70

FREDERICK Now mistress of mine, what do you think of this?

FLORINDA I think he will not, dares not be so barbarous.

FREDERICK Have a care, Blunt, she fetched a deep sigh; she is enamoured with thy shirt and drawers, she'll strip thee even of that. There are of her calling such unconscionable baggages, and such dexterous thieves, they'll flay a man and he shall ne'er miss his skin till he feels the cold. There was a countryman of ours robbed of a row of teeth whilst he was a-sleeping, which the jilt made him buy again when he waked. You see, lady, how little reason we have to trust you.

80 BLUNT 'Adsheartlikins, why this is most abominable!

FLORINDA Some such devils there may be, but by all that's holy, I am none such. I entered here to save a life in danger.

BLUNT For no goodness, I'll warrant her.

FREDERICK Faith, damsel, you had e'en confessed the plain truth, for we are fellows not to be caught twice in the same trap. Look on that wreck: a tight vessel when he set out of haven, well trimmed and laden, and see how a female picaroon of this island of rogues has shattered him, and canst thou hope for any mercy?

BLUNT No, no, gentlewoman, come along; 'adsheartlikins, we must be better
90 aquainted. —We'll both lie with her, and then let me alone to bang her.

FREDERICK I'm ready to serve you in matters of revenge, that has a double pleasure in't.

BLUNT Well said. —You hear, little one, how you are condemned by public vote to the bed within? There's no resisting your destiny, sweetheart.

Pulls her.

FLORINDA Stay, sir. I have seen you with Belvile, an English cavalier. For his sake use me kindly; you know him, sir.

BLUNT Belvile? Why yes, sweeting, we do know Belvile, and wish he were with us now. He's a cormorant at whore and bacon: he'd have a limb or two of thee, my virgin pullet. But 'tis no matter, we'll leave him the bones to
100 pick.

FLORINDA Sir, if you have any esteem for that Belvile, I conjure you to treat me with more gentleness; he'll thank you for the justice.

FREDERICK Hark'ee, Blunt, I doubt we are mistaken in this matter.

FLORINDA Sir, if you find me not worth Belvile's care, use me as you please. And that you may think I merit better treatment than you threaten, pray take this present. *Gives him a ring; he looks on it.*

BLUNT Hum—a diamond! Why, 'tis a wonderful virtue now that lies in this ring, a mollifying virtue. 'Adsheartlikins, there's more persuasive rhetoric in't than all her sex can utter.

110 FREDERICK I begin to suspect something; and 'twould anger us vilely to be trussed up for a rape upon a maid of quality, when we only believe we ruffle a harlot.

BLUNT Thou art a credulous fellow, but 'adsheartlikins, I have no faith yet. Why, my saint prattled as parlously as this does; she gave me a bracelet too, a devil on her, but I sent my man to sell it today for necessaries, and it proved as counterfeit as her vows of love.

FREDERICK However, let it reprieve her till we see Belvile.

BLUNT That's hard, yet I will grant it.

Enter a Servant.

SERVANT Oh, sir, the colonel is just come in with his new friend and a Spaniard of quality, and talks of having you to dinner with 'em. 120

BLUNT 'Adsheartlikins, I'm undone! I would not see 'em for the world. Hark'ee, Fred, lock up the wench in your chamber.

FREDERICK Fear nothing, madam, whate'er he threatens; you are safe whilst in my hands. *Exeunt Frederick and Florinda.*

BLUNT And, sirrah, upon your life, say I am not at home, or that I am asleep, or—or—anything. Away; I'll prevent their coming this way.

Locks the door, and exeunt.

Act V Scene 1

Blunt's chamber
After a great knocking as at his chamber door, enter Blunt *softly crossing the stage, in his shirt and drawers as before.*

[VOICES] (*call within*) Ned! Ned Blunt! Ned Blunt!

BLUNT The rogues are up in arms. 'Adsheartlikins, this villainous Frederick has betrayed me: they have heard of my blessed fortune.

[VOICES] (*and knocking within*) Ned Blunt! Ned! Ned!

BELVILE [*within*] Why he's dead sir, without dispute dead; he has not been seen today. Let's break open the door. Here, boy—

BLUNT Ha, break open the door? 'Adsheartlikins, that mad fellow will be as good as his word.

BELVILE [*within*] Boy, bring something to force the door.

A great noise within, at the door again.

BLUNT So, now must I speak in my own defence, I'll try what rhetoric will do. —Hold, hold, what do you mean gentlemen, what do you mean? 10

BELVILE (*within*) Oh, rogue, art alive? Prithee open the door and convince us.

BLUNT Yes, I am alive gentlemen, but at present a little busy.

BELVILE (*within*) How, Blunt grown a man of business! Come, come, open and let's see this miracle.

BLUNT No, no, no, no, gentlemen, 'tis no great business. But—I am—at—my devotion. 'Adsheartlikins, will you not allow a man time to pray?

BELVILE (*within*) Turned religious! A greater wonder than the first! Therefore open quickly, or we shall unhinge, we shall.

BLUNT [*aside*] This won't do. —Why, hark'ee, colonel, to tell you the plain 20 truth, I am about a necessary affair of life: I have a wench with me. You apprehend me? —The devil's in't if they be so uncivil as to disturb me now.

WILLMORE [*within*] How, a wench? Nay then, we must enter and partake. No resistance—unless it be your lady of quality, and then we'll keep our distance.

BLUNT So, the business is out.

WILLMORE [*within*] Come, come, lend's more hands to the door. Now heave, altogether. (*Breaks open the door.*) So, well done, my boys.

313

Enter Belvile [*and his* Page], Willmore, Frederick *and* Pedro. Blunt *looks simply, they all laugh at him; he lays his hand on his sword, and comes up to* Willmore.

BLUNT Hark'ee, sir, laugh out your laugh quickly, d'ye hear, and begone. I
30 shall spoil your sport else. 'Adsheartlikins, sir, I shall. The jest has been
carried on too long. —(*Aside.*) A plague upon my tailor!

WILLMORE 'Sdeath, how the whore has dressed him! Faith, sir, I'm sorry.

BLUNT Are you so sir? Keep't to yourself then sir, I advise you, d'ye hear, for I
can as little endure your pity as his mirth.   *Lays his hand on his sword.*

BELVILE Indeed Willmore, thou wert a little too rough with Ned Blunt's
mistress. Call a person of quality whore, and one so young, so handsome,
and so eloquent? Ha, ha, he.

BLUNT Hark'ee, sir, you know me, and know I can be angry. Have a care, for
'adsheartlikins, I can fight too. I can sir, do you mark me? No more.

40 BELVILE Why so peevish, good Ned? Some disappointments, I'll warrant.
What, did the jealous count, her husband, return just in the nick?

BLUNT Or the devil, sir. (*They laugh.*) D'ye laugh? Look ye settle me a good
sober countenance, and that quickly, too, or you shall know Ned Blunt is
not—

BELVILE Not everybody, we know that.

BLUNT Not an ass to be laughed at, sir.

WILLMORE Unconscionable sinner, to bring a lover so near his happiness—a
vigorous passionate lover—and then not only cheat him of his movables,
but his very desires too.

50 BELVILE Ah, sir, a mistress is a trifle with Blunt. He'll have a dozen the next
time he looks abroad: his eyes have charms not to be resisted; there needs
no more than to expose that taking person to the view of the fair, and he
leads 'em all in triumph.

PEDRO Sir, though I'm a stranger to you, I am ashamed at the rudeness of my
nation; and could you learn who did it, would assist you to make an
example of 'em.

BLUNT Why aye, there's one speaks sense now, and handsomely. And let me
tell you gentlemen, I should not have showed myself like a jack pudding
thus to have made you mirth, but that I have revenge within my power. For
60 know, I have got into my possession a female who had better have fallen
under any curse than the ruin I design her. 'Adsheartlikins, she assaulted me
here in my own lodgings, and had doubtless committed a rape upon me,
had not this sword defended me.

FREDERICK I know not that, but o' my conscience thou had ravished her, had
she not redeemed herself with a ring. Let's see't, Blunt.

Blunt *shows the ring.*

BELVILE [*aside*] Ha! The ring I gave Florinda, when we exchanged our vows.
—Hark'ee Blunt—   *Goes to whisper to him.*

WILLMORE No whispering, good colonel, there's a woman in the case. No
whispering.

70 BELVILE [*aside to* Blunt] Hark'ee fool, be advised, and conceal both the ring
and the story for your reputation's sake. Do not let people know what
despised cullies we English are; to be cheated and abused by one whore, and
another rather bribe thee than be kind to thee, is an infamy to our nation.

WILLMORE Come, come, where's the wench? We'll see her, let her be what she will, we'll see her.

PEDRO Aye, aye, let us see her. I can soon discover whether she be of quality, or for your diversion.

BLUNT She's in Fred's custody.

WILLMORE Come, come, the key—

> To Frederick, *who gives him the key; they are going.*

BELVILE [*aside*] Death, what shall I do? —Stay, gentlemen. —[*Aside.*] Yet if I   80
hinder 'em I shall discover all. —Hold, let's go one at once. Give me the key.

WILLMORE Nay, hold there colonel, I'll go first.

FREDERICK Nay, no dispute, Ned and I have the propriety of her.

WILLMORE Damn propriety! Then we'll draw cuts. (Belvile *goes to whisper* Willmore.) Nay no corruption, good colonel. Come, the longest sword carries her.

> They all draw, forgetting *Don Pedro, being a Spaniard, had the longest.*

BLUNT I yield up my interest to you, gentlemen, and that will be revenge sufficient.

WILLMORE (*to* Pedro) The wench is yours. —[*Aside.*] Pox of his Toledo, I had   90
forgot that.

FREDERICK Come, sir, I'll conduct you to the lady.

> Exeunt Frederick *and* Pedro.

BELVILE (*aside*) To hinder him will certainly discover her. —Dost know, dull beast, what mischief thou hast done?

> Willmore *walking up and down, out of humour.*

WILLMORE Aye, aye, to trust our fortune to lots! A devil on't, 'twas madness, that's the truth on't.

BELVILE Oh, intolerable sot—

Enter Florinda *running, masked,* Pedro *after her;* Willmore *gazing round her.*

FLORINDA (*aside*) Good heaven defend me from discovery!

PEDRO 'Tis but in vain to fly me; you're fallen to my lot.

BELVILE [*aside*] Sure she's undiscovered yet, but now I fear there is no way to   100
bring her off.

WILLMORE [*aside*] Why, what a pox, is not this my woman, the same I followed but now?

> Pedro, *talking to* Florinda, *who walks up and down.*

PEDRO As if I did not know ye, and your business here.

FLORINDA (*aside*) Good heaven, I fear he does indeed!

PEDRO Come, pray be kind, I know you meant to be so when you entered here, for these are proper gentlemen.

WILLMORE But sir, perhaps the lady will not be imposed upon: she'll choose her man.

PEDRO I am better bred than not to leave her choice free.   110

Enter Valeria, *and is surprised at sight of* Don Pedro.

VALERIA (*aside*) Don Pedro here! There's no avoiding him.

FLORINDA (*aside*) Valeria! Then I'm undone.

VALERIA (to Pedro, *running to him*) Oh, have I found you, sir!
The strangest accident—if I had breath—to tell it.

PEDRO Speak—is Florinda safe? Hellena well?

VALERIA Aye, aye, sir. Florinda is safe. —[*Aside.*] From any fears of you.

PEDRO Why, where's Florinda? Speak!

VALERIA Aye, where indeed sir; I wish I could inform you. But to hold you no
longer in doubt—

120 FLORINDA (*aside*) Oh what will she say?

VALERIA She's fled away in the habit—of one of her pages, sir—but Callis
thinks you may retrieve her yet, if you make haste away; she'll tell you, sir,
the rest. —(*Aside.*) If you can find her out.

PEDRO Dishonourable girl, she has undone my aim. —[*To* Belvile.] Sir, you
see my necessity of leaving you, and I hope you'll pardon it. My sister, I
know, will make her flight to you; and if she do, I shall expect she should
be rendered back.

BELVILE I shall consult my love and honour, sir.   *Exit* Pedro.

FLORINDA (*to* Valeria) My dear preserver, let me embrace thee.

130 WILLMORE What the devil's all this?

BLUNT Mystery, by this light.

VALERIA Come, come, make haste and get yourselves married quickly, for
your brother will return again.

BELVILE I'm so surprised with fears and joys, so amazed to find you here in
safety, I can scarce persuade my heart into a faith of what I see.

WILLMORE Hark'ee colonel, is this that mistress who has cost you so many
sighs, and me so many quarrels with you?

BELVILE It is. —[*To* Florinda.] Pray give him the honour of your hand.

WILLMORE Thus it must be received then. (*Kneels and kisses her hand.*) And
140 with it give your pardon too.

FLORINDA The friend to Belvile may command me anything.

WILLMORE (*aside*) Death, would I might; 'tis a surprising beauty.

BELVILE Boy, run and fetch a Father instantly.   *Exit* Page.

FREDERICK So, now do I stand like a dog, and have not a syllable to plead
my own cause with. By this hand, madam, I was never thoroughly
confounded before, nor shall I ever more dare look up with confidence, till
you are pleased to pardon me.

FLORINDA Sir, I'll be reconciled to you on one condition, that you'll follow
the example of your friend in marrying a maid that does not hate you, and
150 whose fortune, I believe, will not be unwelcome to you.

FREDERICK Madam, had I no inclinations that way, I should obey your kind
commands.

BELVILE Who, Fred marry? He has so few inclinations for womankind that had
he been possessed of paradise he might have continued there to this day, if
no crime but love could have disinherited him.

FREDERICK Oh, I do not use to boast of my intrigues.

BELVILE Boast! Why thou dost nothing but boast. And I dare swear, wert thou as innocent from the sin of the grape as thou art from the apple, thou might'st yet claim that right in Eden which our first parents lost by too much loving. 160

FREDERICK I wish this lady would think me so modest a man.

VALERIA She would be sorry then, and not like you half so well. And I should be loth to break my word with you, which was that if your friend and mine agreed, it should be a match between you and I.

She gives him her hand.

FREDERICK Bear witness, colonel, 'tis a bargain. *Kisses her hand.*

BLUNT (*to* Florinda) I have a pardon to beg too, but 'adsheartlikins, I am so out of countenance that I'm a dog if I can say anything to purpose.

FLORINDA Sir, I heartily forgive you all.

BLUNT That's nobly said, sweet lady. —Belvile, prithee present her her ring again; for I find I have not courage to approach her myself. 170

Gives him the ring; he gives it to Florinda.

Enter Page.

PAGE Sir, I have brought the Father that you sent for. [*Exit* Page.]

BELVILE 'Tis well. And now, my dear Florinda, let's fly to complete that mighty joy we have so long wished and sighed for. —Come Fred, you'll follow?

FREDERICK Your example, sir: 'twas ever my ambition in war, and must be so in love.

WILLMORE And must not I see this juggling knot tied?

BELVILE No, thou shalt do us better service, and be our guard, lest Don Pedro's sudden return interrupt the ceremony.

WILLMORE Content; I'll secure this pass. 180

Exeunt Belvile, Florinda, Frederick *and* Valeria.

Enter Page.

PAGE (*to* Willmore) Sir, there's a lady without would speak to you.

WILLMORE Conduct her in; I dare not quit my post.

PAGE [*to* Blunt] And sir, your tailor waits you in your chamber.

BLUNT Some comfort yet: I shall not dance naked at the wedding.

Exeunt Blunt *and* Page.

Enter again the Page, *conducting in* Angellica *in a masquing habit and a vizard.* Willmore *runs to her.*

WILLMORE [*aside*] This can be none but my pretty gipsy. —Oh, I see you can follow as well as fly. Come, confess thyself the most malicious devil in nature; you think you have done my business with Angellica—

ANGELLICA Stand off, base villain!

She draws a pistol, and holds it to his breast.

WILLMORE Ha, 'tis not she! Who art thou, and what's thy business?

ANGELLICA One thou hast injured, and who comes to kill thee for't. 190

WILLMORE What the devil canst thou mean?

ANGELLICA By all my hopes to kill thee—

317

Holds still the pistol to his breast, he going back, she following still.

WILLMORE Prithee, on what acquaintance? For I know thee not.

ANGELLICA Behold this face so lost to thy remembrance.
And then call thy sins about thy soul,

Pulls off her vizard.

And let 'em die with thee.

WILLMORE Angellica!

ANGELLICA Yes, traitor! Does not thy guilty blood run shivering through thy veins? Hast thou no horror at this sight, that tells thee thou hast not long to
200   boast thy shameful conquest?

WILLMORE Faith, no, child. My blood keeps its old ebbs and flows still, and that usual heat too, that could oblige thee with a kindness, had I but opportunity.

ANGELLICA Devil! Dost wanton with my pain? Have at thy heart!

WILLMORE Hold, dear virago! Hold thy hand a little. I am not now at leisure to be killed. Hold and hear me. —(*Aside.*) Death, I think she's in earnest.

ANGELLICA (*aside, turning from him*) Oh, if I take not heed,
My coward heart will leave me to his mercy.
—What have you, sir, to say? —But should I hear thee,
210   Thoud'st talk away all that is brave about me.
And I have vowed thy death, by all that's sacred.

Follows him with the pistol to his breast.

WILLMORE Why then, there's an end of a proper handsome fellow, that might 'a lived to have done good service yet. That's all I can say to't.

ANGELLICA (*pausingly*) Yet—I would give thee time for—penitence.

WILLMORE Faith, child, I thank God I have ever took care to lead a good, sober, hopeful life, and am of a religion that teaches me to believe I shall depart in peace.

ANGELLICA So will the devil! Tell me how many
Poor believing fools thou hast undone?
220   How many hearts thou hast betrayed to ruin?
Yet these are little mischiefs to the ills
Thou'st taught mine to commit: thou'st taught it love.

WILLMORE Egad, 'twas shrewdly hurt the while.

ANGELLICA Love, that has robbed it of its unconcern,
Of all that pride that taught me how to value it.
And in its room
A mean submissive passion was conveyed,
That made me humbly bow, which I ne'er did
To any thing but heaven.
230   Thou, perjured man, didst this; and with thy oaths,
Which on thy knees thou didst devoutly make,
Softened my yielding heart, and then I was a slave.
Yet still had been content to've worn my chains,
Worn 'em with vanity and joy for ever,
Hadst thou not broke those vows that put them on.
'Twas then I was undone.

All this while follows him with the pistol to his breast.

318

WILLMORE Broke my vows! Why, where hast thou lived? Amongst the gods? For I never heard of mortal man that has not broke a thousand vows.

ANGELLICA Oh impudence!

WILLMORE Angellica, that beauty has been too long tempting,   240
  Not to have made a thousand lovers languish,
  Who in the amorous fever, no doubt have sworn
  Like me. Did they all die in that faith, still adoring?
  I do not think they did.

ANGELLICA No, faithless man; had I repaid their vows, as I did thine, I would have killed the ingrateful that had abandoned me.

WILLMORE This old general has quite spoiled thee: nothing makes a woman so vain as being flattered. Your old lover ever supplies the defects of age with intolerable dotage, vast charge, and that which you call constancy; and attributing all this to your own merits, you domineer, and throw your   250 favours in's teeth, upbraiding him still with the defects of age, and cuckold him as often as he deceives your expectations. But the gay, young, brisk lover, that brings his equal fires, and can give you dart for dart, he'll be as nice as you sometimes.

ANGELLICA All this thou'st made me know, for which I hate thee.
  Had I remained in innocent security,
  I should have thought all men were born my slaves,
  And worn my power like lightning in my eyes,
  To have destroyed at pleasure when offended.
  But when love held the mirror, the undeceiving glass   260
  Reflected all the weakness of my soul, and made me know
  My richest treasure being lost, my honour,
  All the remaining spoil could not be worth
  The conqueror's care or value.
  Oh, how I fell, like a long worshipped idol
  Discovering all the cheat.
  Would not the incense and rich sacrifice
  Which blind devotion offered at my altars
  Have fallen to thee?
  Why wouldst thou then destroy my fancied power?   270

WILLMORE By heaven thou'rt brave, and I admire thee strangely.
  I wish I were that dull, that constant thing
  Which thou wouldst have, and nature never meant me.
  I must, like cheerful birds, sing in all groves,
  And perch on every bough,
  Billing the next kind she that flies to meet me;
  Yet, after all, could build my nest with thee,
  Thither repairing when I'd loved my round,
  And still reserve a tributary flame.
  To gain your credit, I'll pay you back your charity,   280
  And be obliged for nothing but for love.

Offers her a purse of gold.

ANGELLICA Oh, that thou wert in earnest!
  So mean a thought of me
  Would turn my rage to scorn, and I should pity thee,
  And give thee leave to live;
  Which for the public safety of our sex,
  And my own private injuries, I dare not do.

Prepare— *Follows still, as before.*
I will no more be tempted with replies.

290 WILLMORE Sure—

ANGELLICA Another word will damn thee! I've heard thee talk too long.

She follows him with the pistol ready to shoot; he retires, still amazed. Enter Don Antonio, *his arm in a scarf, and lays hold on the pistol.*

ANTONIO Ha! Angellica!

ANGELLICA Antonio! What devil brought thee hither?

ANTONIO Love and curiosity, seeing your coach at door. Let me disarm you of this unbecoming instrument of death. (*Takes away the pistol.*) Amongst the number of your slaves, was there not one worthy the honour to have fought your quarrel? —[*To* Willmore.] Who are you, sir, that are so very wretched to merit death from her?

WILLMORE One, sir, that could have made a better end of an amorous quarrel
300 without you, than with you.

ANTONIO Sure 'tis some rival. Ha! The very man took down her picture yesterday—the very same that set on me last night! Blessed opportunity—

Offers to shoot him.

ANGELLICA Hold, you're mistaken, sir.

ANTONIO By heaven, the very same! —Sir, what pretensions have you to this lady?

WILLMORE Sir, I do not use to be examined, and am ill at all disputes but this—

Draws; Antonio *offers to shoot.*

ANGELLICA (*to* Willmore) Oh hold! You see he's armed with certain death.
—And you Antonio, I command you hold,
310 By all the passion you've so lately vowed me.

Enter Don Pedro, *sees* Antonio, *and stays.*

PEDRO (*aside*) Ha! Antonio! And Angellica!

ANTONIO When I refuse obedience to your will,
May you destroy me with your mortal hate.
By all that's holy, I adore you so,
That even my rival, who has charms enough
To make him fall a victim to my jealousy,
Shall live; nay, and have leave to love on still.

PEDRO (*aside*) What's this I hear?

ANGELLICA (*pointing at* Willmore) Ah thus, 'twas thus he talked, and I
320 believed,
—Antonio, yesterday
I'd not have sold my interest in his heart
For all the sword has won and lost in battle.
—But now, to show my utmost of contempt,
I give thee life, which, if thou wouldst preserve,
Live where my eyes may never see thee more,
Live to undo someone whose soul may prove
So bravely constant to revenge my love.

Goes out, Antonio *follows, but* Pedro *pulls him back.*

PEDRO Antonio, stay.

ANTONIO Don Pedro! 330

PEDRO What coward fear was that prevented thee
    From meeting me this morning on the Molo?

ANTONIO Meet thee?

PEDRO Yes, me; I was the man that dared thee to't.

ANTONIO Hast thou so often seen me fight in war,
    To find no better cause to excuse my absence?
    I sent my sword and one to do thee right,
    Finding myself uncapable to use a sword.

PEDRO But 'twas Florinda's quarrel that we fought,
    And you to show how little you esteemed her, 340
    Sent me your rival, giving him your interest.
    But I have found the cause of this affront,
    And when I meet you fit for the dispute,
    I'll tell you my resentment.

ANTONIO I shall be ready, sir, e'er long to do you reason. *Exit* Antonio.

PEDRO If I could find Florinda now whilst my anger's high, I think I should
be kind, and give her to Belvile in revenge.

WILLMORE Faith, sir, I know not what you would do, but I believe the priest
within has been so kind.

PEDRO How? My sister married? 350

WILLMORE I hope by this time she is, and bedded too, or he has not my
longings about him.

PEDRO Dares he do this? Does he not fear my power?

WILLMORE Faith, not at all; if you will go in and thank him for the favour he
has done your sister, so; if not, sir, my power's greater in this house than
yours: I have a damned surly crew here that will keep you till the next tide,
and then clap you on board for prize. My ship lies but a league off the
Molo, and we shall show your donship a damned Tramontana rover's trick.

Enter Belvile.

BELVILE This rogue's in some new mischief. Ha! Pedro returned!

PEDRO Colonel Belvile, I hear you have married my sister. 360

BELVILE You have heard truth then, sir.

PEDRO Have I so? Then, sir, I wish you joy.

BELVILE How?

PEDRO By this embrace I do, and I am glad on't.

BELVILE Are you in earnest?

PEDRO By our long friendship and my obligations to thee, I am;
    The sudden change, I'll give you reasons for anon.
    Come lead me to my sister,
    That she may know I now approve her choice.

Exit Belvile *with* Pedro.

Willmore *goes to follow them. Enter* Hellena, *as before in boy's clothes, and
pulls him back.*

WILLMORE Ha! My gipsy! Now a thousand blessings on thee for this kindness. 370
Egad, child, I was e'en in despair of ever seeing thee again; my friends are all
provided for within, each man his kind woman.

HELLENA Ha! I thought they had served me some such trick!

WILLMORE And I was e'en resolved to go aboard, and condemn myself to my lone cabin, and the thoughts of thee.

HELLENA And could you have left me behind? Would you have been so ill-natured?

WILLMORE Why, 'twould have broke my heart, child. But since we are met again, I defy foul weather to part us.

380 HELLENA And would you be a faithful friend now, if a maid should trust you?

WILLMORE For a friend I cannot promise; thou art of a form so excellent, a face and humour too good for cold dull friendship. I am parlously afraid of being in love, child; and you have not forgot how severely you have used me?

HELLENA That's all one, such usage you must still look for; to find out all your haunts, to rail at you to all that love you, till I have made you love only me in your own defence, because nobody else will love you.

WILLMORE But hast thou no better quality to recommend thyself by?

HELLENA Faith, none, captain. Why, 'twill be the greater charity to take me for
390 thy mistress. I am a lone child, a kind of orphan lover, and why I should die a maid, and in a captain's hands too, I do not understand.

WILLMORE Egad, I was never clawed away with broadsides from any female before. Thou hast one virtue I adore: good nature. I hate a coy, demure mistress, she's as troublesome as a colt; I'll break none. No, give me a mad mistress when mewed, and in flying, one I dare trust upon the wing, that whilst she's kind will come to the lure.

HELLENA Nay, as kind as you will, good captain, whilst it lasts. But let's lose no time.

WILLMORE My time's as precious to me as thine can be. Therefore, dear
400 creature, since we are so well agreed, let's retire to my chamber; and if ever thou wert treated with such savoury love! Come, my bed's prepared for such a guest, all clean and sweet as thy fair self. I love to steal a dish and a bottle with a friend, and hate long graces. Come, let's retire and fall to.

HELLENA 'Tis but getting my consent, and the business is soon done. Let but old gaffer Hymen and his priest say amen to't, and I dare lay my mother's daughter by as proper a fellow as your father's son, without fear or blushing.

WILLMORE Hold, hold, no bug words, child. Priest and Hymen? Prithee add a hangman to 'em to make up the consort. No, no, we'll have no vows but
410 love, child, nor witness but the lover; the kind deity enjoins naught but love and enjoy! Hymen and priest wait still upon portion and jointure; love and beauty have their own ceremonies. Marriage is as certain a bane to love as lending money is to friendship. I'll neither ask nor give a vow, though I could be content to turn gipsy, and become a left-handed bridegroom, to have the pleasure of working that great miracle of making a maid a mother, if you durst venture. 'Tis upse gipsy that, and if I miss I'll lose my labour.

HELLENA And if you do not lose, what shall I get? A cradle full of noise and mischief, with a pack of repentance at my back? Can you teach me to weave inkle to pass my time with? 'Tis upse gipsy that, too.

420 WILLMORE I can teach thee to weave a true love's knot better.

HELLENA So can my dog.

WILLMORE Well, I see we are both upon our guards, and I see there's no way to conquer good nature but by yielding. Here—give me thy hand: one kiss, and I am thine.

HELLENA One kiss! How like my page he speaks! I am resolved you shall have none, for asking such a sneaking sum. He that will be satisfied with one kiss will never die of that longing. Good friend single-kiss, is all your talking come to this? A kiss, a caudle! Farewell, captain single-kiss!

Going out; he stays her.

WILLMORE Nay, if we part so, let me die like a bird upon a bough, at the sheriff's charge. By heaven, both the Indies shall not buy thee from me. I adore thy humour and will marry thee, and we are so of one humour it must be a bargain. Give me thy hand. (*Kisses her hand.*) And now let the blind ones, Love and Fortune, do their worst.

430

HELLENA Why, god-a-mercy captain!

WILLMORE But hark'ee: the bargain is now made, but is it not fit we should know each other's names, that when we have reason to curse one another hereafter, and people ask me who 'tis I give to the devil, I may at least be able to tell what family you came of?

HELLENA Good reason, captain; and where I have cause, as I doubt not but I shall have plentiful, that I may know at whom to throw my—blessings—I beseech ye your name.

440

WILLMORE I am called Robert the Constant.

HELLENA A very fine name; pray was it your faulkner or butler that christened you? Do they not use to whistle when they call you?

WILLMORE I hope you have a better, that a man may name without crossing himself, you are so merry with mine.

HELLENA I am called Hellena the Inconstant.

Enter Pedro, Belvile, Florinda, Frederick, Valeria.

PEDRO Ha! Hellena!

FLORINDA Hellena!

450

HELLENA The very same. Ha! My brother! Now captain, show your love and courage; stand to your arms, and defend me bravely, or I am lost for ever.

PEDRO What's this I hear? False girl, how came you hither, and what's your business? Speak! *Goes roughly to her.*

WILLMORE Hold off sir, you have leave to parley only.

Puts himself between.

HELLENA I had e'en as good tell it, as you guess it. Faith, brother, my business is the same with all living creatures of my age: to love, and be beloved—and here's the man.

PEDRO Perfidious maid, hast thou deceived me too, deceived thyself and heaven?

460

HELLENA 'Tis time enough to make my peace with that;
     Be you but kind, let me alone with heaven.

PEDRO Belvile, I did not expect this false play from you. Was't not enough you'd gain Florinda, which I pardoned, but your lewd friends too must be enriched with the spoils of a noble family?

BELVILE Faith sir, I am as much surprised at this as you can be. Yet sir, my friends are gentlemen, and ought to be esteemed for their misfortunes, since they have the glory to suffer with the best of men and kings. 'Tis true, he's a rover of fortune, yet a prince aboard his little wooden world.

470 PEDRO What's this to the maintenance of a woman of her birth and quality?

WILLMORE Faith sir, I can boast of nothing but a sword which does me right where e'er I come, and has defended a worse cause than a woman's; and since I loved her before I either knew her birth or name, I must pursue my resolution, and marry her.

PEDRO And is all your holy intent of becoming a nun debauched into a desire of man?

HELLENA Why, I have considered the matter, brother, and find the three hundred thousand crowns my uncle left me, and you cannot keep from me, will be better laid out in love than in religion, and turn to as good an 480 account. Let most voices carry it: for heaven or the captain?

All cry, A captain! A captain!

HELLENA Look ye, sir, 'tis a clear case.

PEDRO (*aside*) Oh, I am mad! If I refuse, my life's in danger. —Come, there's one motive induces me. Take her; I shall now be free from fears of her honour. Guard it you now, if you can; I have been a slave to't long enough. *Gives her to him.*

WILLMORE Faith sir, I am of a nation that are of opinion a woman's honour is not worth guarding when she has a mind to part with it.

HELLENA Well said, captain.

490 PEDRO (*to* Valeria) This was your plot, mistress, but I hope you have married one that will revenge my quarrel to you.

VALERIA There's no altering destiny, sir.

PEDRO Sooner than a woman's will; therefore I forgive you all, and wish you may get my father's pardon as easily, which I fear.

Enter Blunt *dressed in a Spanish habit, looking very ridiculously; his* Man *adjusting his band.*

MAN 'Tis very well, sir—

BLUNT Well, sir! 'Adsheartlikins, I tell you 'tis damnable ill, sir. A Spanish habit! Good Lord! Could the devil and my tailor devise no other punishment for me but the mode of a nation I abominate?

BELVILE What's the matter, Ned?

500 BLUNT Pray view me round, and judge. *Turns around.*

BELVILE I must confess thou art a kind of an odd figure.

BLUNT In a Spanish habit with a vengeance! I had rather be in the Inquisition for Judaism than in this doublet and breeches; a pillory were an easy collar to this, three handfuls high; and these shoes, too, are worse than the stocks, with the sole an inch shorter than my foot. In fine, gentlemen, methinks I look altogether like a bag of bays stuffed full of fool's flesh.

BELVILE Methinks 'tis well, and makes thee look e'en cavalier. Come sir, settle your face, and salute our friends. Lady—

BLUNT (*to* Hellena) Ha! Say'st thou so, my little rover? Lady, if you be one, 510
give me leave to kiss your hand, and tell you, 'adsheartlikins, for all I look
so, I am your humble servant. A pox of my Spanish habit!

WILLMORE Hark—what's this? *Music is heard to play.*

Enter Boy.

BOY Sir, as the custom is, the gay people in masquerade, who make every
man's house their own, are coming up.

*Enter several men and women in masquing habits, with music; they put
themselves in order and dance.*

BLUNT 'Adsheartlikins, would 'twere lawful to pull off their false faces, that I
might see if my doxy were not amongst 'em.

BELVILE (*to the masquers*) Ladies and gentlemen, since you are come so *a
propos*, you must take a small collation with us.

WILLMORE (*to* Hellena) Whilst we'll to the good man within, who stays to 520
give us a cast of his office. Have you no trembling at the near approach?

HELLENA No more than you have in an engagement or a tempest.

WILLMORE Egad, thou'rt a brave girl, and I admire thy love and courage.
   Lead on; no other dangers they can dread,
   Who venture in the storms o'th' marriage bed.

Exeunt.

THE END

Epilogue

The banished cavaliers! A roving blade!
A popish carnival! A masquerade!
The devil's in't if this will please the nation
In these our blessed times of reformation,
When conventicling is so much in fashion.
And yet—
That mutinous tribe less factions do beget,
Than your continual differing in wit;
Your judgment's, as your passion's, a disease:
Nor muse nor miss your appetite can please;
You're grown as nice as queasy consciences,
Whose each convulsion, when the spirit moves,
Damns everything that maggot disapproves.
    With canting rule you would the stage refine,
And to dull method all our sense confine.
With th'insolence of commonwealths you rule,
Where each gay fop, and politic grave fool
On monarch wit impose, without control.
As for the last, who seldom sees a play,
Unless it be the old Blackfriars way,
Shaking his empty noddle o'er bamboo,
He cries, 'Good faith, these plays will never do!
Ah, sir, in my young days, what lofty wit,
What high-strained scenes of fighting there were writ:
These are slight airy toys. But tell me, pray,
What has the House of Commons done today?'
Then shows his politics, to let you see
Of state affairs he'll judge as notably
As he can do of wit and poetry.
The younger sparks, who hither do resort,
Cry,
'Pox o' your genteel things, give us more sport!
Damn me, I'm sure 'twill never please the court.'
    Such fops are never pleased, unless the play
Be stuffed with fools as brisk and dull as they:
Such might the half-crown spare, and in a glass
At home behold a more accomplished ass,
Where they may set their cravats, wigs and faces,
And practise all their buffoonry grimaces:
See how this huff becomes, this damny, stare,
Which they at home may act because they dare,
But must with prudent caution do elsewhere.
Oh that our Nokes, or Tony Lee, could show
A fop but half so much to th' life as you.

Postscript

This play had been sooner in print, but for a report about the town (made by some either very malicious or very ignorant) that 'twas *Thomaso* altered, which made the booksellers fear some trouble from the proprietor of that admirable play, which indeed has wit enough to stock a poet, and is not to be pieced or mended by any but the excellent author himself. That I have stolen some hints from it may be a proof that I valued it more than to pretend to alter it, had I had the dexterity of some poets, who are not more expert in stealing than in the art of concealing, and who even that way outdo the Spartan boys. I might have appropriated all to myself, but I, vainly proud of my judgment, hang out the sign of Angellica (the only stolen object) to give notice where a great part of the wit dwelt; though if the *Play of the Novella* were as well worth remembering as *Thomaso*, they might (bating the name) have as well said, I took it from thence. I will only say the plot and business (not to boast on't) is my own; as for the words and characters, I leave the reader to judge and compare 'em with *Thomaso*, to whom I recommend the great entertainment of reading it. Though had this succeeded ill, I should have had no need of imploring that justice from the critics, who are naturally so kind to any that pretend to usurp their dominion, especially of our sex: they would doubtless have given me the whole honour on't. Therefore I will only say in English what the famous Virgil does in Latin: I make verses, and others have the fame.

Notes

Title-page

The Rover, or, The Banished Cavaliers: In the seventeenth century the term 'rover' could signify a pirate, a male flirt, an inconstant lover, or, simply, a wanderer. The reference to 'banished cavaliers' indicates that the action of the play takes place in the 1650s, between the end of the Civil Wars in England and the Restoration of Charles II to the throne in 1660. Many Royalists ('Cavaliers') who fought for Charles I and Charles II against Oliver Cromwell and the Parliamentary armies left England to follow the court of Charles II into exile on the Continent.

Prologue

Prologue: Restoration plays always began with a prologue and ended with an epilogue. These might be written by a friend of the playwright, and would be spoken by one of the actors. The prologue would be spoken in front of the curtain, which would then be raised and would not fall until after the epilogue had been delivered.

line 1 *Wits*: the fashionable literary set who frequented the theatre and whose opinions could often determine the success or failure of a new play.

line 3 *Rabell's Drops*: the 'Styptick Drops' patented by a well-known medical man, Monsieur Rabell.

line 9 *cabal*: secret group or faction.

line 10 *hit your humour right*: describe your characteristics accurately.

line 12 *elves*: malicious creatures.

line 23 *bating*: excepting.

line 33 *lampoon*: a virulent satire upon an individual.

line 37 *the author*: when first published *The Rover* was anonymous. Behn only claimed authorship on the title-page of the third issue of the first edition in 1677.

line 42 *debauches*: that is, debauchees, or people who give themselves over to indulgence in sensual pleasures.

line 43 *cits*: short for citizens; used contemptuously of ordinary townspeople, shop-keepers and the like.

line 43 *May-Day coaches*: it was the custom for pleasure parties to drive round Hyde Park on May Day.

Characters

the Viceroy's son: 'Viceroy' is the title of one who acts as the governor of a country or province in the name of the supreme ruler, in this case the King of Spain. Naples came under Spanish control in 1503 and remained so until 1707. For much of the seventeenth century most of Italy was under Spanish domination, and was treated as part of the wider Spanish Empire. Spanish rule was by no means universally unpopular, but there were outbreaks of resentment from time to time in Naples, particularly when taxes rose or food became expensive. In 1647 there was a full-scale rebellion which frightened the Viceroy into temporary concessions before the revolt was finally crushed.

gallant: lover, paramour.

pimp: one who procures clients for a prostitute.

bravoes: daring ruffians, or hired bodyguards.

courtesan: high-class 'kept woman'. (In theory a courtesan had only one lover at any given time.)

jilting wench: deceitful, wanton woman.

masqueraders: a masquerade was a masked ball or party, often also involving fancy-dress.

Carnival: in Italy, and indeed throughout most of Roman Catholic Europe, the period before Lent was given over to revelry and riotous amusement.

Act One

I.1.1 *bred*: educated, brought up.

I.1.23 *Anglese*: Englishman.

I.1.41 *devote*: nun.

I.1.43 *siege of Pamplona*: Pamplona, the fortified capital of the province of Navarre in Spain, was frequently besieged during the long war between France and Spain which ended in 1659. A number of English Royalists, exiled after the civil wars, joined the French army, which would explain how Belvile came to be on the French side at this siege.

I.1.48 (stage direction) *masquing habit*: carnival costume, including a face mask.

I.1.63 *licensed lust*: according to the rules of war, victorious armies had the right to plunder and rape.

I.1.67 *jointure*: an amount of money made over to a wife on marriage, to guarantee her an income in the event of her husband's death.

I.1.77 *bags*: wealth.

I.1.89–90 *Indian breeding*: Don Vincentio had been brought up in, or spent much of his life in, the West Indies (that is, the Americas).

I.1.90 *dog days*: the hottest part of summer.

I.1.92 *Sancho the First*: Sancho the Great, king of Navarre in the early eleventh century.

I.1.95 *furbushed*: cleaned up, renovated (obsolete form of 'furbished').

I.1.97 *coxcomb*: foolish, conceited man.

I.1.97 *uncase*: undress.

I.1.112 *Hostel de Dieu*: hospital founded by a religious order.

I.1.113 *lazars*: poor diseased people, especially lepers.

I.1.118 *Gambo*: Gambia in West Africa was an important source of slaves for English and Portuguese merchants during the seventeenth century. It eventually became a British colony.

I.1.119 *bell and bauble*: worthless object, trifle.

I.1.127 *grate*: barred convent window.

I.1.160 *ramble*: during the seventeenth century, but particularly in the Restoration period, 'to ramble' frequently meant 'to go out looking for sex'; hence a prostitute might be described as a 'rambler'. Compare the use of the phrase 'upon the ramble', IV.5.62.

I.2.13 *'adsheartlikins*: a mild oath, meaning 'by God's little heart'. In the first edition it is rendered variously as 'sheartlikins and 'dsheartlikins, as well as 'adsheartlikins, which is adopted here throughout.

I.2.33 *hogoes*: spicy relishes or flavourings.

I.2.42–4 *Parliaments and Protectors ... cavaliering*: under Cromwell, who became Lord Protector in 1653, many estates belonging to Royalists were confiscated.

I.2.48 *pick a hole in my coat*: blame me.

I.2.49 *Commonwealth*: following the execution of Charles I in 1649, England was ruled by Parliament as a 'Commonwealth'. Although strictly speaking this gave way to a 'Protectorate' under Cromwell in 1653, the term 'Commonwealth' is often used to describe the whole period of the English Republic from 1649 to 1660.

I.2.56–7 *the Prince*: the exiled Charles II.

I.2.68 *chapmen*: merchants.

I.2.81 *still*: presumably a reference to the distilling of perfume from roses.

I.2.86 *pest-house*: a hospital for plague victims.

I.2.100 *horns*: traditionally the sign of a cuckold (a husband whose wife has been unfaithful).

I.2.108 *monsieurs*: Frenchmen.

I.2.110–13 *But here in Italy ... the New Bridge*: this rather obscure speech seems to be saying that the French have not been able to import their custom of duelling into Italy, where quarrels are settled by using hired ruffians. The only 'duels' here are between Frenchmen and the hangman in the public square, where the hangman is as hard on them as they have recently been on the Dutch. (France had gone to war against the Dutch in 1672, and 'New Bridge' may refer to Nieuwerbrug, which the Dutch lost in 1673.)

I.2.116–17 *cross their hands*: give them payment.

I.2.126 *Egad*: a softened form of 'By God!'.

I.2.130 *parlous*: shrewd, keen.

I.2.157 *Jephtha's daughter*: before Jephtha sacrificed his only daughter in fulfilment of a sacred vow he granted her wish to be left for two months to bewail her virginity. See Judges 11: 30–40.

I.2.160 *took orders*: became a nun.

I.2.174 *swinging*: a variant of 'swingeing', meaning immense.

I.2.189 *This woman*: that is, Callis.

I.2.245 *Let her alone for that*: trust her to arrange that.

I.2.249 *bellman*: town crier.

I.2.252 *sell him for Peru*: that is, into slavery to work in a Spanish silver mine.

I.2.265 *stock*: money.

I.2.267 *piece of eight*: Spanish dollar.

I.2.276 *honest*: chaste, respectable.

I.2.282 *Paduana*: native of the Italian city of Padua in Northern Italy, part of the Venetian Republic which was outside Spanish control.

I.2.283 *mistress*: beloved (that is, mistress of his heart).

I.2.286 *as on a monarch's birthday*: it was the custom at court to dress up in honour of the king's birthday.

Act Two

II.1.1 (stage direction) *vizard*: mask.

II.1.4 *buff*: leather coat worn by soldiers.

II.1.16 *the picture*: Angellica's portrait; see stage direction below line 83.

II.1.39 *clap*: gonorrhoea.

II.1.54 *bottom*: ship's hold.

II.1.57 *cozened*: cheated, tricked.

II.1.65 *right*: genuine.

II.1.66 *plate*: silver or gold table utensils.

II.1.67 *errant*: downright, thorough.

II.1.69 *ycleped*: called. (A comic archaism.)

II.1.71 *Essex calf*: dolt, fool (Blunt is, of course, from Essex).

II.1.101 *a portion for the Infanta*: a dowry for the Spanish royal princess. In 1666 the Princess (Infanta) Margarita, daughter of Philip IV, was married to the Emperor Leopold I of Austria, bringing with her an immense dowry.

II.1.135 (stage direction) *anticly attired*: dressed outlandishly.

II.1.185 *Molo*: a stone pier or quay (known in English as a 'mole'). In many Italian sea-ports the Molo was a well-known meeting-place or thoroughfare.

II.1.252 *patacoon*: a Portuguese and Spanish silver coin.

II.1.259 *saluting*: that is, with a kiss.

II.2.18 *Worcester*: a Royalist army led by Charles II was routed by Oliver Cromwell at the Battle of Worcester in 1651.

II.2.23 *troop*: be off.

II.2.31 *pistole*: Spanish gold coin.

II.2.39–40 *sell upon the Friday's mart at 'Who gives more?'*: sell by auction at the market on Friday.

II.2.138 *awful*: reverential (full of awe).

II.2.149 *shameroon*: deceitful, shameful fellow, trickster.

II.2.151 *tatterdemalion*: ragamuffin.

II.2.151 *picaroon*: pirate, brigand.

Act Three

III.1.4 *mewed up*: confined.

III.1.7 *Loretto*: Italian town in the province of Ancona near the Adriatic coast, the site of the Santa Casa, or Holy House of the Virgin, a shrine much visited by pilgrims.

III.1.32 *the pip*: originally a disease of poultry, but often applied in a jocular way to ailments, or fits of depression, in humans.

III.1.42 *cast*: throw of the dice.

III.1.64 *laid the soft-winged god in your hearts, or broke the bird's nest*: beaten down Cupid and your feelings of love.

III.1.85–6 *bona roba*: courtesan.

III.1.86 *in fresco*: in cool fresh air.

III.1.88 *Canary*: a light sweet wine from the Canary Islands.

III.1.89 *spigot*: wooden stopper of a barrel.

III.1.89 *butt*: wine barrel.

III.1.94 *hungry balderdash*: unsatisfying mixture of liquors.

III.1.94 *sack*: a type of white wine from Spain and the Canaries.

III.1.116 *dog me, or stay me*: follow me, or prevent me from going.

III.1.128 *Capuchin*: member of an austere Fransciscan order founded in 1528 whose friars wore a distinctive hooded cloak.

III.1.137 *collation*: light meal, often cold.

III.1.194 *jewel*: ornament (in this case a locket).

III.1.194–5 *bills of exchange*: written orders for the payment of money.

III.1.219 *budget*: leather pouch or wallet.

III.2.14 *settlements*: legal arrangements before marriage granting money or property to a wife.

III.2.28 *Justice of Peace*: obsolete form of 'Justice of the Peace', or local magistrate, a more important official in the seventeenth century than now.

III.3.38 *eighty-eight*: a reference to the Spanish Armada which attempted to invade England in 1588, during the reign of Elizabeth I.

III.3.40 *bowed*: bent or curved.

III.3.44 *common shore*: main sewer.

III.4.2 *clue*: alternative spelling of 'clew', a ball of yarn or thread, and hence figuratively anything which acts as a guide or thread to find a way out of a maze or complicated situation.

III.4.3 *quean*: harlot, strumpet.

III.4.13 *Prado*: a fashionable park or promenade.

III.4.21 *cullies*: dupes, gulls.

III.5.2 *cabinet*: private chamber.

III.5.8 *jessamine*: jasmine.

III.5.21 *parlous*: exceedingly.

III.5.25 *disguised*: intoxicated.

III.5.50 *coil*: fuss, disturbance.

III.6.22 *awful*: profound.

III.6.37 *baggage*: a term often applied to prostitutes, but also used jocularly of any young woman.

III.6.47 *chase-gun*: a gun placed in the bow or stern of a ship, for use in pursuit.

III.6.59 *St Jago!*: Santiago, or St James, the patron saint of Spain.

Act Four

IV.1.7 *quality*: high birth or rank.

IV.1.50 *discounting*: paying off.

IV.2.30 *Or*: either.

IV.2.108 *nicely punctual*: scrupulous.

IV.2.165 *fourscore*: an eighty-year-old.

IV.2.193 *mumping*: sulky, grimacing.

IV.2.253 *dressed*: ready waiting.

IV.2.262 *prater*: chatterer.

IV.2.329 *cogging*: pleading, wheedling.

IV.2.340 *motion*: puppet show.

IV.2.361 *foppery*: foolishness.

IV.2.398 *nice*: fastidious.

IV.2.403 *soothed*: flattered.

IV.3.5 *Augustine nuns*: nuns obeying the rule of St Augustine.

IV.3.39 *clapped*: infected with venereal disease.

IV.3.59 *prize*: a ship captured at sea under the rules of war.

IV.5.6–7 *like a morris dancer*: that is, because he is wearing white underwear (Morris dancers traditionally wore white).

IV.5.98 *cormorant*: a large sea-bird, renowned for its greed; hence used figuratively of any greedy person.

IV.5.99 *pullet*: young hen.

IV.5.112 *ruffle*: handle rudely, or roughly.

Act Five

V.1.29 (stage direction) *simply*: foolishly.

V.1.58 *jack pudding*: buffoon.

V.1.81 *one at once*: one at a time.

V.1.90 *Toledo*: finely tempered sword blade made in Toledo, Spain.

V.1.158 *sin of the grape*: drunkenness.

V.1.177 *juggling*: deceitful.

V.1.205 *virago*: originally a female warrior or amazon, the term came to be used of a scolding or impudent woman.

V.1.254 *nice*: hard to please or satisfy.

V.1.358 *Tramontana rover*: a barbarous foreign pirate. (Italians described anyone from beyond the Alps as 'tramontano'.)

V.1.392 *clawed away*: beaten off (by another ship's guns).

V.1.392 *broadsides*: discharges of all the guns on one side of a ship simultaneously.

V.1.394–5 *a mad mistress when mewed*: that is, one who cannot bear to be confined. (Mewed was a hawking term.)

V.1.396 *kind*: grateful, satisfied.

V.1.405 *old gaffer Hymen*: Hymen, in Greek and Roman mythology the god of marriage, was usually represented as a young man, but is here referred to as an elderly man.

V.1.408 *bug words*: words meant to frighten.

V.1.409 *consort*: combination of voices or instruments.

V.1.416 *upse gipsy*: after the manner of a gipsy.

V.1.419 *inkle*: linen tape.

V.1.428 *caudle*: a warm drink given to the sick, and also to women after childbirth.

V.1.443 *faulkner*: one who keeps falcons or hawks.

V.1.495 (stage direction) *band*: collar, neck-band.

V.1.506 *bays*: spices used in cooking.

V.1.517 *doxy*: wench.

V.1.520–21 *to give us a cast of his office*: to let us have a sample of his speciality, that is, to marry us.

Epilogue

line 1 *blade*: rakish fellow.

line 5 *conventicling*: it was against the law during the Restoration period to worship outside the Church of England; illegal meetings of Dissenters were known as conventicles.

line 7 *mutinous tribe*: Dissenters who refused to conform to the Church of England.

lines 11–13 *You're grown ... disapproves*: Theatre audiences have become hard to please, just like Dissenters who reject everything that does not accord with their conscience. (A 'maggot' is a whimsical fancy.)

line 14   *canting*: affected, hypocritical. (Dissenters were frequently derided as 'canting'.)

line 20   *Blackfriars*: Blackfriars Theatre was one of the main indoor theatres during the first half of the seventeenth century. It was pulled down in 1655.

line 21   *bamboo*: a walking stick.

line 35   *brisk*: used in an unfavourable sense, meaning smart, or 'fast'.

line 40   *damny*: more usually 'damme', short for 'damn me!'. In the seventeenth century Cavaliers and Restoration wits were noted for their profanity, and were often referred to as 'Dammes'.

line 43   *Nokes, or Tony Lee*: James Nokes and Anthony Leigh were the most popular comedians of the time. They were both with the Duke's Company and appeared in a number of Behn's comedies.

Postscript

Thomaso altered: *Thomaso, or, The Wanderer*, was a play in two parts by Thomas Killigrew, written in 1654 but not published until 1664 in his *Comedies and Tragedies*. Making use of earlier material, *Thomaso* was far too long and rambling ever to be performed and was meant for reading only. Behn was not alone in drawing upon or adapting existing plays, or in being accused of plagiarism for so doing; it was common practice throughout the seventeenth century.

only stolen object: Behn is not being entirely truthful here: much of *The Rover* is based on *Thomaso*.

Play of the Novella: *The Novella*, a verse comedy by Richard Brome, acted in 1632 and published in 1653. It provided some ideas which Behn adapted.

Virgil ... fame: According to legend, some verses written anonymously by Virgil were claimed by a hack writer. Virgil then produced some more, each line of which required completion, and preceded these with the quotation here. Since only Virgil could complete the new lines, his authorship of the others was established.

Bibliography

Andreas, J.R. (1995) '*Othello*: African American progeny', in Kamps, I. (ed.) *Materialist Shakespeare*, Verso.

Barber, C.L. (1963) *Shakespeare's Festive Comedy*, Princeton University Press.

Belsey, C. (1985) 'Disrupting sexual difference: meaning and gender in the comedies', in Drakakis, J. (ed.) *Alternative Shakespeares*, Methuen.

Bloom, H. (1973) *The Anxiety of Influence*, Oxford University Press.

Bloom, H. (1994) *The Western Canon*, Harcourt Brace.

Bradbrook, M. (1980 edn) *Elizabethan Tragedy*, Cambridge University Press (first published 1935).

Bristol, M.D. (1990) 'Charivari and the comedy of abjection in *Othello*', *Renaissance Drama* XXI, pp.3–21.

Copeland, N. (1992) '"Once a whore and ever"? Whore and virgin in *The Rover* and its antecedents', *Restoration*, 16, pp.20–27.

Cotton, N. (1991) 'Aphra Behn and the pattern hero', in Schofield, M.A. and Macheski, C. (eds) *Curtain Calls: British and American Women and the Theatre, 1660–1820*, Ohio University Press.

DeRitter, J. (1986) 'The gypsy, *The Rover*, and the wanderer: Aphra Behn's revision of Thomas Killigrew', *Restoration*, 10, pp.82–92.

Diamond, E. (1989) '*Gestus* and signature in Aphra Behn's *The Rover*', *English Literary History*, 56, pp.519–41.

Donaldson, P.S. (1990) *Shakespearean Films/Shakespearean Directors*, Unwin Hyman.

Duffy, M. (1977) *The Passionate Shepherdess: Aphra Behn 1640–89*, Cape.

Eagleton T. (1983) *Literary Theory: An Introduction*, Basil Blackwell.

Eagleton, T. (1986) *William Shakespeare*, Basil Blackwell.

Elam, K. (1984) *Shakespeare's Universe of Discourse*, Cambridge University Press.

Elsom, J. (ed.) (1989) *Is Shakespeare still our Contemporary?*, Routledge.

Empson, W. (1977 edn) *The Structure of Complex Words*, Chatto & Windus (first published 1951).

Ferguson, M. (1993) 'Transmuting *Othello*: Aphra Behn's *Oroonoko*', in Novy, M. (ed.) *Cross-Cultural Performances*, University of Illinois Press.

French, M. (1983) *Shakespeare's Division of Experience*, Abacus.

Gay, P. (1994) *As She Likes It: Shakespeare's Unruly Women*, Routledge.

Goodman, L. (1993) *Contemporary Feminist Theatres: To Each Her Own*, Routledge.

Goodman, L. (1993) 'Women's alternative Shakespeares and women's alternatives to Shakespeare in contemporary British theatres', in Novy, M. (ed.) *Cross-Cultural Performances*, University of Illinois Press.

Goodman, L. (ed.) (1996) *Literature and Gender*, Routledge/The Open University.

Goreau, A. (1980) *Reconstructing Aphra: A Social Biography of Aphra Behn*, Oxford University Press.

Greenblatt, S. (1988) *Shakespearean Negotiations: The Circulation of Social Energy in Renaissance England*, Oxford University Press.

Gurr, A. (1987) *Playgoing in Shakespeare's London*, Cambridge University Press.

Hapgood, R. (1990) 'Othello', in Wells, S. (ed.) *Shakespeare: A Bibliographical Guide*, Oxford University Press.

Harrop, J. (1992) *Acting*, Routledge.

Holderness, G. (1991) 'What is my nation? Shakespeare and national identities', *Textual Practice*, vol. 5, no. 1, pp.74–93.

Holderness, G. (1992) *Shakespeare Recycled*, Harvester Wheatsheaf.

Howe, E. (1992) *The First English Actresses: Women and Drama, 1660–1700*, Cambridge University Press.

Hutner, H. (1993) 'Revisioning the female body: Aphra Behn's *The Rover*, Parts I and II', in Hutner, H. (ed.) *Rereading Aphra Behn: History, Theory and Criticism*, University of Virginia Press.

Jardine, L. (1994) 'Canon to left of them, canon to right of them', in Dunant, S. (ed.) *War of the Words: The Political Correctness Debate*, Virago.

Jones, J.E. (1991) 'Foreword', *Othello: The Everyman Shakespeare*, in Andrews, J.F. (ed.) Doubleday.

Jordan, R. (1972) 'The extravagant rake in Restoration comedy', in Love, H. (ed.) *Restoration Literature: Critical Approaches*, Methuen.

Kennedy, D. (1993) *Looking at Shakespeare: A Visual History of Twentieth Century Performance*, Cambridge University Press.

Kermode, F. (1985) *Forms of Attention*, University of Chicago Press.

Kernan, A. (1975) '"Ducdame": Shakespearean comedy to Twelfth Night', in Barrell, J.L. *et al.* (eds) *The Revels: History of Drama in English, vol. III 1576–1613*, Methuen.

Kettle, A. (1983 edn) *An Introduction to the English Novel*, vol. 1, Hutchinson (first published 1951).

Kott, J. (1967 edn) *Shakespeare our Contemporary*, trans. by B. Taborski, Methuen (first published Doubleday, 1965).

Langdell, C.D. (1985) 'Aphra Behn and sexual politics: a dramatist's discourse with her audience', in Redmond, J. (ed.) *Drama, Sex and Politics*, Cambridge University Press.

Langhans, E.A. (1966) 'Three early eighteenth-century promptbooks', *Theatre Notebook*, 20, pp.142–50.

Leavis, F.R. (1948) *The Great Tradition*, Chatto & Windus.

Leavis, F.R. (1952) *The Common Pursuit*, Chatto & Windus.

Leavis, F.R. (1962 edn) 'Diabolic intellect and noble hero', *The Common Pursuit*, Penguin Books, pp.136–59 (essay first published in *Scrutiny* 6 (1937), pp.259–83; book first published 1952).

Link, F. (ed.) (1967) Aphra Behn, *The Rover*, University of Nebraska Press.

Loughrey, B. (ed.) (1984) *The Pastoral Mode*, Macmillan.

Margolies, D. (1992) *Monsters of the Deep: Social Dissolution in Shakespeare's Tragedies*, Manchester University Press.

Mendelson, S.H. (1987) *The Mental World of Stuart Women*, Harvester Press.

Mulryne, R. and Shewring, M. (eds) (1989) *This Golden Round: The Royal Shakespeare Company at the Swan*, A.H. Jolly.

Munns, J. (1988) 'Barton and Behn's *The Rover*: or, The Text Transpos'd', *Restoration and Eighteenth Century Theatre Research*, 3, pp.11–22.

Newman, K. (1987) '"And wash the Ethiop white": femininity and the monstrous in *Othello*', in Howard, J.E. and O'Connor, M.F. (eds) (1987) *Reproducing Shakespeare: The Text in History and Ideology*, Routledge.

Patterson, A. (1988) *Pastoral and Ideology: Virgil to Valéry*, University of California Press.

Pearson, J. (1988) *The Prostituted Muse: Images of Women and Women Dramatists 1642–1737*, Harvester Press.

Poole, A. (1987) *Tragedy: Shakespeare and the Greek Example*, Basil Blackwell.

Rogers, K.M. (1982) *Feminism in Eighteenth-Century England*, Harvester Press.

Rosenberg, M. (1961) *The Masks of Othello*, University of California Press.

RSC Study Pack for David Thacker's 1992–3 production of *As You Like It*.

Russell Brown, J. (1973) *Shakespeare in Performance: An Introduction through Six Major Plays*, Harcourt Brace Jovanovich.

Ryan, K. (1995 edn) *Shakespeare*, Prentice Hall/Harvester Wheatsheaf (first published 1989).

Sackville-West, V. (1927) *Aphra Behn: The Incomparable Astrea*, Gerald Howe.

Shakespeare, W. (1968 edn) *As You Like It*, ed. by H.J. Oliver, Penguin Books.

Shakespeare, W. (1968 edn) *Henry V*, ed. by A.R. Humphreys, Penguin Books.

Shakespeare, W. (1968 edn) *Othello*, ed. by K. Muir, Penguin Books.

Singh, J. (1994) 'Othello's identity, postcolonial theory, and contemporary African rewritings of *Othello*', in Hendricks, M. and Parker, P. (eds) *Women, 'Race' and Writing in the Early Modern Period*, Routledge.

Speiaght, R. (1973) *Shakespeare on the Stage*, Collins.

Spencer, J. (ed.) (1995) Aphra Behn, *'The Rover' and Other Plays*, Oxford University Press.

Taylor, G. (1990 edn) *Reinventing Shakespeare: A Cultural History from the Restoration to the Present*, Hogarth Press.

Tillotson, G. (1933) 'Othello', *The Times Literary Supplement*, 20 July, p.494.

Todd, J. (ed.) (1992) Aphra Behn, *Oroonoko, The Rover and Other Works*, Penguin Books.

Trussler, S. (ed.) (1986) *An Adaptation of 'The Rover' by Aphra Behn: A Programme/Text*, Methuen, in association with the Royal Shakespeare Company.

Voltaire (1961 edn) *Philosophical Letters*, trans. by E. Dilworth, Bobbs-Merrill.

Williams, R. (1976) *Keywords: A Vocabulary of Culture and Society*, Fontana.

Williams, R. (1981) *Culture*, Fontana.

Williams, R. (1991 edn) *Drama in Performance*, The Open University Press (first published by Frederick Muller, 1954).

Williams, R. (1992 edn) *Television: Technology and Cultural Form*, Wesleyan University Press (first published 1976).

Wilson, J.D. (1962) *Shakespeare's Happy Comedies*, Faber.

Wilson Knight, G. (1949 edn) *The Wheel of Fire: Interpretations of Shakespearian Tragedy, with Three New Essays*, Methuen (first published Oxford University Press, 1930).

Woolf, V. (1929) *A Room of One's Own*, Hogarth Press.

Wynne-Davis, M. (1995 edn) *Bloomsbury Guide to English Literature*, Bloomsbury (first published 1992).

Audio and video cassettes associated with this book

As You Like It (1995) BBC/Open University video, with student workshops, interviews with actors and directors, extracts from the Cheek by Jowl production directed by Declan Donnellan, and an extract from the banishment scene directed by Fiona Shaw; video produced and directed by Amanda Willett.

As You Like It (1995) BBC/Open University audio cassettes; produced by Amanda Willett.

The Authentick and Ironicall Historie of Henry V (1996) BBC/Open University television programme; produced and directed by Tony Coe.

Henry V (1995) BBC/Open University audio cassettes; produced by Nick Levinson.

Othello (1995) BBC/Open University audio cassettes; produced by Tony Coe.

Producing The Rover (1995) BBC/Open University; an illustrated interview by Lizbeth Goodman, with Jules Wright (WPT theatre director) and Tony Coe (BBC/OUPC).

The Rover (1995) BBC/Open University video cassette, WPT/OU/BBC co-production directed by Jules Wright; video produced and directed by Tony Coe.

Index